OTHER PEOPLES,
OTHER CUSTOMS

The Landing of Columbus, a woodcut print that accompanied an Italian printing of the first letter by Columbus, which appeared in Florence in 1493 (from Winsor 1889, vol. 2).

OTHER PEOPLES, OTHER CUSTOMS

World Ethnography and Its History

Wendell H. Oswalt
University of California
Los Angeles

Holt, Rinehart and Winston, Inc.

NEW YORK   CHICAGO   SAN FRANCISCO   ATLANTA
DALLAS   MONTREAL   TORONTO   LONDON   SYDNEY

Also by Wendell H. Oswalt
Mission of Change in Alaska
Napaskiak: An Alaskan Eskimo Community
This Land Was Theirs
Alaskan Eskimos
Understanding Our Culture

Cover and text design by Colin Chow
(print adapted for cover from Winsor 1889, vol. 2:19).

Copyright © 1972 by Holt, Rinehart and Winston, Inc.
All rights reserved
Library of Congress Catalog Card Number: 70–183347
ISBN: 0–03–085192–0
Printed in the United States of America
23456 038 987654321

TO: Cornelius Osgood
ethnographer

PREFACE

This book is an invitation
to learn about peoples who have been variously described as low races;
savages, both ignoble and noble; barbarians; nonliterates or even illiterates;
primitives; simple, backward, indigenous, small-scale, or tribal peoples;
natives, and aborigines. Our changing attitudes toward this ever-diminishing
block of humanity are well reflected in these words which we have used
in referring to them. Not considered here are peoples who are for the most
part literate or civilized and are most often referred to by proper nouns
such as Islamics, Chinese, East Indians, Europeans, or Euro-Americans.

The introduction seeks to probe the universal dimensions of humanness in search of an answer to the intriguing question, "What is it that all
men have in common?" The reader who is familiar with the field of anthropology will be well aware of these findings, but for someone unexposed to
the diversity of human ways, this information should provide a useful overview. The latter part of the introduction is devoted to the clarification of
pertinent terms. This discussion is somewhat pedantic, but it offers insight
into the meanings of words used frequently in ethnographic studies.

The first and second chapters provide background material from which
the reader derives an awareness of the diverse circumstances under which
peoples first were contacted and portrayed. The purpose of the opening
chapter is to discuss the manner in which European or American explorers,
travelers, missionaries, and others described their early encounters with the
members of small-scale societies. This presentation does not pretend to be
a comprehensive history of such depictions; instead it is a broad sampling
of the spectrum. In the historical survey only Euro-American discoveries of
aboriginal peoples have been considered. What Arabic, Chinese, or other
literate peoples have written about aboriginal societies has not been con-

sidered. The second chapter is in part an extension of the first, for it too offers a historical perspective about accounts of nonliterate peoples. The stress, however, shifts to a concern with the rise of professionalism in the collection of pertinent data about exotic peoples. The careers of certain persons are discussed briefly in order to illustrate turning points in the history of ethnography.

The following five chapters are devoted to ethnographic sketches of select peoples. The purpose of this core of the text is to present descriptive accounts of aboriginal peoples who represent the five major geographical areas of the world. Peoples were selected for inclusion on the basis of the quality of the data concerning them, their ethnographic importance, and the pertinence of a particular aspect of their lifeway to the anthropological understanding of man. Throughout these chapters I have attempted to offer information about these small-scale societies as they existed in their aboriginal state or at a point as near this condition as possible. As the chapters unfold, the reader will increasingly share my awareness that the accounts about some peoples do not reflect that ideal. The problem of separating aboriginal and acculturative data is not resolved in a consistent manner, nor can it be, given the available information.

In the thirty-five ethnographic vignettes no effort has been made to describe the peoples in a parallel manner. In many instances I have attempted to describe a particular way of life in sufficient detail so that the reader has at least some idea about the appearance of the people, their clothing, house forms, and so on, and yet even basic information of this nature has not been included for all of the peoples described. Some sketches are designed to stress one or more ethnographic points at the expense of basic particulars, and others are more balanced, although they too may center about comparatively few characteristics. The purpose of this approach is to avoid repetitious minutiae and to concentrate on vital human differences. Each ethnographic sketch closes with an interpretation bearing on the focal points in the descriptions.

The broader uses of ethnographic data are considered in the closing chapter. Here the overwhelming stress is on the different taxonomies which have been devised to classify data about ethnics. Above all else these frameworks are means for ranking, in terms of comparative complexity, the achievements of different ethnics.

It is legitimate for the reader to ask, particularly at this point, "Why should I read a book about various primitive peoples around the world?" Anyone remotely interested in the subject of anthropology soon realizes that the heart of the discipline is the lifeways of small-scale societies, and this book draws together information about such peoples. Furthermore, worldwide ethnographic information provides the basis for testing crosscultural theories about the nature of human behavior. These considerations alone make a knowledge of world ethnography imperative for any serious student of man's social and cultural ways. From a less technical point of view, a book which presents a worldwide variation of life styles among peoples called primitive may help provide a contemporary reader with a far greater appreciation of universal humanism.

A number of comments concerning the format and style of the text are necessary at this point. Since many sources were consulted in compiling the material for the two opening chapters, exact references are cited in the pertinent text, although the biographical information drawn from diverse standard dictionaries of national biography has not been referenced. In the five ethnographic chapters various sources were integrated in presenting information about each people, and since citing specific references would have been textually cumbersome, the consulted works have been listed at the end of each ethnographic sketch. Finally, the ethnographic descriptions have been presented consistently in the past tense. Although it is an accepted anthropological convention to use the "ethnographic present" (i.e., the present tense, irrespective of whether or not the way of life described is extinct), I decline to follow this pattern, if only because it tends to create the false impression that many extinct cultures continue to exist.

W. H. O.

Los Angeles, Calif.
February 1972

ACKNOWLEDGMENTS

My foremost thanks are to my personal critic and editor, Helen Taylor Oswalt. Furthermore, I am grateful to a number of anthropological colleagues who have advised me in preparing this manuscript. My greatest debt is to George D. Spindler for his insightful reviews of the manuscript in two different drafts. William A. Lessa, Michael Moerman, and Bobby J. Williams aided me in settling particular problems, while Barbara Collins was most helpful in locating source materials.

The International African Institute granted permission to reproduce the text of a Bushman prayer which appeared in an article titled "Bushman Folklore" by Dorothea F. Bleek, published in *Africa*, vol. 2. The Jivaro war song from "The Head-hunters of Western Amazonas" by Rafael Karsten, *Commentationes Humanarum Litterarum*, vol. 7, 1935, is reproduced with the permission of the Societas Scientiarum Fennica. The selections of Yakut poetry are reprinted with permission of the publisher from A. P. Okladnikov, *Yakutia before Its Incorporation into the Russian State*, edited by Henry N. Michael (Montreal: McGill-Queen's University Press, 1970), pp. 264–265, 268–270, 271–272. © Arctic Institute of North America 1970. The quotation from Herodotus appears with permission from G. P. Putnam's Sons, and the portion of a letter by Christopher Columbus is reproduced by permission of the Hakluyt Society.

CONTENTS

OTHER PEOPLES,
OTHER CUSTOMS

INTRODUCTION

Travelers today as in the past return from distant lands, seat themselves comfortably before a stay-at-home audience, and begin to tell of the realms they have seen. At some point in the narration the wayfarer may be expected to nod his head and say something to the effect that people are really the same everywhere. At yet another point he is almost certain to shake his head in virtual disbelief as he relates the strange customs of a bizarre people. The contradiction is real and obvious, but it troubles neither the storyteller nor his listeners. In differing contexts each statement is valid. At certain levels of behavior some people do one thing as others do another in order to attain a particular goal, but at other, more abstract levels all people react in a similar manner. To identify those forms of behavior shared by all mankind is to isolate the universal basis for humanness, and from this point one may consider with more understanding the ways of peoples who seem so very different from each other.

As an introductory precept, it should be understood that this book is concerned only with learned human behavior, that which a child is taught by its parents or adults by one another. No attention whatever is allotted to the biology of being human. Human physiology and morphology are accepted as givens and as being broadly similar for people everywhere. Our topic is ethnography, and it is concerned with the knowledge and understanding that people acquire from each other and the utilization of this learning in developing distinctive ways of life. Man alone possesses an ability for the complex abstract thinking which is the basis of cultural knowledge, and his learned and shared behavior, passed from one generation to the next, constitutes the essence of humanness.

Visualize *Homo sapiens* standing on the baseline of a triangle en-

1

compassed by a circle. The circle represents the natural setting within which the individual lives; among its characteristics are features of the landscape and other qualities of the natural world which would be present even if no man existed. The environment contains energy sources, such as foods, water, and air, as well as other organic and inorganic forms which have potential utility for men. Thus, all men occupy settings which are at least to some degree "natural" and from which they take substances to further their survival. In all inhabitable areas of the earth certain materials exist which may be combined or reformed by man in various ways to create aids to his way of life. These productions, called artifacts, are represented by the base of the triangle on which man stands. The most essential cultural forms are those which are directly instrumental in providing food and water for their makers. No group of men can sustain itself long without artifacts such as digging sticks, plows, or bows and arrows. A man might on occasion run down an animal and kill it with his hands or use his hands to snatch a fish from a stream, but these nonartifactual means of acquiring sustenance cannot maintain life over an extended period of time anywhere in the world. Not only do peoples everywhere manufacture artifacts to aid them in making a living, but they also make objects which are nonessential in terms of physical survival but fill secondary needs. Thus, all men stand on a technological base in order to survive physically and emotionally.

Even though it is stressed that man first must learn how to employ technical devices in order to subsist, it is equally important to note that he normally will function in the company of other persons. This is the social side of living and is represented by the second segment of the triangle. The sociality of men and women probably arises from the long period of physical dependency during human maturation and from sexual drives rather than from any instinctive gregariousness. People living in the company of others organize themselves for social action in different patterns, but these patterns always reflect positions or statuses. These statuses, since they represent the formal relationships which guide one man's behavior toward another, require brief elaboration. A status is an abstract social position, and an individual occupies multiple statuses, each representing a distinctive relationship between himself and various other members of his society. *Ascribed statuses* are those into which a person is born, including race, sex, and kinship distinctions; the individual has no control over his positioning in these terms. *Achieved statuses* are those attained by personal actions. Technical or artistic accomplishments, political or religious positions which are gained on an individual basis serve as examples. Likewise the position of parent, general of an army, self-made man of wealth, or member of any voluntary organization is achieved.

The third side of the triangle involves ideas and behaviors of a supernatural order. This constitutes the sphere of sacred activities as opposed to secular involvements. Supernaturalism is the basis for religion and requires belief, faith, trust, control, and submission. That supernaturalism is a universal dimension in human living systems might be questioned, since secular rationalism appears to be replacing it in some societies. However, this concept, which is emerging among some Euro-Americans and others, is unknown among small-scale societies and at this point remains relatively untried in large-scale or civilized societies.

In abstraction, the three sides of the triangle are equal, but in actual fact, the length of the arms may differ greatly. One people may have placed great emphasis on material objects, another on supernaturalism, and yet another on man's associations with other men. It also is necessary to recognize that the triangle is bonded by many different integrative networks. These involve the mutual adjustment and unification of behaviors which are social, supernatural, or technological. In one society, artifacts of a symbolic nature represent the links which men have with the supernatural, whereas in another society, group activities may connect man and the supernatural. Great differences exist in the forms of integration, but each society depends on its own functioning links between artifacts, men, and supernaturals. To triangulate man's action patterns is a step toward understanding what it is that all men have in common; it offers a gross overview of human behavior and suggests an orderliness in human actions.

An operational approach for the analysis of culture and society may be derived from this triangulation by thinking in terms of the patterns or actions which form coherent, integrative networks. A *pattern* of this nature is an implicit plan or organizational framework of behavior which gives stability and order to the lives of a people. Within each population isolate patterns mesh to form a unique sociocultural system. A general and universally applicable means of classifying those manifestations of man's learned behavior into *universal culture patterns* was offered by Clark Wissler (1923:74). He suggested that there were nine such behavioral patterns, most of them with recognizable subordinate divisions. They are as follow:

1. Speech
    Languages, writing systems, etc.

2. Material Traits
    a. Food habits
    b. Shelter
    c. Transportation and travel

    d. Dress
    e. Utensils, tools, etc.
    f. Weapons
    g. Occupations and industries

3. Art. Carving, painting, drawing, music, etc.

4. Mythology and Scientific Knowledge

5. Religious Practices
    a. Ritualistic forms
    b. Treatment of the sick
    c. Treatment of the dead

6. Family and Social Systems
    a. The forms of marriage
    b. Methods of reckoning relationship
    c. Inheritance
    d. Social control
    e. Sports and games

7. Property
    a. Real and personal
    b. Standards of value and exchange
    c. Trade

8. Government
    a. Political forms
    b. Judicial and legal procedures

9. War

In order to derive the universal culture patterns, Wissler studied accounts about peoples around the world and sought to identify the gross behavioral involvements which all peoples shared. His concern was with the commonalities in the structure of human behavior as these had been perceived by Euro-Americans in their studies of other peoples. The usefulness of Wissler's divisions is reflected in the tables of contents for most comprehensive ethnographic studies. At the same time it must be remembered that the universal culture pattern classification is based on observed behavior above all else. It might be more legitimate to label the units as "empirical universals" following Clyde Kluckhohn (1953:508) or "cultural constants" as they have been designated by Alfred L. Kroeber (1949:187–188). These patterns, no matter what they are termed, are no more nor less than gross abstractions about human behavior as interpreted by persons from a Western cultural tradition.

    Within the universal culture pattern concept, Wissler's subordinate divisions may be reduced to more refined categories which are still universal in scope. These have been termed *common denominators* by George P. Murdock (1945:124), who prepared an extended list applicable to all mankind. The universal culture patterns identified by Wissler, with modifications, have been used to group Murdock's common denominators in the list below. Murdock's denominators of government and language have been omitted since they occur as universal culture patterns, and some of the headings have been altered slightly.

UNIVERSAL CATEGORIES OF HUMAN BEHAVIOR

Speech
kinship nomenclature
personal names

Subsistence
cooking
ethnobotany
feasting
mealtimes
trade

Material Culture
bodily adornment
fire making
housing
tool making

Art
decorative art

Knowledge (scientific, folk, mythological)
calendar
cosmology
dream interpretation
eschatology
ethics
folklore
taboos (incest, food)
luck superstitions
medicine
music
mythology
numerals
obstetrics
postnatal care
pregnancy usages

surgery
weather control

Supernatural
divination
faith healing
funeral rites
magic
mourning
propitiation of supernatural beings
religious ritual
soul concepts

Society
age-grade
athletic sports
cleanliness training
cooperative labor
courtship
dancing
division of labor
education
etiquette
family organization
games
gestures
gift giving
greetings
hair styles
hospitality
hygiene
joking
kin-groups
marriage
marriage residence

modesty
puberty customs
sexual restrictions
status differentiation
visiting
weaning

Property
inheritance rules
property rights

Government
community organization
population policy
penal sanctions
law

Violence
feuds

The placement of common denominators within the universal culture pattern headings required many arbitrary decisions. Certain denominators might have been placed under more than one heading, and some represented categories of unequal proportions. Nonetheless, the unification of the universal culture patterns and the common denominators of culture provides a manageable classification of all learned behavior among humans.

Traits are the specific manifestations of common denominators. A trait, as a particularization of a common denominator, is found among one or more peoples but is not universal. Consider the common denominator of mourning. The people in one society may cry bitterly at the death of a member; those in another group may amputate a finger, and still other people pretend that the death did not take place and keep the body in the house. Thus, in terms of specific mourning behavior widespread differences exist. In a like manner all people adorn their bodies in some fashion, but no single technique or decorative element is universal. Again all societies have numerical systems, but no one method of counting is reported everywhere. Although certain traits have undeniable parallels in totally unrelated societies, no particular cultural trait is found everywhere, and no specific social custom is reported for all societies.

If we are to categorize culture on the basis of universal patterns and common denominators, we should try to understand why these concepts are applicable to all societies. The often-stated reason is that they are basic to the nature of the human animal, but this is a simplistic answer. Perhaps a better approach is to identify those principles which govern human behavior in any society. David F. Aberle and others (1950:104–111) have offered a framework in which they seek to isolate the "functional prerequisites" of societies. They attempt to identify what must be accomplished in any society if it is to be an ongoing system. According to their presentation, a society must adapt to and manipulate the environment effectively and must sustain itself biologically. It must arrive at a stable division of activities in terms of role allotment among the members and be able to communicate the values of the society from one generation to the next while at the same time effectively socializing members. Furthermore, members must share cognitive orientations and goals as well as the means for attaining these goals.

To return to our original generalization, people are alike the world over in terms of universal culture patterns and common denominators; on the other hand, the nonuniversal manifestations of these categories, traits, are distinct and combine to form a unique life style for any particular society. Thus, all peoples are either very much alike or very different, depending on the level of abstraction at which their behaviors are conceptualized.

In terms of the tripartite classification of peoples as savage, barbarian, and civilized which prevailed until quite recently, our concern is with those called savages or barbarians. The word "savage" was applied to those peoples who hunted, fished, and collected their foods in order to survive (e.g., foragers or gatherers), while "barbarians" referred to horticulturalists, who now may be called tribal, small-scale, or protostate societies. In current usage these terms mean precivilized peoples without a writing system of their own and outside the political control of a contiguous society which was dominant and often was civilized. "Primitive" replaced the terms savage and barbarian in more recent times, but to many people this word implies deficiencies. A new word is badly needed in order to clear the semantic field, and I offer *ethnic* as a noun to mean any politically independent and economically self-sufficient nonliterate, nonpeasant, noncivilized, nonstate society regardless of where or when it occurs on earth. Small-scale society and primitives will be considered terms synonymous with ethnic.

The word "ethnography" appears to have been coined by English speakers in 1834 (*Oxford Universal Dictionary* 1955:637). By this time the "ethno-" portion of the word was long established as referring to heathen peoples. In the past, and often at present, it has been customary to limit the scope of ethnography to the study of small-scale societies. Kroeber (1957:191) wrote, "By usage rather than definition, ethnography deals with the cultures of the nonliterate peoples." Some anthropologists would prefer to expand the meaning of ethnography, making the concept more all-inclusive. In this vein John J. Honigmann (1959:5) wrote that it is "the process of actually acquiring data about a living culture," and E. Adamson Hoebel (1966:562) considers it to be "the division of anthropology devoted to the descriptive recording of cultures." I prefer the original definition and consider *ethnography* to be the descriptive framework for behavioral information about a population of ethnics at a particular point in time. "Descriptive" refers to the recording of primary data which are not interpretive, although many descriptions will include some statements of a narrowly analytical nature. The word "framework" is meant to exclude those superficial remarks made about a people from those carefully gathered with a greater or lesser degree of conceptual rigor. An explorer's casual account of a rite observed or similar impressions reported by a tourist, traveler, or journalist would not be acceptable in terms of this definition. The data must be collected with care and precision, efforts must be made to verify the accuracy of what is recorded, and the findings must be described as an integrated whole. This implies an intensity of observation and a utilization of other forms of data in order to check the validity of materials presented. "Behavioral information" in this context means that which is learned and may concern relations between siblings, the methods of manufacturing a boat, hair styles, ideas about deities, or even the amount of water typically consumed by an individual at a particular meal. An ethnographer deals with a life system which he observes, participates in, counts, measures, "feels" mentally or physically, and discusses with his subjects. The specific unit for description is a "population," a purposefully vague term since its precise range hinges on the researcher's focus. A population may refer to a tribe, hamlet, camp, band, horde, or barrio, depending on the investigator's point of reference. By "a particular point in time" is meant a single calendar year within which a complete cycle of seasonal activities will be observed. In terms of this definition an ethnography is an objective, descriptive record about a living population of ethnics as it functions during a single year. It is systematic versus pedestrian; it is idiographic and essentially static or synchronic.

Several types of ethnographies may be distinguished on the basis of the aboriginal "purity" of the ethnics studied or on the basis of the source of information. A *baseline ethnography* is a description of a people as they existed just before contact with civilized peoples. Exotic change might begin when European trade goods or a smallpox epidemic first reached a people through other aborigines, preceding any direct contact with Europeans. In other instances the first contact was face to face and unexpected, with no prior indirect contacts. As will be detailed later, only rarely has it been possible for ethnographers to assemble their information at this ideal point—the time when contact brings its first changes.

In the absence of a baseline study, we must often utilize the often imprecise observations of explorers, missionaries, and others. These will have been recorded at various points in time, will reflect differing points of view, and usually will not be systematic studies. We also may have the field observations of an ethnographer-come-lately. A composite description of the probable baseline behavior of a people, one in which time is loosely held constant and which is drawn from diverse sources, is a *reconstructed baseline ethnography.* Here the ideal is to establish as nearly as possible an aboriginal baseline from which to plot changes resulting subsequently from direct or indirect historic contact. It should be noted that if the reconstruction is made more than forty years after the point of direct contact, the baseline data often are difficult if not impossible to establish. Assume, for example, that the first European contact with a people took place in A.D. 1880 and that by 1900 the people had become Christianized and drawn into a wage-labor economy. An ethnographer who arrived on the scene in 1920 could record viable behaviors from his personal observations and from this derive a postcontact ethnography. However, in order to assemble baseline information for the 1870s, he would be forced to depend on the verbal accounts of those old people who might be able to recall pre-Christian ceremonial life or the aboriginal hunting methods no longer employed. It would be very difficult to check the validity of such informants' statements without historical records for the period. As time passes, these attempts at reconstruction, especially when they rely on fieldwork, become progressively less reliable since the sources become increasingly scarce and the validity of the data collected becomes more questionable.

Any recorded descriptive information which pertains to a particular population of ethnics during a number of time periods may be combined into an *ethnohistory*. Included as sources would be baseline ethnographies, reconstructed baseline ethnographies, information derived from commercial records, maps, diaries, and so on. The key characteristics of an ethnohistory are that the information pertains to an identified population, that it has been recorded somewhere in written or graphic form, and that it represents a temporal sequence. Ethnographies deal with static, idiographic data (a single year); when time depth is added, we have ethnohistory, which is idiographic but temporal or diachronic. In these terms, all ethnographic studies are possible components on which ethnohistories may be built.

When data about an identified population are obtained through archaeological methods, the study is *ethnoarchaeology*. It is of no import whether the archaeological leavings are from a historic or prehistoric context or whether the artifacts and other data-revealing forms were found on the ground surface, excavated from the soil, or retrieved from the sea. The critical characteristics of ethnoarchaeology are that the remains be linked to an identified population and that they be recovered through the employment of archaeological methods. If the remains cannot be linked to a particular people, the results will be archaeology rather than ethnoarchaeology. Thus ethnoarchaeology, like ethnohistory, is idiographic and temporal or diachronic.

When all information of a verbal, historical, and archaeological nature about a people is combined, the compilation is of a different order of magnitude. *Ethnistics* is suggested as a term which would mean the collection of all available descriptive and analytical information about the behavior of an identified human population through time; ethnistics would be the complete anthropological history of a particular human population.

ONE

THE BEGINNINGS
OF ETHNOGRAPHY

The earliest ethnographic information was disseminated by the first person to visit another group of humans and return home to recount what he had learned. In all likelihood the most appealing topic was the unfamiliar customs of the foreigners. Who this traveler was, where and when he lived, we are never likely to know. Unquestionably he embarked on his venture many thousands of years ago, and in all probability the text of his report has been repeated time and again by both ancient and contemporary travelers. Today, as in the past, most visitors seldom linger among exotic peoples long enough to gain more than superficial verbal and visual impressions. The observations, deductions, and inferences of these persons, although of an ethnographic nature, usually do not rise to the objective level of an ethnography. Most untrained observers, both living or dead, are so enmeshed in their own society that they cannot accurately view or comprehend the living designs of other peoples. Two factors above all others inhibit the ordinary traveler, and most others, from assembling an ethnography; these are the casual nature of his exposure to strangers and the attitude that one's own ways are the most human.

What constitutes an ethnography? First, the information must be reported as objectively as possible. It is presumptive to suppose that a fully objective account of any people ever will be assembled, but objectivity nonetheless remains a major goal. Each observer, no matter where or when, has blindnesses and biases of which he is unaware and prejudices which often are difficult to perceive, let alone overcome. Errors of observation and misinterpretations are a probable, if not an inevitable, result of the observer's age, sex, national background, and so on. Nonetheless, a trained ethnographer attempts to negate the fact that he is a person and

11

strives to become a recording machine. Second, an ethnography must include descriptions covering a very broad range of behavior for the people involved. As usually conceived, the topics for inclusion are the universal culture patterns presented in the introduction. One pattern unit often slighted is mythology, and as Melville Jacobs (1964:120, 305, 346) has pointed out, it also is unlikely that ethnomusicology, the dance, or humor will be presented in a reasonably adequate manner. Furthermore, quantitative information seldom plays a significant part in ethnographic reporting. The perfect ethnography of a people has never been written, and to write even an adequate one is a difficult task.

One very good reason that no perfect ethnography exists is that there is no perfect set of questions to be answered by ethnographic data. This leads the diligent observer to inquire into everything and to become very frustrated because he can never hope to complete his task. At one period ethnographers devoted an inordinate amount of time to collecting information about material culture; at another time kinship systems commanded a great deal of attention; more recently both of these topics have become secondary to the study of social institutions and ecological problems. In a like manner, information about culture and personality or ethnic origins wax and wane as subjects for serious consideration. The most enduring ethnographies are those which include a broad range of detailed information collected with as few biases as possible.

TRAVELERS AND ENCYCLOPEDISTS

It is customary to credit Herodotus (c. 484–c. 425 B.C.) as fathering history and anthropology, and I do not dispute either of these claims. He begins by stating, "What Herodotus the Halicarnassian has learnt by inquiry is here set forth; in order that so the memory of the past may not be blotted out from among men by time. . . ." (Godley 1920: vol. 1, 3). In the era of Herodotus "history" meant inquiry or research and by extension information resulting from inquiry; by the second century B.C., however, the word had come to mean the particular kinds of descriptions recorded by Herodotus. *Histories* by Herodotus is primarily an account of the Greco-Persian War, with the additional presentation of related and unrelated information ranging topically from anthropology to zoology; about one-ninth of this work is devoted to ethnographic data (Bagby 1963:24–25). Herodotus personally visited Egypt and much of the Near East (Godley 1920: vol. 1, viii–ix); the quality of his description of Egyptian homelife speaks for itself.

But concerning Egypt I will now speak at length, because nowhere are there so many marvellous things, nor in the whole world beside are there to be seen so many works of unspeakable greatness; therefore I shall say the more concerning Egypt.

As the Egyptians have a climate peculiar to themselves, and their river is different in its nature from all other rivers, so have they made themselves customs and laws of a kind contrary to those of all other men. Among them, the women buy and sell, the men abide at home and weave; and whereas in weaving all others push the woof upwards, the Egyptians push it downwards. Men carry burdens on their heads, women on their shoulders. Women make water standing, men sitting. They relieve nature indoors, and eat out of doors in the streets, giving the reason, that things unseemly but necessary should be done in secret, things not unseemly should be done openly. No woman is dedicated to the service of any god or goddess; men are dedicated to all deities male or female. Sons are not compelled against their will to support their parents, but daughters must do so though they be unwilling.

Everywhere else, priests of the gods wear their hair long; in Egypt they are shaven. With all other men, in mourning for the dead those most nearly concerned have their heads shaven; Egyptians are shaven at other times, but after a death they let their hair and beard grow. The Egyptians are the only people who keep their animals with them in the house. Whereas all others live on wheat and barley, it is the greatest disgrace for an Egyptian so to live; they make food from a coarse grain which some call spelt. They knead dough with their feet, and gather mud and dung with their hands. The Egyptians and those who have learnt it from them are the only people who practise circumcision. Every man has two garments, every woman only one. The rings and sheets of sails are made fast elsewhere outside the boat, but inside it in Egypt. The Greeks write and calculate by moving the hand from left to right; the Egyptians do contrariwise; yet they say that their way of writing is towards the right, and the Greek way towards the left. They use two kinds of writing; one is called sacred, the other common (Godley 1920: vol. 1, 315–319).

The brevity, clarity, and scope of this passage is striking. Admittedly we would prefer to know more about each topic discussed, but what is more important in the present context is that this description has a calm and studied objectivity. To Herodotus the Egyptians were different from the Greeks, but they were not quaint or bizarre. In his accounts of them he usually described what he had seen or heard. His record of the esoteric Egyptian embalming practices, for example, could only have been obtained through lengthy and systematic interviews, and the same is true of his discussion of their religion, to which he gives an ethnological perspective by comparisons with Greek ideas. On the basis of this Egyptian material, Herodotus should be credited with fathering ethnography.

A further search for the beginnings of ethnography within the Western tradition of learning leads to the Middle Ages of Europe. Early in this era Europe was fringed on the west by unknown seas and on the north by cold foreign lands; to the east was seemingly endless steppe country from which barbaric peoples emerged, bringing terror and destruction. To the south along the Mediterranean Sea lived alien people who were but vaguely familiar. Medieval minds most often were turned inward to matters of theological concern, and for this reason non-Europeans were seen as souls to be saved and infidels to be conquered, rather than as peoples with customs to be described. Expanded interests did emerge at times, but geographical knowledge was such that peoples beyond the boundaries of Europe often could be conceived only fancifully. Isidore (c. A.D. 560–636), Bishop of Seville and an outstanding medieval encyclopedist, compiled his *Etymologies* or *Origins* between the years 622 and 632. This was a compendium of seventh century learning presented in a dictionary format; references to people's customs are few and scattered throughout. The more distant a people were from Europe the more monstrous they became; for example, far to the east there were reportedly noseless races and others whose mouths were so small that their sustenance was drawn through wheat stems. This work was cited authoritatively until the thirteenth century (Hodgen 1964:49–59). Between 1240 and 1260 another encyclopedia was assembled, one which was to become an accepted reference for the next three hundred years. It was *De proprietatibus rerum* by Bartholomaeus Anglicus, a Franciscan. Written for a wide audience, it proved to be immensely popular. *Etymologies*, the Bible, and earlier compilations were the primary sources utilized, and again the diversities of human ways usually were described in highly imaginative terms. As Margaret T. Hodgen (1964:68) has written of these works, "Ethnographical knowledge was choked by a blanket of luxuriant superstition, and erroneous beliefs of a classical origin were joined to others of a Germanic, Celtic, or Oriental provenance. Sheer magic, incantation, divination, and witchcraft, abetted by alchemy and astrology, all flourished and mingled, overshadowing whatever sound knowledge there was of nature, man, and culture."

It is surprising that early travelers to far-off lands did little to dispel erroneous views (Hodgen 1964:49–87). Among the early extended travels beyond Europe were the pilgrimages of Christians to Jerusalem. Because the pilgrims were concerned primarily with spiritual matters and with visiting sacred places, their accounts add little to our understanding of other peoples. Their significance lies in the fact that they are records of initial exposures to non-Europeans (Jenkins 1926:39–69). With the beginning of the Crusades in A.D. 1096 the Near East attracted tens of thousands of Europeans, ranging from peasants to adventurers and kings. Crusaders often observed other peoples for extended periods of time, and sometimes after their return they recorded what they had seen

(Wright 1925:292–293). These contacts with exotic cultures, far removed from the European cultural tradition, often produced a lasting "cultural shock," which was not a state of mind conducive to objective reporting. Furthermore, since the crusaders were bent on the holy conquest of infidels, they could not be expected to be unbiased observers.

By the thirteenth century central Europeans were not obliged to leave their homeland in order to be exposed to foreigners. In 1206 Genghis Khan (1162–1227) consolidated many Mongol peoples and led them westward. After his death the armies continued to fight in the west until they were forced to retreat to the Russian steppes after 1243. A description of these invaders by Matthew Paris is graphic but does not approach objectivity.

That the joys of mortal men be not enduring, nor worldly happiness long lasting without lamentations, in this same year (i.e., 1240) a detestable nation of Satan, to wit, the countless army of the Tartars, broke loose from its mountain-environed home, and piercing the solid rocks (of the Caucasus), poured forth like devils from the Tartarus, so that they are rightly called Tartari or Tartarians. Swarming like locusts over the face of the earth, they have brought terrible devastation to the eastern parts (of Europe), laying it waste with fire and carnage. After having passed through the land of the Saracens, they have razed cities, cut down forests, overthrown fortresses, pulled up vines, destroyed gardens, killed townspeople and peasants. If perchance they have spared any suppliants, they have forced them, reduced to the lowest condition of slavery, to fight in the foremost ranks against their own neighbours. Those who have feigned to fight, or have hidden in the hope of escaping, have been followed up by the Tartars and butchered. If any have fought bravely (for them) and conquered, they have got no thanks for reward; and so they have misused their captives as they have their mares. For they are inhuman and beastly, rather monsters than men, thirsting for and drinking blood, tearing and devouring the flesh of dogs and men, dressed in ox-hides, armed with plates of iron, short and stout, thickset, strong, invincible, indefatigable, their backs unprotected, their breasts covered with armour; drinking with delight the pure blood of their flocks, with big, strong horses, which eat branches and even trees, and which they have to mount by the help of three steps on account of the shortness of their thighs. They are without human laws, know no comforts, are more ferocious than lions or bears, have boats made of ox-hides, which ten or twelve of them own in common; they are able to swim or to manage a boat, so that they can cross the largest and swiftest rivers without let or hindrance, drinking turbid or muddy water when blood fails them (as beverage). They have one-edged swords and daggers, are wonderful archers, spare neither age, nor sex, nor condition. They know no other language than their own, which no one else knows; for until now there has been no access to them, nor did they go forth (from their own country); so there could be no knowledge of their customs or persons through the common intercourse of men. They wander about with their flocks and their wives, who are taught to fight like men. And so they came with the swiftness of lightning to the confines of Christendom, ravaging and slaughtering, striking every one with terror and incomparable horror (Rockhill 1900:xiv–xvi).

The Mongol inroads gave pause to Christians, who first felt that the anti-Christ had arrived and that destruction of the world was imminent. Yet after the Mongols withdrew, Christians sought accommodation with their leaders, so recently thought by some to have emerged from Hell (Hodgen 1964:88–89).

Fancy and fable began to fade, at least in the easterly direction, when Marco Polo (1254–1324) returned from China and wrote an account of his travels undertaken during 1271 to 1295. Unfortunately, he was a merchant above all else, and his observations are not well rounded. The separate eastward ventures of two Franciscans provide the most notable accounts of non-Europeans subsequent to the descriptions by Herodotus. Friar John de Plano Carpini (c. 1182–1252) bore a papal commission to travel among the Tartars and describe their ways, while Friar William Rubruck (c. 1220–1293) was sent by Louis IX of France to describe and Christianize the same people. The 1253–1255 travel account of Friar Rubruck is commendable especially with respect to non-religious subjects (Rockhill 1900). Some of the reports by these and other travelers eastward were excellent, but they made remarkably little impact on the views of stay-at-home Europeans (Hodgen 1964:88–104; Wright 1925:269–270). For the most part the crusaders, missionaries, and merchants from the late tenth to the end of the fifteenth century described peoples who were Islamic or Chinese, or were on the fringes of these centers of civilization. This body of descriptive literature has little direct relevance to the less civilized peoples of prime anthropological concern, but it is important to note that adventurous Europeans during this span became increasingly exposed to foreign ways. This background served as a valuable prelude for the subsequent exposures to ethnics which took place during the great era of maritime exploration, from the fifteenth through the nineteenth centuries.

When ships ranged beyond Europe to discover near and distant lands, the explorers most often found continents and islands with established populations. Although some large-scale societies were contacted in Africa, Asia, Middle America, and South America, the greatest expanses of these landmasses were occupied by ethnics. Antarctica alone among the continents has never had a lasting human population. A few uninhabited islands were located by adventuring Europeans, the largest cluster being the Arctic Archipelago of northern Canada. Also unpopulated were the Commander Islands off eastern Siberia; Iceland was unoccupied prior to the Norse arrival there around A.D. 870. It also is notable that some continental areas were without indigenous peoples when Europeans arrived. These included a section of the Barren Grounds in the central Canadian Arctic and the sterile deserts of southern Africa and central Australia. By and large, however, few unoccupied islands or continental areas existed when Europeans ventured to the far corners of the earth. It was more likely that travelers to an area would discover that they had been preceded by long-established but hitherto unknown peoples.

The great age of European discoveries is bracketed by the voyages of Bartholomeu Dias (c. 1450–1500) and James Cook (1728–1779). Between the time of the journey of Dias from Portugal to the Cape of Good Hope in 1487–1488 and the conclusion of the third Cook expedition in 1780, most of the world's indigenous peoples were discovered by Westerners. However, from an ethnographic point of view it does not follow that the peoples located after 1780 are of no consequence—quite to the contrary. Since persons have been trained as ethnographers only in very recent times, any ethnics surviving into the modern world are important because they can be studied by more perceptive observers than was possible earlier. Fortunately, even now a few localities have aboriginal populations beyond the control of any nation. In Australia as recently as 1961 some aborigines probably had been in no direct, or at least no lasting, contact with Europeans. A few hundred individuals who possibly had never been contacted lived in the deserts of Western Australia, and approximately 7,000 who lived in either the Northern Territory or Western Australia were defined as having had minimal contact with Europeans by 1961 (Berndt 1963:385–408). The last stronghold of primitive man, however, is New Guinea. The coast of the island was not mapped until 1873, and the southeastern sector of New Guinea, Papua, was not fully explored until 1938. Some peoples in highland localities did not come into direct contact with Europeans until the early 1960s (Souter 1963: 19–20, 173, 234–235).

In all of Africa the most pristine ethnics are the Bushmen. Of the 44,100 Bushman total in 1964, only 9,300 remained hunters and collectors; the others were farm workers, herders, farmers, or incipient farmers. Irrespective of their current economic base, however, all Bushmen have had access to metal weapons and other products of European manufacture for at least forty years (R. B. Lee ms.:20–22).

Eurasia and North America have no pristine aborigines today, but some still exist in South America. Permanent contact was made in 1950 with some of the Yanomamö of southern Venezuela and northern Brazil, but by the late 1960s many villages of these farming people, whose total population was estimated to be nearly 10,000, had not yet been contacted by outsiders (Chagnon 1968:1, 4). In the interior of Surinam a people called the Wama were still subsisting by hunting and collecting when contacted in 1968. They probably are the most primitive surviving New World Indians. Although discovered in 1937, the Wama maintained their Stone Age technology and appear to have been fully aboriginal in their way of life in 1968 (Schoen 1969).

EXPLORERS

It is safe to write that most people around the world—both primitive and civilized—were, and are, ethnocentric racists believing in the superiority of their particular way of life and their racial group. A racist philosophy has dominated the attitudes of Europeans toward Mongolian and Negro peoples into the present century, as we all are quite aware. A prime tenet has been that Europeans, usually meaning white Christians, are innately superior to all other peoples. Contrary and compromising views have existed and clearly continued to exist, and yet this general characterization has a clear historical basis. The philosophy of European superiority was fully compatible with the era of international colonialism which followed most discoveries. Actual behavior toward aboriginal peoples by Europeans has ranged from acceptance and paternalistic economic exploitation to enslavement and genocide.

Given the conditions surrounding most early geographical discoveries, the explorers usually were anxious over their personal safety, shipboard intrigues, the adequacy of their transport, and their ability to return home safely. It is little wonder that their observations of aboriginal peoples were often pedestrian and that the strangeness of distant peoples was exaggerated. They sometimes brought back with them some captured indigenous peoples to exhibit as curiosities before commoners and kings. Perhaps the most notable of "human zoos," before the creation of modern "reserves" and "reservations," was constructed in Bordeaux in 1565. Here a Brazilian village setting was recreated, and several hundred recently captured South American Indians were placed on exhibit (Hodgen 1964:112). Such a method of presenting peoples from distant lands did little to change the prevailing European attitude—that these were bizarre peoples with grotesque customs and appearances.

Another factor affecting the descriptions by explorers was the purpose behind their travels. Expeditions with a prime objective of geographical discovery were likely to linger in far-off places, but those of explorer-traders, whose purpose was to exchange their goods for local products, departed as quickly as possible. Other voyagers searched for slaves, lands to colonize, souls to save, or mineral wealth to retrieve. Given the variability of purpose, it is not surprising that the quality of ethnographic descriptions varied, especially since there were further differences among explorers in terms of their personalities and training, their national origins, and the intellectual climate at the time of their adventure.

In general the Europeans were accepted peaceably, except on islands in the Pacific Ocean. Aboriginal populations most often were noted to be "childlike," "timid," and "afraid" rather than "warlike" and "aggressive." The descriptions which resulted from these contacts usually are best classed as "strange customs of quaint peoples." Observations were confined largely to bodily adornments, forms of dress, manners, dwellings, and manufactures, these being aspects of behavior which were visually apparent during even a brief encounter. Reports of most other customs were likely to be inaccurate, since these observers had no knowledge of the people's language. Accounts of this nature are of limited utility to an ethnographer. They may be tantalizing, but they are very frustrating to consult, the only consolation being that incomplete data and casual observations may serve better than no account at all.

The contributions of most explorers to our understanding of ethnics are few, but some noteworthy examples should be considered briefly. Early and notable contacts between tribal peoples and Europeans took place along the west coast of Africa when Portuguese explorers met tribal Negroes. Infante Enriques (1394–1460), Prince Henry the Navigator, had ordered his ship captains to bring back African captives, and in 1441 one voyager, Antam Goncalves, returned with ten Negroes, a little gold, an oxhide shield, and a number of fresh ostrich eggs (Hart 1950:13). In a short while the west coast of Africa became a region of well-established trade, and explorers then turned their efforts toward finding a sea route to India. The original account of the voyage Dias undertook in 1487 to the Cape of Good Hope and somewhat beyond the cape is not known to exist, but extant remarks about this momentous discovery include brief mention of the people encountered. When the Dias party landed at Mossel Bay and attempted to present gifts to a group of Hottentots who were herding cattle nearby, the Africans fled. When the sailors began to fill their water casks at a stream, the Hottentots attempted to drive them away by throwing stones; they were not afraid of the strange weapons of the explorers. Dias killed one Hottentot with an arrow shot from a crossbow and the others fled; such was the initial white-African contact in the south. This Dias expedition marked a great moment in the history of exploration, for the waterway to the Indies was now apparent. It was also important because of its influence on Christopher Columbus (1451–1506), who was present at the Portuguese court when Dias reported his findings to King John II (Hart 1950:24–40).

The 1492 voyage of Christopher Columbus is not only a watershed in the history of exploration, but an ethnographic landmark as well. The original letter in which Columbus reported the results of his first adventure is not known to exist, but an approximation of the primary text is available from copies (Jane 1930:cxxiii–cxliii). Two of the eight printed pages of text are devoted to Indians of the Caribbean, and those met on the island of Haiti are described in the following words.

> The people of this island, and of all the other islands which I have found and of which I have information, all go naked, men and women, as their mother bore them, although some women cover a single place with the leaf of a plant or with a net of cotton which they make for the purpose. They have no iron or steel or weapons, nor are they fitted to use them, not because they are not well built men and of handsome stature, but because they are very marvellously timorous. They have no other arms than weapons made of canes, cut in seeding time, to the ends of which they fix a small sharpened stick. And they do not dare to make use of these, for many times it has happened that I have sent ashore two or three men to some town to have speech, and countless people have come out to them, and as soon as they have seen my men approaching they have fled, even a father not waiting for his son. And this, not because ill has been done to anyone; on the contrary, at every point where I have been and have been able to have speech, I have given to them of all that I had, such as cloth and many other things, without receiving anything for it; but so they are, incurably timid. It is true that, after they have been reassured and have lost their fear, they are so guileless and so generous with all they possess, that no one would believe it who has not seen it. They never refuse anything which they possess, if it be asked of them; on the contrary, they invite anyone to share it, and display as much love as if they would give their hearts, and whether the thing be of value or whether it be of small price, at once with whatever trifle of whatever kind it may be that is given to them, with that they are content. I forbade that they should be given things so worthless as fragments of broken crockery and scraps of broken glass, and ends of straps, although when they were able to get them, they fancied that they possessed the best jewel in the world. . . . And I gave a thousand handsome good things, which I had brought, in order that they might conceive affection, and more than that, might become Christians and be inclined to the love and service of their highnesses and of the whole Castilian nation, and strive to aid us and to give us of the things which they have in abundance and which

are necessary to us. And they do not know any creed and are not idolators; only they all believe that power and good are in the heavens, and they are very firmly convinced that I, with these ships and men, came from the heavens, and in this belief they everywhere received me, after they had overcome their fear. And this does not come because they are ignorant; on the contrary, they are of a very acute intelligence and are men who navigate all those seas, so that it is amazing how good an account they give of everything, but it is because they have never seen people clothed or ships of such a kind (Jane 1930:6–10).

What is most significant about this ethnographic sketch is the author's attitude of objectivity, which resulted in a report unadorned with embellishments and exaggeration. At the same time we miss details and note that most of the account deals with cultural dimensions which need only have been seen to be described. One would gather that Columbus had an attitude toward the people which would have led to a competent account if he had been interested enough to compile it.

Many explorers had no profound interest in what they saw, or they allowed their cultural biases to distort their recording of the unfamiliar. In contrast, Antonio Pigafetta (c. 1480–1534), a member of the Magellan expedition which circled the world from 1519 to 1522, was in many respects a notably straightforward observer. He spent about three months among the Indians along the Patagonian coast of South America, and he tells of their appearance, subsistence activities, and certain aspects of their material culture. The account has a pleasing clarity and seems exaggerated primarily with respect to the physical characteristics of the people. The Indians consistently were described as being of giant stature, running faster than horses, and drinking half a pail of water at a single gulp. The breasts of women were said to be over two-and-a-half feet in length (Nowell 1962:101–108). Observations such as these about the physical characteristics of the Patagonians were not confirmed by later travelers and must be regarded as fanciful. We must therefore conclude that even a reasonably competent early observer found it difficult to limit himself to factual reporting when he saw conditions which seemed to him extraordinary. Although in certain respects Pigafetta's account is disappointing, it is remarkable that he troubled to write about the people at all, considering the many difficulties which the expedition faced.

Early explorers spent years among aboriginal peoples only if some misadventure occurred. Cabeza de Vaca (c. 1490–1557) was an explorer of note who found himself in such a situation. He served as the second in command of the Narvaez Expedition charged with the conquest of Florida. In 1528 the party of 300 men landed along the western sector of the peninsula and subsequently ventured westward in an effort to reach

Mexico City, which they mistakenly thought was only a short distance away. After a series of mishaps, over ninety of them reached an area near present-day Galveston, Texas, in which a group of Karankawa Indians lived. A few men survived the winter there and subsequently lived among the Coahuiltecans of western Texas. When the expedition reached Mexico and civilization in 1537, only four men, including de Vaca, had survived. The first published record of the incredible 6,000-mile trek appeared as *The Relation* in 1542. Nearly a quarter of the text is ethnographic information about Indians, especially those of Texas; this is particularly fortunate since very little else has been recorded about some of these tribes (Newcomb 1961:29–81). De Vaca was in an excellent position to observe Indian life in detail since he was first a captive and later a trader and curer (Covey 1961). His information is graphic, seemingly very accurate, and not given to stressing the bizarre.

Probably the most honored name in the history of modern exploration is that of the English sea captain James Cook. His three far-reaching voyages spanning 1768–1779 must be judged as extraordinary in terms of geographical discovery and varied original contacts with diverse isolated peoples. Cook recorded what he saw and heard with clarity and objectivity. While we may lament that he did not linger longer at many of his landings, when he did stay long enough to observe a people, his record is notable. On his first voyage he circumnavigated New Zealand, and he was the first to describe the Maori in any detail (Beaglehole 1955:vol. 1, 167–288). Fortunately he had aboard a Malayo-Polynesian speaker who could facilitate communication; nonetheless, the fierce nature of the New Zealanders led to frequent hostilities. Cook described the Maoris' appearance, clothing, weapons, tools, and certain other manufactures, as well as the general nature of their domestic life. On the other hand, Cook's summary of the aboriginal peoples encountered along the eastern shores of Australia indicates the limited amount to be learned if contacts were fleeting and communication was by signs alone.

Among those explorers in the service of the Hudson's Bay Company who have left important accounts of aboriginal peoples, Samuel Hearne (1745–1792) is notable. In the quest for a reportedly fabulous copper deposit in northwestern Canada, Hearne made two memorable trips with different parties of Chipewyan Indians. The first was from Fort Prince of Wales (near Churchill, Manitoba) into the northern Barren Grounds during 1770; on this trip, he failed to attain his goal. Within less than a month after his return, he set out again, and this time he reached the Coppermine River and the Arctic Ocean, finally returning to the fort in late 1772. During these travels he was the only European among the Chipewyan and other northern Athapaskan Indians, and he was a faithful observer of their customs. His account (Hearne 1958), which deals largely with the Chipewyan, was published first in 1795 under the title *A Journey from Prince of Wales's Fort, in Hudson's Bay to the Northern Ocean*. Most of what is known about the Chipewyan Indians during the early historic period is from the writings of Hearne. His descriptions of their seasonal activities, supernatural system, and a raid against a group of Copper Eskimos are particularly notable.

Of all the initial contacts between explorers and ethnics, none was more spectacular than the meeting in 1818 between the Polar Eskimos and the members of an English naval expedition. The reason for its import is that these Eskimos had thought that they were the only people in the world. John Ross (1777–1856) of the Royal Navy led two ships between Baffin Island and Greenland in search of a northwest passage. As the vessels were negotiating ice floes adjacent to northwestern Greenland, four dog sleds approached the ships but stopped at a distance. Fortunately Ross had aboard a Greenlandic Eskimo, John Sacheuse, who had accompanied the expedition from England. It was he who ventured forth alone and unarmed to meet the Eskimos, and John Ross (1819:83–84) described this fascinating episode in the history of ethnography.

> Sacheuse, after a time, thought he could discover that they spoke the Humooke dialect, drawling out their words, however, to an unusual length. He immediately adopted that dialect, and, holding up the presents, called out to them, *Kahkeite*, "Come on!" to which they answered, *Naakrie, naakrieai-plaite*, "No, no—go away;" and other words which he made out to mean, that they hoped we were not come to destroy them. The boldest then approached to the edge of the canal, and drawing from his boot a knife, repeated, "Go away"; "I can kill you." Sacheuse, not intimidated, told them he was also a man and a friend, and, at the same time, threw across the canal some strings of beads and a chequed shirt; but these they beheld with great distrust and apprehension, still calling, "Go away, don't kill us." Sacheuse now threw them an English knife, saying, "Take that." On this they approached with caution, picked up the knife, then shouted and pulled their noses; these actions were imitated by Sacheuse, who, in return, called out, *"Heigh, yaw!"* pulling his nose with the same gesture. They now pointed to the shirt, demanding what it was, and when told it was an article of clothing, asked of what skin it was made. Sacheuse replied, it was made of the hair of an animal, which they had never seen; on which they picked it up with expressions of surprise. They now began to ask many questions; for, by this time, they found the language spoken by themselves and Sacheuse, had sufficient resemblance to enable them to hold some communication.
>
> They first pointed to the ships, eagerly asking, "What great creatures those were?" "Do they come from the sun or the moon?" "Do they give

us light by night or by day?" Sacheuse told them that he was a man, that he had a father and mother like themselves; and, pointing to the south, said that he came from a distant country in that direction. To this they answered, "That cannot be, there is nothing but ice there." They again asked, "What creatures these were?" pointing to the ships; to which Sacheuse replied, that "they were houses made of wood." This they seemed still to discredit, answering, "No, they are alive, we have seen them move their wings." Sacheuse now inquired of them, what they themselves were; to which they replied, they were men, and lived in that direction, pointing to the north; that there was much water there; and that they had come here to fish for seaunicorns.

The English remained in the area only briefly, but the resultant descriptions of the people, while short, are quite comprehensive, unquestionably facilitated by the Eskimo interpreter.

Because detailed descriptions of the way any aboriginal people lived during their first year of direct historic contact are nearly unknown, the initial study of the Angmagsalik Eskimos in eastern Greenland is particularly valuable. Despite the fact that southwestern Greenland had been colonized by Icelanders in the tenth century, contact with eastern Greenland Eskimos in their homeland did not take place until 1884. The Norse and the later explorers of Greenland avoided the eastern coast because of the great ice masses which flowed southward from the arctic ice pack. The first party to venture along the southeastern coast in the vicinity of Angmagsalik was led by Gustav Holm (1849–1940). His expedition originated at a southern Greenland trading station and traveled northward by umiak, or large, open skin boat. Holm had good reason to believe that he could reach the Eskimos since occasional trading parties from their area had visited the southern coast. During the late summer of 1884, Holm (1914:6–13) and his party arrived at Angmagsalik, and they remained among the people until June of the following year. Their goals included mapping the area, collecting information about its natural history, and locating any settlements occupied by historic Scandinavians. They found no such remains in the area; instead, "We found at *Angmagsalik* a branch of Eskimo who had not previously been into contact with Europeans. We investigated the mode of life, customs, language and legends of this tribe, and brought home from there a collection of ethnographic objects" (Holm 1914:16). Holm's original account of these 413 Angmagsalik Eskimos appeared first in 1888–1889, and in 1914 it was published in English. It is a well-balanced ethnography of nearly 150 pages, and to this have been added compilations of the ethnographic data collected by Holm and others during the first contact year or shortly thereafter. This total text, of about 730 published pages (Thalbitzer

1914), is devoted to the aboriginal life of one small homogeneous group of Eskimos as they were observed at the time of historic contact.

The descriptions of ethnics by most explorers seldom are adequate because of the very nature of explorations. The peoples discovered may have been considered as quaint and friendly or barbaric and fierce, but more significantly, the observational demands on the discoverers were so great that indigenous populations were but one among many matters for attention. When the physical difficulties and privations of explorations are considered also, it is remarkable that we have any accounts at all of the peoples encountered. Understandably the most satisfactory records are those made by individuals who were long exposed to a particular people; for this reason the descriptions by de Vaca and Hearne are far superior to those of Pigafetta and Ross. Intimate and long-term contact with a people tended to dissipate the cultural differences which separated the observer from the observed, and this was a more important factor than the particular century in which the contact occurred. For this reason, the thirteenth-century writings of Rubruck about the Tartars are superior to most of the information provided about ethnics by Cook in the eighteenth century. In summary, we may expect most ethnographic accounts by explorers to be superficial because their exposures to tribal peoples were brief and their orientation was not ethnographic. Perhaps our greatest debt to these discoverers of small-scale societies is that through their published descriptions people first became aware of the remarkable range of human diversity.

TRADERS

Occasionally traders were the first to establish contact with tribal peoples, but more often they followed explorers, entering the new area at about the same time as missionaries. Although exploring parties carried some trade goods as a means for establishing contacts with aboriginal peoples, in the present context a "trader" is defined as a person whose primary reason for being in a locality was monetary gain. Some traders were transient, whereas others established residence among the people. The former included trading parties traveling overland or on vessels which anchored first off one coastal settlement and then another in pursuit of their commercial activities. In these circumstances the contacts with any particular people usually were superficial, and any sophisticated understanding was unnecessary. Transient traders often feared for their lives, and they were unlikely to risk close contacts with their clients. Thus, social intercourse was strained or cautiously maintained, and meaningful interaction was minimal. We can expect only limited descriptions of ethnics in the accounts of such traders; only under exceptional conditions did they leave useful information of an ethnographic nature.

The first notable contacts of European traders took place in the Middle Ages with the peoples of Maghreb, as North Africa was termed. Here Christians exchanged goods with their Moslem counterparts at ports along the Atlantic Ocean and southern Mediterranean Sea. Although Christian traders succeeded in entering Asia, they were prohibited from venturing into Africa beyond the coastal fringe. Jewish merchants who penetrated the Sahara and the Sudan provided the earliest information about these areas. The most important initial item of trade was gold, but soon slaves and ivory were widely sought. The fifteenth-century Portuguese attempted to gain direct access to African wealth, but their overland ventures met with little success. This in part spurred Prince Henry the Navigator to sponsor explorations by sea. The earliest extant account of contacts in western Africa is that of Alvise Cadamosto (c. 1426–1483), a Venetian in the service of Portugal. He made two trading ventures, possibly in 1455 and 1456, sailing as far south on his second voyage as the Jeba River, located just south of the westernmost point of Africa. His descriptions of Negroes living on the southern fringe of direct Moslem influence are important not only because of their early date, but because his narrative suggests the texture of the accounts of fifteenth-century traders. He dwelt primarily on matters of trade and navigation but recorded some information about peoples and places. Notably he did not exaggerate or stress the bizarre. Although his stay in Negro Africa was brief and he was handicapped at this southernmost landfall by not having an interpreter, he described with reasonable thoroughness that which could be observed in a short time (Crone 1937).

Negroes were valued not only as souls to be saved, but more importantly as a ready source of labor which could contribute significantly to the economic growth of Portugal. An active slave trade developed rapidly, and eventually this led to the enslavement of over twelve million Africans. The attitude of men who traveled to Africa solely to capture the people there was not one conducive to ethnographic recordings; this is well reflected in a fifteenth-century description of a raid by a Portuguese party on an island off the Guinea coast.

The "Moors" [a general Portuguese term for Africans] having evidently had unfortunate experience with former white visitors, with their women and children were already coming as quickly as they could out of their houses, because they had caught sight of their enemies. But they, crying "St. James," "St. George," and "Portugal," attacked them at once, killing and taking all they could. Then might you see mothers forsaking their children, and husbands their wives, each striving to escape as best he could. Some drowned themselves in the water; other sought to escape by hiding under their huts; others concealed their children among the seaweed (where our men found them afterward), hoping that they would thus escape notice. And at last our Lord God, who giveth a reward for every good deed, willed that for the toil they had undergone in his service, they should that day obtain victory over their enemies, as well as a guerdon and a payment for all their labor and expense; for they took captive of those Moors, what with men, women and children, 165, besides those that perished and were killed (Hart 1950:14–15).

Men who held such views were not likely to record the cultural ways of their captives. Furthermore, in an effort to retain a monopoly on the African trade, the Portuguese revealed little about their discoveries; maps and travel accounts were not only scarce but were kept secret (Hart 1950:12–31).

Traders of the second type, those residing at a particular locality for some time, were forced to maintain more lasting relationships with the peoples trading at their establishment, be it a store, fort, post, factory, or redoubt. Although resident traders often feared for their physical safety when they first opened their business, in time most of them came to trust their clientele, at least to a limited degree. Resident traders usually were literate and often had been selected because of their abilities to interact successfully with other people. These qualities made them likely to be better observers than their transient counterparts. In addition they acquired at least some proficiency in a local language or languages, and this ability to communicate led to a broader understanding of local customs.

According to Clark Wissler (1942:196) the first colonial American to write an extended interpretive account of Indians was the trader James Adair (c. 1709–c. 1783). He traveled, lived, and traded among Indians in the southeastern United States, particularly among the Chickasaw and Cherokee. By the time of his observations, which began in 1735, the people of this area had been rather badly buffeted by Europeans who contested each other and the Indians for control and occupancy of the region. Adair is known best for his thesis that the ancestors of Indians were Jews. This view of American Indian origins is no longer accepted, but the ethnographic data which he collected is quite valuable in ethnohistorical terms.

Another trader of note in early American history is Alexander H. Murray (1818–1874), who founded the Hudson's Bay Company post of Fort Yukon along the Yukon River near the Alaskan and Canadian border. He began constructing the fort in 1847, and his journal (Murray 1910) spans approximately this first year. This area had witnessed little prior contact since it had not been explored by Hudson's Bay Company employees until 1839. Although commercialism was Murray's first and foremost concern, his journal is notable for its information about the local Kutchin Indians and for his often reproduced pen-and-ink sketches of these Indians.

Extended and acceptable accounts by traders are comparatively unusual, but there are some examples worthy of citation. The Hollanders William Ten Rhyne (c. 1640–?) and Johannes G. Grevenbroek (c. 1644–c. 1726), both in the service of the Dutch East India Company, compiled valuable early accounts of the Hottentots in South Africa (Grevenbroek 1933; Ten Rhyne 1933). The East India Company merchantman Henry Wilson, who was shipwrecked on the Palau Islands in 1783, was the first European to contact these Pacific islanders. An account of this adventure was compiled by George Keate (1803), and although the party was there only for a brief period, the ethnographic information is valuable because of the fully aboriginal conditions prevailing. The trader Alfred Tetens (1835–1909), who lived on the Palau and adjacent islands in the 1860s when the region still was largely inaccessible, wrote about these people also (Tetens 1958), as did his contemporary and one-time business associate Andrew Cheyne (1852). Joel S. Polack (1807–1882), a trader in New Zealand from 1831 to 1837, developed an interest in the Maori to the point that he learned their language and wrote a two-volume work about these people (Polack 1840). Published personal accounts of traders are comparatively few and often disappointing, and yet traders were great keepers of records and of general information for their home company. Archival sources sometimes contain ethnographic data of immense value, but they usually have not been consulted in a meaningful manner by ethnographers. When the commercial archives of such organizations as the Hudson's Bay Company, Dutch East India Company, or Russian-American Company are researched, the yield will unquestionably be great.

CAPTIVES AND OTHERS

Possibly the accounts of an ethnographic nature which have the greatest reader appeal are those written by persons held in captivity by an aboriginal people. Writings by captives, especially those taken prisoner by Indians on the American Plains, may be quite fanciful, but some of them are useful if not valuable sources of ethnographic data. One of the most respected captive accounts was written by Richard Alsop (1967) based on interviews with John R. Jewitt (1783–1821), a man of English birth who was forced to live among the Nootka Indians for about two years. Jewitt was a blacksmith at the port of Hull, and when a New England trading vessel, the *Boston,* docked there, he signed on as the armorer for a trading venture to the Northwest Coast of North America. At the time the ship arrived in 1803, the British, Russians, and New Englanders were plying the coast, all engaged in the highly profitable sea otter trade to the Orient. The *Boston* anchored at Nootka Sound on Vancouver Island in order to obtain supplies of wood and water before sailing northward. While his ship was anchored, the captain of the *Boston* insulted the leader of the local Nootka Indians. These Indians had had intermittent contact with trading vessels since the 1770s and had been ill-treated before by some of the traders, but had not been in a position to retaliate. Now the opportunity presented itself, and the Indians killed and decapitated all of the crew except Jewitt, whose life was spared because they recognized his metalworking skill, and John Thompson, the sailmaker, who was spared because Jewitt insisted this man was his father. Jewitt worked as the personal blacksmith of his benefactor, who was a Nootka chief. Although he was capriciously treated, Jewitt soon acquired a wife and slaves of his own, and he learned to speak the Nootka language. From the time of the massacre until his escape on another trading vessel some twenty-eight months later, Jewitt lived as an Indian, and he kept a journal of his experiences. In one printed version written by Richard Alsop certain aspects of Nootka life are portrayed extremely well. The descriptions of the appearance of these people and of their clothing are notable, as illustrated by the remarks which follow.

The women keep their garments much neater and cleaner than the men, and are extremely modest in their deportment and dress; their mantle or Katsack, which is longer than that of the men, reaching quite to their feet, and completely enveloping them, being tied close under the chin, and bound with a girdle of the same cloth or of sea otter skin around their waists; it has also loose sleeves which reach to the elbows. Though fond of ornamenting their persons they are by no means so partial to paint as the men, merely colouring their eye-brows black and drawing a bright red stripe from each corner of the mouth towards the ear. Their ornaments consist chiefly of ear-rings, necklaces, bracelets, rings for the fingers and ankles, and small nose jewels, (the latter are however wholly confined to the wives of the king or chiefs) these are principally made out of copper or brass, highly polished and of various forms and sizes; the nose jewel is usually a small white shell or bead suspended to a thread. The wives of the common people frequently wear for bracelets and ankle rings, strips of the country cloth or skin of the Metamelth painted in figures, and those of the king or principal chiefs bracelets and necklaces, consisting of a numbre of strings of *Ife-waw* [dentalium shells], an article much prized by them, and which makes a very handsome appearance (Alsop 1967:62–63).

Elsewhere Jewitt recorded the erection of a plank house with a crafts-man's eye for details, and he provided specifics about domestic life, subsistence activities, and artifacts used in the village. The reader also be-comes privy to conflicts and intrigues which only a resident normally could know. This provides a revealing glimpse of Nootka political struc-ture; on the other hand, the presentation of religious and ceremonial life is almost superficial. Perhaps the greatest value of his account is the wide range of information covered; his is a far more balanced account than could be compiled by any explorer. It might be added that Jewitt's com-panion, Thompson, was very hostile and violent among his captors. He never thought well of the Indians and in fact was delighted to kill as many as he could when he accompanied the Nootka on a raid against their enemies. After being rescued, Jewitt went to Boston, Massachusetts, where he married, but he apparently could not settle down. He seems to have capitalized on his adventure by selling the book about his captivity in one community and then another. He also appeared in a play dealing with his adventures; titled *The Armourer's Escape*, the play ran in Phila-delphia briefly. Later Jewitt dressed as a Nootka and sang Indian songs at an amusement park.

One of the most remarkable adventures of a quasicaptive was that of William Buckley (1780–1856), who spent thirty-two years among aboriginal Australians near the modern city of Melbourne. One account of Buckley's adventures was assembled by William T. Pyke (1916) from contemporary published sources, and another was written by John Morgan (1967) after he had interviewed Buckley at length. In 1803 Buckley was among the first English convicts sent to the penal colony founded temporarily at Port Phillip in southeastern Australia. He escaped with three others, and although his companions soon decided to give themselves up, Buckley refused to do so. Since the administrators had abandoned the original colony in the meantime, Buckley's companions had nowhere to surrender, and they appear to have died soon after. Buckley went his own way, but he feared being discovered by the aborigi-nal people. For months he lived a solitary wandering life, often finding barely enough food to keep him alive. His description of his first contact with aboriginal Australians is worth quoting.

One day when I was indulging in these meditations, and gazing round from my Robinson Crusoe hut upon the surface of the waters, I thought I heard the sound of human voices; and, on looking up, was somewhat startled at seeing three natives standing on the high land immediately above me. They were armed with spears, and had opossum skins thrown over their shoulders, partially covering their bodies. Standing as they did, on an elevated position, armed too, and being myself totally defenceless, I confess I felt alarmed; so that hoping I had not been seen, I crept into a crevice in a rock near at hand, where I endeavoured to conceal myself. They were however soon upon my track, and shouting what I considered to be a call for me to come out, I resolved to do so; indeed I could not have remained there long on account of the water. With but faint hopes of meeting with good treatment at their hands, I crawled out from my shelter, and surrendered at discretion. They gazed on me with wonder: my size probably attracting their attention. After seizing both my hands, they struck their breasts, and mine also, making at the same time a noise between singing and crying: a sort of whine, which to me sounded very like premeditated mischief. Pointing to my hut, they evinced a desire to examine it—so we entered. My new friends, if friends they were to be, made themselves very much at home, although uninvited. One made up a large fire, another threw off his rug and went into the sea for crayfish, which, on his return, he threw alive into the flame—at the same time looking at me with an expression as much as to intimate that they intended to grill me next, by way of a change of diet. I can afford to smile, and even laugh now at the recollection; but, at the time, I assure the reader, I was by no means satisfied with the prospect before me, or with my visitors. At length my suspense ended, by their taking the fish, fairly dividing them, and handing to me the first and best portion. Having finished our meal, they gave me to understand they wished me to follow them (Morgan 1967:15–16).

Buckley returned as soon as possible to his solitary existence. At a later date, when he was exhausted and very hungry, Buckley was found by a small party of natives. He was carrying a spear that he had taken from a grave, and the people believed that he was a reincarnation of the spear's original owner. Within a few days he was well received at the camp of his "brother" and was invited to remain. Buckley soon lost all record of time except for the passing of the seasons, but he knew that he remained with his "relatives" for an extended period. On one occasion the people presented him with a wife, but she soon left him. Later he was joined by another woman, with whom he lived for a much longer period of time. The body of his narrative stresses the frequent and violent quarrels between his people and others; these disputes usually were caused by women in one way or another. His protectors were nearly annihilated at one point, and he returned to a solitary life for a year or two, being visited by friends only intermittently. Finally in 1835 settlers returned to Port Phillip, and Buckley was reunited with whites. He received a pardon and remained in the area serving as an interpreter for the settlers. In 1838 he moved to Hobarth, Tasmania, where he married a widow in 1840, but his life after leaving Port Phillip was relatively uneventful. At the time Buckley arrived in Australia, it was estimated that from 5,000 to 7,000 aborigines lived in the Victoria colony area, but by 1889 no more than 500 aboriginal Australians, including those of mixed ancestry, remained alive in this region. The Buckley tale, as it was reported by Morgan and Pyke, includes surprisingly little solid ethnographic information considering the length of time Buckley lived with aborigines. The stress is on the strangeness of the Australians' ways, their brutality, and their fierceness. Admittedly some useful descriptions are scattered through the text, but by and large Buckley's account illustrates that lengthy exposure to tribal peoples and a knowledge of the language does not necessarily lead to a well-rounded presentation of them.

One of the more widely known accounts of a small-scale society was written by an American sailor, and the editors to whom the manuscript was submitted originally doubted its authenticity—for good reasons. The book is best known under the title of *Typee*, and it was written by Herman Melville (1819–1891). He was twenty-one years old when he signed on the whaler *Acushnet*, and in 1842 he jumped ship at an island in the southern Marquesan Islands in the South Pacific Ocean. For a brief period he lived with a group of Marquesans, and *Typee* was supposedly based on his experiences. In actual fact, however, portions of the text were taken from accounts of previous travelers to the islands (Anderson 1939:117–195).

Autobiographies of aborigines are relatively common, especially after about 1900, and biographical accounts are even more plentiful. A bibliography of these works has been prepared by Lewis L. Langness (1965:59–82); as he points out, personal documents offer insight not only into the lives of individuals but also into the manner in which particular cultures functioned. Accounts of this nature will not be detailed because they most often are about highly acculturated individuals from societies which have become far removed from the baseline studies under prime consideration. In passing, however, it might be noted that one of the first biographical documents published by a professional anthropologist was a collection of three Gros Ventre war stories which Alfred L. Kroeber (1908) recorded in 1901. The earliest and most notable autobiography recorded in detail by an anthropologist is that of the Winnebago Indian, Sam Blow Snake. Titled *Crashing Thunder*, this work was compiled by Paul Radin and appeared first in 1920, an enlarged edition being printed in 1926. One of the most insightful life histories is that of Don C. Talayesva, a contemporary Hopi. Titled *Sun Chief*, the volume was prepared for publication by Leo W. Simmons (1942). The autobiography *Zulu Woman*, about Christina Sibiya (1948), the wife of the Zulu king Solomon, is a revealing portrait of a sensitive woman but again is essentially a contemporary account. Roy F. Barton lived and worked as a teacher among the Ifugaos of northern Luzon Island from 1908 to 1915. When he returned there in 1937, he recorded three significant biographies, which were published under the title of *Philippine Pagans* (1938). The most engaging study to appear in recent years about an aborigine is the biographical study *Ishi*. A Yana Indian of California, Ishi was the "last wild Indian in North America" when he was discovered in 1911. The record Theodora Kroeber (1961) assembled of his life and adventures is a sensitive and significant document.

The qualities limiting the usefulness of life histories usually apply as well to those ethnographies compiled by aborigines about their own people. Despite the fact that they usually are recorded late in a people's history, some of them have a real value. An exceptional record was compiled by Garcilaso de la Vega (1539–1616), whose mother was of the line of Inca nobility and whose father was Spanish. He was born eight years after the Spanish conquest of Peru, and his *Royal Commentaries of the Incas* is a wide-ranging history and ethnography of Inca life compiled from the author's experiences, historical sources, and verbal traditions of the Inca (de la Vega, 1966). David Malo (c. 1793–1853), a Hawaiian associated with the household of a high chief, was born shortly after Captain Cook discovered the islands. He had a keen and retentive mind and was in a social position to learn the ways and traditions of his people. Although his enthnography, *Hawaiian Antiquities* (1951), is colored by biases toward Christian norms, the work is nonetheless an extremely valuable commentary. An ethnography of the Lapps was written by Johan O. Turi, a Finnish Lapp, in 1907–1908 with the encouragement of Emilie D. Hatt, a Danish anthropologist. *Turi's Book of Lappland* (1931) is a fascinating and highly informative account. The same is true of the book written by Lucy Thompson called *To the American Indian* (1916), a misleading title. This book is in fact a fine account of the Yurok Indians of northern California.

Ethnographic information may be conveyed visually as well as verbally, and thus it is pertinent to mention a few of the more notable illustrations of aboriginal peoples. Accompanying one Italian printing of the first letter by Columbus, which appeared in Florence in 1493, is an imaginative woodcut which depicts the landing of Columbus and gives a vague impression of the people discovered (see Frontispiece). Between 1497 and 1504 there appeared what is reportedly the first graphic representation of American Indians based more on fact than on imagination. Reprinted herein as a plate on page 34, the accompanying caption is as revealing as the illustration itself (Winsor 1889:vol. 2, 19, 52).

The first artist to make a set of watercolors of the Indians in present-

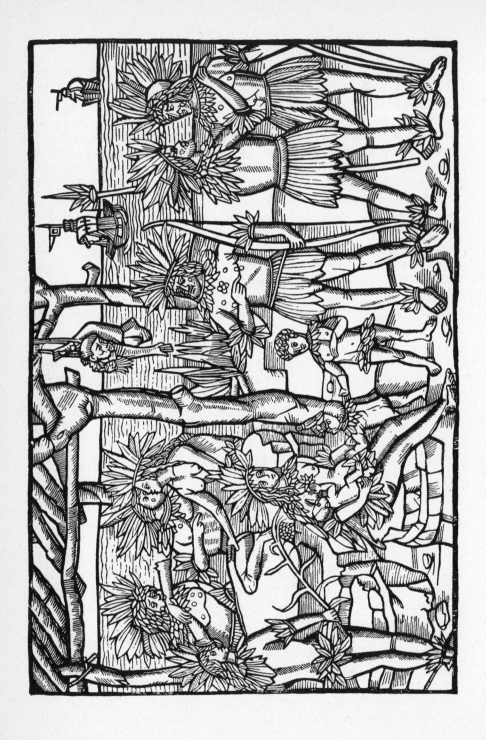

day United States was John White. He arrived in 1585 on one of the vessels outfitted by Walter Raleigh to colonize Virginia, and he remained at the settlement on Roanoke Island for a year before returning to England with Francis Drake. White sailed back to the colony in 1587, but he soon returned to England for additional supplies. Due to a war with Spain, vessels were not sent back to the Roanoke colony until 1590. When White and the others arrived, there was no sign of the settlers, and so they returned to England, leaving the disappearance of the original Roanoke settlement an unsolved mystery to this day. During his stay in Virginia, White made sixty-three watercolors, some of which were reproduced as engravings in A *Brief and True Report of the New Found Land of Virginia*, a book about the colony authored by Thomas Hariot and published in 1590 by Theodore De Bry. White's original paintings were not published in color until 1946 (Lorant 1965). Of the sixty-three pictures of fauna, flora, maps, scenes and people, twenty were of Indian subjects and have been reproduced frequently because of the valuable ethnographic details provided (see the plate on p. 36).

CHRISTIAN MISSIONARIES

Roman Catholic missionaries assembled better early ethnographic accounts than did any explorers, traders, or other missionaries, and diverse circumstances contribute to this fact. First and foremost, the Roman Catholic Church was the most powerful and best organized institution in all of Europe during the great era of maritime expansion. The primary purpose of the church was to save souls, and the countless tribal peoples discovered were all persons to be converted. From Europe,

Aboriginal Americans as first depicted from observation. The print was issued in Augsburg sometime between 1497 and 1504. The text accompanying the illustration is as follows, "This figure represents to us the people and island which have been discovered by the Christian King of Portugal, or his subjects. The people are thus naked, handsome, brown, well-shaped in body; their heads, necks, arms, private parts, feet of men and women, are a little covered with feathers. The men also have many precious stones on their faces and breasts. No one else has anything, but all things are in common. And the men have as wives those who please them, be they mothers, sisters, or friends; therein make they no distinction. They also fight with each other; they also eat each other, even those who are slain, and hang the flesh of them in the smoke. They become a hundred and fifty years of age, and have no government" (Winsor 1889: vol. 2, 19).

John White's watercolor of the town of Pomeiock in North Carolina (from Swanton 1946).

Roman Catholic missionaries ventured forth to proselytize, and in many instances they encountered formidable, state religious systems whose representatives were not only hostile but well organized. In contrast, the opposition aroused when ethnics were contacted usually was disorganized, and their hostile feelings were of shorter duration than those encountered among complex societies. For these reasons Roman Catholics felt that they could work most successfully among ethnics. These men were literate and very well educated by the standards of the times, and as a result they were better than ordinary observers and recorders. Because they were obligated by higher authorities to keep accurate records and to make periodic reports about their progress, their accounts had coherence and continuity. Furthermore, a missionary often arrived early in the contact period, either with explorers or shortly thereafter. A missionary usually devoted years to working with a particular people, and of great importance, he was obligated to learn the language of those that he hoped to convert. The greatest single drawback to missionary accounts, from the standpoint of modern ethnography, is that the records often were overly concerned with religious matters. Nonetheless, the best sources of documentary information about many small-scale societies for the early period of European contact are church archives.

No clergy accompanied Columbus on his first voyage, but on the second, 1493–1496, Friar Ramon Pane was included in the party. Pane's goal was to convert the Taino of Haiti, but Columbus also asked him to collect information about the "ceremonies and antiquities" of these people. His account is devoted primarily to myths, curing practices, and his efforts to convert the people. Pane learned the Taino language, and he employed surprisingly modern field techniques in certain respects. He named his primary informants, defined their statuses, and noted the source of his information. At one point he mentioned that he was reporting only what he had heard, and elsewhere he stated that he had seen some of the reported events. Pane also noted in one description that he recorded the informant's statements in writing at the time of the interview. The information which he collected is not nearly as extensive as the accounts soon to be collected by other Roman Catholic missionaries, but *Ramon Pane is important as the first person to systematically assemble ethnographic information in the New World* (Bourne 1907).

Unquestionably, the first great missionary-ethnographer was the Franciscan, Fray Bernadino de Sahagun (1499–1590), who arrived in Mexico in 1529 and remained there until his death. The Aztec had been defeated by the Spanish in 1521, and Sahagun's purpose was to proselytize these Indians. However, he soon became primarily absorbed in recording information about the Aztec; he learned to speak Nahuatl, the language of the Aztec, and systematically began to record their customs and history, even to the point of chronicling the Spanish conquest from the Indian point of view. His efforts to preserve pagan beliefs were poorly received by some Franciscans, but in 1558 a sympathetic superior encouraged him to continue his work. It was in *Historia general de las cosas divinas, humans y naturales de Nueva Espana* that Sahagun set forth the core of his ethnographic research, rationalizing as its purpose that evangelizing the Indians would be more successful if the cultural and social norms for the aboriginal period were available. His methods included recording data in the aboriginal language, conducting open-ended interviews, selecting informants with great care, using questionnaires, having informants respond to his questions by writing their answers in the aboriginal pictorial texts, consulting old pictorial records, training Aztec assistants to collect information for him, and crosschecking the information provided by informants. Since the Aztec had developed a writing system of their own in aboriginal times, they are not technically within the range of ethnics. I have included Sahagun, however, because his account of the Aztec is one of the most comprehensive ethnographic studies ever assembled for a non-European population early in its history. (d'Olwer n.d.).

The Society of Jesus was founded in 1540 by Ignatius Loyola, who espoused that the members support "the knowledge necessary to be a good Christian, the humane sciences, from the rudiments of grammar to the highest branches of study." In its organizational framework missionary work was not stressed but teaching was. Soon the order became embroiled in bitter theological conflicts, from which it emerged with a liberal educational philosophy. When the opportunity presented itself to conduct missionary activities in eastern Canada, the society was financially and organizationally ready to undertake the task with dedication. Each year between 1611 and 1768 the Jesuit missionaries sent their letters, journals, and reports to Quebec, where they were incorporated into the annual report or *Jesuit Relations*. Reuben G. Thwaites edited and translated the original reports and combined them with supplementary materials into seventy-three volumes titled *The Jesuit Relations and Allied Documents* (Kenton 1927: vol. 1, xiii–xvii; Mealing 1967: vii–xii; Thwaites 1896–1901). Thwaites' work is a notable contribution to modern scholarship, and the Jesuit reports he incorporates are among the best of early ethnographic accounts.

If we hesitantly set aside Sahagun since he worked among a literate people, then *the first field ethnographer of recent times, meaning after 1700, was Joseph-Francois Lafitau (1681–1746)*. Lafitau was a French Jesuit missionary who worked among the Canadian Iroquois from 1712 to 1717. Most of these Indians were Mohawk who settled at Caughnawaga near Montreal at the inducement of the missionaries and became known as the "French Praying Indians." In 1724 Lafitau published a two-volume work in French titled *Customs of the American Savages, Compared with Customs of Earliest Times*. Surprising as it may seem, this work has not yet appeared in English, although William N. Fenton and Elizabeth L. Moore are in the process of preparing an English edition. As Fenton (1969) points out in an article, Lafitau never received just recognition by his contemporaries, and even today his contributions are largely unrecognized in the United States. The work of Lafitau is an ethnographic landmark in a number of important respects: He wrote about a broad range of topics knowingly and in detail; he anticipated Clark Wissler's universal culture pattern system in the descriptive arrangement of his text, and he described the Iroquois in terms of their own norms rather than those of Europeans, indicating acceptance of the concept of cultural relativity (Fenton 1969; Harris 1968:17).

The information collected among ethnics by Protestant missionaries is less impressive than that compiled by their Roman Catholic counterparts. Most Protestant denominations were relatively late entrants into the missionary field, and some peoples among whom they worked had prior long-term exposure to Roman Catholics. Often the organizational support behind Protestant workers in the field was poor and funds extremely limited. The missionaries from some denominations were poorly trained and were very intolerant of the customs of the peoples they hoped to convert. Some were short-term workers who made few reports and gained only a superficial understanding of the peoples among whom they proselytized. These statements are by no means intended as a blanket indictment of Protestant missionaries as ethnographers, for some of them collected valuable information. It is in general true, however, that by comparison with Roman Catholic reporters they are a poor second.

Because of their late arrival among most ethnics, Protestant missionaries were not in a position to compile baseline ethnographic data. Nonetheless, Clark Wissler (1942:197) expressed the opinion that "the first great leaders in American ethnography" were David Zeisberger (1721–1808) and John G. E. Heckewelder (1743–1823), who were Moravian Church missionaries. It is apparent, however, from the dates of their lives alone that the information which they recorded, largely in Ohio, deals primarily with the acculturation of Indian refugees from other areas. The information which they assembled, along with that of most other early Protestants, is valuable primarily as ethnohistorical data.

Protestant missionaries commonly published books about the peoples they proselytized, and the best of these works are more than simple, general accounts about heathen peoples in strange lands. Among the notable contributions from Africa is the study by John Roscoe (1861–1932) of the Ganda, who lived along the northwestern shore of Lake Victoria. Roscoe was a member of the Church Missionary Society and lived in Uganda for eighteen years, during which time he assembled the information for his book *The Baganda* (1966). Possibly the most respected missionary account from Africa was that of Henri A. Junod (1863–1934), who was Swiss and a member of the Swiss Romande Mission. He arrived in Mozambique in 1889 and worked in the area intermittently until 1921. His account, *The Life of a South African Tribe*, appeared first in 1912; it was extensively revised for a second edition published in 1926 and was reprinted in 1962 and 1966. The work is about the Thonga (Bathonga) of Mozambique and serves as a baseline ethnography for the precolonial era. In the Pacific region one of the most notable Protestant missionaries was the Methodist Missionary Society worker, Thomas Williams (1815–1891). Williams lived among the Fijians from 1840 to 1853, and his book as well as his journals are superior ethnographic sources (Henderson 1931*a*, 1931*b*; Williams

1858). These examples serve to illustrate the nature of the better studies by Protestants; each, however, was written long after initial historic contact with the peoples involved.

OVERVIEW

When Europeans first sailed south of the equator along the western shore of Africa and when they forged overland routes into Asia, they found men of strange but not unexpected appearance. Their scriptures provided the key to these differences. Noah had three sons, and from the one called Japhet Europeans were derived, from Shem arose the Asiatics, and from Ham the Africans were descended. These all were normal men, but it was also thought that at the ends of the earth there were monstrous beings of quasihuman form. The discovery of the New World was disconcerting, for the humans occupying it were not monsters nor was their skin color clearly black, white, or yellow (Lee 1929:263–265). Amerigo Vespucci (1454–1512) by 1506 considered that the skin color of Indians was a reddish cast because the sun had discolored their white skin, and he compared them with the Tartars in appearance (Huddleston 1967:6). But were Indians really human? The Spanish conquistadores reasoned that they appeared human in form but were not true men; therefore their property could be seized and they could be enslaved. Francis of Vittoria (c. 1480–1546), a Spanish theologian and the founder of modern international law, argued that Indians were human beings whose land and other possessions were to be respected and that their enslavement could not be justified (Cohen 1960:288–290). In 1537 Indians were recognized as "truly men" in a papal bull issued by Pope Paul III.

The English of the sixteenth century were unable to match the colonizing successes of the Spanish and Portuguese, but they often brought aborigines to England, voluntarily or otherwise. One reason offered was the need to teach such persons to speak English so that they might serve as interpreters on later ventures. Another rationalization was that the heathen could observe Christianity functioning in England and then would appreciate its merits so much that on returning to their homeland they would impart their enlightenment to others. Most of all, however, exotic peoples were transported to England because Englishmen were extraordinarily curious to see them. The first such strangers to arrive were Eskimos; they soon were followed by an Indian chief from Brazil, an African Negro—who married an Englishwoman—, and several Indians from Virginia and Venezuela. In time the difficulty of transforming such persons into Englishmen was realized; nonetheless, they usually were judged as human and not infrequently as quite intelligent. When it came to an abstraction of an aborigine, however, such as Shakespeare's Caliban in *The Tempest*, the character was much more brutish than human (Lee 1929).

To generalize on explorers' views of aboriginal peoples is nearly impossible. Ethnics first were thought to be without human qualities, but after they were contacted in their own environment, they often were idealized as perfect beings living in utopian bliss. Sooner more often than later, conflicts developed, however, and the aborigines would be dealt with firmly, with or without justice. These and other perspectives ebb and flow through the writings of the time (e.g., Jones 1964). What is most important from the viewpoint of ethnography is that rarely were exotic peoples described in a reasonably thorough manner, irrespective of what the observers might have thought about them. Contacts between explorers and ethnics often were of such brief duration that all resultant remarks are superficial. As captives or missionaries, some Europeans later had more extended contacts, but they were not always good observers. Even if their perception was keen, the range of data noted usually was restricted. Only in rare instances did an explorer, missionary, or other observer attempt to record systematically a wide range of information about any particular small-scale society. Since ethnographic information usually was compiled tangentially to the observer's primary purpose for being among the people involved, it was largely a matter of chance whether he would be of the type to assemble good or poor descriptions. What we seek but find only rarely at this stage are men who were perceptive enough to record detailed ethnographic data before formal training in such endeavors became a reality.

TWO

THE RISE OF ETHNOGRAPHY

The systematic collection of descriptive information about aboriginal peoples had no clear beginning, and no distinct historical break separates adequate or superior ethnographic reports from accounts which are superficial and pedestrian. To the question, Who is to be accorded the distinction of being the first ethnographer?, there is no ready answer. In a broad sense of the word, it is Herodotus among the ancients and Sahagun in the late Middle Ages. A purist would set aside the works of these men because they described literate peoples and name Lafitau as the first true ethnographer because of his work among ethnics, the thoroughness of his reporting, and his relative freedom from biases.

The distinctions between levels of ethnographic reporting also may be considered on a different basis. In certain respects it is reasonable to assume that an individual becomes an ethnographer when the subject dominates his intellectual life, does not serve as a means to any other end, and leads to an account having breadth and quality. By intensively studying the lives of an aboriginal people, an ethnographer comes to understand the organization of their society and the nature of their culture in a manner distinct from that of a casual observer or even of an aboriginal member of the society involved. The professional ethnographer is able to generalize effectively about the behavior of a people studied. (Lafitau anticipates this perspective, but since he made no impact on the intellectual climate at the time, he will not be considered.) Professional ethnography originated when persons were hired or commissioned by museums, learned societies, governmental agencies, or universities to assemble a broad range of ethnographic data about ethnics, information which served no immediate or practical purpose but which provided broad insight into the nature of the lifeways of the peoples studied. If a museum commissions someone simply to buy artifacts, the collector is not an ethnographer, since his involvement is far too limited in scope. Likewise, an individual hired to make a highly restricted and specialized study is not in a formal sense an ethnographer since he deals with a limited aspect of ethnographic data. Explorers, missionaries, and similar persons are not ethnographers, although a few are far better observers and recorders than some professionally trained persons. For an individual to be designated an *ethnographer* his primary job must be that of an anthropologist, and he must have made at least one comprehensive study of ethnics, whether it be a baseline ethnography, ethnographic reconstruction, acculturation study, or ethnohistory. Many, but not all, anthropologists who are at least part-time ethnographers blanch at being called by the latter terms. Since by definition the subdiscipline is solely a descriptive compilation, some anthropologists consider ethnography to be work more fitting for graduate students than for themselves.

As the geographical knowledge of Europeans broadened and familiarity with both local and distant peoples expanded, compendiums of customs, both real and imagined, attracted readers. Sebastian Muenster (1489–1552) authored *Cosmographia*, which was a popular compilation in the tradition of the encyclopedists and *the first modern work about peoples of the world*. It was published originally in 1544 and for 100 years remained an appealing source; this work was translated into six languages and appeared in forty-six editions. Muenster briefly described some forty different peoples of Europe, Asia, and the New World. The sketches were of an ethnographic nature but were very brief except for those about the Germans, Tartars, and Turks. He relied heavily on earlier sources which were by tradition acceptable. Recently acquired knowledge of New World peoples had no effect on the manner in which these people were represented; collectively, they were considered to be cannibals (Hodgen 1964:127–128, 143–151).

The earliest book-length study of ethnics was about the Lapps and was published in 1673 by Johannes Scheffer (1621–1679). Scheffer was a classical philologist with an interest in history as well as archaeology. He had never visited Lappland; instead he derived his information from historical sources as well as from clerics and officials who were familiar with the Lapps. This work, *Lapponia*, which was published originally at Frankfurt, is the first lengthy ethnographic reconstruction of a tribal people (Casson 1939:118–122; Slotkin 1965:96).

The first academic center for anthropological studies was at Goettingen, which was established as a university in 1734 (Ackerknecht

1955:83). It was here that the intellectual father of physical anthropology, Johann F. Blumenbach (1752–1840) taught from 1775 to 1840. The physical anthropologist Christoph Meiners (1747–1816) also taught for many years at Goettingen. Although he wrote about races and cultures and recognized the need for a distinct "history of humanity," Meiners was himself comparatively uninterested in the ways of tribal peoples (Lowie 1937:10–11). Johann Georg A. Forster (1754–1794), usually known as George Forster, was associated with Goettingen and received an honorary degree there. He was born near Danzig where his Scottish father, Johann R. Forster, was a pastor. The elder Forster abandoned the ministry when George was a youth in order to pursue literary and naturalistic interests. Together they went to Russia in 1765 and on to England the following year. They translated into English and then published Bougainville's travels, and the father became the naturalist on Cook's second voyage, 1772–1775, his son serving as an assistant. Johann Forster had expected to publish an account of the voyage, but since Cook was determined to do so himself, the admiralty ordered Forster not to write about the voyage. However, George published such a narrative in 1777, just before Cook's own account appeared. As a result of his two-volume work George became well known as a naturalist, but he and his father were criticized for failing to live up to the spirit of their agreement with Cook. In 1778 George left England permanently and for a short while taught natural history at Wilna, but he was restless by nature and never settled long at any particular location. According to Erwin H. Ackerknecht (1955:85–86),

> Up to Forster's time and long thereafter, ethnography was written by sedentary scholars, using not always discriminately the reports of travellers who neither were qualified nor cared to generalize on their observations. Forster was the first ethnographic observer who was also a scientist, not only more capable of observing, but also more willing to analyze and generalize his observations . . . His goal was to study the totality of a culture, and to study the cultures of primitives on their own merits rather than merely to compare their traits with 'superior' Western behavior.

It was naturalists in the tradition of George Forster who were among the first to describe ethnics in a reasonably adequate manner.

Currently the words "natural history" most often are used to mean the popularized presentation of information about plants, animals, minerals, and man, but their former meaning was far less pedestrian. Natural history once was considered a branch of knowledge dealing with the description and classification of all natural objects. The English words "natural history" came into use in 1555, while "naturalist" originated in 1587 (*Oxford Universal Dictionary* 1955:1312). The term "natural history" has not yet been abandoned to the amateurs entirely; it still may be used to mean the natural development of something over a period of time or the relationship of a form to its general or ecological setting (*Webster's Third New International Dictionary* 1961:1507). Natural history was alternatively called natural theology in nineteenth-century England, and it was an honorable pursuit for clerics, who studied the natural world in attempts to learn more about the infinite variety of God's created forms. It was in this vein that William Paley published a book in 1802 titled *Natural Theology; or, Evidences of the Existence and Attributes of The Deity*. This work was above all else an attempt to reconcile the order in the natural world with a divine design. The volume was to make a profound impression on Charles Darwin during his student days at Cambridge, and Paley's thesis lingered to trouble Darwin later in his life (Himmelfarb 1962:35–36).

Above all else a naturalist traditionally was a meticulous observer and a careful recorder of what he saw and heard. Furthermore, he described his subjects as objectively as possible. These methodological ideals were approximated rather than realized even when studying spiders or kangaroos. No matter where a naturalist traveled or when he lived, he remained a person whose own culture colored his objectivity because he had no training in methods of minimizing cultural biases. A naturalist may have thought of himself as completely objective when examining a mineral specimen under a microscope, watching a bird through binoculars, or examining a plant community growing on a hillside, but his background influenced his description of such observations despite his best intentions.

When a naturalist studied men, his ability to achieve objective reporting was even more strained. The observer had to be proximal to his subjects, and consequently he disturbed, or even disrupted, their life rhythm. A white naturalist in a community of Negroes stood out as obviously different. The same was true of a female intent on studying hunters or a young man attempting to collect tribal lore within the realm of the aged. Furthermore, and of more critical importance, the observer of exotic peoples usually did not speak the language of his subjects, and this posed a serious barrier. Most naturalists who worked in foreign settings for relatively brief periods of time required the services of sophisticated interpreters. To these handicaps must be added others which resulted from one's particular cultural background and personality. When totaled, the difficulties inherent in assembling undistorted natural histories about ethnics are so many that one may marvel that they were attempted at all and furthermore that some have remained respected even in the present.

The goals of a naturalist were to record, describe, and arrange, but a naturalist was not a scientist. Scientists search for rules or laws which govern the association of natural forms and behaviors, whereas naturalists assemble the raw materials or data with which the scientist can work. The great age of naturalists, which was between about 1750 and 1900, came gradually to an end after most natural forms throughout the world had been located, described, and broadly classified. The rise of intensive scientific specialization which began about 1840 ultimately put the old-time naturalists into eclipse.

With respect to the study of man, we find that in its essence the natural history stage struggles somewhat feebly on. Some, perhaps only a few, anthropologists feel that we should follow the naturalists' tradition and concentrate our efforts on broadly describing the last ethnics before they become extinct. According to this point of view, there will be time enough to analyze the descriptive reports after the data are collected. Others consider this position nonsense and argue that the task is to collect and to analyze concurrently, since only in this manner is it possible to determine which data are most pertinent and should be most diligently sought. When weighed against the historical background of other fields of human knowledge, the latter position seems more reasonable. (A third view must be acknowledged as growing in acceptance. It is that the anthropologists' involvement with primitives is a disgraceful exercise in intellectual masturbation and that the real task before him is that of a social scientist, to work actively and diligently in order to plan the future of man.)

PIONEERS

A notable naturalist whose work was oriented toward ethnography was Henry R. Schoolcraft (1793–1864). He was born in New York State, and as a young man he became a glassmaker, soon rising to the position of superintendent of various factories. However, the unsettled economic conditions produced by the War of 1812 led him to abandon this occupation. In 1818 he headed westward, intent on writing a natural history and engaging in business. His first book, *A View of the Lead Mines of Missouri* (1819), led to his participation as the mineralogist in the Cass Expedition, which sought to establish the source of the Mississippi River. The expedition's goal was not realized, but the semiofficial record of the trip published by Schoolcraft (1821) established his reputation as an authority on the area. As a result of this and other writings he was appointed in 1822 as Indian agent in charge of tribes in the Lake Superior region. The following year, while still serving as an agent, he married Jane Johnston, who was seventeen years old and had just returned from Europe, where she had been educated for nine years. Jane Johnston's father was a white fur trader, and her mother was a Chippewa (Ojibwa). Until her death in 1842, Schoolcraft's wife helped him collect ethnographic data, particularly folklore. She spoke a number of local Indian languages and had access to information which was unavailable to an outsider. As an Indian agent Schoolcraft supported laws to prohibit the sale of intoxicants to Indians, helped arrange treaties, and in 1830–1831 was sent to end the hostilities between the Chippewa and their Siouan-speaking enemies. The following year he made another trip, this time with the purposes of vaccinating Indians, collecting information about the fur trade, and compiling statistics about the Indians in his area. All of these tasks were accomplished at least in part, and in addition he discovered the true source of the Mississippi River, a lake which he named Lake Itasca (Mason 1958:xi–xx). The first important book written by Schoolcraft about Indians was titled *Algic Researches* (1839). "Algic" was a word derived from Allegheny and Atlantic which Schoolcraft coined to refer to those Indians who had lived in these areas at the beginnings of their history (Schoolcraft 1839:vol. 1, fn., 12–13). This work, produced originally in two volumes, was reissued three times, each under a different title (Pearce 1965:121). *Algic Researches* is a compilation of folklore collected from tribes in the eastern part of the United States. In an introduction to the stories and tales Schoolcraft (1839:vol. 1, 11–12) explains that his purpose in collecting oral literature was to make Indian institutions and Indian thought patterns more comprehensible. In a further introductory statement he casually reviews the history of European and Indian relations in order to demonstrate that through most of the history of contact between these peoples circumstances prevented the collection of systematic information about Indian lifeways. He further discusses the complexity of Indian languages and a diversity of other matters pertaining to Indians, but he leaves the modern reader with very uncomfortable feelings about his unity of purpose and his objectivity. The Indian "does not seem to open his eyes on the prospect of civilization and mental exaltation held up before him, as one to whom the scene is new and attractive" (Schoolcraft 1839:vol. 1, 50–51). Schoolcraft sees the Indian as both good and evil and regrets his failure to recognize the superiority of the ways of civilized man.

Oneota, which first appeared serially in 1844–1845, was published nine times as a book. Although it had five different titles, this work appeared most often as *The Indian in His Wigwam* (Pearce 1965:121, 123). The 1848 edition of this work opens with an account of Schoolcraft's first westward trip and closes with an Indian war song. In parlance now current, it is a nonbook. As in *Algic Researches*, Schoolcraft reasoned that the key to understanding Indians was to be found in their religion, which he felt formed their character and guided their behavior. "By it [religion] he preserves his identity, as a barbarian, and when this is taken away, and the true system substituted, he is still a Red Man, but no longer, in the popular sense, an *Indian*—a barbarian, a pagan" (Schoolcraft 1848:67). He did not develop this theme extensively but went on to make other generalizations which can only be considered as quaint by a modern reader. For example, he noted that Indians have continued to live in a state of barbarism because of their "false" religion and the absence of political organization among them, although he exempted the Aztec and Iroquois from the latter void. At the same time he felt that Indian ways must be considered in terms of Indian life: "If he does not come to the same conclusions, on passing questions, as we do, it is precisely because he sees the premises, under widely different circumstances. The admitted errors of barbarism and the admitted truths of civilization, are two very different codes" (Schoolcraft 1848:69). This volume is a series of eclectic ramblings, most of which are of dubious merit, yet during his lifetime Schoolcraft was considered an outstanding authority on Indians. As a governmental official, Schoolcraft was above all else an agent to civilize the Indians, but in his writing about them he attempted to be as objective as possible. (The factual background for Henry W. Longfellow's poem "Hiawatha" was drawn from *Algic Researches*; see Osborn and Osborn 1942.) Schoolcraft's reputation as an authority on Indians did not endure very long after his death. In the history of ethnography his place is insecure; his principal contributions were in the fields of folklore and acculturation.

Lewis H. Morgan (1818–1881), born near Aurora, New York, was the son of a successful farmer and landowner. He studied law at Union College and was admitted to the bar, but because of the economic conditions following the Panic of 1837, he could not find employment as a lawyer. For a number of years he helped manage the family farms and wrote articles for literary journals, particularly on the subject of ancient history. In 1844 Morgan moved to Rochester, New York, where he opened a law office and became increasingly successful by concentrating on railroad and mining business. At this period fraternal organizations were popular, and Morgan had organized one called the Order of the Gordian Knot. The group was reorganized in 1843 as a social and study club called the Grand Order of the Iroquois. At their meetings the members wore clothing patterned after that of the Iroquois, carried tomahawks, and orated in a manner which they considered appropriate for Indians. Some members, including Morgan, sought to place increased stress on learning more about Indians, and after an internal struggle a "literary committee" was formed to study writings about the Iroquois. Morgan soon realized that comparatively little was known about the Iroquois League, which was composed of the Cayuga, Mohawk, Seneca, Oneida, Onondaga, and Tuscarora tribes. He began making inquiries, and while in an Albany bookstore in 1844, he met Ely Parker, the son of a Seneca chief. Parker had been educated in a Baptist mission school, and he was chosen by members of his band, the Tonawanda, to study law in order to defend their legal rights. The same day that they met, Parker invited Morgan to meet and talk with other Seneca in their hotel room, with Parker serving as the interpreter. During the two days which followed, Morgan continued with further interviews concerning the organization of the Iroquois League and other ethnographic topics. Parker enlisted the aid of Morgan and the Grand Order of the Iroquois to help fight the Ogden Company's efforts to gain title to Seneca lands, and in 1846 Morgan delivered a petition to the President of the United States and to the Senate in behalf of the Seneca. The response was minimal, but in the spring of the same year, hearings were held before the U.S. Senate Committee on Indian Affairs about the Tonawanda land dispute. Schoolcraft and Parker served as expert witnesses to interpret Iroquois legal norms; *this has been reported as the beginning of applied anthropology in the United States* (Resek 1960:1–32).

When it appeared that the Seneca would be moved from their lands, Morgan intensified his efforts to collect ethnographic information. Parker contributed a great deal of information, and Morgan visited several Iroqouis reservations to gather still more data. The Tonawanda were especially responsive to his inquiries since he had come to their aid, and in 1846 Morgan was adopted as a Seneca warrior in the Hawk clan (sib). His newly achieved status made it possible for him to obtain information of an even more esoteric nature from his informants. The Grand Order of the Iroquois dissolved in 1847, but the intensity of Morgan's interest in the Iroquois had established him as a leading authority on their way of life. In 1847–1848 he published a series of fourteen articles which appeared as "letters" in the *American Whig Review*. Each article dealt with Iroquois ethnography, and he soon reworked the series into a book titled *League of the Ho-de-no-sau-nee or Iroquois. Published in 1851, the volume was the first comprehensive field ethnography ever written which was to make a strong impact on the emerging field of anthropology.*

The table of contents of *League of the Iroquois* reflects the breadth of Morgan's inquiries into the lives of these Indians. He discussed their setting, history, political organization, religious system, social life, manufactures, and certain dimensions of historic changes which affected them. He dealt with most topics in a clear expository style. His rationale for writing the book was set forth in the first sentence of the preface. "To encourage a kinder feeling towards the Indian, founded upon a truer knowledge of his civil and domestic institutions, and of his capabilities for future elevation, is the motive in which this work originated." This was the statement that Morgan had composed earlier as the preamble to the constitution of the Grand Order of the Iroquois (Porter 1954:vol. 2, 155, note 3). His purpose was humanistic, yet his reference to the "future elevation" of the Indian is a good indication of what he considered the Indian's position to be in relation to whites. This attitude does not emerge as dominant, however, until he discusses the future of American Indians in the closing chapter. When compared with contemporary writings about aboriginal peoples, Morgan's League is outstanding, first because he presented such a breadth of subject matter and second because he approached his task with objectivity. His relative freedom from bias is particularly impressive when compared with other authors of his time, especially Schoolcraft. The League has continued to be the best general source about the Iroquois. Unquestionably an ethnohistorian today could compile an Iroquois ethnography far superior to that of Morgan, since a vast amount of additional information about these Indians has been recorded (Fenton 1951:296–310), but no one has made the attempt. Thus Morgan's book stands firm and is rivaled only by Annemarie A. Shimony's study of a segment of the Canadian Iroquois population (Shimony 1961).

What are the failings of Morgan's Iroquois ethnography? First, he did not compile an aboriginal baseline study as he seems to have intended but rather wrote a composite ethnographic reconstruction and ethnohistory. Second, the book is about the Iroquois in general only when dealing with League matters; it is above all else a description of one group of Seneca. The work may best be considered an account of Seneca acculturation. Since the Iroquois were in rather intensive contact with the Dutch, English, and French by around 1650, for Morgan to gather data about aboriginal conditions from informants nearly two hundred years later is not realistic, especially in light of the changes in Iroquois life shortly before and after the Revolutionary War. As the recent ethnohistorical researches of Cara B. Richards (1957, 1967) and Mary E. F. Mathur (1969) demonstrate, the Iroquois had undergone profound changes before Morgan's time. The chapters he devoted to history, geography, and language are weak, and his understanding of subsistence activities was poor. Strangely enough, he was convinced that the Iroquois subsisted primarily by hunting, yet they clearly had a well-developed farming economy at the time of historic contact and later. Morgan is best in his discussions of material culture and of the organization of the League (Stern 1931:62–72).

Alfred C. Haddon (1855–1940), born in London, was trained as a zoologist at Cambridge, and in 1880 he began to teach in Dublin. His interest in marine zoology led him on a collecting trip taken among the islands of Torres Strait between Australia and New Guinea. Here he became interested in the local people, and his recording of information about them led to a lasting involvement with ethnography.

After a preliminary cruise in the Straits, I stayed at Mabuiag during the month of October in 1888 and spent five months at Mer in 1888–9. I also paid short visits to various islands. Throughout this time I was in close contact with the islanders, especially when dredging and collecting plankton. I found them a cheerful, friendly and intelligent folk, and soon became friends with many of them. Naturally, when opportunity offered, I spoke to them about their past and soon found that the young men knew extremely little about it and they always referred me to the old men. I had previously found that practically none of the Europeans in the islands knew or cared anything about the customs of the natives or their former beliefs, and I also discovered that all that was known about them was contained in the accounts given by Jukes, by Macgillivray, and in the sketches and often inaccurate notes by Wyatt Gill and a few others. I therefore considered it my duty to record as much as was possible in the circumstances, so I induced the old men to come in the evenings and talk about old times and tell me their folk-tales. In this way, without any previous experience or knowledge, I worked single-handed among the Western islanders and amassed a fair amount of information (Haddon 1935:vol. 1, xi).

When he returned to the British Isles in 1889, he spent a few months in London arranging his collection of material culture and preparing his enthnographical notes for publication before returning to his teaching post in Ireland. During that time he was encouraged by some persons to abandon zoology for anthropology, but he was not prepared to do so. Over the next few years he became increasingly involved in problems of an anthropological nature, and he left his post as zoologist at Dublin for Cambridge in 1893. By the turn of the century he was devoting all of his energies to anthropology. Haddon organized the Cambridge Anthropological Expedition to Torres Straits, which was *the first anthropological field study to involve a group of highly trained observers* (Quiggin and Fegan 1940:98). They arrived at Torres Strait in April of 1898 and left in October of the following year. Haddon, Charles G. Seligman, and Anthony Wilkin collected ethnographic information, while William H. R. Rivers, C. S. Myers, and W. McDougall recorded data about diverse physiological responses. Rivers also gathered most of the data about kinship systems and social organization, while the linguistic materials were assembled by Sidney H. Ray. Between 1901 and 1935 the results were published in six volumes, titled *Reports of the Cambridge Anthropological Expedition to Torres Straits*. One volume was devoted to linguistics, another to physiology and psychology, and the others to general ethnographic information.

The Torres Strait area was chosen for study because Haddon recommended it. No problem of a general nature drew them to the islands other than the desire to fill a gap in the ethnographic literature and to apply physiological techniques to persons in an exotic setting. The choice of this area for study was good but not the best, since many other peoples had retained their aboriginal ways more fully. Torres Strait was discovered sometime around 1600, and the people were discussed briefly by Cook in 1770. Systematic ethnographic information was collected first by the naturalist John Macgillivray while on the H.M.S. *Rattlesnake* in 1849. The beginnings of the pearl shell industry in 1868 brought dramatic outside influence since the islanders were exploited ruthlessly as divers, but regulations put an end to the gross abuses in 1881. The first permanent London Missionary Society workers were stationed in the area in 1872. Thus, although a few of the islands reportedly were untouched by these and other outside influences, Haddon and his coworkers did not enter a generally pristine setting. Considering the very broad scope of the Torres Strait study, the early death of Wilkin, and the absence of precedent, the expedition results are impressive if not monumental. The published data are on the whole best viewed as normative ethnographies for a geographical region, although some highly specific information applies only to given islands. The most satisfying descriptions were written by Rivers whose contributions Sol Tax (1965:472) judged to be "the first somewhat scientific accounts of native societies ever written."

William H. R. Rivers (1864–1922) was born at Luton, Kent, and was trained as a medical doctor. He lectured on psychology at Guy's Hospital and in 1893 began similar lectures at Cambridge. Some years before his death, however, he resigned from Cambridge and thereafter held no university post. Throughout his life Rivers made contributions to the field of experimental psychology, and as a result of his participation in the Torres Strait expedition he developed an additional keen and lasting interest in ethnographic research. On the Torres Strait islands he administered certain physiological tests, hoping to determine whether certain response patterns were characteristic of related persons. In order to verify relationships he collected genealogies, and he soon realized that tracing family lines enabled him to deal precisely with vital statistics, kinship terms, and the rights and duties of family members. *Rivers (1900) is credited with originating the genealogical method as a means for recording sociological information about individuals.*

Rivers next studied the Toda of the Nilgiri Hills in South India in 1901–1902, and his book, *The Todas* (1906), set the standard for modern ethnographic field studies. Few persons would deny the advances made by Rivers in ethnographic methodology. His field techniques, reported in the introductory chapter of *The Todas*, are particularly worthy of summary. He was especially careful to select translators who would render statements by informants exactly and without interpretation, and he always used the Toda names in making inquiries about objects, individuals, and places, in order to avoid misunderstandings. By obtaining independent accounts of the same general subject from many persons he was able to crosscheck for discrepancies. He also attempted to cover one subject or event by different means; for example, he might obtain a descriptive account of a ritual and later record the event as it actually occurred. By using hypothetical cases he was further able to check the general patterning and specific details of behaviors. He, of course, used the genealogical method extensively in his inquiries, and he sought out persons who were knowledgeable about particular subjects. Under normal circumstances he paid informants, not for information, but for the time that they spent with him. Rivers also was able to have one of his knowledgeable interpreters collect additional information and send it to him after leaving the field.

When these pioneering ethnographers began their studies, their livelihoods were derived from occupations which were somehow related to an aboriginal people or their setting. Morgan's legal skills led him to assist in Indian land claims, and his broad interest in the Iroquois was additionally a result of living in an area steeped in their lore. His successful legal practice and profitable business ventures made it possible for him to devote much of his adult life to ethnography and anthropology in general. Haddon was a professional zoologist with an academic appointment before his interests shifted to the peoples he observed while on a zoological field trip.

The entry of Franz Boas (1858–1942) into anthropology from the field of physics appears to have been more subtle. Boas was born into a prosperous, liberal family in Minden, Germany. His university education was at Heidelberg, Bonn, and Kiel, where he earned his doctorate in 1881 after completing a dissertation titled "Contributions to the Understanding of the Color of Water." Even before Boas had completed his degree requirements, his interests had shifted from physics to geography, which overlapped with ethnology, and through the latter to the psychological interpretation of behavior (Kardiner and Preble 1963:117–119; Stocking 1965:53–58).

When Boas joined an expedition to Baffin Island in 1883, he was primarily concerned with studying Eskimo geographical knowledge in terms of the relationship between perception and reality. On his return to Germany he still regarded himself primarily as a geographer, but he began working at the Royal Ethnographic Museum under the ethnologist Adolf Bastian. In 1888 Boas published an ethnographic study of the Baffin Island Eskimos, and in it his geographical interests are clear but not overwhelming. This work is said by some to be the only systematic account Boas ever published about any people that he studied, and yet he is better known for his work among Indians along the Northwest Coast of North America. His interest in the latter area appears to have been stimulated by contact with a group of Bella Coola, whom he interviewed when they were in Berlin. Between 1886 and 1931 Boas spent nearly twenty-nine months in the field studying Northwest Coast peoples; his longest stay was in 1897, when he was in the area for about three months. He made thirteen visits to the Vancouver Island region and collected a vast amount of anthropological information, with a stress on tribal distributions, art, mythology, language, and religion. During his lifetime Boas published over 5,000 pages dealing with the Kwakiutl Indians (Boas 1966:xiv; Codere 1959:62; Kardiner and Preble 1963:117–120; Rohner 1966: 153; Stocking 1965:53–63).

The field methods of Boas were essentially the same as those of his contemporaries, except that he was likely to collect a broader range of information than some investigators. If he stressed any specific field techniques, they were that one should learn the language of the people involved, encourage local residents to compile ethnographic data after the ethnographer had gone, and above all else collect extensive texts in the original languages studied. In an evaluation of Boas' position as a field-worker, Mariam W. Smith states that he viewed his subjects for study from the perspective of a natural historian. He was most concerned with the question of how to collect ethnographic data and impose the fewest possible biases on it. Boas felt that the best approach was to record texts from informants verbatim; he then published these in the aboriginal language with interlinear English translations. Apparently Boas made comparatively little effort to guide his informants toward discussing particular topics; instead he attempted to make a systematic record of all that they had to say. In this manner he documented their language and literary style and at the same time collected information on cultural and social behavior. It is difficult to conceive of a more objective approach without the use of electronic or mechanical aids. By exhaustively using his transcription technique, Boas was able to amass a wealth of primary information about the Kwakiutl and other Indians along the Northwest Coast (Smith 1959:46–51).

It has been asserted that Boas had a packrat approach to the collection of ethnographic data and that he was negatively eclectic, but there is only a modicum of truth in such remarks. If we grant that his thinking about the collection of information was in the naturalist tradition, then his efforts are understandable, but if we consider Boas to be a scientist, as many persons are prone to do, then his approach to the collection of ethnographic data is indeed inadequate. The ideal naturalist treats all facts as equal and deplores subjective judgments; he strives for a fully objective report. Since one never knows precisely what is important, everything must be collected systematically. Interpretations are to be made only after the field data have been collected, thereby avoiding biases when collecting information. This seems to have been the position of Boas (Smith 1959:52–53), and his success in the broadscale collection of raw data is unparalleled in the history of ethnography.

It sometimes is stated that a wide-ranging and thorough approach to the collection of field data originated with Boas, and in a sense this is true, but he too had a teacher, or more precisely an exacting mentor, early in his career. The second and third trips which Boas made to the Northwest Coast of North America, in 1888 and 1889, were funded entirely or in part by the British Association for the Advancement of Science, and Horatio Hale (1817–1896) assumed the responsibility for guiding Boas' field studies. Hale had served as an ethnologist and philologist on the first "expedition" organized in the United States which had as one of its broad goals the collection of information about ethnics. He spent four years with this United States Exploring Expedition (Wilkes Expedition), and his published findings are largely of a linguistic nature. Hale's interests were diverted from ethnographic matters temporarily, but by the 1880s he had emerged as a prominent figure because of his early work and more recent studies among the Iroquois. At the time he began guiding the early fieldwork of Boas, Hale already had a great deal of experience on which to draw, and he had prepared a questionnaire to guide others whose work was contracted by the British Association for the Advancement of Science. In a series of letters written to Boas before, during, and after the field trips of 1888 and 1889, Hale made his precise requirements abundantly clear. Among his strictures were: An ethnographic map was to be prepared; the ethnographic findings were to be by region, rather than by tribe; observations were to be made about the physical characteristics of the peoples; and representative linguistic materials for one language in each stock was to be provided. Furthermore, as Jacob W. Gruber (1967:32) writes in his notable study of Boas as an emerging fieldworker, "There can be no question, I think, of Hale's influence on Boas in his use—by himself and through his students—of the native narrative, gathered in the native text, as both a source of linguistic data and as means of recapturing lost elements from the remnants of an already disorganized and disappearing society." It was Hale who made Boas aware that the collection of texts provided both linguistic and ethnographic data, and furthermore, as Gruber has noted, "Hale laid the conceptual foundations for the 'general anthropology' whose holistic approach to the study of man distinguished Boas and his followers so clearly from their contemporaries."

Following his first field trip to the Northwest Coast, Boas returned to New York, and from 1888 until 1892 he served as a faculty member at Clark University. Under his supervision *the first Ph.D. degree in anthropology in the United States was granted to Alexander F. Chamberlain (1865–1914) at Clark University in 1892.* It has been stated (e.g., Tanner 1959:76) that the dissertation concerned the heights and weights of children, but it was in fact about the language of the Mississaga Indians, a group of Algonkian (Chamberlain 1892; Gilbertson 1914:338, 344). After Boas left Clark University, he held a number of different positions briefly, and then in 1889 he became a professor of anthropology at Columbia University, where he remained for the balance of his academic career (Kardiner and Preble 1963:120).

Franz Boas made enduring original contributions in the field of ethnography, but he did still more—he made the anthropology department of Columbia University into the foremost training center for anthropologists in this country during the first three decades of the present century. Of his outstanding students, those who made substantial or major ethnographic contributions include Ruth F. Benedict (1887–1948), Ruth Bunzel, Melville J. Herskovits (1895–1963), Alfred L. Kroeber (1876–1960), Robert Lowie (1883–1957), Margaret Mead, Paul Radin (1883–1959), Frank G. Speck (1881–1950), and Leslie Spier (1893–1961).

Between 1896 and 1905 Boas was directly or indirectly associated with the American Museum of Natural History, and in this capacity he was responsible for organizing the Jesup North Pacific Expedition, 1897–1902 (Boas 1905:91–100). Unlike the Torres Strait expedition, the one arranged by Boas focused on a particular problem. It was to establish the nature of the physical, linguistic, and cultural ties between peoples living on both sides of the northern Pacific Ocean. The most notable fieldwork in Siberia was carried out by Waldemar Bogoras (1865–1936), an exiled revolutionary recommended by the St. Petersburg Academy of Sciences (Boas 1937:314). His study of the reindeer-herding Chukchi is the finest account of a people recorded by any member of the expedition (Bogoras 1904–1909).

In the professional origins of ethnography Morgan, Haddon, and Boas are towering figures. Contemporary with these men were a host of other persons who made important contributions to the field of ethnography. Many of these individuals viewed ethnography as their avocation while earning their livings by other means. They most often became interested in one or a few tribal peoples with whom they happened to have long contact because of their particular work situations. Brief biographical sketches for a number of such persons will illustrate the nature of their backgrounds and activities.

Lorimer Fison (1832–1907) was born in England and studied briefly at Cambridge before going to Australia in 1856. He received his degree at the University of Melbourne and soon afterward was ordained as a Methodist minister. He was a missionary in Fiji from 1863 to 1871, and from 1875 to 1884. When in Fiji he became interested in the customs of the people, and he published an article on Fiji land tenure. He supplied Morgan with Tongan and Fijian kinship schedules, and when he returned to Australia in 1871, he was determined to study kinship and marriage among the aboriginal Australians. In Australia at this time Fison became acquainted with Alfred W. Howitt (1830–1908), who was English and, like Fison, had emigrated to Australia in search of gold. In 1859 Howitt explored the Lake Eyre area, and he later led a prospecting party into Gippsland in southeastern Victoria. He is most famous, however, as the leader of a party to Cooper's Creek to find the sole survivor of the ill-fated Burke and Wills Expedition which attempted to cross the continent from south to north. Howitt became police magistrate and warden for Gippsland in 1863 and held these posts for a quarter of a century. During these years and later he contributed Australian data to the fields of botany, geology, and ethnography. In the 1870s Fison and Howitt made field studies and circulated questionnaires to knowledgeable persons in order to acquire information about the aboriginal Australians. Together they wrote a book titled *Kamilaroi and Kurnai* (1880), prefaced by Morgan and considered by James G. Frazer (1920:220) to have "unquestionably laid the foundations of a scientific knowledge of the Australian aborigines." When Fison returned to Fiji, he continued his inquiries into the customs of these people, and he later published articles as well as a book on his findings. During the many years that Howitt was stationed in Gippsland he traveled widely and came to know the members of the diverse local tribes well. In 1904 he published a book titled *The Native Tribes of South-East Australia*, which is the standard work on the people of this area (Frazer 1920:210–259).

As the names of Fison and Howitt are associated, so it is with two other men who are chronologically more recent but are of greater importance in the history of Australian ethnography. Walter B. Spencer (1860–1929) was born in Lancashire, England, and his early interest in art was subordinated to the study of biology at Owens College and at

Oxford. After completing his studies, he was appointed to a university teaching post in Australia, and in 1894 he joined the W. A. Horn Expedition to explore central Australia. At Alice Springs he met Frank J. Gillen (1855–1912), a man born in Australia of Irish parents. At that time Gillen was employed by the telegraph service and served also as the government subprotector of the local aborigines. The two men worked in close association from 1896 to 1898 and again in 1901 collecting ethnographic information about peoples in central and northern Australia; their joint efforts led to the publication of two books (1899, 1904). In 1911 Spencer returned to the Gulf of Carpentaria, an area which he had visited in 1901 with Gillen, and after considerable travel and research he wrote a book about the local peoples (1914). In 1923 and again in 1926 he revisited the area of Alice Springs, and he subsequently published *Arunta: A Study of a Stone Age People* (1927), with Gillen as a posthumous coauthor. Spencer considered himself to be primarily a biologist, but at Oxford he had been exposed to anthropology through Edward B. Tylor and through a biology teacher, Henry N. Moseley. This led him to an interest in anthropology, and despite his role as a biologist and the numerous contributions he made to this field, he is best known and highly regarded as an ethnographer. It is fitting that he died in Tierra del Fuego while studying the peoples there (Marett and Penniman 1931:14–46).

One of the most colorful pioneers was Frank H. Cushing (1857–1900), frequently described as a genius and equally as often characterized as strange or peculiar. He was born in western Pennsylvania and was plagued with poor health throughout his life. As a youth he was intrigued by Indians, and in his efforts to emulate them he reproduced their artifacts with great skill. When he was eighteen years old, he attended a natural science course at Cornell University and wrote a paper about archaeological finds in New York. It was brought to the attention of the secretary of the Smithsonian Institution and was published by that organization (Cushing 1875). As he matured, Cushing seemed to think of himself as an Indian. In 1879 he accompanied a Smithsonian party to the Southwest and persuaded them to leave him at the pueblo of Zuni in order that he might learn the language. Here he remained for five years, and before long he spoke as a Zuni, dressed as one, and even became a priest in the Bow Society following a long and complex initiation. Ill health forced him to return to the East for medical attention, but he made still another trip to study archaeological remains, this time in Florida, before his death. Cushing wrote comparatively little about the Zuni considering his breadth of knowledge about them. *Zuni Folk Tales* (1901) and *Zuni Breadstuffs* (1884–1885) are his major published works (Holmes 1900: 356–360; Judd 1967:58; Powell 1900:360–367).

During the development of ethnography a number of women made substantial contributions. Unlike the social sciences in general and other fields in particular, anthropology has not blatantly discriminated against women as professionals. It is not that anthropologists were inordinately enlightened, but they realized that many facets of life among ethnics were closed to men and could be penetrated only by women doing fieldwork. Erminnie A. P. Smith (1836–1886) holds a number of firsts among women in anthropology in the United States. *She was the first woman to achieve professional standing,* and her fieldwork, probably undertaken in 1878, was another first for a woman. Although trained originally in mineralogy, she turned to anthropology and wrote with authority on the language and mythology of the Iroquois (Lurie 1966:40–42). The contributions of Smith, however, are far less important than those of Alice C. Fletcher (1838–1923). She first became interested in Indians through philanthropic activities and did not begin her fieldwork until she was about forty years old. She does not appear to have had any formal academic training, but through Frederic W. Putnam of the Peabody Museum at Harvard, she received funds to conduct studies of Plains Indian tribes. Her major work was about the Omaha and was written in collaboration with Francis La Flesche (1857–1932), the son of a principal chief. This ethnography, which is based on twenty-nine years of work by Fletcher and the lifetime remembrances and cultural knowledge of La Flesche, is one of the most comprehensive accounts about a people ever published by the Bureau of American Ethnology (Fletcher and La Flesche 1911; Lurie 1966:43–48). This work was the firm base on which Mead (1932) built her acculturation study of the same people; the volume by Fletcher and La Flesche is not a baseline ethnography, however, for the Omaha had been changed a great deal by their contacts with whites prior to this report.

Among the pioneers of ethnographic field studies, Morgan, Haddon, Rivers, and Boas are outstanding. In sketching the lives of these men and others who contributed to ethnography in its early stages, my purpose has been to point out their diversity of background, their most significant contributions, and something about the methods which they used. The failings in their works are legion and might also be considered. Schoolcraft generalized to a painful degree and often was naively biased in favor of civilized man; Morgan did not write a baseline ethnography of the Iroquois as he purported to do, but rather published an account largely about the acculturation of one particular Seneca band; Boas was inordinately concerned with diverse particulars but seldom integrated them into a coherent whole. Minutiae are the concern of a few, while generalizations without clearly defined population referents are common to many. Often the recorder was a sympathetic outsider who saw the culture through the eyes of a few bilingual informants and from this limited viewpoint proceeded to generalize about the entire group. And how was the information obtained? Usually in interviews with very few persons during short visits to the field. Most often too it is unclear whether the recorded information referred to contemporary behaviors, was recalled about the specific past, or described the traditional past. Concepts and terminology often were vaguely applied, and abstract questions seldom were asked, leading to the collection of a broad but superficial range of information. Some individuals stand immune to these criticisms, but they are justified for the group as a whole. In spite of these inadequacies, however, the pioneers of field ethnography and the naturalists who reported about the ways of ethnics deserve our lasting praise. No clear precedents existed for them to follow, and their only guideline was to record as much accurate information as possible about a broad range of topics. Beyond this primary goal their personal interests and intellectual backgrounds served to focus their studies. To these individuals our debt is great because through them we can know of some peoples and ways of life which no longer exist.

Men such as the cleric Lafitau and the naturalist Forster were among the first to describe peoples in comparatively objective terms. A diligent naturalist wrote about everything which he observed in a particular setting: animals, fish, trees, minerals, and man competed for his descriptive attention. An observer might be more interested in peoples than in trees, but he felt obligated to describe both because they were natural phenomena. The naturalists most important to later anthropologists are those who tended to concentrate on the description of aboriginal peoples. They attempted to gather innumerable specifics about ethnics, often in an eclectic manner. These investigators, naturalists and pioneering ethnographers alike, might be labeled as particularists since they stressed the collection of many bits and pieces of descriptive data. Schoolcraft was such an individual, a largely self-educated man who was a generalized naturalist until he limited himself to the description of Indians; only after years of Indian studies and even then reluctantly did he give up his broader interests. The most outstanding pioneers of more formal ethnography shared certain major qualities which made their contributions both lasting and important. Each set himself a goal which he felt was unassailable: to collect as much specific or particular information as possible about nonliterate peoples before the data were forever lost. Morgan feared that the Seneca soon were to be removed from their lands, and Haddon saw before him on the islands of Torres Strait the rapid disappearance of aboriginal ways, with few persons even concerned about the loss. Boas shared similar views with reference to the Northwest Coast Indians of North America. Each of these men was concerned mainly with collecting as much information as possible about the waning ways of the peoples he saw changing so rapidly. After making these ethnographic studies, each went on to make major contributions to other aspects of anthropology. Furthermore, both Haddon and Boas held influential university teaching positions and thereby exerted a powerful influence on the first generation of professional ethnographers.

PROFESSIONALS

Alfred L. Kroeber (1876–1960) was born in Hoboken, New Jersey, into an upper-middle-class family of German background. His early training was at home under the guidance of his parents and a tutor; later he entered a college preparatory grammar and high school. At the age of sixteen he enrolled at Columbia University to pursue his interests in languages, classical history, and natural history. The subject of English was most appealing to him as a college student, and after receiving an undergraduate degree he earned an M.A. degree in English. Curiosity led Kroeber to take a seminar offered by Boas on American Indian languages, and the following year he returned to the seminar to work with Eskimo informants whom Robert Peary had brought to New York City. Kroeber became increasingly involved in anthropology; he made a three-month field trip to study the Arapaho Indians in 1899 and another trip to study other western Indians in 1900. In 1901 he received his Ph.D. degree under Boas; the subject of his dissertation was Arapaho Indian art. He began to teach anthropology at the University of California, Berkeley, in 1901, and he remained associated with this institution throughout his long professional career. He retired in 1946 but continued to make significant contributions to anthropology until his death (Steward 1961:1038–1060).

Kroeber, who was a humanist and naturalist in his approach to anthropological data, is best known as an ethnographer for his work among the Indians of California. His major ethnographic monograph, completed in 1918 (Lowie 1936:xxi) and based on seventeen years of fieldwork, is titled *Handbook of the Indians of California* (1925). This work, which is nearly a thousand pages in length, was reissued in 1953. In this volume Kroeber sought to record aboriginal baseline data obtained from informants representing nearly fifty tribes in California. Most of the ethnographic sketches are brief, and only the one about the Yurok Indians is reasonably detailed. This account and other writings about the

Yurok are Kroeber's major contributions in terms of well-rounded ethnography.

At the time professionalism in anthropology was developing appreciably, which was near the turn of the present century, investigators were strikingly aware that small-scale societies were disappearing rapidly before their eyes. Many ethnographers worked almost feverishly and often with the zeal of secular missionaries to collect as much information as possible from expiring ethnics. The prefaces and introductions to their published works reflect these feelings of urgency. They almost always attempted to compile aboriginal baseline accounts, but in most instances the task proved to be extremely difficult. Many of the early professional ethnographers visited tribal peoples who already had come under the direct influence of Europeans or Americans and were wracked by alcoholism, disease, poverty, economic exploitation, and religious oppression. Given such a setting, the ethnographer's goal often was difficult if not impossible to achieve. Ethnographers faced the very real problem of learning about behavior which no longer existed, and they applied the same general techniques to their work in most areas of the world. The ethnographer located knowledgeable, elderly persons to interview systematically about the past. In addition, after the investigator had spent a few weeks or months among his subjects, he began noting behavior which seemed to represent continuity with the aboriginal past, and he recorded this information as well. Another approach to the same problem was to consult nonaboriginal informants who had either long-term or intimate familiarity with a people in question. In either of these instances an ethnographer attempted to derive a baseline study, reconstructing the aboriginal past on the basis of fieldwork.

A number of distinct disadvantages are inherent in such studies. The first is that the time factor is held constant in only a very loose manner. When aboriginal peoples are attempting to recall the past, it frequently is difficult for them to be any more exact than to say that a particular custom prevailed "when I was a boy" or "when my father was a young man." In most instances data of this nature were lumped by the recorder to form a composite view about the distant and not-so-distant past. Another problem is that informants are likely to recall ideal rather than real behaviors, which results in a distorted view of the past. An informant might say that there was no divorce among his people because he thought in terms of this ideal even though it was untrue in fact. If the ethnographer did not check with care, he might be led to accept statements of ideals as being statements of facts. Quite frequently too the investigator is able to locate only a very few persons to interview, which makes it impossible for him to systematically check the accuracy of statements.

After spending many hours with a few individuals, the recorder is able to crosscheck his notes for internal consistency, and although this is inadequate, it often is the only possible form of data control.

Most baseline ethnographies collected during this time period are reconstructions, especially those obtained in the Americas. An example will illustrate the point. Robert H. Lowie (1883–1957), a student of Boas who received his Ph.D. degree at Columbia in 1908, worked with the Crow in 1907 and again each summer from 1910 through 1916 (Lowie 1959:41, 175–176). The Crow were Siouan speakers who lived along the Yellowstone River and were related closely to the Hidatsa. Before 1800 European trade goods had begun to reach the Crow, who at that time numbered about 3,500. White traders moved into the area before many years had passed, and by 1833 these Indians had firearms, ammunition, iron tools, cloth, and other trade items. As the bison herds declined rapidly during the last quarter of the nineteenth century, the economic base for their lifeway was destroyed, and some of them were influenced by whites to turn to farming. By 1890 they numbered only slightly more than 2,000, and by 1904 the population had fallen somewhat below this number. When Lowie arrived in 1907, the Crow lived on reservations, and their glory as warriors was part of the past. At that time the Crow must have been overwhelmed by the largely negative aspects of their acculturative setting, but Lowie (1956:xvii) wrote that during his fieldwork among them, they were "spiritually very much alive." During the seasons that he spent with the Crow, great war chiefs still recounted their achievements at public meetings, men could show scars from arrow wounds of old, and hunters told stories about great bison hunts. Some of the less dramatic aspects of their old lifeways continued still and could be observed (Lowie 1959:50–58). By such observation and through prolonged interviews with the aid of capable interpreters, Lowie reconstructed bygone patterns among the Crow. As another aid in his reconstructions he drew on earlier published sources for information; these included the account of James P. Beckwourth, who lived among the Crow in the 1820s and 1830s (Bonner 1965), and Thomas H. Leforge, who lived among the Crow during the latter half of the nineteenth century (Marquis 1928). By combining these sources, Lowie was able to write his widely respected Crow ethnography. Even with these reasonably adequate sources, however, he was forced to hold the time element loosely constant.

Only rarely today does an ethnographer find indigenous peoples beyond the grasp of Western culture. In the deserts of western Australia, the highlands of New Guinea, and the interior jungles of northern South America—the ever-diminishing enclaves of primitive man—it is possible to collect field data unobtainable previously and to compile an ethnography which is a historic baseline study. In general, however, most ethnics by now have been in contact with civilized peoples for many generations, and it has become increasingly difficult for a field investigator to produce even a reconstruction. As the Western world intruded increasingly on living peoples who were or are pristine savages, it became necessary to acknowledge that the information obtained on an Indian reservation or reserve, at a mission outpost, or administrative enclave did not in all honesty pertain to aboriginal conditions. The response was a shift, not toward the study of pertinent historical documents as might be expected, but rather toward field studies with a different goal, to determine how peoples had changed their ways to accommodate intruders from civilized societies, e.g., acculturation. The first lengthy field study of this type was the book by Margaret Mead titled *The Changing Culture of an Indian Tribe* (1932) based on her 1930 study of the Omaha Indians. It is surprising that acculturation as an explicit and acknowledged focus for fieldwork did not formally emerge until the 1930s. It may be that many aboriginal peoples had retained some of their traditional ways with great tenacity, and in addition it is clear that many ethnographers deceived themselves, and continue to deceive themselves, into believing that they were gathering field data about an aboriginal baseline hundreds of years after a people were contacted first by Europeans.

Alfred R. Radcliffe-Brown (1881–1955) was born in England and was educated at Cambridge, where he became the first student of Rivers after the latter's interests had come to include anthropology. As a result of the influence of Rivers and Haddon, he traveled to the Andaman Islands in the Sea of Bengal, where he spent 1906–1908 studying the local Negrito inhabitants. The English had established a penal colony at Port Blair in 1858, and by the time Radcliffe-Brown arrived the Negritos were a remnant population, although some local groups had remained relatively isolated from contact. Radcliffe-Brown's thesis, written at Cambridge in 1908–1909, was a reconstruction of Andamanese culture history, but he did not publish it until 1922 because of his dissatisfaction with the original conceptual framework. After completing his studies at Cambridge, he taught at the London School of Economics and later at Cambridge, and during this time he developed an increasing awareness of the researches of French sociologists, particularly Emile Durkheim. These sociological studies made a profound impression on Radcliffe-Brown's later work. From 1910 to 1912 he studied aboriginal peoples in Australia, and soon after World War I he taught at the University of Cape Town, later at Sydney, and at the University of Chicago from 1931 to

1937. In 1937 he returned to England to fill the newly created chair of Social Anthropology at Oxford; following World War II he taught in Egypt and once again in South Africa. Although Radcliffe-Brown made no major contributions to ethnographic field method, he is notable because he broke with the Haddon-Boas pattern of data collection and interpretation to initiate a program of problem-centered research which stressed the collection of information about social activities within a more rigid conceptual framework than had been attempted previously (Eggan and Warner 1956:544–547; Radcliffe-Brown 1948:vii).

The modern focus on social structure in anthropology was formalized by Radcliffe-Brown, and researchers working within this orientation have come to be called British social anthropologists, social anthropologists, or comparative sociologists. The best explicit statements about the concepts involved were offered in 1940 by Radcliffe-Brown (1952:188–204) and later were republished in a collection of his essays. He considered culture to be a vague concept because it was abstracted from reality; he felt it was more valuable to devote attention to the actual networks of social relations between persons. Included were all person-to-person social relations, and the differentiation of individuals and classes by their social roles was noted. From this point of view, social structure begins with social relations and focuses on the adjustment, convergence, or conflict of individual interests as well as on the norms of the institutions involved. It should be made quite clear that Radcliffe-Brown viewed his approach to social structure not only as a perspective for data collection, but more importantly in his eyes, as a step toward formulating a natural science of society. When Radcliffe-Brown was at the University of Chicago in the 1930s, he exercised a profound influence on anthropology, first through the students he trained and second on American anthropologists in general. His approach to the study of societies was quite different from that which had prevailed previously. Radcliffe-Brown was not interested in the "descriptive integration" of culture which is said to characterize the ethnographic work of Boas and his students, nor was he concerned with historical reconstructions. His primary thrust was to study the dynamics of social interaction and by generalizing from his observations, to formulate laws governing human social behavior.

Possibly no ethnographer works solely as a "structuralist" in a strictest interpretation of the word's meaning, because he must necessarily take into account the fact that every structure serves a purpose or "function."

Bronislaw K. Malinowski (1884–1942) was born in Cracow, Poland, of parents who were landed gentry, and he attended the Polish

University of Cracow where he studied chemistry. In order to fulfill his language examination in English for a Ph.D. he read James Frazer's *Golden Bough*, and this book changed the course of his career. Frazer's work had captured his imagination, and after he graduated in 1908, Malinowski traveled to England and enrolled in the London School of Economics in order to study anthropology. From 1910 to 1913 he worked with the anthropologists Edward Westermark, Charles G. Seligman, and Leonard T. Hobehouse, and the sociologist Martin White, who occupied the first chair in sociology in the British Isles. Malinowski's first book, *The Family Among the Australian Aborigines* (1963, first published 1913), was based on the fieldwork of others and was begun before he left Poland. The volume is described by M. F. Ashley Montagu (1942:147–148), "As a monographic treatment of a single social institution in a single region of the world it is a model of how ethnographic evidence should be collected, presented, and analyzed." Between 1914 and 1918 Malinowski spent most of his time on field trips to New Guinea and northwestern Melanesia. His most intensive studies were carried out on the Trobriand Islands; he learned the local language and became one of the first ethnographers to conduct his research in the language of the people involved. In 1922 he published *Argonauts of the Western Pacific*, which was about the Trobrianders and is considered by some to be an anthropological classic. Not only does Malinowski's literary style provide a delightful relief from the bland writings of most ethnographers, but he also brought a new perspective to ethnographic data collection. He was most concerned with the manner in which diverse aspects of a sociocultural system were integrated into an operating whole; this functional approach gave new depth to ethnographic data collection and interpretations. From 1923 until the end of his life Malinowski traveled widely around the world and lectured at diverse universities. His first teaching position was at the London School of Economics and his last at Yale University. Among the noteworthy books he wrote on the basis of fieldwork were *Crime and Custom in Savage Society* (1926) and *Coral Gardens and Their Magic* (1935). Even the titles of these volumes are appealing, and the contents sustain the major concept of cultural integration which Malinowski spent his lifetime developing (Ashley Montagu 1942: 146–150; Evans-Pritchard 1962:74; Firth 1960:4–6; Kaberry 1960:77).

Malinowski is renowned among ethnographers for his clear, published statements about field methods. In many respects his sections devoted to methodology in *Argonauts of the Western Pacific* form a superior introduction to the subject of ethnography. Another very different perspective of Malinowski and his fieldwork may be realized by reading his diaries (Malinowski 1967). However, as Marvin Harris (1967:72) noted in a review of the volume,

> . . . these are the inner thoughts of a man under great stress, rather than the professional log of an anthropologist on a field trip . . . They are astonishingly barren of direct insight into Malinowski's professional plans and procedures. They consist instead almost entirely of expressions of the inner psychological turmoil that lay beneath the brilliantly poised exterior of this supreme field worker.

The particularist approach to ethnographic data collection, of the pioneers and early professionals, stressed specifics without any clearly formulated context in which to integrate the findings; the structuralists emphasized form in a limited or expanded context of its meaning. The functionalists, on the other hand, stressed the contexts of usage and the meaning of forms rather than focusing on the forms themselves. No name is associated with the origins of a functional perspective more than Malinowski. For him artifacts and sociofacts were explained in terms of their functions, "by the part which they play within the integral system of culture, by the manner in which they are related to each other within the system, and by the way in which this system is related to the physical surroundings" (Malinowski 1932:864). Because of his functional view of field data, Malinowski presented particulars against the backdrop of the whole culture and the setting in which they occurred. He was uninterested in information which was not derived from specific observations or reported by informants. Malinowski further viewed cultural forms as filling needs of biological, psychological, and social origins. Thus, if a form were present, no matter how bizarre it might appear to be, he considered that it fulfilled a need and was thereby a necessary component in the cultural matrix. The distinct tendency was to conceive of cultures as delicately balanced wholes in which all components were necessary and served an integral purpose in the maintenance of the total system. Malinowski's position was that every social form operates with almost equal force in order to sustain the whole, and each form results from a learned social heritage in order to fulfill cultural needs. Malinowski's discussion of the *kula* ring, a network of intertribal trade relations of the Trobriand Islands, is the classic example of a functional presentation. Involved in the kula were various components: the technological skills necessary to produce items for exchange and canoes in which the daring voyages could be undertaken; magical formulas which were recited to ensure the safety of the travelers, and trading parties which were established on far-flung islands for the purpose of receiving one another and negotiating exchanges. The kula complex could be conceived of as a method of integrating the cultural whole. To Malinowski description could not be separated from explanation, and an ethnography became the vehicle of integrated expression (Malinowski 1961; Richards 1960:15–31).

In order to describe the Trobriand Islanders, Malinowski selected key institutions around which he built his ethnography. He did not report on the culture as a whole, but in flowing prose he explained how these islanders sustained their way of life—in other words, he focused on the functioning of their sociocultural system. The fact that he worked among the inhabitants of small, isolated islands might in itself have been important in the development of his ethnographic approach, for he could see before him an integrated system and the ways in which it sustained the whole. It will be recalled that Radcliffe-Brown too worked among islanders and developed an explicit concern with describing their way of life as an integrated system. Unlike Malinowski, however, Radcliffe-Brown formulated his structural units with considerable rigidity and stressed the manner in which they formed articulated structures meant to fulfill particular purposes.

It appears that an awareness of structure by ethnographers emerged as a result of intensive field studies in which the investigators became at least partially immersed in the lives of the peoples that they studied. This emphasis is not found in the works of Morgan and Boas because they viewed Iroquois and Kwakiutl culture as an outsider looking in, despite the fact that they made field studies among these peoples. Rivers, who worked more intensively with the Toda, seems to have become more involved with the peoples and their lifeway. Radcliffe-Brown on the Andaman Islands and Malinowski on the Trobriands were each in a position to see before them both narrow and broad structural networks. The detailed study of structure, social or otherwise, is quite in keeping with the earlier observations by naturalists, but Radcliffe-Brown initiated a major change in this tradition when he attempted to describe Andamanese social life in such a manner that the information could be compared with similar observations among other peoples. Malinowski's Trobriand study did not break with the naturalist pattern but rather extended it by seeking to fathom the operation of a cultural whole. Thus he was concerned with the broadest meanings of particulars in the lives of the Trobianders, but he did not seek to establish crosscultural comparisons.

Radcliffe-Brown's most important contribution to ethnography was the fact that he directed attention to the structuring of the social relationship networks. Malinowski's major contribution was that he pointed out the interrelatedness of structural forms by stressing the purposes which they served. Radcliffe-Brown sought to be a scientist, but because he dealt with data for a single time period, he could not effectively accommodate change in his statements about structure and its related function. He could not predict even though he recorded information in a manner which could lead to comparisons, because he had no gauge against which to measure and anticipate behavior. The value of his structural approach was that a wealth of detail was collected about particular societies and fitted together as an articulated whole, but the emphasis on the uniquely interconnected parts made crosscultural comparisons difficult because the dominant patterns in one lifeway might be unimportant or nonexistent among other peoples.

The only view into the past accepted by structural-functional ethnographers was through the peoples themselves. Malinowski, for example, gladly collected myths, tales, and folk history because he felt that these served functional ends among the peoples themselves. Documentary sources had no place in the works of early structuralists and functionalists because they felt that even if such information was available, it was not pertinent to their purpose. The most pronounced reaction within social anthropology to this antihistorical position was expressed by E. E. Evans-Pritchard in 1950. His attitude was that the functionalist view, as valuable as it might be as a guide to field methodology, could contribute little without a historical perspective in which to fit the ideas presented. He felt that the time element must be added in order to make useful comparisons and that since ethnographers would deal increasingly with societies which are being drawn into the sphere of Western culture, historical information, which in fact is clearly available, would be pertinent. In a broad context the ethnographic information collected by social anthropologists is a form of historiography, and Evans-Pritchard (1962:144–154) reasoned that the accounts prepared by ethnographers form blocks of historical information. However, he would go much further and maintain, "The thesis I have put before you, that social anthropology is a kind of historiography, and therefore ultimately of philosophy or art, implies that it studies societies as moral systems and not as natural systems, that it is interested in design rather than in process, and that it therefore seeks patterns and not scientific laws, and interprets rather than explains" (Evans-Pritchard 1962:152).

Another view of the direction in which functional studies might well move has been articulated by Michael G. Smith (1962:81–84). He stresses that particular units should be studied as a continuum in terms of diachronic processes. This approach denies that the gross units for study are balanced and closed self-sufficient wholes functioning in equilibrium.

It is advanced that the "unit is or forms part of, a system, many elements of which are somehow interrelated" (Smith 1962:82). The actual network of relationships is determined by empirical study conscious of both continuity and change, with each plotted through time for the varying units in order to establish the nature of regularities. Thus, Smith considers the proper aim of social anthropology to be the scientific explanation of process, whereas Evans-Pritchard supports the humanistic search for patterns as the most valid goal.

The early functional approach to recording ethnographic data often has been faulted for unduly stressing articulations of the components making up sociocultural systems. The integration sometimes has been presented as complete and as virtually perfect, so much so that alternative explanations of how a culture might successfully function could not be accommodated. When it subsequently was demonstrated that one institution could in fact fulfill different functions and that all traits were not in perfect accord with one another, the functional perspective received harsh criticism. The functionalists had derived self-contained systems which did not allow for tests of the integrative networks described. A more fruitful approach to a functional analysis of ethnographic data did not become possible until the variables involved were isolated with greater precision and the environmental setting was more thoroughly considered.

It is difficult to know which contemporary and near contemporary field workers should be considered and to what extent. In any accounting of this nature, however, certain individuals clearly deserve recognition as outstanding ethnographers, and one such person is Cornelius Osgood. Osgood received his graduate training in anthropology at the University of Chicago, and in order to collect information for his doctoral dissertation he decided to work among Athapaskan Indians in northwestern Canada. In 1927 he visited the Chipewyan, but he had comparatively little success working with these and other nearby Indians. In 1928–1929 he wintered among Indians of the Great Bear Lake area, but again the scientific rewards of the venture were few. His experiences at Great Bear Lake are recorded in a book which does not pretend to offer systematic information about either fieldwork or Indians, but it does vividly convey how difficult it may be to conduct ethnographic fieldwork (Osgood 1953). In spite of two unproductive seasons he returned north in 1931, this time to work along Cook Inlet in Alaska among the Tanaina Indians, who were sea-mammal hunters and salmon fishermen; in 1932 he visited the Canadian and Alaskan Han and Kutchin, who lived by hunting and fishing; and finally he worked among the salmon-fishing Ingalik of the lower Yukon River in 1934, 1937, and 1956. The published results of these studies (Osgood 1936*a*, 1936*b*, 1937, 1940, 1958, 1959) helped to fill a major regional blank which had existed on the ethnographic map of the world.

Unlike most ethnographers, Osgood is very precise in stating his purposes, his methods, and the limitations of his work. His primary goal was to assemble a descriptive record of aboriginal lifeways among diverse Northern Athapaskans, but he never deluded himself into thinking that the behaviors which he observed were more than clear echoes of the past. Contact with Euro-Americans had taken place among these peoples from 75 to 150 years ago, and therefore his task clearly was one of ethnographic reconstruction. As was true of other ethnics shortly after historic contact, most Northern Athapaskan Indian tribes were exposed to new diseases which decimated them and left them disorganized in terms of their manner of living. In their contacts, which were with traders and missionaries primarily, these Indians had found comparatively little that was appealing in the ways of whites by the time Osgood arrived among them. Consequently, they had preserved many of their traditional behaviors and values, if not in living fact at least in the memories of older Indians. Osgood's major problems were to locate informants who were knowledgeable about the past without idealizing it and to gain the services of satisfactory interpreters. After he had searched out knowing persons on whom he could rely, Osgood worked with them intensively. His most able informant by far was Billy Williams, an Anvik Ingalik, and by working primarily with Williams, who consulted others concerning subjects about which he knew little, Osgood wrote one of the more comprehensive ethnographies compiled by an individual investigator. The nearly one thousand pages of text are a monument to one man's persistence, skill, and enviable perception.

The goal of naturalists and early professionals was to compile compendiums of particulars, but this focus first gave way to an emphasis on social structure and then to stress on the function of sociocultural forms. Investigators consequently were drawn in diverse directions when conducting subsequent field studies, and yet the compilation of baseline ethnographies remained a frequent goal, although it might be masked with more specific interests. However, a new direction was pioneered by Julian H. Steward, who worked among the Paiute and Shoshoni of Nevada and adjacent areas mainly in 1935 and 1936. Given the difficulties of survival faced by these Indians Steward (1938) came to focus on the influence of the environment on their lives. The limited resources exploited by the Shoshoneans in their great arid valleys resulted in a population density which averaged about one person per twenty to thirty square miles. Plants offered only sparse quantities of food, while the most important meat animals, antelope and hares, were limited in number and could be hunted only at infrequent intervals. Given the scarcity of food resources and the unpredictable nature of most harvests, small family groups wandered from place to place in search of food; the resources of the country were open to exploitation by all. In years of good harvests and in order to participate in cooperative hunts, families banded together for brief or extended lengths of time. During these periods of group living, leadership was transient but important. Because of the nature of the food quest the sustaining unit of the culture, however, was the independent nuclear family.

Steward (1955:30–42) defined the nature of man's environmental relationships by setting forth a procedural approach to the study of cultural ecology. He felt that environmental characteristics require analysis and are critical, especially in the case of people whose lives were affected daily by the climate, fauna, flora, and drainage systems. To him the technological devices employed should be considered in terms of their environmental usages; their origins or the manner in which they reached a particular people were not directly significant. His next step was to investigate the social implications of the use of technological devices in exploiting the environment. Some plant foods might be efficiently collected by individuals, while others might be harvested more successfully by groups of persons; the same would apply to exploitation of the fauna. In a like manner the matter of transporting foods involved people, technology, and environment. Finally it was necessary to establish the manner in which these exploitative behaviors impinged on other aspects of culture. The essence of this method was to isolate and analyze the *cultural core*, which is defined by Steward (1955:37) as "the constellation of features which are most closely related to subsistence activities and economic arrangements. The core includes such social, political, and religious patterns as are empirically determined to be closely connected with these arrangements."

By identifying the ecological variables which furthered the survival of gatherers and by isolating the concept of cultural core, Steward paved the way for integrating a functional approach to ethnographic data collection with the presentation of environmental factors. This has at least in part contributed to the increasing tendency to view culture and ecology within broader, more all-encompassing frameworks such as ecosystems. The latter focus attention both on the living and nonliving aspects of an environment without isolating man as a separate and distinct entity. A volume edited by Anthony Leeds and Andrew P. Vayda (1965) includes a number of articles which are specifically concerned with the relationships between men and animals in their joint setting. For example, Leeds

(1965:87–128) demonstrates the very positive relationship between reindeer herd size and sociocultural factors among the Chukchi of Siberia. Louise E. Sweet (1965:129–152) discusses the Bedouin of northern Arabia and the relationship between the flexibility of their social units and their ability to maintain mobile herds of camels. Specific studies of this nature appear to utilize an integrated ecological approach most successfully.

NEW DIRECTIONS

Each succeeding generation of students who attempted to follow the anthropological tradition of collecting baseline ethnographic information struggled increasingly to encourage remnant aborigines to recall the half-forgotten past, with the ever-diminishing likelihood of reasonable success. It was not until the early 1930s that ethnographers in the United States finally were forced to admit that they were not assembling baseline ethnographic data. (And even then it probably was not the professors who led them into the study of acculturation as much as the pangs of conscience that began to gnaw at social scientists as a result of the depression in the 1930s. The case may be overstated, yet in its essence it is reasonable.)

New directions to ethnographic research were in the intellectual wind as acculturation studies posed an exciting challenge to a new generation of ethnographers. But one field study seemed to produce essentially the same results as the next and yet another. A vast amount of new information was collected, but no theory or underlying purpose, except data collection in the natural history tradition, drew it together. The dissatisfactions of some investigators led them to try other approaches.

Students with compelling interests in ethnography and in the past have begun turning to libraries and archives for their information rather than to living peoples with nonliterate backgrounds. These investigators are ethnographically oriented historians. The focus of ethnohistorians is on peoples defined as ethnics, members of small-scale societies, as opposed to that of traditional historians on large-scale or civilized peoples. An ethnohistorian draws his information from any and all data sources irrespective of the compiler or the format in which the data exist. Historical baseline ethnographies, acculturation or community studies, histories, diaries, and any other forms of evidence are admissible so long as they pertain to the particular people concerned. (For a more restricted use of the term ethnohistory, see Sturtevant 1966:6.) Thus, an ethnohistorian utilizes all forms of written and verbal information about ethnics and presents his information in a temporal perspective. Ethnoarchaeology is an adjunct to ethnohistory and serves to extend and supplement the findings of an ethnohistorian. The ethnoarchaeologist recovers his information from the ground rather than from libraries and archives, but it applies to known and clearly identified populations. Pushing backward in time to a point when the peoples involved cannot be identified, ethnohistory fades into culture history, and ethnoarchaeology becomes archaeology.

The basic data for one of the early modern ethnohistorical studies were compiled in 1928–1930 by Felix M. Keesing (1939). His monograph about the Menomini of northern Wisconsin was based primarily on documentary sources. Keesing's purpose was not only to present the changes resulting from three centuries of Menomini-white contact, but to assess the accuracy of ethnographic reconstructions which had been compiled recently from Menomini informants. It was his judgment that certain aspects of the culture were retained with notable tenacity, especially the methods of obtaining food, the artifacts associated with religion, the primary group relationships, and the language; all of these were judged as "closely connected either with the immediate environment or with deep-seated mental and emotional patterns" (Keesing 1939:221). It was possible to establish that these dimensions were stable only after an ethnohistorical study.

As recently as 1942 Oscar Lewis (1914–1970) could write that anthropologists neglected written history in their efforts to resolve particular historical problems. It was historians, not anthropologists, who studied written records systematically. Ethnographers made their reconstructions from essentially static ethnographic data. Thus, Lewis wrote of anthropologists making "minimum use of documented history" and "their systematic neglect of documentary material," while Boas and Kroeber "tacitly assumed that the paucity of historical material makes it negligible for the anthropologist." Obvious exceptions were researches concerning Mexico and Peru, for which excellent documentary sources exist which literally have forced themselves into the hands of ethnographers (Lewis 1942:1–3). It was with these thoughts about the usefulness of historical data that Lewis introduced his study titled *The Effects of White Contact upon Blackfoot Culture.* As the title suggests, his purpose was to plot chronologically the changes in the lives of these Indians in order to assess the importance of the horse in the spread of Plains Indian culture. By means of written sources, he concluded that the fur trade, the gun, and the horse as a combination brought about the greatest change but that the fur trade was the most critical single factor. Furthermore, Plains Indian life as it usually is conceived did not emerge among the Blackfoot until 1830, which is nearly two hundred years later than had been presumed by most observers who utilized ethnographic information in their efforts to reconstruct history. Here we have a striking example of the contrasting results between an ethnohistorical study and surmised ethnographic history.

Whereas ethnohistorical studies are diachronic and span considerable lengths of time, another type of combination study is duosynchronic. The first segment of this combination usually is an ethnographic field study of a people for one point in time in the recent past, and then in later years the original investigator or another makes a "restudy" of the same unit. Descriptive accounts such as these provide a logical temporal extension forward from a baseline ethnography. In 1928–1929 Margaret Mead (1930) studied the Manus settlement of Peri on one of the Admiralty Islands. She returned to this Melanesian island in 1953–1954 to work again among the village inhabitants and their descendants (Mead 1956). Raymond Firth spent a year with the Tikopia, Melanesians of the Solomon Islands, in 1928–1929 and returned in 1952–1953 to record the changes which had occurred (Firth 1936, 1959). In the early 1930s Robert Redfield (1941) and his coworkers studied the Maya of the Yucatan Peninsula in Mexico; in 1948 Redfield returned to one settlement, Chan Kom, which had been a focal point earlier, and made a restudy (Redfield 1950). In 1926–1927, Redfield (1930) studied the south-central Mexican village of Tepoztlan, which is near Mexico City. Oscar Lewis (1951, 1960) made his first study of the same community in 1943 and returned in 1956–1957 to make subsequent reports.

Each of the ethnographic approaches presented thus far is a broad description rather than a rigid conceptual division. The general thesis has been that the earliest ethnographic descriptions were assembled in the naturalists' tradition of reporting. Morgan, Haddon, and Boas were considered particularists in order to emphasize their stress on orderly and specific descriptions. Morgan and Boas performed feats of salvage ethnography because the peoples they described had been in intensive contact with Europeans long before they were studied; only the Haddon party working among some of the Torres Strait islanders contacted essentially pristine peoples.

The names of Morgan, Haddon, and Boas stand out as eminent because these men collected detailed information about particular peoples and thereby revealed the nature of the culture and society under study. The breadth and intensity of their recordings was generally unparalleled in the accounts of nontrained observers. The works of Boas and Haddon had the greatest impact, in part because they held prominent university teaching positions. Morgan influenced far fewer persons, but through his extensive correspondence he was a persuasive exponent of ethnographic data collection. After publishing his Iroquois study Morgan tended to focus on the social lives of peoples, and he was aided by men such as Fison and Howitt. These men as well as Spencer and Gillen and others became immersed in problems of social organization, totemism, and religion, often under the direct guidance of James Frazer and Edward B. Tylor. It was not, however, until the Andamanese study by Radcliffe-Brown that the integrated nature of social activities was presented with great clarity. A student of Haddon who came to be influenced strongly by Emile Durkheim and other French sociologists, Radcliffe-Brown isolated the key cross-societal units for social description and analysis and contributed directly to the formal emergence of social anthropology. He also described the integrated ways in which social structure served a people, but it was Malinowski who best articulated, and even dramatized, the intertwining functional networks of behavior.

The structural-functional approach, with its stress on social life, did not make any immediate impact on ethnographic data collection in the United States. The students of Boas went their particularist way, and the salvage approach to data collection became the standard method of the time. In this era one recorded what informants happened to be able to recall, and only rarely did a researcher function without a translator. Given the likelihood of social disorganization among the peoples involved, the investigators necessarily stressed cultural survivals. This particular emphasis culminated in works such as that of Frank G. Speck, a man who devoted his life to recording survivals among Indians in the eastern United States. Among researchers from England there tended to be much less stress on recording the aboriginal ways of a people studied and more emphasis on a thorough presentation of conditions at the time of the field study. Furthermore, an investigator from England was likely to learn the language of the people studied more thoroughly than did his American counterpart, and he usually spent a longer period of time among his subjects. One important fact helps to explain why most British social anthropologists did not attempt to make aboriginal baseline studies. By the time their discipline emerged, most peoples around the world had long been under the influence of one colonial power or another. It is true that Radcliffe-Brown and Malinowski worked among isolated and relatively unacculturated peoples, but their students were drawn primarily to Africa with its long prior history of European contacts. The first professional ethnographers to work in Africa were Charles G. and Brenda Z. Seligman in 1909–1910, and the first social anthropologist there, Evans-Pritchard, worked among the Azande beginning in 1927 (Evans-Pritchard 1962:75).

The arrival of Radcliffe-Brown at the University of Chicago in 1931 provided students in the United States with the first significant alternative to a Boasian approach to ethnographic data collection. In this era, "American anthropologists were not going to be hasty in accepting any conclusions; there were to be no rules of method except painstaking research in the minutiae of recorded and reasonably reconstructed history; every theory would have to stand the test of common sense" (Tax 1965:475). Radcliffe-Brown, whose concern was with general principles, offered a position antithetical to that of the Boasians. Students at the University of Chicago were challenged and engaged by his approach. At the same time they did not abandon their interest in recording the past of the American Indians whom they were most likely to study. The net result, best exemplified by the works of Fred R. Eggan and Edward H. Spicer, was a concentrated analysis of social structure and function through time.

The concepts of culture and society are intertwined but separable. In England the tendency has been to stress the nature of social relations over a brief span of time, while in the United States stress has been on cultural patterns over longer periods of time. However, with the exchange of ideas between these two groups of ethnographers we find that some social anthropologists are now primarily concerned with historical patterns, while others are most interested in processual change and still others are content to concentrate on the more traditional area of structural and functional relationships. Cultural anthropologists have demonstrated an increasing willingness to employ the concepts of social anthropology if only to provide a behavioral dimension previously deemphasized or ignored. The two schools are not integrated, but the extent of mutual borrowings has influenced the positions of enough persons in the respective camps to justify joining them under the label of Anglo-American.

While Anglo and American approaches to collection of ethnographic data are moving nearer one another in their methods and goals, the natural history tradition is declining as a focus; it retains a certain degree of continuity only in the perspectives of some ecologists. Rarely does a modern ethnographer venture into the field with the goal of collecting particulars about every possible subject in the naturalist tradition. Before most contemporary students venture to make a field study they clearly define a specific topic for concerted attention. They formulate a series of questions which bear on the topic so that they can concentrate their attention on these. Their problem may be stated as a tightly conceived hypothesis or as a more loosely formulated area of interest, but in either case information is collected which bears most directly on the preconceived question. Ethnographers no longer expect to be able to collect every type of data about a people they study.

Likewise, some modern ethnographers are not dedicated to making field studies among pristine savages. This is in part due to the disappearance of most of these peoples, but also there is an increasing realization that if the focus for study is to be on the structure and dynamics of small group behavior, as usually is the case, then it matters little whether the people studied are derived from an aboriginal, a peasant, or some other form of background. In fact, for many investigators *aborigines are undesirable subjects for study* because their ways of life are frequently wracked with so many adjustment problems that they are doomed to extinction and provide insight only into societal death.

Innovations in the perspectives for collection and interpretation of ethnographic data are rare, but in recent years considerable energy has been expended on pioneering a novel methodology termed "ethnoscience," "folk science," or more presumptively, the "New Ethnography." In essence the method is designed to reveal, through a study of linguistic expression, the manner in which ethnics have come to conceive of their world. The purpose of the investigator is to bring the rigor of a scientific methodology to ethnography by replacing the nonstandard selection of information emphases with a precise framework for data collection and interpretation. Boas made a major attempt to break the bonds of ethnocentrism by utilizing a linguistic approach, recording texts in the words of his Kwakiutl informants. The cognitive approach too focuses on the languages of peoples in order to establish their conceptions of reality free from the ethnographer's constructs. Since it is largely through language that thoughts are expressed and actions are conceived, it is felt that the nature of reality for a people most readily will be perceived through an analysis of their linguistic means of expression. As a leading exponent of the cognitive approach, Charles O. Frake (1962:74) has written, "An ethnographer should strive to define objects [anything construed as a member of a category, whether perceptible or not] according to the conceptual system of the people he is studying." One begins by recording words which in and of themselves reflect the cognitive or perceived world and express the basis for empirical knowledge. Determining linguistic structure is not in itself a goal but is a first step in establishing meaningful units for behavior. The investigators seek to determine categories of contextual responses which are important in conveying distinctive, significant meanings. Thus, the concern is with morphemes as they reflect the "boundaries of a culture's cognitive map."

The cognitive approach to ethnographic data collection involves a set of precise techniques designed to expose the workings of particular cultural taxonomies. At present no analysis of a complete cultural system from a cognitive point of view has been concluded, and possibly a considerable length of time will pass before this goal is achieved. To date we have numerous studies of particular taxonomies, such as those of disease among the Eastern Subanun (Frake 1961:113–132) and color categories among the Hanunoo (Conklin 1955:339–344), both peoples living on the Philippine Islands. The cognitive method, since it has not as yet been applied to the complete cultural system of any people, is more confining than the other approaches to ethnographic data which are being considered in this volume. The method is in one respect quite exciting since it yields results which are free from the more obvious confines of Western taxonomies and since it most nearly approaches being a culture-free means of recording the multiple ramifications of human thought. On the other hand, an anonymous critic of the method described the approach as "an attempt to understand the mood and temper of men through empty words. Vacuous, sterile, inconclusive, programmatic, hyperprofessionalized, and the product of apolitical, asexual, amoral, asocial anthropology" (Berreman 1966:346). These remarks are harsh but quite responsible within the multiple traditions of ethnographic data collection.

PROJECTIONS

Once upon a time travelers were satisfied to describe a people just because they existed and were unknown to potentially interested readers. Accounts of ethnics often were written not only to inform but also to entertain. As the reporters became more culture conscious, they sought to be as fully objective in their descriptions as time and circumstances allowed. Within the humanistic tradition some naturalists became ethnographers; as such they refined but never significantly departed from the previously established descriptive goals. Techniques improved and perspectives became broader, but the methodology and overall purpose remained largely unchanged and unchallenged. As time passed, pangs of intellectual conscience were to ring in the ears of persons who had come to be known as ethnographers. All around them they saw naturalists becoming scientists, and a conscious attempt to make many aspects of anthropology more exact was begun. Some ethnographers thought that patterning data collection along structural or functional approaches would make it possible for ethnography to join the expanding throng of exacting craftsmen and technicians whose background and orientation was scientific. It would appear that this goal has proven to be largely unattainable through these methods. The present-day ecological studies are experimental gropings which appear to be developing firm methodological grounds, yet the study of cognitive systems, while it may be a panacea for some, is far from acceptable to all. Those who are ethnohistorians appear to be little troubled by the turmoil and are by and large content to be unreconstructed humanists. In reading ethnographic accounts the impression gained is that every investigator succeeds to a greater or lesser degree in attaining his descriptive purpose and arrives at conclusions acceptable within his framework of reference. Every published ethnography has virtues, primarily because we have no clear standards by which to measure the adequate against the misleading. If an ethnography is labeled as extraordinary in a reviewer's judgment, it usually is because the author and reviewer have a like perspective; the reverse of this combination occurs as well.

How may we establish whether an ethnography is "good" or not? One method would be to have a study replicated by an independent investigator. It is most unlikely that this test ever will be effected widely, if only because ethnographers overwhelmingly prefer to study peoples who are largely unknown prior to their fieldwork. Another factor limiting the possibility of a duplicative study is the time element. If a second person studies a particular people, the effort is likely to be made long after the original study, and this negates a fully comparable field situation. When two different anthropologists have described the same people, the results have been contrasting more often than parallel. The often cited example of this is the contrast in the studies of Tepoztlan, Mexico, by Robert Redfield and Oscar Lewis.

Team research would appear to be a logical means for correcting possible distortions by a lone investigator and for providing immediate crosschecks on the validity of information obtained. Again, however, distinct limitations are encapsulated in this approach. A group of investigators entering a small community may be viewed by the residents as an unclear but apparent threat, and local hostility rather than rapport may be engendered. Assuming that a cooperative field ethnography is to be compiled, it often is difficult, at times impossible, to have all participants complete their manuscripts for joint publication. The net result is that the printed report is often incomplete, uneven, or both. At a more personal level many field ethnographers prefer to work alone and to be as far away from students and colleagues as possible; for this reason, sometimes above all others, they resist cooperative field studies.

Another means of establishing the merits of an ethnography is to evaluate the text in terms of an author's central interests or theme offered in a preface or introduction. The major foci should be elaborated fully and well, with conclusions being insights which are testable rather than a simple textual summary. Internal consistency is another measure of a report's adequacy, but reasonably perceptive editors and copyreaders can often mask these failings of an author. Finally, if an ethnographer understands a particular people well, he might be expected to anticipate significant trends in their future.

My purpose is not to write a critique of ethnographic field methods, but to point out some of the past difficulties which might be considered in determining future directions. As for the future itself, there is every indication that the humanistic tradition for recording ethnographic data is losing ground rather rapidly to more precisely conceived frameworks for data collection, frameworks which attempt to bring a scientific perspective to bear on fieldwork. The cognitive approach is one such effort, and another is found in the statistical orientation of behavioral scientists. The humanistic and scientific approaches give comparatively little indication of reaching mutual accommodation, which possibly is understandable. However, as Gerald D. Berreman has suggested, one means for bringing a more exact approach to the collection of field data would be for workers to pay greater attention to what they do, why, and how they do it.

I would suggest that extensive, explicit, and perceptive field notes, self-analytical reporting of research procedures and research contexts, documentation of sources, documentation of the bases for inferences, and documentation of the ethnographer's theories of society and his biases, are steps which work toward the same end and with greater promise than the cognitive approach. What I would call for, in short, if verification is to be enhanced, is a *sociology of ethnographic knowledge*; an *ethnography of ethnography* (Berreman 1966:350).

Perhaps one of the most satisfying means for improving the quality of ethnographic reporting would be to rely more on accounts by individuals from among the ethnics described. If local persons could be encouraged to describe the manufacture of a canoe, the purpose of a ceremony, the details of a ritual, their view of the nature of the universe, or anything else which interests them, original documents of considerable value would soon be accumulated. This of course is nothing more than the recording of informal and formal texts, which is a long-established technique, but one which is not now employed as widely or intensively as might be desired. However, records of this nature need to be accompanied by extensive interpretations. In the texts the people speak for themselves, while in a subsequent discussion the ethnographer places the accounts in an anthropological context. In this manner a number of distinctly important goals are attained. The first is to bypass the ethnocentric trap by recording and publishing the precise statements of individuals. A clear distinction would be seen between ideal and real behaviors. The informant's abstract discussion of divorce would be a generalizing document about normative behavior, whereas his account of an actual divorce would be of a very different order and would be more likely to satisfy critics of the normative approach to ethnographic data collection. Either record, or preferably both, could then be analyzed and interpreted in an anthropological context. In this manner original data and the interpretation of it would be distinguished with clarity rather than appearing as a jumble, as is now likely to be the case. Extended texts rarely have been collected and interpreted insightfully.

Perhaps the time has come to encourage more ethnics to become professional ethnographers and to record the ways of their own people. In the past there have been a few such persons who made notable contributions. These include the Maori Te Rangihiroa or Peter H. Buck (1877–1951), as well as William Jones (1871–1909), who was part Fox Indian. Jones received his Ph.D. at Columbia in 1904 and worked largely among the Algonkian-speaking Indians of the eastern United States. Two American Indians who became professional anthropologists and ethnographers are Edward P. Dozier, who was raised in the pueblo of Santa Clara, New Mexico, and Alfonso Ortiz, a Tewa-speaker from the pueblo of San Juan in New Mexico. Both of these men have written insightfully of their own people (Dozier 1954, 1966; Ortiz 1969). As has been pointed out by John R. Bodine (1969:2), a part-Indian who was born at Taos, New Mexico, lived there much of his life, and was fully accepted by some segments of the community, there are obvious advantages and distinct disadvantages when working among one's own people. Among the important assets he noted were the ease with which information could be obtained without the formalities of interviews, the functions which could be attended that were closed to outsiders, and the ability to gain insightful information on the basis of what he was presumed to know. A major disadvantage was that by not openly acknowledging his anthropological purpose he risked engendering widespread hostility against himself as a community member. Furthermore, it was difficult for him to keep his roles clearly in mind when interacting with informants who were actually a part of his community and his life.

ORGANIZATIONS

The first anthropological society was the Société des Observateurs de l'Homme, *founded in Paris during 1799* by Louis F. Jauffret (1770–1850), a minor French philosopher. In a statement of purpose recorded in an introduction to the group's unpublished memoirs, Jauffret proposed that a very broad range of anthropological data be collected; race, language, culture, and society each were subjects for attention. When a proposal by Nicholas Baudin for a scientific expedition was accepted by the French government, the organizers turned to the society for a format within which to collect anthropological information. Joseph-Marie Degérando (1772–1842) prepared the guide, which bore the published title "Considerations on the Various Methods to Follow in the Observation of Savage Peoples." The importance of this virtually unknown but strikingly significant document first was discussed by George W. Stocking (1964), and in 1969 an English translation of the original was published.

Degérando felt that after carefully observing and recording the ways of primitive peoples their behaviors could be compared and "general laws" formulated in order to explain human development and diversity. In order to achieve this end he systematically discussed the range of information to be gathered and the manner in which it was to be collected. To learn the language of the people studied was essential, and he outlined the step by step techniques by which this could be accomplished. The environment, the physical characteristics of a typical individual, family life, societal norms, and so on all were to be recorded with ordered care. Degérando listed eight faults of previous observers of savage peoples, which merit repeating. He noted that their work was incomplete, not well authenticated, poorly organized, based on questionable judgments because of analogies drawn with European customs, lacked precision in linguistic terms, did not sufficiently allow for inaccuracies resulting from the circumstances of contact, failed to record the language in a meaningful manner, and finally did not convey important shades of meaning (Degérando 1969:65–70). The expedition, which had no full-time anthropological observer, set forth in 1800, but the leader, Baudin, could not cope with the differences among those who accompanied him. Scientists and crew members alike deserted, while scurvy, dysentery, and death plagued the party. The anthropological efforts of the expedition were minor, and by the time its members returned in 1804, the society guiding their efforts had become moribund.

Another society which was to concern itself with the ways of aboriginal peoples had a modest beginning but an illustrious development. Soon after Benjamin Franklin (1706–1790) had arrived in Philadelphia, he founded a club called Junto in 1727, whose purpose was the mutual improvement of the individuals involved. The fortunes of the group waxed and waned, depending on the amount of time that Franklin was able to devote to it; in 1766 it appears to have emerged as the American Society for Promoting and Propagating Useful Knowledge. As early as 1743, Franklin had proposed founding the American Philosophical Society, and within a year the group was formed and began to function. It was relatively inactive until 1767, when there was a resurgence of interest. In 1769 the members joined with the American Society to establish the

American Philosophical Society on a reorganized basis (Dercum 1927: 19–24; Conklin 1948:7–12). The primary purpose of this society was to be the promotion of research, and special attention soon turned to the past and present of the United States. In terms of Indian studies, particular attention came to center on recording and comparing diverse languages. A prominent member of the society, Thomas Jefferson (1743– 1826), began to organize the linguistic manuscripts prepared before 1780 and to collect additional vocabularies. However, it was not until the Historical and Literary Committee was founded in 1815 that the society as a group set about systematically collecting such materials. The contributions of Peter S. Du Ponceau (1760–1844), and Albert Gallatin (1761–1849) are particularly notable (Wissler 1942:189–204). Over the years the American Philosophical Society has sustained its early interest in aboriginal Americans to the point that it is now a major archive, and its publications continue to include diverse studies about Indians.

The government of the United States has been relatively uninterested in the direct sponsorship of ethnographic studies. The index of Anderson H. Dupree's comprehensive study of federal involvements with science prior to 1940 is respectable in length and scope, but it includes neither anthropology nor ethnography as headings although two entries are noted under the heading of ethnology (Dupree 1957). These facts reflect partially on the quality of the book's index but more significantly on the overall paucity of ethnographic researches within the broad scope of federal scientific activities. While ethnography was for many years a peripheral area of federal interest, it was nonetheless under government sponsorship that much of the ethnographic information about North American Indians was collected.

Unquestionably the greatest proponent of governmental support of exploration and research in the early history of the country was Thomas Jefferson. His move to explore the Missouri and Columbia rivers to reach the "Western Ocean" was presented to Congress as a commercial undertaking, but in reality it was to gain an empire (Dupree 1957:26). Congress appropriated the money, and the military was charged with pursuing the project under the leadership of Meriwether Lewis (1774–1809) and George R. Clark (1752–1818). Jefferson's instructions to these men about the range of information to be collected concerning Indians are notable because of their comprehensive nature, indicating an awareness of pertinent knowledge which was rare at this time. An article by Verne F. Ray and Nancy O. Lurie (1954) discusses the ethnographic results of the Lewis and Clark Expedition, 1804–1806, in light of what generally is accomplished by explorers and also in terms of the impact of such information on later ethnographers dealing with the same area. Both Lewis and Clark were experienced military men, and they were operating under clear, reasonable instructions, with capable assistants, and with supplies which most often were adequate. Neither man regarded Indians as innately superior or inferior, but rather as regionally quite varied in temperament. The personalities of both men were well suited for ethnographic studies; they were tolerant and outgoing, with Lewis in particular being a superior observer. They were careful to identify the sources for their data; as we might expect, their information is best concerning technology and economics. In fact, Ray and Lurie (1954:359) venture that their "descriptions of aspects of material culture are time and again equal or superior to accounts in modern ethnographies." While they had something to say about most topics in the questionnaire, they did not systematically record a broad range of data for any tribe with the exception of the Shoshoni. Their findings about religion and social life are inadequate, but occasionally such matters are mentioned. Like most early explorers they frequently were hampered by linguistic barriers which made it virtually impossible to obtain information about most abstract subjects. Ray and Lurie are impressed by the valuable information contained in the expedition reports, but they note that the use of such data by later researchers is fraught with problems, especially in terms of the correct identification of peoples and places. They found that as of 1954 most ethnographers interested in the area through which these explorers passed had not consulted the journals in an orderly or very fruitful manner.

After the auspicious beginning under the aegis of Jefferson and similar men of vision, the momentum for federal involvement with scientific pursuits was not maintained. The reports of later exploring and survey parties sent westward often included ethnographic information, but it is far from adequate. Although of relatively insignificant ethnographic yield, the United States Exploring Expedition to Latin America, Antarctica and the Pacific, led by Charles Wilkes in 1838–1842, readmitted the federal government into the serious pursuit of scientific goals (Dupree 1957: 56–61). Horatio Hale, who has been discussed earlier in this chapter, was responsible for the collection of linguistic and ethnographic data for the expedition. His contributions consisted largely of linguistic material for Polynesia and the Pacific Northwest of the United States.

The relationship of the federal government to science was to be changed, strangely enough, by a British chemist of nonlegitimate birth who had spent much of his life in France and had no obvious ties with the United States. He was James Smithson (1765–1829), a bachelor with no near relatives and with considerable wealth. His will stated that if his third nephew died, "I then bequeath the whole of my property . . . to the United States of America, to found at Washington, under the name of the

Smithsonian Institution, an Establishment for the increase and diffusion of knowledge among men" (Dupree 1957:66). The legacy amounted to half a million dollars when the bequest was made available in 1836, and after some debate in Congress it was accepted. At first it appeared that the money would be used to found a national university, but each voice heard from supported a different plan. Finally in 1846, Congress created the Smithsonian Institution as a rather vaguely defined organization, under congressional control, which was to house a library, museum, chemical laboratory, and art gallery. The first secretary was Joseph Henry (1797–1878), an eminent American physicist who visualized a research-oriented organization with carefully conceived projects and provision for the publication of results. He was beset by the herculean task of fending off special interest groups, some of whom would have done away with the institution altogether, while others would have turned it into a museum, library, or forced it to deal only with practical problems. Henry resisted the permanent combination of the National Museum with the Smithsonian; when this change did take place later, public funds were made available in addition to the Smithson endowment of some $30,000 a year. The first volume in the original publication series, *Smithsonian Contributions to Knowledge*, was "Ancient Monuments of the Mississippi Valley," by Ephraim G. Squier and Edwin H. Davis (1848). The Civil War restricted funds, and the interests of the personnel did not lead to any concerted study of living Indians until after the war. It was to be a largely self-educated man, one who had risen to the rank of major in the Union Army and had lost his right forearm at Shiloh, who would make ethnography a realistic concern of the institution. He was John W. Powell (1834–1902), and in 1867 he led a party of students on a trip to the Colorado Rockies. The following year he went to Washington, D.C., with a plan to survey the Colorado River. He proposed to fill the last great void on the map of the United States, contribute geological knowledge of potentially great importance, and study Indians. With Henry's support the exploration was undertaken, and Powell's 1869 trip down the Colorado River made him famous. He later undertook a number of western surveys under federal sponsorship, and he became the head of the U.S. Geological Survey soon after it was created in 1879. Furthermore, Powell was the first man in charge of the Bureau of Ethnology, founded in 1879; the bureau functioned under this name until 1894 when it became known as the Bureau of American Ethnology (Dupree 1957:66–90, 199–211; Judd 1967:3, 6).

The publications issued by the Bureau of American Ethnology are a major source of information about American Indians; however, most of the studies deal with conditions among peoples who had been exposed to

Euro-Americans long before they were described. The first publication series of the bureau was the eight volumes of *Contributions to North American Ethnology* (1–7, 9) which appeared between 1877 and 1893. Each annual report of the bureau included ethnographic information, from the issuance of the first volume for 1879–1880 until the forty-seventh for 1929–1930. A third major series was called the *Bureau of American Ethnology Bulletin*, of which 199 were published between 1887 and 1967 (Judd 1967:6, 78–95, 126–129). The most recent series, *Smithsonian Contributions to Anthropology*, originated in 1965.

In terms of the rise of professional ethnography, it is notable that when the Bureau of Ethnology began to function in 1880, the staff included six men with a wide variety of backgrounds. For example, Henry W. Henshaw (1850–1930) was a self-trained naturalist whose greatest interests were in ornithology. He joined the bureau only because he could not obtain a position in the field of ornithology, and in later years he returned to this discipline, having made no lasting original contributions to ethnography. Clay MacCauley (1843–1925) was a Unitarian clergyman who was commissioned to write a study of the Seminole Indians after he resigned his pastoral duties because of ill health. Garrick Mallery (1831–1894) was a lawyer who became an officer during the Civil War and afterwards was assigned to Fort Rice, Dakota, where he became interested in Indian sign language and pictorial records. In 1879 he retired from the army and became associated with the Bureau of Ethnology, which published his findings primarily in two annual reports (1886, 1893).

In the rise of professional societies with ethnography as a major interest, one of the most fascinating developments took place in London. In 1837 the Aborigines Protection Society was founded as a result of efforts by a Quaker physician, Thomas Hodgkin (1798–1866), the discoverer of Hodgkin's disease. The earliest members appear to have been drawn largely from the ranks of Quakers and physicians. They soon separated into two wings, those most interested in the objective study of aborigines and those who preferred to crusade for the welfare of indigenous peoples. The group interested in study founded the Ethnological Society in 1843, and Hodgkin was among the members. One of the first efforts of the newly formed group was to prepare a questionnaire designed to elicit systematic information about aboriginal peoples from travelers and others. This was published as the earliest edition of *Notes and Queries on Anthropology*; appearing in a sxith edition in 1951, it is still the best book-length guide to the collection of ethnographic information. One of the primary purposes of the organization was to assemble information about peoples, and the first volume of reports appeared in 1848.

The membership, which was never very large, had by the early 1860s divided into two factions. James Hunt was intent on leading the rather staid group into the political arena and an involvement with "the whole science of man." He was so persuasive that by 1863 he succeeded in founding a splinter group, the Anthropological Society. Initially his efforts to popularize anthropology were quite successful, and the new society soon far outstripped the parent organization in membership and influence. The group began to move away from anthropological concerns, however; one of its members, Algernon C. Swinburne, lectured on American poets and their works. Financial difficulties and Hunt's early death led to a rejoining with the parent group in 1871 under the name of the Anthropological Institute of Great Britain and Ireland, to which the word "Royal" was added in 1907 (Burrow 1963:137–154; Keith 1917:13–22; Penniman 1965:53, 91).

In the United States the first learned society devoted entirely to comprehensive anthropological research was the American Ethnological Society, founded in 1842 by the linguist Gallatin and the ethnographer Schoolcraft. "The objects of this Society shall comprise inquiries into the origin, progress, and characteristics of the various races of man" (Transactions of the American Ethnological Society 1845:vol. 1, iii). From the time of its founding until approximately 1869 the group centered in New York City. Although it was reasonably active at first, it later became dormant. In 1896 Boas organized an Anthropological Club in New York City, and it amalgamated with the American Ethnological Society in 1899, leading to the revitalization of the latter organization (Boas 1943: 7–8; Osborn and Osborn 1943:161–162; Smith 1943:181–184; Stocking 1960:1–2). During the latter part of the nineteenth century, however, most anthropologists were drawn together for the mutual exchange of ideas at meetings of the American Association for the Advancement of Science, which was founded in 1848. Initially the programs were divided into loosely-conceived "sections," but with a reorganization in 1874 these became more formalized. At the 1875 meeting Morgan established a "Permanent Sub-Section of Anthropology," which became Section H in 1882 (Kiger 1963:134–137; Lurie 1966:41–42; Resek 1960:133). During this era most persons interested in the study of man in the United States were concentrated in the general vicinity of Washington, D.C., which led to the organization in 1879 of the Anthropological Society of Washington (Lamb 1906:564–579).

The person most directly responsible for founding the American Anthropological Association, which began functioning in 1902, was W J McGee (1853–1912). Although his full name was William John McGee, he signed his given name with initials only and refused to place periods after them. Born in Iowa, McGee's formal classroom education ended when he was fourteen years old. He became a surveyor and then a geologist for the U.S. Geological Survey, and from 1893 until 1902 he was the acting head of the Bureau of American Ethnology. McGee is best known for his work as an administrator and as an ethnographer of the Seri Indians, who lived in northwestern Mexico. In 1901 McGee proposed the formation of an anthropological organization at a national level which could embrace professionals and amateurs alike. Boas opposed the inclusion of nonprofessionals and proposed instead that the group be professionals exclusively. McGee prevailed, however, and the society which was formed included diverse persons interested in the subject of anthropology (Hodge 1916:63–68; Judd 1967:21–23; Stocking 1960:1–17).

In this chapter it has been presumed that the primary purpose of professional ethnography has been to record the sociocultural ways of peoples defined as ethnics before they were influenced by Euro-Americans. The goal of writing aboriginal baseline ethnographies was foremost in the minds of most pioneers and early professionals. This fond ideal with all of its purity of purpose steadily has been eroded because of the inroads made by Western societies among all but the most isolated of ethnics. Ethnographers have responded in very different ways. British workers often have disregarded the ideal of an aboriginal baseline because they have worked largely in Africa and arrived on the scene late as well as without an interest in the precontact setting. United Statesian fieldworkers most often either have turned to acculturation studies or have bypassed the problem to describe peasant peoples as they lived at a particular moment. Some workers have sought documentary data to supplement their own field studies; still others have used documentary studies as basic data in an ethnohistorical approach. In each instance, save among a few British anthropologists, the original goal has been revised in a rather striking manner. It often is asked of ethnographers, whom will they study after the last primitives have abandoned their ways? The answer is in part supplied by these new directions in which ethnography has moved. Yet another direction is being pioneered by employing accepted ethnographic techniques and new "social science" techniques in combination in order to study small groups.

Recently, and largely for the first time, professional ethnographers have directed attention to their field methodology and the field "experience." This concern is reflected in the publication of six books between 1967 and 1970 (Freilich 1970; Golde 1970; Henry and Saberwal 1969; Jongmans and Gutkind 1967; Naroll and Cohen 1970; Spindler 1970) which include over sixty articles by ethnographers about their fieldwork.

Such an outpouring suggests that a critical threshold has been reached in ethnography. The old ethnography, along with its subjects for study, is expiring rapidly. Without suggesting a moratorium on ethnographic data collection, it might be well to consider devoting greater energy to an analysis of the vast number of accounts about ethnics which we have before us. Seemingly the natural history phase of ethnography is past. If so, we might rejoice in the fact and employ our impressive body of factual details in the broader causes of social science and history. *To better understand ourselves and our future through the experiences of ethnics is a selfish but worthwhile human goal.*

THREE

AFRICA

In any presentation of ethnics on a worldwide basis it is fitting to begin with the peoples of Africa. A primary reason for this ordering is that man seemingly originated in Africa over two million years ago. Furthermore, more distinct cultural traditions were reported from among ethnics here at the beginnings of history than from those on any other major landmass; this belies the common assumption that groups of Africans were very much like each other. However, this does not mean that cultural diversity among ethnics was greatest in Africa. The major drawback in the ethnographic information for this continent is the scarcity of baseline studies. Accounts by travelers and missionaries are numerous, but these usually do not convey a breadth of baseline data. As stressed previously, the accounts by professional anthropologists date from the early 1930s or later, well after the disruption of indigenous societies by colonial Europeans and long after the intrusions by Islamic peoples into sub-Saharan Africa. Islamic influence had disrupted the aboriginal ways of some peoples and strongly influenced those of others. Thus, the adequate records of ethnic ways were primarily from those people who lived south of the Sudan and its lateral fringes.

Topographically the continent includes few great mountain ranges, and there were no major barriers to the movement of peoples. Most of Africa is comprised of plateaus ranging from 1,000 to 4,000 feet above sea level with few sharp ecological breaks. These plateaus often terminate at or near the coast, which means that the coastal plain usually is narrow and good harbors few. The drainage pattern consists of comparatively few but long rivers, whose slow movement sometimes is interrupted by great waterfalls. Some rivers are landlocked and form great interior drainages. In geographical terms Africa is divided horizontally by the equator, and the climate is grossly similar north and south of this band. The Equatorial Zone is a tropical region with an average of sixty or more inches of rainfall per year, which in some areas has given rise to the development of dense forest cover. To the north and south of this band and blending into the tropical forests, the Sudanic Zone occurs; here the rainfall averages between twenty and sixty inches, producing great grasslands, the predominant form of vegetation on a continentwide basis. Beyond these regions are great deserts, but they did not lie across the paths of major population shifts. At the northern and southern extremes of the continent the climate is mild throughout most of the year.

In economic terms very few peoples based their subsistence on gathering (hunting, fishing, and collecting, or a combination of these methods). Some gatherers, such as the Bushmen, had very simple technologies and a great deal of physical mobility in their subsistence round. Others, such as the Pygmies, were economically dependent on settled farmers. Most African ethnics had economies based on farming, herding, or a combination of these subsistence orientations. Freshwater fishing was comparatively rare, in part because of the absence of extensive lake systems. Similarly, coastal fishing tended to be unimportant, partially because the deepness of the ocean near the shore prevented the development of fishing banks.

Cultivators were divided into two primary groups, depending on whether they lived in temperate areas and raised primarily grains or were in tropical regions where root crops were most important. The prevailing farming implements were the iron-bladed hoe and the digging stick. The most common means for preparing the soil for cultivation was by cutting the brush and trees on a plot and later burning them (slash-and-burn). The ash served to fertilize the ground, and after a plot had declined in productivity, another was prepared by the same method. This pattern of shifting cultivation led to the periodic abandonment of homesteads and villages in order to form new settlements near new farmlands. Among cultivators productive land was the most important form of wealth, and much of the religious life of the people focused on fertility, both of the land and of the peoples themselves. In farming, the use of the plow, draft animals, or purposeful fertilization of the soil was unknown or rare, but crop rotation sometimes was practiced. Among herders cattle usually were the most important domestic animal. Cattle-based economies were distributed widely but were limited to the nontropical areas, which were free from the tsetse fly. Among peoples focusing on cattle, wealth was represented by these animals, and a great deal of social and religious attention centered on them.

In order to generalize about the sociocultural diversity among Africans at the time of effective historic contact, it is desirable to group ethnics. The necessity for some system of lumping becomes obvious when it is realized that over 800 languages were spoken in Africa at the time of historic contact and that an even larger number of ethnics existed. One means for classifying these people is the culture area system, which often has been maligned but does offer an overview of regional similarities and differences. Harold E. Driver (1961:12) defines the concept: "A culture area is a geographical area occupied by a number of peoples whose cultures show a significant degree of similarity with each other and at the same time a significant degree of dissimilarity with the cultures of the peoples of other such areas." The culture area approach makes it possible to group ethnics into a relatively small number of manageable units on the basis of shared characteristics which make such units distinctive. The culture area map for Africa (Map 1) does not include peoples along the southern coast of the Mediterranean Sea nor Egypt; these regions and the fringes of others designated as ethnic culture areas were dominated by nonethnic states and nations. Ethnics included on Map 1 are those discussed in the text and others selected on the basis of their ethnographic or geographic importance.

Sources: Herskovits 1924, 1930, 1945; Honigmann 1959; Murdock 1959; Ottenberg and Ottenberg 1960; Spencer and Johnson 1968.

KNOWLEDGE AMONG THE BUSHMEN

The biological unity of mankind is evident for all to see amidst the mixtures and blendings of human races, yet the cultural separation between ethnics and other persons is in many respects very profound. The dichotomy is to a great extent based on the ability of nonethnics to read and to write. Literacy implies much more in cultural terms than the simple presence of authors and books; the written word profoundly changes the quality of learning in those societies where it has arisen or to which it has spread. The volume of cumulative writings has expanded today beyond realistic calculation and represents an almost unfathomable storehouse of information. In literate societies formal institutions of learning attempt to disseminate this knowledge in an orderly manner, and the primary obligations of parents have been reduced to feeding and bedding-down their young. Most of a child's formal training is allocated to educational organizations rather than to his parents, and much of his informal learning is acquired from peers. Among all men understanding is cumulative, but among ethnics it has been passed from one generation to the next more directly than among ourselves, through conscious or unconscious instruction by parents and elders. Thus, a child usually learned

Table 1. CULTURE AREAS OF AFRICA (Information is presented in the following sequence for each culture area: the area name; language; major economic foci; social factors; political organization; religious activities; manufactures; and additional key characteristics.)

Bushmen: Khoisan or "Click" languages; mobile hunters and collectors; small family units, bilateral descent, band exogamy; band organization; the sun and moon honored as supernaturals; simple manufactures; bow and poisoned arrows critical in hunting.

Hottentot: Khoisan or "Click" languages; cattle pastoralists; patrilineages and patriclans; hereditary chiefs; ceremonial focus on rain; dome-shaped houses of poles with mat or skin covers, the spear as the primary weapon; cattle tended by women and functioning as beasts of burden and the most important form of wealth.

Eastern and Western Cattlemen: Bantu and Sudanic (Macro-Sudanic) languages; men as cattle pastoralists and women as millet farmers; patrilineal descent, age grades, cattle as bridewealth, polygyny; large-scale political organization in some areas; focus on cattle in religious life, rites of passage, ancestral spirits important; round or rectangular, thatched or mud-plastered houses, ironworking a craft specialization; cattle prized and tended by men.

Congo: Bantu languages; root crop farmers, with market centers important; descent patrilineal or matrilineal, hoes and cowrie shells as bridewealth; village chief and council, hereditary offices and courts; masks in ceremonies, secret societies, stress on fetishes and ancestor rituals; rectangular houses with gabled roofs, craft specializations in iron and woodworking, basketry, and pottery making.

Horn: Hamitic (Hamito-Semitic, Afroasistic) languages; cattle, camel and horse pastoralism, plow farming, markets; patrilineal descent, stress on age grades and bridewealth; hereditary leaders; Islamic influence sometimes strong; iron workers formed outcast guilds; cattle cared for by women, camels and horses tended by men.

Guinea Coast: Nigritic (Niger-Congo) languages; root crop farming and markets; bilateral descent; relatively large chiefdoms, royal or chieftain cults; elaborate ancestor rituals, pantheons of nature deities, priesthoods, temples; ironworking and other craft skills in the hands of specialists.

Western Sudan: Nigritic (Niger-Congo) and Songhaic (Songhai) languages; cattle herding, farming, trade, markets; patrilineal emphasis; large chiefdoms and urban centers; Islam and secret societies; round houses with thatched roofs in compounds, woodworking skills notable; cattle raised for meat, sale, or prestige.

Eastern Sudan: largely Sudanic (Macro-Sudanic) languages; camels and horses herded, farming; patrilineal emphasis, bridewealth in cattle; hereditary political leaders; Islam widely important; round houses with thatched roofs or tents; camel's milk important as sustenance.

Desert: Hamitic (Hamito-Semitic, Afroasiatic) languages; pastoralism (camel and horse), oasis cultivation (cereals and dates), caravan trade; stratified social classes; Islamic religion; craft specializations.

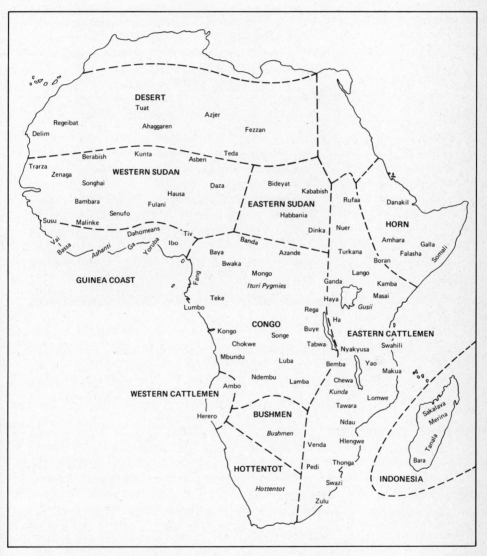

Map 1. CULTURE AREAS AND SELECT ETHNICS OF AFRICA.

A Bushman hunter (Courtesy of Dr. W. Junk Publishers).

by watching a parent perform a task or by listening to what he had to say. In this manner, as well as through personal experience, a child among ethnics acquired his cultural ways and adults learned from one another. To describe the world of knowledge among the Bushmen offers a glimpse of their ideas of reality, both imagined and perceived.

The Bushmen in the not-too-distant past were distributed widely over southern Africa, but they were being displaced from more fertile areas by the Hottentot and by the aggressive Bantu at the time of historic contact. Therefore, those Bushmen who are best known have survived in and around the Kalahari Desert of southwestern Africa. The Bushmen were of short stature and were slim in body build. The black hair on their heads was short and tightly curled in spirals, and elsewhere on their bodies there was little hair. Their skin was brownish-yellow and wrinkled, especially about the face. Bushman women in particular had a tendency to develop especially fat thighs and buttocks (steatopygia), but this physical trait was not as prevalent as is sometimes reported. It was a rather common practice in some localities to remove a finger joint; the operation appears to have been performed on children whose siblings had died in order to protect them from dying. Some Bushmen also made small cuts on the face or elsewhere about the body for beautification or for magical purposes. The Bushmen were divided into three distinct dialect groups, whose members spoke languages distinguished by the importance of "click" consonants. No realistic figure for their aboriginal population is available, but they clearly numbered in the tens of thousands.

The most important male garments were a loincloth and a cloak. The former was a skin which was attached around their loins, passed between their legs, and tied in the back. A skin cloak (kaross) was tied over one shoulder in colder weather. When journeying away from camp, a man carried two separate leather bags suspended from his shoulders. In the smaller bag were food and other necessities; the second bag, which was longer, contained his bow and arrows as well as fire-making equipment. Adult women wore a skin apron in front, which often was adorned with beads or leather tassels at the lower edge. Older women wore an additional apron behind, suspended either from their waist or shoulders. The most popular adornments, worn by all except adult men, were small beads made from ostrich egg shells and strung on sinew threads. These were worn as necklaces or else hung from the hair in a variety of styles. The people did not wash but rubbed their bodies with fat and powdered themselves with a preparation made from an aromatic plant.

All peoples reckon time in some fashion if only because daily and annual variations in light, moisture, and heat occur around the world and because certain activities must be regulated according to the season. The longest span of Bushman time was a season; these numbered either three or four depending on how many dramatic climatic changes occurred annually in a particular area. The coming of a season could be determined by observing particular constellations and their positioning. A separate reckoning of time was made by observing the moon in different phases, but moons were not counted or correlated with seasons. Thus, they did not conceive of the temporal unit we term a year; neither did they count seasons or moons in a cumulative manner. The time at which a child was born soon was forgotten, and no one knew his age. Days appear to have been apportioned according to the sun's location, and distance was calculated in terms of the days required to travel to a particular destination. Their lack of concern with numbers is reflected also in their counting system. Their numbers were one, two, and two and one, standing for three, followed by many. Larger numbers were referred to in terms of the number of digits on their hands or feet, but they seldom had need for these amounts.

The moon figured prominently in the supernatural system insofar as the particulars have been reported. Prohibitions existed against looking at the moon at certain times, or laughing at it, and prayers for food were addressed to the moon, especially when it was new. The text of one particular Bushman prayer recorded by Dorothea F. Bleek (1929:306) is as follows.

Ho, my hand is this,
I shoot a springbok with my hand
By an arrow.

I lie down,
I will early kill a springbok
To-morrow.

Ho Moon lying there,
Let me kill a springbok
To-morrow,
Let me eat a springbok;
With this arrow
Let me shoot a springbok
With this arrow;
Let me eat a springbok,
Let me eat filling my body
In the night which is here,
Let me fill my body.

Ho Moon lying there,
I dig out ants' food
To-morrow,
Let me eat it.

Ho Moon lying there,
I kill an ostrich to-morrow
With this arrow.

Ho Moon lying there,
Thou must look at this arrow,
That I may shoot a springbok with it
to-morrow.

The sun and stars also figured as supernatural aids in the food quest, yet formal rituals to invoke the cooperation of the moon, the sun, or stars rarely are described. The moon not only was associated with rain and food but was linked with death as well. The origin of death was accounted for by a myth about the moon and the hare. In one version the moon asked the hare to tell people on earth that they, like the moon, shall die but return again. The message conveyed by the hare was that men would die and never return. In its anger for this distortion the moon split the hare's lip, but since then death without rebirth has existed among men.

Bushman knowledge about local materials was essential for the manufacture of artifacts on which their lives depended. They knew how to fashion pieces of wood into bows, throwing sticks, digging sticks, bowls, pestles and mortars, and scoops for ashes. Their fire-making equipment consisted of two sticks, one of which was twirled between the hands and pressed against the second stick, held by one foot; once sparks were produced, nearby grass tinder was lighted. Wood fibers were made into snare cordage and less often into bowstrings or netted carrying containers. The shafts of arrows were from reeds, and the same material was woven into mats or bound together to make fish traps. Animal products served diverse purposes; from leather, clothing was prepared and containers made; sinew served for bowstrings, as a mending material, and thread; the stomach of a larger animal was made into a bag for carrying liquids; from bones were produced arrowheads, knives, and awls; horn served as a material for making spoons and whistles; and stones were flaked into arrowheads. The Bushmen also prepared poisons with which they tipped their fragile arrows. It was necessary only to pierce the skin of a prey because of the deadly effect of the poisons employed. The nature of the poisons varied locally, but the essential ingredients consisted of vegetable juices alone, a combination of poisonous plant juices and venom from snakes, or a poison derived from the chrysalis stage of a species of *Cladocera* beetle. One particular form of vegetable poison was made from the wood of a shrishrub. The wood was powdered and boiled in a container; the fiber was removed and the remaining liquid cooked to a glutenous mass. It was mixed with the sap from a particular tree, and the final product had the appearance of beeswax. In order to prepare poison from the venom of snakes such as the cobra or puffadder, their heads were removed and the poison sacs extracted, dried, and pounded into a powder which was mixed with vegetable juice and then boiled down. These poisons were prepared by any hunter and without ritual involvements, but great care was taken not to come into direct contact with them, especially when they had formed a dry coating on arrows. When wounded with poisoned arrows, animals usually ran off but were trailed until they were found dead, either within a short time or hours later, depending on the size of the species.

A technical kind of learning was required in order to make artifacts and poisons, but knowledge of another order was needed to employ these forms with success, especially with respect to taking game. This involved an awareness of environmental factors and of societal structure. Each small cluster of families, a band, defended its area against intruders, but each member was free to range over the band's entire domain. It was at the same time possible for a man to claim ownership to a particular resource. For example, if a man found an ostrich nest with a single egg in it, he stuck an arrow in the ground nearby as a sign of ownership and later returned to gather the eggs when they all had been laid. A similar claim was exercised over a bee's nest to reserve the honey produced. A man was free to hunt anywhere, and he tended to hunt alone, although he might be accompanied by a boy. His most important weapon was the bow, but iron-tipped spears were obtained from the Bantu by the northern Bushmen. Animals such as the duiker, steenbok, and even the larger gemsbok were pursued during the rainy season when their progress was slower than normal and they could be speared. During the dry season wildebeest and zebra were chased until they became so tired that they could be approached and killed with a throwing stick (kirris) or spear. Throughout the year the Bushmen hunted large animals such as giraffe, hartebeest, and ostrich with bows and arrows. A hunter located the fresh trail of an animal and followed it until he was within arrow range, or he might wait near a waterhole or salt lick for the arrival of an unsuspecting animal. Bushmen also lured birds and animals within weapon range by imitating their calls; one particular technique was for a hunter to locate a concealed and newborn animal and imitate its cry in order to attract the mother. A method involving more than one hunter was for a group of men to drive game toward other hunters who were concealed in the vicinity; they might also use dogs for bringing animals to bay.

Burrowing creatures such as the spring hare, anteater, and snakes were taken by probing long poles with hooked ends into their holes. The hook either snagged the animal's skin so that it might be pulled out or it held the prey fast while an excavation could be made into the tunnel to retrieve it. The throwing stick was used as a digging implement, as a club to strike an unwary animal before it could escape, or as a hurling device for birds, hares, and other fast-moving game.

Other means for taking game appear to have been limited to particular ethnic segments, but nonetheless they were important in specific localities. During a drought pitfalls were dug in trails leading to watering places. In some localities a column of earth that did not reach the ground surface was left standing across the middle of the pit. When a large animal tumbled into such a pit, it attempted to jump over the column of earth; its forelegs fell into the forward section, leaving the body suspended because its feet could not reach the bottom of the excavation. Elsewhere pitfalls had stakes driven into the floor; these were sharpened at the upper end to impale a fallen animal. It also is reported that some Bushmen constructed long fences and left openings at intervals where pitfalls were dug. Animals were frightened toward the fence, and as they attempted to escape through an opening, they fell into a pit. Spring-pole snares also were set, and portions of springs might be fenced off and poisoned.

Adequate equipment and objectively perceived skills are essential in taking game, but many people employed supernatural aids as well. It may seem illogical to depend on magical practices when weapons and the abilities of their users were the prime requisites for a successful hunt. However, even the best hunters miss what seem to be sure shots, and seemingly for no good reason a stalked animal might dart away. These situations were dealt with by most ethnics with magical practices; if nothing else, they offered believers at least a degree of psychological assurance. All Bushmen used some form of hunting magic, but it was not the same among different bands. Men of the northwestern area, for example, made incisions on their arms or less often on their cheeks or body. Into these cuts were rubbed ashes from the animals whose outstanding qualities they sought to gain; a man who desired physical speed performed the ritual with springbok meat. In some localities an unsuccessful hunter might explain his ill luck as due to his children playing on his bed at home. There were also other circumstantial explanations for the lack of success in hunting which tended to absolve the hunter of responsibility.

Bushman artifacts classed as containers, tools, implements, and weapons usually were employed directly or indirectly in food-getting activities. Most of their possessions were comparatively lightweight and portable, which facilitated the mobility of their owners. The people ranged from one source of water to another, camping in the general vicinity rather than beside a water supply so that they would not frighten game away. They harvested local resources for a few weeks or months and moved on to another locality when food became scarce. The people lived in caves and rockshelters when these were at hand, but given the nature of the terrain, they most often were obliged to build artificial dwellings. These dome-shaped structures, designed to accommodate a small family, were built from tree branches and covered with grass or else consisted of a bent-pole framework covered with reed mats. In the floor a shallow excavation was lined with grass, and it was here that the family members slept. Food was an almost constant concern, and although the Bushmen were hunters at heart, they disdained few edibles. Roots, bulbs, iguanas, and tortoises were standard items obtained with the aid of a digging stick pointed at one end. Insects such as beetles, locusts, scorpions, and termites were consumed also; in fact, the only tabooed foods were the meat of baboons, because they were so manlike, and hyena meat, because this animal ate human flesh.

The nuclear family, as the habitual food-getting and social unit, was free to camp and seek food anywhere within the band's territory. A man was most likely to have married a woman from another band (band exogamy), and they lived with his band (patrilocal residence). The families of a band usually, but not inevitably, camped in the vicinity of one another for companionship and for mutual protection. These bands, which rarely numbered as many as one hundred persons, formed the largest aggregate for political action. Since the members of some bands spoke a mutually intelligible language, they often have been termed a "tribe," but this was in no sense a unit of political action or one identified by the people themselves. Among some bands decisions about matters of common interest, such as when and where to move, were made by hunters and elders; in other sectors, such as in the Northwest, hereditary leaders along a line of males were recognized. A son succeeded his father, but if a leader had no son, the office was assumed by his closest male relative. A band leader had no badge of office, nor was he the recipient of goods or services because of his position. A man of such standing among ethnics usually is called a "chief," but this term implies that formal power was vested in the office, which was not the case among the Bushmen. He was nonetheless influential in ordinary activities and on special occasions by virtue of his position and because of personal attributes. To lead raiding parties, supervise a hunt, and perform rituals were among his important rights and duties.

People were expected to follow certain behavioral patterns; rewards and punishments relative to these were either in the hands of other men or were controlled by supernaturals. For example, food restrictions were placed on persons of different ages and conditions. Among some bands small children were not permitted to eat the heart of a jackal, apparently for fear that the child would become as timid as this animal. When a hunter had wounded but not yet captured a quarry, he ate no meat from animals that were swift in flight because his doing so might aid the wounded prey in its escape. In these particular bands there was also the belief that a menstruating girl could not eat game killed by a young man because he then would have ill luck on future hunts. Furthermore, in a few bands it was necessary for a leading member to perform a "first fruit" ceremony each year to open the season for harvesting newly available plant products.

Food products and water belonged to the persons who obtained them. A hunter distributed the meat from a kill to those who were present at the time, and a woman likewise shared her takes. The broad effect of these practices was that all the members of a band shared in the food-getting successes of others. Under certain circumstances, especially in sectors of the Kalahari Desert, water was scarce and belonged to the individual who collected it. In order to obtain subsurface water, a spot where the grass was green first was located. A hole was dug here, and a bundle of grass was attached at the lower end of a reed tube inserted in the hole. As the water seeped into the grass bundle, it was sucked through the tube and transferred from the collector's mouth to an empty ostrich egg which served as a storage container. The egg was closed with a wad of grass and buried in the ground or hidden in a tree. The theft of cached water was regarded as an extremely serious offense.

Ideas about property and its ownership were clearly conceived but usually were not an important concern. The lands of the band were exploited equally by all except for the temporary ownership of ostrich nests and beehives mentioned previously. Clothing and adornments belonged to an individual; since a man's clothing and weapons often were buried with him, problems surrounding the inheritance of these items were negligible or nonexistent. During her life a woman gave her ornaments to a daughter, and the eldest son seems to have been the recipient of those items not buried with a man. Adultery, theft, and murder were the most extreme forms of antisocial behavior. An adulterous wife was beaten or divorced, and her lover might be killed. A thief who was caught was expected to restore what he had stolen to the rightful owner, and refusal to do so was grounds for killing the offender. Killings, whether seemingly justified or not, often appear to have led to further murders and blood feuds between the families involved in the original dispute.

When an individual died, he was buried in a flexed position and accompanied by objects that he had used in life. Gravegoods usually are interpreted as items for the use of the deceased in a future life, but in the case of some Bushmen it appears that this property was included with the burial because survivors did not want to see or use the manufactures of someone to whom they had felt so close. The living tended to fear the dead and avoided, at least temporarily, the site of a burial. The exact fate of the dead is not known, but in general these people conceived of an afterlife in which a person assumed human form or became associated with natural phenomena such as the stars or rain.

Bushman knowledge, which includes not only empirical understandings but beliefs as well, has not been reported as thoroughly as might be hoped. Enough data are recorded, however, to realize that the spectrum of their knowledge was broad and in many ways quite systematic. Quite clearly, the Bushmen do not illustrate "prelogical" thinking nor do they manifest "primitive" mentalities. These are misguided concepts and only serve to illustrate the gulf that separates the thinking of the observers and interpreters from the ethnics they seek to characterize. Bushman thoughts about unknown qualities are quite different from our own, yet it is clear that these people had formulated an orderly view of the world in which they found themselves. Their beliefs about the sun and moon have a certain logic and internal consistency, which, while not scientifically valid, do represent a reasoned attempt to explain the nature of the world. The technological skills necessary for making their artifacts, as simple as they may have been, remain impressive if only because the forms produced led to Bushman survival for thousands of years in a very different environment. Their successful production of poisons was a notable accomplishment; considerable experimentation of a scientific nature must have been required in order to derive an effective product. The logic of their environmental adaptations, their originality in making new products, and their imaginative thinking about that which they could not objectively explain combine to make Bushman knowledge an effective means for coping with their world.

The ethnics that ethnographers study usually attach great importance to genealogical ties between individuals. It is less often realized that ethnographers too are linked to one another by sometimes precise bonds of fictive kinship. Basically it is a matter of whom one studies under, and it is intellectual ties that are the important bonds. The preceding account of the Bushmen was drawn from the writings of the anthropologist I. Schapera, who prepared a draft of the text as a Ph.D. dissertation at the University of London. As an undergraduate at the University of Cape Town, Schapera was influenced by the teaching of Radcliffe-Brown, and his doctoral training was guided by Malinowski, who taught at the University of London. Interested as he was in the aboriginal Bushmen and Hottentot, Schapera was almost forced to attempt a reconstructed baseline ethnography of these peoples from the observations of others, since they had changed radically by the 1920s. However, some isolated Bushmen have exhibited more vitality in following their old ways than was realized at that time. In any event Schapera's composite description of the Bushmen, which was skillfully drawn from the fieldwork of others, demonstrated how various structural and functional forms were integrated into coherent behavior patterns. Historical sources were consulted with great care and perception, but an ethnohistory was not attempted; the study avoids any discussion of changes in Bushman life resulting from European intrusions. The work is above all else an integration of data pertaining to aboriginal life, with time and space held loosely constant.

Source: Bleek 1929; Schapera 1930.

ITURI PYGMY HUNTING

In an ethnographic account we expect to learn that a particular people behave toward one another in a specified manner under a given set of circumstances, that they believe in a particular cluster of supernaturals and manufacture specific types of artifacts. If a source is judged reliable, these general descriptive statements are accepted without reluctance; yet at the same time we expect to learn about the differences among local forms, such as the varieties of particular artifact types or the contrasting interpretations of shamans concerning the same event. The generalizations offered by ethnographers often ignore a great deal of variation which probably exists and should be recognized. When variations are noted, as among the forms of arrows, for example, the recorder has made the judgment that the differences are of sufficient magnitude to require recognition as varieties. The problem is one of lumping versus splitting, and the tendency is to lump. If the ethnics described number in the hundreds and are homogeneous in their cultural ways, then the significance of minor local differences which might exist does not seem overwhelming. On the other hand, if a people numbered in the thousands and occupied contrastive ecological settings, with segments of the population out of habitual contact with one another, sweeping characterizations about them are likely to reflect reality only among part of the group. Thus, all-encompassing ethnographic statements about the particulars of behavior among most ethnics must be considered deceptive in their generality. One extreme reaction against overgeneralizations of cultural behavior has been to reject the idea of culture entirely and to maintain that there are only individuals who do different things in terms of personal costs and rewards. The culture versus nonculture issue need not concern us, but the problem it poses is contextually important. The descriptions to follow illustrate rather striking differences between localized segments of the Pygmy population, and to recognize these differences is essential for understanding the nature of culture among Pygmies.

African Pygmies are concentrated to the west of Lake Victoria; they probably occupied the northeastern Congo for thousands of years, and from there they spread westward. The Ituri Forest Pygmy population, which was about 40,000 in 1940, seems to be separated into two distinct clusters: those who hunted primarily with bows and arrows and others who depended most heavily on nets for obtaining game. All Ituri Pygmies lived in a dense forest environment which was productive in terms of foods. The area has little climatic variability throughout the year, and the Pygmies exhibited few seasonal or cyclical differences in their subsistence activities. The area exploited by a band most often had rivers and large streams as boundaries because the Pygmies did not know how to cross bodies of water which could not be forded. At the fringes of the forests occupied by the Pygmies were scattered communities of Negro farmers.

Ituri Pygmy men hunting with nets, with camp in background (detail, Peoples of Africa Hall, Courtesy of the American Museum of Natural History).

They cleared the forest and cultivated large plots of plantains as their most important staple; other cultigens included manioc, peanuts, and rice. In general terms, the Pygmies and Negroes were functionally linked by social, economic, and ceremonial ties. Basically the Negroes provided the Pgymies with domestic plant foods, forged iron spearpoints, axes, knives, and a few other trade items in exchange for meat from forest animals. Thus, the Pygmies are not ethnics in the sense that the word has been used throughout this book because they were not politically or economically self-sufficient. They were quasiethnics with symbiotic ties to the Negroes; that they might have been independent previously is not important in the present context. The Pygmies spoke the same Bantu or Sudanic languages as the Negro farmers, but they usually were familiar with about three distinct languages, indicating their diverse and intense contacts with different groups of settled villagers. The nature of their "original" language is a moot point.

One of the distinctive characteristics of Pygmy material culture is that they rarely used bone, clay, horn, shell, or stone as raw materials for the manufacture of artifacts in spite of the fact that these materials were available to them locally. Furthermore, they made limited use of skin as a raw material for quivers, wrist guards, capes, or belts. Likewise it is surprising that they did not work any wood that was more than about an inch in diameter. Their manufactures of wood included mainly bows, arrows, spear shafts, ax handles, and house frame poles. Plant products were by far the most important raw materials; species of *Ficus* produced bark cloth for clothing; vines were made into hunting nets; fibers formed bow strings, tumplines, and carrying baskets, and broad leaves served as house coverings or water containers.

Among those Ituri Pygmies who employed the bow and arrow as their most important hunting weapon, the band was the most important social unit, and it consisted of a small number of related families who camped together. On an average the members of a band occupied six dwellings, each housing a man, his wife, and their children (nuclear family). A house consisted of a dome-shaped framework of poles covered with large leaves. Inside was a bed consisting of a raised platform supported by sticks or a layer of leaves placed on the ground. Furnishings might include a wooden stool or a chair made from saplings and bound with vines. The core of a band's members were related through males (patrilineage), and their activities were guided by an elder member. Descent ties were acknowledged to exist with the members of distinct bands but were of no great importance, and the concept of "tribal" identity did not exist. A man was likely to take a wife from another band (band exogamy), and the couple lived with the husband's band (patrilocal residence) although there was considerable flexibility in these arrangements.

The only habitual clothing of both sexes consisted of a piece of bark cloth fastened about the waist with a belt and tucked between the legs. The men wore basketry caps, and older men sometimes wore skin capes over their shoulders. Bodily adornments included armbands of fur and fiber cord bracelets with pieces of wood or teeth attached as charms; combs, which usually were obtained in trade from Negroes, were worn in the hair of adults. The people painted their bodies in order to look more attractive and painted their faces for supernatural purposes. Males were circumcised in initiation ceremonies which they held with the village Negroes.

Most of their tools and weapon points, plus some of their containers, were bartered or stolen from village Negroes. These included baskets, wooden mortars and plates, and clay pots as well as spearheads and arrowpoints, knives, and axes of iron. The Pygmies did not know how to kindle fire; therefore, they carried embers when traveling and kept fires burning continuously at their camps. Mute dogs, their only domestic animals, were obtained from the Negroes and were employed in hunting. In order to keep track of their dogs the Pygmies hung wooden bells around their necks.

Among the archers only about 30 percent of the diet consisted of meat. Antelope were an important source of meat, and one way in which they were hunted was for five or six men to track them with dogs. A dog might either kill an antelope or drive it toward a hunter, who then shot it with an iron-tipped arrow. The take was butchered at once and divided among the hunters, each man returning to camp with his share wrapped in leaves. Older men who were unable to track animals depended on their abilities to imitate animal calls in order to lure game within the range of their arrows. The men and women from one or a number of bands might on rare occasions join for a communal hunt. Preparations included a number of ritualistic practices. Herbs were burned in a fire to produce dense smoke; the sight and smell of the smoke was thought to attract supernatural aid. Hunters also rubbed charcoal from the fire around their eyes in order to improve their vision. When the drive began, women hit the ground with cylindrical petards fashioned from leaves in order to make noise and rouse the game into fleeing; they then could be intercepted and killed by the men with their bows and arrows. The harvest from such a communal or multiband hunt was shared by all of the participants. Hunts were not organized to take monkeys although their meat was a favorite food; they were shot with arrows, which on at least some occasions were poisoned. Some of these Pygmies used only bows and arrows, but others supplemented this weapon with spears, which they used in hunting elephants and wild pigs. Particular totemic animals were taboo within specific clusters of patrilineages (patrisibs); a hunter avoided contact with his totemic animal and did not eat meat from the species.

Most food of the bow hunters was procured by women and consisted of a wide variety of fruits, nuts, roots, and wild vegetable products. Although fish were not important in the diet, women did sometimes take them as well as crabs in small streams by using small nets or their hands. Likewise, women collected honey from the nests of stingless bees which lived in the ground. The honey from bees that had stingers and lived in hollows of trees was obtained by men. They smoked the bees out and then used an ax to enlarge the nest entrance in order to retrieve the honeycombs by hand. Plants cultivated by the village Negroes were an important dietary item, especially in times when forest foods were scarce. These Pygmies tended to live near Negro villages in relatively permanent settlements. Here they could depend on obtaining food from villagers, and at the same time they could exploit adjacent hunting areas.

They tended not to affect the local game population drastically because their hunting methods were relatively ineffective.

The Pygmies who depended largely on nets for taking game lived in larger social clusters than did the archers. A band of net hunters averaged about twenty-five households, but the patrilineages of a patrisib were scattered and included some lines which were affiliated with other bands. Dwellings were essentially the same as those reported among the archers, although they tended to have fewer furnishings due to their mobile way of life. The net hunters moved every month or so because they diminished local food sources quickly and because their practice of defecating only a short distance from their dwellings made the area odoriferous. These people had very few dogs, sometimes only one or two per camp. Their clothing was the same as among the bowmen except that charms were worn less often and garments of skin were not worn. Body decorations also were similar to those of the other Ituri Pygmies.

The net hunters did not use deadfalls, pitfalls, or traps even though these were employed by village Negroes; the Pygmies regarded these devices as largely ineffective in taking game. They stressed hunting with nets, which required the cooperation of a comparatively large number of persons. Each man with proven abilities as a hunter, whether he was married or not, owned a net which measured four feet in width and from 100 to 200 feet in length. The minimum number of nets required for a hunt was seven, and the optimum number was about fifteen. In a camp of about seventeen families, all of the occupants participated in a drive with nets. Women carried their small babies along on their backs, and younger children joined the men at the nets. The procedure was to set up a large semicircle of nets, each net being tended by its individual owner. The women assembled noisemakers of branches and twigs, and they arranged themselves in a semicircle facing the nets. They moved toward the nets making as much noise as possible; sometimes during this process they were able to take small game, which they placed in baskets that they carried. Their primary purpose, however, was to drive animals into the nets. The men stood motionless near the nets until an animal was entangled and then speared or killed it with a knife. As many as seven drives might be made in a single day, but if the first few sweeps were largely unsuccessful, they gave up and returned to camp. The animals most often taken were antelope, and the average daily take per family per day amounted to half an antelope, which supplied about as much meat as a goat.

The net hunters made bows and arrows, but they were poor marksmen and did not make frequent use of arrows. The iron-tipped arrows that they had were employed against large game; arrows with poisoned points were shot at birds and monkeys. However, net-hunting Pygmies were excellent trackers; traveling fast and silently through the forests, they often were able to kill game by hand. Elephant hunting was important among Pygmies of this sector, and it tended to be a specialization of some bands. The techniques possibly are of recent origin and stem at least in part from encouragement by Negroes because elephants destroyed their gardens. The individual who was brave enough to hunt elephants used a special spear with a short wooden shaft and a broad metal blade. A hunter silently tracked an elephant by staying upwind from it and approaching at one side. He thrust his spear into the elephant's underside just behind the ribs and then stood motionless. The people said that if you "as much as wink at this moment you are a dead Pygmy." If the opportunity presented itself, the hunter stabbed the elephant again before he returned to camp. If the men there decided from the amount of blood on the spearpoint that the wound was serious, most of the camp members joined in tracking the wounded elephant. Sometimes two to three days of pursuit were required before the elephant died. When the dead animal was located, a man other than the original hunter cut skin and meat from the abdomen in small pieces, and each of the band's members ate some of the raw meat. When the inner wall of the body cavity was reached, the youngest son of the hunter bit into it, and the bloated animal burst; the significance of this ritual was not recorded. After the elephant was butchered, some of the meat was boiled, but other portions were dried to be consumed later or traded to village Negroes; drying meat was the only preservation technique known to the Pygmies. Another means for hunting elephants involved two men. One of them cut the tendon in one leg of an elephant, and the second man cut the opposite tendon, making it impossible for the wounded animal to move. In this condition it usually was blinded, following which the trunk was cut off so that the animal bled to death.

The net hunters appear to have placed greater emphasis on fishing than did the archers. Fishing techniques among the netters included using grubs as bait and preparing fish poison. Plant products and small game were collected by the women. Honey was gathered by men at one particular time of the year; they were accompanied by the women, who were concerned about receiving their share. The collection of honey appears to have been the only harvest of a seasonal nature. Like the bowmen the netters were dependent on village Negroes for iron spearpoints and other trade goods, but they depended less often on them for cultivated plant foods.

It might be supposed that the differences in hunting methods of the bowmen and netters reflect environmental contrasts, but this does not appear to be the case. Some differences may be traced to the cultural ways of the Negroes to whom they were exposed, but the two distinctive hunting orientations cannot be explained as having been derived from these sources. How the netter and archer division arose is not known. It is, nonetheless, clear and important that the contrast in hunting techniques led to distinct differences in the life styles of the two groups. Net hunting required at least seven men working together, and if the number habitually fell below ten, the existence of the band was in jeopardy. On the other hand, if more than about twenty-five men were involved, netting operations could not be conducted effectively. The solution adopted by the netters if their group became too large was for part of a band to net in the forests while the others settled near Negro villagers and became largely dependent on them.

The material culture of the netters was slightly more portable than that of the bowmen, and it also was better adapted to the forest environment. The netters were less dependent on village Negroes for cultivated plant foods to supplement their meat, honey, and wild plant product diet; archers were more permanently settled near, and were more dependent on, Negroes. The netters lived in larger, more cooperative and socially integrated groups. Leadership among the archers tended to be determined by lineage elders, whereas among the netters success as a hunter was a far more important factor than age or lineage background. These and other differences have given rise to cultural orientations which differ significantly.

This survey of the Ituri Pygmies, focusing primarily on their hunting techniques, should serve to illustrate that any broad generalizations about their subsistence methods and social life must ignore differences of considerable magnitude. This raises a number of questions which are perplexing to the fieldworker. One is whether any ethnography should consist of more than a series of minimally normative statements, since there is likely to be a certain amount of unrecorded variability in activities among even the most homogeneous of ethnics. In theory, if observations were thorough enough, most of the differences could be recorded; however, an emphasis on variations might tend to obscure the primary cultural norms. If such a comprehensive account about an ethnic cultural system were written, it is rather doubtful that a publisher could be found for it since it would be of great length. One alternative would be to abandon serious efforts to compile comprehensive ethnographies and concentrate on particular dimensions of life, recording these in terms of most of the existing ramifications. Yet another possibility would be to concentrate solely on a number of small social units, such as two or three families, for broadscale observation. Some ethnographers might bypass the issue and acknowl-edge, unwillingly, that they write "ethnographic fiction" in the humanistic tradition of their discipline, and let the matter rest in discomfort.

Sources: Putnam 1948; Turnbull 1965.

THE HOTTENTOT AND THEIR CATTLE

We usually think of the economies of ethnics as centering around either gathering or farming pursuits. Peoples who were gatherers collected plant foods, hunted meat animals, and fished by diverse techniques. In general they lived in areas where cultivated plants could not be grown successfully because of natural conditions. Those peoples who were farm-ers conveniently may be divided into two groups: horticulturalists, who cultivated small plots or gardens, and agriculturalists, who farmed large fields, usually with the aid of domestic animals. At the time of historic contact most ethnics placed their greatest economic stress on either gath-ering or farming activities. A small cluster of ethnics, however, subsisted mainly on domestic animals and their products, with supplementary sus-tenance derived from gathering efforts. These peoples tended to occupy areas which were so hot or cold that crops could not be raised, but there were gregarious animals present which matured quickly and were tolerant of living in proximity to humans. Pastoral economies such as these usu-ally are identified with populations in northern Africa and central Asia, but the herders of these two regions either raided or traded at nearby settlements in order to obtain vital necessities for living such as grain and iron products. Since they were economically dependent peoples, these pastoralists are more correctly considered quasiethnics. The Hottentot of South Africa, however, were fully autonomous at the beginnings of their history and thus acceptable for presentation as pastoral ethnics.

The Hottentot termed themselves Khoikhoin, which translates "men of men, people of pure race." Designations of this general nature are common among ethnics and are indicative of their ethnocentric attitudes; each group usually felt that its members alone were truly human. Hotten-tots and their Bushman neighbors were from the same racial strain, but the Hottentot came into contact with Hamitic peoples after their separa-tion from the Bushmen and acquired some distinct linguistic and cultural characteristics from these exposures. Like the Bushmen, the Hottentot spoke a language characterized by many clicking sounds; their languages were, in fact, unique among men. Although the Hottentot comprised four distinct dialect groups, all were economically similar. They were pastoral wanderers who never cultivated plants, and their economy was based on the ownership of long-horned cattle and fat-tailed sheep. Milk and milk derivatives were the primary foods; these were supplemented by collecting plant products and hunting game. Meat was a relatively unusual item in their diet since game was scarce and their domestic animals were slaughtered for food only on very special occasions. Since large expanses of grazing land were required to support their cattle and sheep, they lived in small and often widely dispersed settlements centered around waterholes. Within a dialect group, subethnic clusters, which numbered from several hundred to a few thousand persons, exploited a defined territory which was owned in common and could not be alienated permanently. Each cluster consisted of the members of several clans; a clan was patrilineal (claimed descent from a common male ancestor) and named after its presumed founder. The hereditary chief of a subethnic was from the leading lineage of a senior clan, and the heads of other clans served as his advisory council to decide issues of common interest. Clans often feuded with each other, and when these differences erupted into open warfare, allegiance to one's clan overrode all other political ties. Within a clan the most important social unit consisted of a man, his wife, and their dependent children (monogamous nuclear family), but a few wealthy men had multiple wives (polygynous family). Closely related families camped near each other in a settlement which consisted of all the members of a clan or a portion of one clan. The communities were surrounded by an encircling fence of thorns, and the houses were built around the inner margins of the fence with entrances that faced the center. Domestic animals were corralled in the center of a settlement at night, with separate enclosures for calves and lambs. This general information has been summarized from relatively recent ethnographic reports and interpretations, but virtually all of the descriptive material which follows was collected by Europeans soon after they began to settle southern Africa.

European explorers who landed at Table Bay, the site of modern Cape Town, and near the Cape of Good Hope were the first to contact the Hottentot, but as is so often the case, their descriptions of the people were fanciful or else confined largely to straightforward observations that did not require a knowledge of the language. The main body of information about the Hottentot which follows has been drawn from the reports of three men who came slightly later but nonetheless had the opportunity to study the people early in their history, and who were interested enough in aboriginal peoples to record what they had learned. The information which they provide suggests the value of some early ethnographic accounts assembled by nonanthropologists.

Olfert Dapper (1636–1689) was the first person to publish a reasonably expansive and accurate account of the Hottentot. He did not visit Africa but relied on published sources and, more importantly, on the information sent him from the Cape Colony by a correspondent. This person probably was George F. Wreede, a German who went to the Cape

Colony in 1659 and became so familiar with the Hottentot that in the 1660s he often was hired by the Dutch as an interpreter. The information which he apparently provided Dapper (1933) is especially satisfactory with respect to ordinary events in the lives of the people. In 1683 the Dutchman William Ten Rhyne (c. 1640–?), a medical doctor and naturalist, published a short record of the Hottentot based on a stay of about four weeks at the Cape Colony in 1673. Among the topics on which he collected valuable information were the cattle trade with the Dutch, warfare, and physical characteristics of the people. Finally, a long letter written in 1695 by Johannes G. Grevenbroek (c. 1644–c. 1726) to an unnamed Hollander was published in 1933. The writer had been in contact with the Hottentot for about ten years and also had the reports of others on which to draw, when he composed his letter. His report is best when dealing with social and ceremonial life, disease, and warfare. Certain clear exaggerations and demonstrably incorrect remarks in their accounts have been ignored in the presentation which follows.

The Hottentot were slim, of medium stature, with a skin color described as yellowish. Their hair was short and curly, and they covered their faces and bodies with grease. They tended to have large buttocks (steatopygia) and wrinkled skin. Furthermore, their bodies were scarified as a part of certain rituals. Males wore a small pubic apron of skin as an undergarment, and over the upper part of their body was worn a cape of skins stitched with sinew and sewn with the aid of an awl. When traveling they wore a garment which was similar but was made of sheepskin. From a thong around a man's neck hung a small leather pouch in which he carried a wooden amulet as well as miscellaneous items of more direct utility. A woman wore a pubic apron of skin, a short skin outer apron, and a sheepskin cloak with the wool facing inward. The footwear of both sexes consisted of rhinoceros skin sandals. Bracelets of native copper were popular among men as were small copper plates and other ornaments attached in their hair. Portions of a man's scalp also were shaved in patterned designs. People habitually carried an ostrich feather or an animal's tail attached to a stick in order to brush flies and dust from their bodies. It also is reported that women stood upright to urinate but that men squatted to do so. The most unusual physical characteristic was the inordinate elongation of the labia minora often called the "Hottentot apron."

The dwelling frameworks were made from a series of poles set into the ground to form a circle up to twelve feet in diameter; the pole tops were bent and tied together, forming a structure with a height of about five feet. At right angles to the poles withes were woven, and over this

A Hottentot community (from Kolben 1731, vol. 1).

skeleton reed mats or hides were attached, with an opening left for a doorway. Inside the dwelling a central fireplace was constructed; the smoke seeped through openings in the cover and also out the door. These dwellings were highly portable, and the component parts were transported from one settlement to another on the backs of cattle used as pack animals.

Cattle and sheep not only contributed the primary food products but were the major form of wealth. These animals were herded by men but were milked each morning and evening by women. The milk of sheep was consumed only by children. Butter was made in a skin bag turned inside out; the container was filled with milk, closed, and shaken vigorously. Cattle or sheep were killed and their meat consumed only on extraordinary occasions, such as to cure a serious illness or to honor a birth or marriage. The meat of domestic animals and game was boiled or roasted.

Manufactures included fired, clay cooking pots made in a number of different forms as well as wooden containers such as food trays, bowls, and dishes. In addition, baskets woven from reeds served as watertight pails, and horn ladles were made for dipping liquids. The Hottentot not only worked clay, wood, reeds, and horn, but they made satchels of leather for carrying bulky objects.

The most important weapon by far was a spear which was from

three to five feet in length and apparently was headed with a bone point until this came to be replaced by a hand-forged point made from European iron. The points were tipped with the venom of poisonous snakes. Large animals such as elephants, rhinoceros, and elands were surrounded by a group of hunters, and as the circle narrowed, each man launched his spear at the confined animals. The people apparently did not use the bow and arrow at the time of historic contact. In warfare their leather garments served to shield them from the spears of others, and for close combat a wooden club with a knob on the head served as a weapon. An advancing party of warriors sometimes drove specially trained oxen before them to provide a protective screen and to trample their opponents. The primary purpose of a conflict was to gain additional cattle and sheep, and enemies were killed regardless of their age or sex.

Religious life focused on the desire for rainfall, and morning as well as evening invocations were made to the creator for rain. Clouds, lightning, and thunder were considered as manifestations of the creator's positive presence. For festivities men played on flutes while women beat on skins bound over the mouths of pottery vessels or else clapped their hands. The most important dances appear to have been held at the time of a new moon, and there is good reason to believe that the moon was regarded as a supernatural. One insect in particular, the mantis, was singled out for inordinate respect. A mantis could not be injured or killed; if one was found in a house, its presence was taken as a sign that the day would be propitious, and it carefully was removed.

In the writings of the three early observers whose accounts are being considered we find that occasionally a text is rather fully developed. For example, Grevenbroek's description of curing practices is quite explicit about particular procedures. When a man was ill, a cow with its feet tied together was positioned three or four paces from the entrance of the invalid's house. The shaman faced the cow's head to the north and hit it a light blow on the left side with his fist, in order that the animal would fall to the right on an already prepared bed of green branches. With a whetted knife held in his right hand the shaman cut a palm-sized piece of skin from near the cow's navel and immediately bound it on the patient's right wrist. After the cow was skinned alive, the face of the patient was washed with a little blood, and after washing out the cow's gall, the gallbladder was placed on the house roof. Other curing practices included placing the entrails of a sacrificed animal around the neck of a person who was ill, having males urinate on a patient, or washing a wound with boiled-down urine. The chest and sides of the ill might be scarified or an afflicted area might be sucked in order to remove diseased matter. A snake bite was treated by binding the limb above and below the bite; incisions were made around the spot and the poison sucked out. If this method of treatment did not succeed, the venom from snakes or scorpions was mixed with boiled cow's milk and administered to the patient as a last resort.

The Dutch colony in South Africa was founded in 1652, and most of the information about the Hottentot just presented was collected between 1660 and 1695. The observers involved recorded a wide variety of particulars which were of unknown validity at that time, and the truth or fiction of their findings could be established only when still others observed and wrote about the same people. If it were not for additional ethnographic accounts about the Hottentot by writers of that time and later, we might accept some of the fancies of these men as facts. For example, included in one description is the statement that young lions were captured and trained for employment against enemies, but there is no supporting contemporaneous or later evidence for the practice, although they did employ specially trained cattle in essentially this manner. Males are described as having had one testicle removed immediately following their birth, but this reported practice is not validated by later observers, although the idea took the fancy of some so much that they perpetuated it as an ethnographic myth. It is written, too, that babies four months old were taught to smoke tobacco, which had been introduced by Europeans, but proof was never forthcoming. These citations should be sufficient to suggest that early accounts, although sometimes detailed, are not always reliable. Accuracies or inaccuracies and falsifications may be established only by consulting parallel information of still other observers. The total body of information must be analyzed for consistency, and by comparing it with what is known about adjacent peoples, another check of feasibility is provided. The major point is that this or any other cluster of ethnographic accounts cannot in themselves be judged as good or bad without a study of the findings of other observers, and this is a task best attempted by professional anthropologists.

Sources: Dapper 1933; Grevenbroek 1933; Schapera and Farrington 1933; Ten Rhyne 1933.

GUSII SONS AND DAUGHTERS

Given the time span of human physiological maturation, adults must devote a significant portion of their lives to raising children. An offspring's need for parental aid may be considered as barely spanning a decade or it may be regarded as lifelong; child-rearing techniques may be harsh or gentle; and the educational process may be rigid and formal, or barely recognized to exist at all. For all societies the usual means to achieve continuity is through enculturating successive generations of children. Between the unexpandable extremes of birth and death in human existence is a comparatively brief period which is most critical in the lives of ethnics: It is the stage of puberty. At that point in a child's life the physiological changes are almost as dramatic as being born or dying. Puberty was the time chosen by many peoples to teach a child the responsibilities of later life, and to dramatize to family, friends, and strangers that a young adult was in the making. It is particularly instructive to consider the transition from childhood to adolescence among the Gusii, who regarded the accompanying initiation ceremonies as among the most important events in life. Thanks to the 1955–1957 study of one particular settlement by Robert A. and Barbara B. Le Vine, we know a great deal about Gusii sons and daughters as they matured.

The Gusii live in Kenya near its western border and only a short distance from Lake Victoria. Although very near the equator and surrounded by savannahs which are oppressively hot, their homeland is a cool and fertile highland area some 6,000 feet in elevation. Streams and rivers flow between well-watered, verdant hillsides dominated by cultivated fields, pastures, and scattered stands of exotic trees. The native trees were cut when the area came under cultivation in the not-so-distant past. Scattered among the fields, rather than clustered in villages, are the Gusii houses, with roads and paths serving as connecting links.

These Negroid, Bantu-speaking people numbered over 250,000 and considered themselves to be descended from a common progenitor, Mogusii, from whom they have taken their name. They were divided into seven subethnics who fought both common enemies and among themselves. Within a subethnic, members were loosely bound together through patrilineal kinship ties, identification with a specified area, and a common association with a particular totemic animal. Each area was dominated by the members of one or more patrilineal clans (persons who lived in the same area and traced their relationship through males to a presumed common ancestor). Certain clans were regarded as the original occupants, while others were considered as later arrivals and were controlled politically by their predecessors. Clans feuded with one another, but each had an acknowledged area of occupancy and was largely autonomous in political life. Since clans were exogamous (marriages must take place outside of the clan), this factor tended to mute or at least restrict conflicts between them.

In 1907 the Gusii area came under British control, which led to changes which have intensified in recent years. Previously, cattle herding was far more important than farming as an avenue to wealth and to prestige. However, cattle diseases, restrictions of their numbers, and a shortage of grazing lands have reduced the overall economic importance of herding. These factors, combined with a growing emphasis on a cash economy, induced people to put more land under cultivation to raise eleusine (a millet) and corn as staples, with coffee raised as a cash crop and any surplus grain likewise sold. Young men once devoted most of their energies to herding cattle, but in recent years they, as well as adult men, have left the area periodically and found jobs, usually as farm workers. Thus, the people recently have shifted to a livelihood based on farming and wage labor, with herding now secondary. At the same time, since the arrival of the British the population has tripled. This resulted in an increasing scarcity of land, and ownership of it frequently was contested. These conditions, along with the already existing emphasis on wealth and prestige, have led to strained economic conditions which have pitted brother against brother and neighbors against one another.

The segment of the Gusii population studied by the Le Vines was in the administrative unit called the Nyaribari Location, which had a population density of about 450 persons per square mile. Since no striking geographical features divided this unit of scattered households, a cluster of eighteen socially linked households was singled out for intensive attention, and it has been termed Nyansongo. These residences formed three neighborhoods of separate kin groups with a total population of 208. From Nyansongo a road led in one direction to a market center eight miles away, and fifty miles away in the opposite direction were tea plantations where jobs were to be found.

The residents of a homestead included a male head, his wife or wives, all unmarried children, and their married sons with their wives and children. A single homestead included a number of round houses, which had wattle walls covered with mud, conical roofs thatched with grass, and floors covered with a mixture of mud and cow dung. One of the two entrances in each house led to the wife's room, which had a fireplace for cooking and an area where she slept with her husband and children; in a partitioned section near this entrance the adult sons of the woman ate. The second room, where the husband kept his possessions and entertained guests, was entered through another door which opened onto a cattle pen. In the area in front of the main entrance, grain was processed, guests were served meals, and women gossiped as children played. Adjoining each homestead was ground cultivated by the women and pasturage for cattle. Smaller houses with a single room and one entrance, of which there was likely one per homestead, were occupied by boys in their middle childhood, initiated but unmarried bachelors, or an aged widow.

Raising crops in this region was both arduous and time-consuming.

Most of the farming tasks were performed by women since the men generally were away working, and the children as well as the women tended the cattle. Fallow land with heavy brush was cleared cooperatively by groups of men, but women broke up the soil with hoes and planted millet or corn just before the long rains were expected. Corn was raised in roughly cultivated soil, but the form of millet grown required finely pulverized earth and careful weeding, which was done by groups of cooperating women. As harvest time approached, the granaries of a homestead were likely to have been depleted, sometimes leading to serious food shortages. With a good harvest came the time for feasting and ceremonies.

The primary emphasis of economic life may have shifted away from cattle raising, but in their prestige system cattle continued to be extremely important. Most families kept from three to six cows; they could not maintain larger herds because of the scarcity of grazing lands. Milk and milk products were important in their diet, and marriages could be validated only with the exchange of cattle as bridewealth. Cattle were the best investment known, and they were so coveted that disputes over them led to the greatest animosities between men.

Gusii social groups, from the family to the ethnic level, were comprised of men identified with a common male progenitor who lived in their area. The term for such a unit was *egesaku*, and it was in a general sense a patrilineage. The word also was used to refer to the father and sons of a homestead, to a lineage, a clan, or the entire ethnic. The homestead and clan unquestionably were important, but in the course of daily life it was the household that loomed as most significant. A single household consisted of a married woman, her unmarried daughters, and her uninitiated sons. These persons ate and slept together and cooperated in various economic pursuits. After a son was initiated and married, he built a house nearby, cultivated adjacent plots of land, and continued to identify with his mother's household. A woman with her children did not comprise a self-sufficient social and economic unit, for she was customarily only one of a number of women married to the same man (polygyny). In actual fact not all men had multiple wives, but those who did not usually were young and aspired to gain more than their single spouse, since four wives was considered as the ideal number. Each wife had her own separate dwelling and at least one plot of land to cultivate, and the husband slept first with one wife and then another. A husband controlled the activities of his wives by allotting them farming land on a yearly basis. In addition he indicated his displeasure by refusing to sleep with an erring wife. She was reluctant to commit adultery because of negative supernatural sanctions surrounding the practice. Irrespective of her husband's attitudes, she was obligated to take him a basket of porridge daily. Although he was not obligated to consume it all, he was expected to take a mouthful, and the balance was returned to the wife's house for her children. Furthermore, a woman was to be obedient to her husband at all times and consult him regarding all important household decisions. Most wives were quite dutiful; if they were not, they might be beaten. Men knew full well that as desirable as it was to have many wives, the difficulties between them could lead to almost endless turmoil. In fact, the Gusii coined a word which meant "hatred between co-wives." A first wife opposed the addition of another since as a monogamous wife, she could exert some authority by refusing to cultivate the land or denying her husband sexual access. When a man had two or more wives, it was he who could punish. In addition, conflict between wives developed as one accused another of not doing her fair share of the homestead work.

The residents of a homestead formed a polygynous extended family and were separated from others with trees and hedges, although they often shared common pasturages. The male head was the legal owner of the homestead, and it was he who dominated all important economic transactions and thus controlled the destiny of the members. His jurisdiction over cattle as bridewealth was of prime importance; as would be expected, sons obeyed and deferred to their fathers on whom they were so dependent for a wife and land. Relations between a son and his mother were warmer and more casual, for common interests united them. When the patriarch died, the homestead usually disintegrated as a social and economic unit because each married son formed his own homestead with land inherited from his father.

Gusii parents strongly desired children of either sex, for sons brought continuity to a lineage and daughters brought cattle at the time of their marriages. The compelling desire for children is reflected in the fact that sterility or impotence were the most common grounds for divorce, infanticide did not occur, miscarriages were lamented, and abortions were attempted only by the unwed. A woman ideally conceived once every two years, and while half of the offspring did not live to maturity, the desire for children remained great. Cowives competed with one another in the number of offspring each bore, and when a woman was unable to conceive with regularity, the couple grew anxious that supernaturals had been offended or that witchcraft was being performed against them.

Conception was thought to occur when semen combined with the blood of a woman, and this could occur only if intercourse took place when a woman was menstruating. A woman suspected that she was pregnant when she failed to menstruate for two or three months and was pleased to announce the fact to her husband. No special restrictions were placed on the actions of a pregnant woman, and she continued to perform her usual tasks until the time of birth. Childbirth took place within the homestead in the house of the pregnant woman's mother-in-law. A few days after a birth the mother returned home, and a small naming feast was held as soon as the baby's umbilical cord dropped off. Between the time of birth and weaning, a span of nearly two years, the needs of a baby were attended to with the greatest consideration and with the fewest expectations from the progeny. Infants required protection from the "evil eye," cast usually by women. If a baby showed physical signs of illness, a shaman was summoned to effect a cure, at considerable expense to the mother. Under usual circumstances only the mother nursed her baby; it slept with her and was in her almost constant company except when she worked in the house or in her garden plots. At these times the offspring was cared for by an older sibling some six to ten years of age or by a young sister of the mother. An infant was fed when hungry, and if the work of the mother took her some distance from the household, the baby was taken there by its attendant in order that it might nurse. As a baby grew older, it was fed millet gruel; sometimes this was introduced as a milk supplement soon after the offspring was born in keeping with older feeding patterns. A mother began to wean her small child as soon as she realized that she was pregnant again. Up to this point a child was dependent and protected, but the demands of living in Gusiiland soon would make themselves felt. With the birth of another offspring a recently weaned child was displaced by the neonate. It was disturbed and cried or disobeyed, which brought forth reproval, threats, and often punishment such as being struck with a stick. A child from three to eight years of age was introduced to farming activities, and by the end of this time span both boys and girls were expected to help their mothers, especially in hoeing her cultivated plots.

After the harvest each year, a local community composed of diverse homesteads and representing different lineages held initiation ceremonies for both boys and girls. A girl was allowed to decide when to be initiated and usually did so without any encouragement from adults. She was eager to be known as an "unmarried girl" rather than as a "little girl," and only by participating in the initiation rituals was it possible for her to achieve this status change. She then would no longer be a child nurse and perform other childhood chores, and she would be attractive to initiated boys, who were more proper than those who were uninitiated. A further inducement was that she dreaded being left behind by her initiated friends and agemates. Parents often said that they were reluctant to permit a daughter to go through the ceremonies because of the expense and trouble involved.

Their hesitation was much more often feigned than real; it served as an added stimulus to the girl's own desire and made her less afraid of the ordeal she must face. When some of the girls in adjacent homesteads entered the first stage of the initiation, the potential initiate became more eager and insisted that her mother allow her to participate. A mother's seeming reluctance finally was overcome, and one morning the mother set off with her daughter, who was naked except for a cloth on her shoulders. They were joined by other mothers and daughters on a short walk to the home of a particular middle-aged woman. Even when the girls arrived, older women pushed them away and told them to go home as a final test of their determination. From this group of girls, their mothers, and other women, one girl was taken at a time and seated on a stone either just outside or inside the house. Behind her was a woman who held the initiate's arms and attempted to make certain that the girl's hands were firmly over her eyes by holding them in place. Her legs were spread apart and a white flower was placed on her pubic region. With a small knife the head of her clitoris was cut off, and as soon as it was removed, the assembled women shouted, screamed, and even danced about while the girl was seated with the girls who had preceded her. After the clitoridectomies were completed and the operator had been paid, the girls walked stiffly home amidst a joyous throng of women who now said and did things that normally were considered very unwomanly. They might use obscene language, make sexual jokes which they considered as crude, sing songs regarded as bawdy, simulate sexual intercourse, and destroy or take crops from gardens. When a girl arrived home, she was concealed near the house until afternoon, and her mother prepared a special meal. In the afternoon she was led into her mother's house by initiated women amidst more hilarity to begin her postoperative seclusion. The visiting women were fed by the girl's mother, whose hospitality humorously was criticized amidst more frivolity.

For the next month no initiated males were permitted to enter the dwelling, and the girl left the house only to relieve herself. She was overfed in the belief that her wound thereby would heal more quickly. On a number of nights initiated girls visited her and performed a ritual which included sexually oriented dances performed in the nude and the use of a phallic symbol, thereby constituting at least indirect instruction about sexual activities. At the end of her confinement a girl was covered with fat and adorned with beads to show herself off with other newly initiated girls. From this time until her marriage a girl was expected to be clean and well groomed, and she spent many hours each day washing her clothes and herself. After her seclusion she was presented with one or more dresses bought at a store, and she soon was expected to wear a kerchief. For the next four or five years neighborhood girls who had been initiated together formed close social ties by working together and going to market as a group, and they were quite concerned about the physical signs of maturation of one another.

Female adolescence was a time of trauma for parents. They felt that a girl should work hard for the household and make a good marriage that would provide the parents with bridewealth and compensate them in part for the expense of raising her. They most feared that a girl would be lured to elope with a youth who had no cattle but had flattered the girl and given her gifts as well as sexual gratification. Their fears were not unfounded because with the increasing scarcity of cattle as bridewealth, elopements were more frequent. Likewise a daughter might become pregnant before her marriage and thereby earn the title of "slut," which made her a less desirable potential wife. A father was anxious especially about the behavior of his twelve- or thirteen-year-old daughter. Yet if she misbehaved, he was reluctant to punish her for fear she would flaunt him by misbehaving more and even eloping. When a girl was suspected of having sexual intercourse, which was typical by the time she was about fifteen years old, her marriage was arranged as hastily and advantageously as possible.

Although a girl of eight was considered ready to be initiated, her male siblings of about the same age or even somewhat older still were children both in body and in spirit. As a boy matured he began to sleep in the dwelling of unmarried, initiated males, but he often hesitated to leave the security of his mother's bed and tended to fear sleeping away from her side. He was expected to be absent when his father slept with his mother, but his emotional dependency on his mother remained great. As an older boy his primary responsibility was to care for the family's cattle, but he found this task tiresome and often neglected his duties. Sometimes he turned the cattle over to a younger brother who was incapable of handling them and went off to hunt, fish, or play. Older boys wandered far from home and were not dependable in many ways. Their aggressive behavior and sex play with uninitiated girls was accepted, but when they behaved similarly toward a young initiated girl, the angry parents of the girl complained and the boy was reproved or beaten. A father was rather anxious to have his growing son initiated because of the child's nearness to his mother, his growing awareness of sexual activities, and his usual rowdiness. The initiation ceremonies tended to make the boys more responsible. Young sons, like daughters, looked on initiation positively, and most boys were anxious to participate in the rituals at the same time as their age-mates. Nonetheless, a father feigned doubt about his son's ability to endure the pain involved in order to encourage his decision.

A boy chose any initiated but unmarried youth, except a brother, as his sponsor, and the day before the initiation rituals began, the aspirants' heads were shaved. The novices and their sponsors left the house of initiated bachelors in the middle of the night. They were led away and frightened with tales of the pain which they must endure. If a boy did not cry at the prospect, he was allowed to bathe in a stream and then proceed naked to a special tree, where he stood with his back to the tree and his hands held above his head. Older initiated boys and men stood directly behind the operator as he approached the boy. With their clubs and spears poised, they threatened to kill the novice if he moved or showed any signs of pain during the circumcision operation. After it was over, he was led away, holding his penis to retard the flow of blood. Later the same day the circumcised boys were taken away by their sponsors and by men who were termed brothers but were not biological brothers (classifactory brothers). They sang an initiation song and screened the novices from the sight of women during the ritual which followed. Two or three initiates were led into a new house constructed for them to share during their postoperative isolation. Specific rituals were performed in each of these dwellings. During this time the fire within the structure would not be permitted to die, and a particular species of grass which was stuck in the floor was carefully kept from withering. Married persons were not permitted to enter the house, and when the newly circumcised boys went out, which they did most often to go hunting, they carried ashes with them to throw into the air to ward off the approach of anyone of their parents' generation. In general the boys enjoyed their isolation, but there was some hazing. They were forced to eat distasteful substances presented to them by the initiated youths as delicious, they were beaten with nettles, and they had to pull up, by using their teeth, pegs that were set near a fire. It was threatened that they would be eaten by a supernatural animal which they heard; later they were shown that the noise it reportedly made was, in fact, made by a bull-roarer. A boy might also be told to call his mother and then beaten if he did so, since he was supposedly now a man and no longer should require her help. Before their release from isolation, which had lasted several weeks, the initiates participated in cleansing, blessing, and other rituals. One of the blessings involved a father and a son. The father placed white earth on his son's head and vowed to respect the youth as he would expect the boy to respect him.

The yearly Gusii initiation ceremonies required extensive participation by most of the society's members, which in itself suggests the importance attached to the event. The differences between the initiation ceremonies for males and females are rather striking. A girl was forcibly held during her genital operation and later was secluded in her mother's house. A boy endured the pain of his operation unaided by others and was isolated but not secluded. As the Le Vines have written, "In short, initiation encourages boys to be self-reliant, to do without parental support, to endure hardship unflinchingly, to cooperate with related agemates, and to venture with weapons. There is no such encouragement for girls, and this is congruent with the fact that the girl leaves her mother's house, not at initiation but at marriage, five or six years later" (Le Vine and Le Vine 1963:200).

Initiations frequently have attracted the widespread attention of observers because they so often were dramatic and also because they differ markedly from the nonceremonial transition from childhood to youth in most of our society. (We do, however, have coming-out parties for debutantes, bar mitzvahs for Jewish males, and hazings for youths joining exclusive groups.) Among ethnics the ceremonies were widespread, often elaborate, and left physical evidence that the transition to adulthood had been recognized. Above all else, initiations such as those performed by the Gusii dramatized to the community as a whole that a girl or boy was no longer to be regarded as a child but as an aspiring adult. The pain involved reinforced the gravity of the transition, and the manner in which youths were treated during and shortly after the rituals began to instill in them the essential values and attitudes of adult life. Thus, initiation ceremonies are not simply strange customs, but are one important means by which the social goals of a society are furthered.

The general ethnographic account of the Gusii by the Le Vines is brief, but of sufficient breadth to enable the reader to understand what is of major importance in the peoples' lives. The authors' purpose was not to write an in-depth report about the entire culture but to stress one dimension, child-rearing practices. A study of this nature, which concentrates on a topic of comparatively limited scope, is in many respects more valuable than a broad-scale ethnographic account which never adequately explores any specific social or cultural dimension. As we increasingly realize that particular dimensions of behavior among ethnics are quite complex, the distinct tendency is to concentrate on the field study of specific topics usually conceived around a set of clear conceptual questions. This trend, if it is a trend, suggests growing methodological sophistication and a greater realization of the aims of problem-centered research.

Source: Le Vine and Le Vine 1963.

KUNDA DESCENT

Humans share the characteristic of living in social groups with many other creatures, ranging from certain varieties of termites to caribou and bison. What is most notable about the nature of human society is the diversity of ways in which people have organized themselves for cooperative action. In our society today, as is true of most other peoples, social life is built around a man, his wife, and their children. Among ourselves this unit is in many respects self-sufficient, but among ethnics the small family often was subordinated to larger family groups. This broader social matrix is familiar to us to the extent that we know of rural family life in some sectors of the United States. More remote to our understandings is an extended system such as the Scottish clan, and many other means of distinguishing and depending on relatives are even more foreign to us. Some of the possible variations in social structure already have been described in this volume, but one of the often occurring patterns has not been stressed. This is the custom of tracing one's relatives primarily through the female line and attaching great social importance to these ties. Kunda social life will illustrate the pattern and the point.

These people numbered about 20,000 and lived mainly along a section of the Luangwa River in northeastern Rhodesia at the time they were studied by J. P. van S. Bruwer in the 1950s. The Kunda appear to have emerged as a distinct ethnic in the 1840s when they arrived in their historic homeland from the northwest. According to their traditions, before the move they were a subject people under a powerful Bisa (Wisa) chief, but when they entered the Luangwa area it was uninhabited. In this new territory the founder of the Kunda, Mambwe, established geographical areas or districts with fixed boundaries and allotted these to subordinate chiefs named from among his competent relatives. The office of subchief was hereditary, and it passed along a line which was considered senior to all others within a district. In judicial matters the subchiefs had considerable power, which they exercised after consultations with senior males of their districts. Before the early decades of the present century, during which the British began to control the Kunda politically, the subchiefs were largely autonomous administrators. Within each district were numerous villages, each of which had its own allotted lands. Unoccupied areas were open to exploitation by any members of adjacent villages for hunting, fishing, and collecting. While the limits of the districts were fixed, the villages as physical settlements often were abandoned for new sites.

In the routine of Kunda life the village was the most important social and political entity. In 1950 there were nearly 250 villages, each of which was an interdependent unit with its own local leader. The villages ranged in size from 28 to 250 persons, averaging about 80 residents each. Each settlement consisted of a core of persons related through females; in this group, which had founded the settlement, genealogical ties could be traced precisely (matrilineage). In addition to the core, one or more similar groups had become attached to the community through marital ties. The leader of a village was the senior male of the core female descent group. The office of village leader usually passed from the current leader to his sister's oldest son (matrilineal descent and primogeniture). Each additional and distinct matrilineal group in a village had its own senior "guardian," who assisted the village leader and together with him formed an informal council which dealt with minor local affairs.

Each village was comprised of households which were independent subsistence units. Every married woman had her own dwelling, garden, granaries, and sleeping quarters which she shared with her husband and younger children. Older children slept in separate quarters or with their grandparents. Household members cooperated in the cultivating, building, and manufacturing activities which were related to their unit.

The principle of matrilineal descent permeated all Kunda social life, whether at the family, village, district, or ethnic level. In these terms relationships traced through females were overwhelmingly important. In the broadest possible application of this concept, everyone, whether living or dead, who was descended from a known common ancestor belonged to the same matrilineage. Most matrilineages traced these ties over six generations, four of which were represented by living persons. In most cases an individual's matrilineage meant to him those living persons to whom actual relatedness could be traced along the female line (e.g., brothers and sisters, sister's children, sister's daughter's children, mother's sister's children, mother's sister's daughter's children, and mother's mother's sister's daughter's children). Thus, the members of each matrilineage had a common ancestress from whom the line of descent was sustained or expanded through females. A matrilineage was a corporate group, meaning that it had established rules of conduct as well as continuity through time as a social institution. Individuals were born into matrilineages and died, but the matrilineages lived on. Within each matrilineage men dominated social, religious, and political life, but they derived their rights entirely through relationships with females.

In order to establish the hereditary standing of any person, birth order within a lineage was the most important factor. Among a group of daughters with the same mother (uterine siblings), the firstborn girl was called the "great womb," and each of her younger sisters was termed "small womb." The eldest female's children comprised the leading family within the matrilineage. The firstborn male of an eldest female was the senior guardian for the entire matrilineage. Thus one's mother's brother was an important person in his sibling group as well as for the children of his sisters. His responsibilities were greatest toward his sisters' children, especially those of his eldest sister. In a parallel manner a second-born son was responsible mainly for the welfare of his second-born sister's children, and so on along the sibling line. In perfect harmony with this system, any office ranging from chief to subchief and village leader was inherited by an eldest sister's oldest son.

Each matrilineage was one segment of a larger matrilineal grouping whose members were distributed widely in Kunda country and among whom actual genealogical ties could not be traced but were presumed to exist (matrisib or "matriclan" in British terminology). Members of the eighteen named matrisibs could not marry anyone within their respective groups (matrisib exogamy). Although the core of relatives was always mother-related, a man's children were linked indirectly with his matrisib. Identity with the father's matrisib is reflected in the fact that a person was addressed by naming the matrisib of the father, not the mother. The dichotomy between father's and mother's relatives was also reflected with clarity in the distinct sets of kinship terms for these persons.

The village associated with the origins of a matrilineage always was dominated by the leading line within that matrilineage. The eldest male of this line was the ranking lineage guardian and held the office of village leader, subchief, or chief. Any settlement was comprised of persons representing two or more matrilineages, of which one was dominant because of its local origins. A Kunda man married a woman of a different matrisib, but she usually was from his settlement (village endogamy), and he became associated with her residence unit (matrilocal marital residence). The only men who were likely to have spouses from other settlements (village exogamy) were office holders, and their wives became associated with the dwelling units of the males involved (patrilocal marital residence). In general, and in keeping with the rule of sib exogamy, a man married a real of fictive father's sister's daughter or a mother's brother's daughter (cross-cousin marriage) from his own village.

This brief summary of Kunda social structure has been introduced in order to illustrate the nature of an organizational system which is not only widespread among ethnics but is quite different from our own. It sometimes is assumed that in societies where descent is traced through females the women control the course of social life (matripotestal), yet this clearly was not the case among the Kunda. Quite to the contrary, for among them men made all important decisions (patripotestal). Similarly the Kunda matrilineal descent system demonstrates that this form is one of the very viable alternatives to tracing primary ties of kinship through males (patrilineal descent) or along both sides of one's family line (bilateral descent). Why did matrilineal descent systems emerge among some peoples? The most widely accepted answer is that they were likely to develop in those societies where the farming activities of women contributed more to the group's subsistence welfare than did the subsistence pursuits of the men.

Sources: Bruwer 1958; Poole 1949.

ASHANTI POLITICAL ORGANIZATION

In the gross classification of mankind it has been customary to place peoples in either the literate and civilized or nonliterate and primitive camps. Such a dichotomy has the advantage of being precise, for people either knew how to read and write or they did not. The difficulty in dividing peoples on the basis of a single cultural criterion is that no single factor is consistently a just basis for a qualitative division. Anthropologists are in part responsible for the importance attached to the literate and nonliterate separation, yet they recognize clearly that such a distinction is in many instances very misleading. The primary reason is that many ethnics, while not literate, had highly complex patterns of behavior which seem in many ways comparable to literacy in significance. Nowhere in the world is this truth more obvious than in sectors of West Africa where political organization was extraordinarily sophisticated in nonliterate populations.

Among the Akan-speaking peoples of Ghana, the Ashanti are best reported in the ethnographic literature. The Ashanti kingdom, or perhaps more properly the Ashanti chiefdoms, began amalgamating about A.D. 1700. Subsequent conquests were in part facilitated by the availability of European firearms, and the Ashanti came to dominate other Akan peoples until they in turn submitted to British control in 1896.

The king, as the head of the Ashanti kingdom, had the exclusive right to make war and to quell insurrections; he alone taxed the entire nation, and he held the ultimate power of life and death over all of his subjects. In arriving at all of his important decisions, however, the king was guided by elders, whose positions as councilors were largely hereditary. Collectively the king and his council functioned primarily as a judicial body, but they also had legislative and executive powers. A further check on the powers of the king was held by the queen mother (sister queen), whose duty it was to speak out against any misconduct by the king. On assuming office a new king pledged his loyalty to the regional chiefs, to his councilors, and to the laws and customs of the nation. Likewise, when a new regional chief was installed, he pledged loyalty to the king; as a symbolic gesture of authority the king placed his bare right foot on the chief's head during the latter's installation ceremony. Each of the chiefs possessed a stool which represented his authority as the leading officeholder in his district or chiefdom. A similar organizational pattern, headed by lesser officials, prevailed down to the village level. A chiefdom was a territorial unit organizationally centered at a capital, and each chief controlled those lands associated with his stool. He allotted unused lands to individuals for their use (usufruct), but subsurface rights remained in control of the stool. The king directly controlled the lands only within his own chiefdom, and even so he was obligated to transmit his orders down through the structure of lesser authorities.

When the Ashanti state was founded, it was comprised of nine component chiefdoms, of which the Kumasi chiefdom was the most powerful. Its leader became the head of state, or king, and although he exercised no control over the ordinary internal affairs of the other chiefdoms, his office symbolized national unity. The king's power over the other chiefdoms was based in part on the superiority of his military force. The gold on Kumasi land had provided the wealth to purchase those firearms which had aided significantly in the original consolidation. From subsequent political expansions the king received further economic advantages in terms of the slaves and material goods which he obtained; this tribute paid by subdued chiefs added to his wealth and power. Military ventures were undertaken in order to gain wealth, to make trade routes safe, and to glorify the king. The ruler controlled national wealth through palace officials who were appointed and were responsible to him in fiscal matters. The office of king was associated intimately with a particular golden stool which had a symbolic value comparable to or even greater than that of a European king's crown and throne.

According to a verbal accounting of the origin of the stool, in about A.D. 1700 a priest had claimed that through him the God of the Sky would make the Ashanti a great state. The Kumasi chief, Osai Tutu, learned of this man's power and assembled the leading members of the nobility as well as a great throng of other persons to view a demonstration of his inordinate abilities. The priest appeared before them and caused a black cloud to descend from the sky amidst rumblings and the air to thicken with white dust. In the cloud was a wooden stool partially covered with gold which descended and alighted on the knees of Osai Tutu; then, as later, the stool was never to have contact with the ground. This sacred stool was regarded as the soul of the nation; it symbolized Ashanti vitality and bravery and was never sat upon by anyone. At great ceremonies the king pretended to sit on the stool, but in fact sat on his own stool and rested an arm on the Golden Stool. The power of the stool was thought to have led the Ashanti to independence soon after they received it. When Osai Tutu had assumed his office as chief of the Kumasi, the Ashanti were a subject people, but soon thereafter they were given the Golden Stool. One year, when a representative of their overlord came to demand the annual tribute of gold as well as the favored wife and son of every Ashanti chief, the messenger was killed. Each chief placed his finger in the dead man's blood and vowed to defeat the oppressor. They achieved this goal and felt that the power of the Golden Stool had made the victory possible. During the reign of a later Ashanti king, the leader of another state was so presumptive as to have a golden stool made for himself. The Ashanti were greatly affronted; they defeated the ruler's armies and beheaded their leader. The false golden stool was melted down and cast into two masks representing the dead man's face, and these were hung on either side of the Golden Stool. Each subsequent Ashanti king added something to the stool, but no addition appears to have been as striking as the masks of gold. When confronted by the overwhelming power of the British in 1896, the Ashanti decided to submit without fighting because they could not bear to think of the Golden Stool as being associated with defeat. The British searched unsuccessfully for the stool, and when they failed to locate it, a government representative asked why he was not permitted to sit on the stool. The very idea so offended the Ashanti that they felt obligated to fight the British, in spite of all the implications, and they soon were defeated.

Among the Ashanti, who numbered around 250,000 in recent historical times, most people were farmers who raised yams, guinea corn (sorghums) and vegetables. Hunting and fishing for food were of lesser importance. Some persons were specialists, serving the king or a major chief as craftsmen, musicians, and courtiers. This led to a great deal of variability in individual rank and wealth. The backgrounds of persons differed as well, since some were descended from war captives, slaves, or refugees. In terms of Ashanti political ideals, foreigners could become accepted as citizens, and the attitude toward their acceptance was so strong that no Ashanti was supposed to reveal the origins of another. Freeborn citizenship was a birthright inherited from an Ashanti mother. For non-Ashanti to become citizens it was necessary for them to become identified with or adopted into an Ashanti lineage. Throughout the entire nation at every level, descent was traced exclusively through the female line (matrilineal descent). An individual was identified with his or her matrilineage (persons related through females when actual genealogical ties were known), which in turn was identified with a particular chiefdom's stool. This meant that one's allegiance was to a particular female descent group irrespective of his place of residence, although most often a person appears to have resided in the chiefdom of his matrilineage. The importance of lineage ties is illustrated further by the fact that even though a lineage elder might have lived and died in an area not identified with the stool of his birth, his body was returned to its ancestral home for burial in the appropriate lineage cemetery.

The rights of citizens and their duties were defined with precision. Within the lands of the chiefdom with which a person was identified he might hunt, fish, and collect, or bring virgin lands under cultivation. The most esteemed members of certain lineages were permitted to serve as political officeholders, and ordinary persons in these lineages could participate in political discussions and at least in part influence political decisions. If wronged, a person had the ultimate right to appear before the court of the king to seek justice. During his lifetime an individual could expect hospitality from his chief, and he knew that at his death his chief would contribute to the funeral expense. It was anticipated that citizens would bear arms in defense of stool lands, would contribute labor to the chief's stool lands, make first-fruit contributions, provide animals for sacrifices to important ancestors, and contribute wealth to the chief's stool in times of need. These obligations were fulfilled by a quota system which was based on an individual's lineage and rank. At the death of a person a portion of his personal wealth went to the officeholder immediately superior to him; this applied from the lowest rank up to that of the king. Thus, an individual's behavior throughout his life was guided by political and judicial norms which were both sacred and secular.

One safeguard against misconduct on the part of a chief was the fact that he could be replaced during his tenure. Charges of misusing stool wealth, corruption, authoritatively making decisions without the advice of the councilors and elders, adultery, or lack of dignity were among the grounds for seeking to destool a chief or even a king. If the accusations were proven valid, the person was replaced by another individual in the lineage associated with that office. In other words, an individual might fail in his obligations, but the office itself was not subject to manipulation from one lineage to another.

The spheres for judicial action as well as the rights and obligations of individuals formed a precisely conceived system. The major division was between obligations defined by law as opposed to those which were dictated by custom. Misbehaviors in the former category, or public wrongs, were referred to the appropriate political officeholders for adjudication. Major offenses included murder, sexual crimes, treason, and disrespect for the Golden Stool of the king. These were punished by death or alternatively by the seizure of property or loss of citizenship. These wrongs were "tribal sins" and had negative moral, political, and religious implications; the supernatural associations were drawn because such acts were offensive to one's ancestors and the gods as well. Any person aware that these transgressions had been committed was obligated by tradition to convey his knowledge to the proper jurisdictional level.

The violations of customs, or the "household cases," were related to persons and their property. Cases dealt largely with problems surrounding personal property ownership, land disputes, marriage, divorce, theft, trespassing, and insults. These were settled within a lineage or between lineages through arbitration by lineage leaders, and judgment was in terms of a "pacification fee," redress, or compensation. Decisions were supported by public opinion based on respect for the customs, and thus penal sanctions were absent. Some wrongs which occurred were judged differently because of the standing of the persons involved. Adultery by an ordinary citizen with a brother's wife was a household case, whereas if the woman were the wife of the king or a chief, the wrong was a tribal sin. In the event that a dispute could not be satisfactorily adjudicated at one level, an appeal might be made to a higher court level.

Throughout all levels of Ashanti social and political life one organizational unit was deemed more important than any other. It was the matrisib and was comprised of component matrilineages whose residents lived in more than one settlement (clan in British social anthropology). An Ashanti proverb states "one matrisib one blood," and the eight sibs were presumed to have been derived from one maternal ancestor. Members of the same sib were prohibited from marrying each other (sib exogamy), they were unified by common descent, and members had the right to hold the political offices passed along particular lines within the sibs. The sibs were dispersed widely among the chiefdoms, held no property in common, and were not unified political action groups. Nonetheless, feelings of solidarity among members were strong and were equated with brotherhood. Thus, descent along the female line was the kinship basis which united lineages, extensions of these ties gave rise to sib identification, and all the sibs combined to form the nation. The dispersal of sib members among the chiefdoms and the power of the leading chiefs in particular territories gave rise to a state built on far-reaching bonds of kinship and governed by representatives of each major kin group.

The ethnographic literature about the Ashanti is not only comprehensive, but it has depth in time as well. The most outstanding field studies appeared in a series of books by Robert S. Rattray (1881–1938). His first trip to Africa was as a soldier, and when he returned to England, he studied at Oxford and received an undergraduate degree in anthropology. Rattray went back to the Gold Coast in 1907 and served with the colonial administration. He became the first head of the Anthropological Department, which was created in 1921 as a venture in applied anthropology but was disbanded in 1930. What is particularly notable about his ethnographic studies is that he had the support of the colonial administration by whom he was employed. Their goal, however, was to obtain ethnographic data that would be useful for administrating local affairs. The Ashanti studies of Rattray attest to the fact that interested administrators with an anthropological background often were in a favored position to assemble a wealth of data. His investigations provided a firm base for later ethnographers, particularly Meyer Fortes, to extend and expand. One of the important points made often by Fortes is the degree of continuity in Ashanti life that exists down to the present time. This is clear evidence that a political system based on custom rather than written law can and does function in the modern world.

Sources: Fortes 1969; Rattray 1923.

FOUR

ASIA

The vast continent of Asia, with its geographical variability, climatic contrasts, and diversity of ecological settings, might be presumed to have been widely populated with ethnics in early historic times. In truth, however, these peoples were found mainly in the marginal regions where it was too cold or too dry to farm, or where cultivation was for some other reason impractical. Islands sometimes became refuge habitats for ethnics, but even here intrusions by large-scale, complex societies were more likely than not to occur. To understand why ethnics were so poorly represented in Asia on a continentwide basis we must consider the diffusion of cultural ideas.

The expansiveness of the Asian landmass meant that concepts developed there could spread over great distances with comparative ease, leading to relatively rapid culture change. From about two million years ago until just 10,000 years ago, all of the world's peoples were ethnics. They lived in comparatively small, autonomous groupings in which the communities and localities were bound by bonds of blood and marriage. Conflicts between groups probably were feuds more often than wars of conquest. Supernaturalism focused on the fertility of the most important plants and animals, on curing, and on the life cycle of individuals. In the Near East about 8000 B.C. people began to raise domestic grains, and before long wheat and barley were cultivated with ever-increasing intensity over a rapidly broadening area. Plant cultivation served as the catalyst for a quantum leap in culture; the techniques of farming, and usually the plants as well, spread from the Near East to India and on to China as well as into Africa and southeast Asia. By about 4000 B.C. the productivity of cereal crops had made it possible for peoples to raise predictable food surpluses, which in turn led to craft specializations and the emergence of cities and states; in short, this was the base on which civilization was to be built. Farming was an irresistible lure. No doubt some societies of gatherers in areas with great cultivation potential refused to become farmers, but sooner or later they were either destroyed or assimilated into the network of cultivators.

Since large-scale and territorially aggressive societies had developed early in Asia, it is not surprising that so few peoples on the continent remained ethnics at the time of historic contact. Only in Siberia did a large cluster endure. They often were reindeer herders such as the Chukchi or Yakut and more peripherally the Lapps; their way of life was not an isolated development, however, but owed its inspiration to pastoralists in the south. In all of Asia only the Siberian culture area had a conceptual integrity equal to that of sub-Saharan Africa or the New World in general. In comparatively recent historical times, when the large-scale cultures based in China, India, or Europe were expanding into marginal regions over most of the continent, Siberian hunters were the least influenced, although they were not free from the side effects. For example, iron knives and other trade goods probably reached most of them hundreds of years before any direct contact.

In considering the distribution of Asian ethnics other than those in Siberia, the classification on a culture area basis is not very satisfactory. The pastoralists of the Steppe probably were far less independent of settled peoples with farming-based economies than has been suggested in most of the ethnographic literature, as Kroeber (1947:323–324) has pointed out. The integrity of Southwest Asia as a culture area probably is subject to other doubts. Although some peoples were free from state control, others were not, and the pastoralists, such as those of the Steppe, appear to have been economically tied to towns and cities.

In most presentations of culture areas for Asia we find that China, India, Japan, Tibet, and Southeast Asia are considered distinct. They are characterized in terms of the large-scale groups of civilized peoples dominating the region, with asides to refer to the ethnics in their midst. In terms of the goals of this book, these political entities cannot be considered as meaningful culture areas. The only reasonable alternative seems to be to violate the principle behind the culture area concept and to label the isolated pockets of small-scale societies, which were not found contiguously, as "Indian-Southeast Ethnic Enclaves." In this manner people such as the Andamanese, Chenchu, and Toda are separated from surrounding large-scale societies. This is far from satisfactory, but it seems the most plausible alternative.

Sources: Bacon 1946; Honigmann 1959; Kroeber 1947; Naroll 1950; Spencer and Johnson 1968.

Table 2. CULTURE AREAS OF ASIA

Siberia: Ural-Altaic and Paleo-Siberian languages dominate; hunting and fishing or reindeer herding; patrilineal or bilateral emphasis; autonomous villages or bands; shamanism; conical skin-covered tents or semisubterranean houses; tailormade skin clothing, dog- or reindeer-drawn sleds.

Steppe: Ural-Altaic languages; pastoralists stressing horses or less often cattle or camels; strong patrilineal emphasis; large-scale band organization; shamanism and Islam; dome-shaped skin tents; domestic pack animals (this possibly is not a valid culture area due to the dependence of the peoples involved on clusters of sedentary farming communities and towns).

Southwest: Hamito-Semitic, Ural-Altaic, and Indo-European languages; wheat and barley cultivation with plow, irrigation important, sheep and goats raised for food; patrilineal emphasis; despotic bureaucracy; Islam dominant; untailored or tailored garments, flat-roofed mud houses within a protective wall; ass, camel, horse, and ox for transport or as draft animals.

Indian-Southeast Ethnic Enclaves: diverse languages; gathering, herding, and farming—sometimes in combination; small, kin group focus; autonomous bands or villages; shamans important but religious activities highly variable; manufactures tend to be simple.

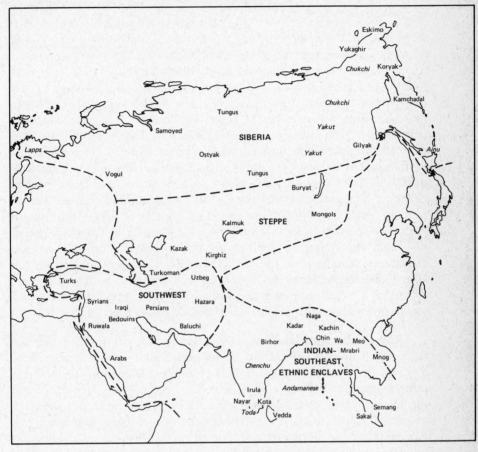

Map 2. CULTURE AREAS AND SELECT ETHNICS OF ASIA.

ANDAMANESE SUBSISTENCE ARTIFACTS

It sometimes is stressed in comparative ethnography courses that there is a great difference between the number of objects used by most ethnics and those used in modern Euro-American nations. This instructional emphasis is reasonable and cannot justly be challenged. If we were to inventory the man-made objects that we touch or see during a typical day, we probably would be staggered by the total. Even if all but "absolute necessities" were excluded from the list, the total would remain impressively high. Ethnics, especially hunters, had comparatively few manufactures, if only because a limited number of items can conveniently be transported by small groups of persons without the aid of animals or machines. Thus, their artifact inventories are slender, and if we were to eliminate dispensable objects, the list would sometimes be almost embarrassingly small. To annotate one people's inventory of necessities makes it possible to arrive at a more reasonable understanding of the word "necessity," and also suggests something about the technological achievements of gatherers, who were the precursors of us all. The people chosen for this exercise are the Andamanese, who lived on a cluster of islands in the Sea of Bengal. Before considering the artifacts by which they lived it is necessary to comment on the people themselves and their general setting.

The Andaman Islands support a dense tropical forest vegetation from which diverse roots, fruits, seeds, and honey were collected. Wild pigs and the civet cat are the only large indigenous mammals, but many different species of birds and some reptiles are present. The frequently indented coastline offers marine resources such as crustaceans, mollusks, and small fish in tidal pools; farther seaward are large fish, green and hawksbill turtles, porpoise, and dugong. The Negrito inhabitants are estimated to have numbered some 5,500, and they occupied nearly 2,500 square miles. One early observer, Edward H. Man (1883:343), estimated that one third of their food consisted of roots, fruits, and honey; the balance of their diet was comprised primarily of meat from pigs, supplemented with the flesh of the civet cat, iguana, sea turtles, fish, and mollusks.

If we consider the Andamanese to be an ethnic, they may be divided into the Great and Little Andaman island subethnics, each of which was comprised of separate and largely independent bands. Some bands confined their activities to the coastal area, one exploited only the resources of the interior, but most bands frequented both the coast and interior forests. A band numbered possibly fifty individuals, and within each were small nuclear family units. A single subethnic whose bands exploited both

Andamanese temporary shelter (Courtesy of the American Museum of Natural History).

inland and coastal areas of Great Andaman Island (which is in fact two islands) will be considered insofar as it is possible to isolate information about these people. Each band had a favored camping site which was likely to be occupied for the longest part of any year; other camps were frequented by family groups for no more than a few months at a time. Throughout the year people fished and collected mollusks, but during the five-month rainy season the men concentrated mainly on hunting pigs in the forests and netting turtles at sea.

At the larger, more permanent camps a single large structure housed an entire community. These buildings were circular, about sixty feet in diameter, roughly dome-shaped, and built of upright posts covered with timbers. Palm mats formed an attached covering, which was broken by a single doorway. Individual families or bachelors occupied separate sections along the periphery. The central area was the dance floor, and meals were cooked over a fireplace either inside or outside the house. Smaller more temporary dwellings, which were occupied by either nuclear families or bachelors as a group, consisted of a frame of four posts arranged in a square with two longer posts at the front and much shorter ones at the rear. Poles were lashed on the top of the frame and covered with palm leaf mats, but the sides were left open. These dwellings were built facing three sides of an open rectangular area reserved for dancing, and the occupants cooked at a common hearth off to one side. Each family also kept a small fire burning continually in its dwelling since the Andamanese did not know how to kindle fires.

Among these islanders the fiber rope around a man's waist was his only garment. A woman wore a wide belt woven from pandanus leaves, to which a tassel of leaves might be added at the back. Both sexes adorned themselves with necklaces made from fiber strings, and garterlike bands were worn below the knees. They added a wide variety of other adornments about their neck or waist, particularly for special occasions such as dances and ceremonies. In the normal routine men hunted in the forests in small groups consisting of from two to five men, and they might remain away several days at a time if necessary. In the meantime the persons remaining in the village collected local plant products for food. Young and inexperienced men tended to attach themselves to those older men who were generous and also were skillful hunters and warriors of repute. Such an older person supervised the food-getting efforts of his group and used his influence to persuade people to settle personal differences. Usually there were two or three persons in each subethnic who were considered as leaders on the basis of their wisdom.

One of the most notable characteristics of Andamanese subsistence is that food preservation techniques were practically unknown. Their setting yielded food products at a reasonably constant rate throughout the year, and at least part of most days was devoted to the procurement of edibles. Reliable food-getting practices are a requisite to the physical survival of any ethnics, and at the time of historic contact all peoples employed certain forms they found vital in subsistence activities. No specific word has been used to denote those objects which contribute directly to subsistence welfare, and yet it would be helpful to be able to distinguish them terminologically. Thus, I take the liberty of introducing the term "subsistant"; it will mean any extrasomatic form which is used by man in the actual procurement of food. The word is derived from "subsist," meaning "to support with provisions," and the suffix "-ant," meaning "the agent that performs a specific action or process." Andamanese subsistants will be specified and discussed in the following pages, and consideration also will be given to the overall complexity of each object.

The simplest device made and used in order to obtain food was a stick sharpened at one or both ends. This form, usually termed a digging stick, was used by women to dig up edible plant roots. Another subsistant was made from a stick having a natural hook at one end and was more specialized since its purpose was to hook crabs. Both of these forms were made by reducing the size of a naturally occurring form; types such as these presumably are among the oldest forms of manufactures among men. Another instrument was made in order to pick otherwise inaccessible fruit. It consisted of a bamboo pole with a small piece of wood attached at one end, presumably with a fiber string. The fruit-picking hook was of a more complex order than the digging stick or crab hook since joining one material to another is a more involved technological process than simply reducing a stick in physical size. Although we usually think of an adz as a tool, it too may be a food-getting instrument. Among the Andamanese an adz served to cut mollusks free from rocks and to remove honeycombs from hollow trees. This artifact is more complex than those cited previously because it consisted of three components of very different materials: a blade, which was processed from a shell; a wood handle, and a piece of fiber to bind the two together. These manmade forms were vital in food-getting activities, yet none of them had more than three basic components.

Among ethnics, artifacts employed in collecting activities were less complex in their overall design than were those used as weapons for capturing animals. One Andamanese weapon was a spear designed to take small fish in reef pools. These fish spears (leisters) consisted of about a dozen long splints of wood sharpened at one end. The pointed ends of the splints were spread outward and held apart with crosspieces bound to the splints. At the other end the splints were bound together to form a handle. This type of leister had seventeen distinct elements, but most of them were actually counterparts. Thus, the form was much simpler than an enumeration of parts would indicate. Any weapon with seventeen components, all of which were different, would be much more complex. The point is that reduplicated parts contribute comparatively little to the overall complexity of a form.

The leister and the bow and arrow were the only weapons known to the Andamanese. The self bow, meaning that it was a simple shaft of wood, had lashings at each end to prevent the bowstring of fiber from slipping down the narrow ends of the bow. The string itself had a loop at one end so that the bow could be unstrung when not in use. The bowstring was covered with wax, and there was a finger grip of string at the center. Used with this form of bow were three different arrow types; all had bamboo foreshafts and were unfeathered. The arrow used to take fish had a foreshaft pointed at the distal end and barbed with a piece of bone. The string which fastened the barb to the foreshaft was covered with a waterproofing compound made from wax, resin, and ocher. One of the two varieties of pig arrows had a fixed point made from shell to which barbs of bone were lashed. The second pig arrow had a detachable fore-shaft, and to this a shell point and bone barbs were bound with a section of cord. When a pig was struck with this arrow, the foreshaft-point unit dislodged from the shaft but remained connected to it with the cord. As a wounded pig fled, the shaft which trailed behind caught in the under-growth, and the cord held the pig until the hunter arrived to kill it. The components of these arrows have not been described in all of their detail; to do so would reveal that the fish arrow has six parts, the fixed-headed pig arrow has seven components, and the detachable-headed pig arrow a total of eleven parts. Since none of the components on the third variety of arrow fully duplicates another, it appears to be the most complex form in terms of manufacture.

Weapons and instruments for collecting were two major categories of aids employed in obtaining food, and to them must be added facilities. These are holding devices which usually do not kill the species captured. For example, the Andamanese used a dip net which consisted of a netted bag attached to the end of a pole. Fish were caught but not killed in this device. The form appears to have had a total of six components, whereas a net set at sea for turtles had eight different components, some of which partially reduplicated others. The only other facility manufacture used in procuring food was an outrigger canoe, which was most important in tending turtle nets. This conveyance was the most complex of any manu-facture the Andamanese produced. It had sixteen components, some of which duplicated one another in their form.

As surprising as it may seem, only nine different subsistants were used by the Andamanese. Furthermore, each of these was comprised of surprisingly few parts. Yet another gauge to the complexity of subsistence methods is to determine how many separate forms were used with one another. The bow and arrow would be excluded since they form a single type; that is, neither component ever functioned alone as a subsistant. The use of a turtle net with an outrigger canoe was the single instance in which clearly distinct subsistants joined to function as an integrated unit.

The Andamanese were not selected from among ethnics because they had a minimal number of subsistants, since any number of peoples used fewer forms of simpler design. At the same time these islanders clearly are representative of a people who made few artifacts for obtaining food and water. Above all else, the Andamanese example provides insight into the meaning of the word "necessity" and something about the nature of technological complexity.

Sources: Man 1883; Radcliffe-Brown 1948.

THE CHENCHU LIFE CYCLE

Anthropologists often express themselves in terms of "culture" and "society" because these reflect a conceptual core around which many important ideas have developed. We may occasionally lose sight of the fact that what we observe, describe, and analyze are the ways of individuals as they relate to their setting and to one another in both narrow and broad contexts. In order to stress the importance of the individual, some workers prefer to consider themselves as behavioral scientists and concentrate on learned behavior at the individual level. In somewhat the same vein, ethnographers describe customs among ethnics but tend to slight the fact that their descriptions are above all else cross-sections of people's lives. We also tend to think that the lives of ethnics are rigidly restricted by innumerable cultural conventions. This vignette about the Chenchu of India will deal largely with the degree of freedom each individual had in determining his own course of action.

In 1941 the Chenchu of Hyderabad numbered about 3,300 persons. Most of them had become agricultural laborers strongly influenced by the nearby population of Hindus, but about 400 still followed an independent and traditional way of life in the forests of the Amrabad Plateau, a sector of the Nallamali Hills. Since this elevated, hilly country of south-central India was formed of sandstone and quartzite, the soil was much less satisfactory for cultivation than that of the adjacent plains, and its nonproductiveness probably was the major reason that the Chenchu way of life had not been impinged on earlier. In this region four months of the year are hot and very dry; these are followed by four months of intermittent rains, bringing about twenty inches of precipitation; the balance of the year is cool, rather dry, and occasionally cold. The rolling hills comprising the plateau are separated by deep and narrow drainages, with streams which flow in torrents during the rainy season but are dry most of the year. The major river of the region is the Kistna, which runs throughout the year. The hilly landscape is covered with open forests of deciduous trees, which sometimes are broken by fields of grasses. When elevations of 2,800 feet are approached, the vegetation is more lush, and the same is true along the deep ravines where the jungle growth is dense. The seasonal contrasts in the appearance of the vegetation are striking; at the end of the dry season the trees are without leaves and the grasses tindery. With the arrival of the monsoon rains the landscape changes almost overnight into a profusion of blossoming trees and a rapid development of lush grasses and tree foliage. The region supported diverse animals in the

A Chenchu couple in search of food (Courtesy of Macmillan, London and Basingstroke; from Fürer-Haimendorf 1943).

varied ecological niches represented. Among the more important mammals were antelope, deer, bears, tigers, panthers, and hyenas; of lesser significance were the wild cats, dogs, and goats. A wide variety of birds and reptiles such as snakes and lizards complete the basic list.

The people were of medium height, slender, and dark-skinned. They paid little attention to their general appearance, but combed their hair daily. The men wore their hair in a knot, tied with a piece of hair string, at the top or side of their head. Women parted their hair in the middle and twisted it into a knot at the back of the neck. In the recent past these people wore garments made from leaves, but by the time of the study clothing made of cotton cloth prevailed. This was bought either from wandering traders or at markets in the plains. A man wore a breechclout and a piece of cloth which served as a cape in colder weather. They often added a separate leather belt in which a knife was stuck and from which a small leather pouch was suspended. The clothing of a woman consisted of a short cloth undergarment which covered the lower portion of her body, a short-sleeved bodice held in place by knotting it between the breasts,

146

A Chenchu summer camp (Courtesy of Macmillan, London and Basingstroke; from Fürer-Haimendorf 1943).

and a calf-length wraparound *sari*. As adornments the men sometimes wore small metal rings in the helix and lobes of their ears. Women wore necklaces of seeds in the recent past, but in general these have been replaced by glass bead necklaces purchased from markets in the plains. The women also adorned themselves with metal bracelets, finger rings, and earrings; some wore a metal ornament in a hole above one nostril.

Their semipermanent settlements included six houses on the average, and it was in these dwellings that the people associated with a particular sector lived during the rainy season and the cold months. The sites for these communities were determined by the long-term availability of food; favored were open ridge tops which were above the forests and away from water, where game would not be disturbed. Each house was circular in outline and up to fifteen feet across. The low walls were framed with upright poles between which were woven sections of bamboo. The conical roof of a dwelling was thatched with grass and was supported by a forked centerpost from which poles extended to the sidewalls. The dwelling was entered through a rectangular doorway, and a hearth of three stones was built a short distance from the centerpost. At the time of the year when food plants and animals were most available the people scattered and occupied temporary camps, where they built cone-shaped dwellings framed with poles and covered with grass. Other even less permanent structures were built from leafy branches in a variety of shapes. Household objects included a broom of grass bound at the upper end and used to sweep out the interior of a dwelling as well as the space just outside the door. Animal skins served as bedding, and household utensils consisted of wooden, bamboo and gourd containers until they were recently replaced with imported pottery vessels. For stirring and serving food, ladles of wood were used. Only the men made wickerwork baskets, and these were produced in a variety of forms. Some were used as collecting containers, others for drying food products, and still others for storage.

These people did not usually store food for future consumption, but instead obtained it on a day-to-day basis. They made little effort to conserve the environmental offerings which were not critical to immediate survival. A productive wild fruit tree might be cut down for a honeycomb in it or to obtain a single lizard. Yet they replaced the creepers of a plant after they had gathered the tubers as food. Most subsistence activities were undertaken on an individual basis, although women might set out on collecting trips in groups. In the economic sphere people cooperated with one another only in the construction of permanent dwellings. Even the sexual division of labor was not as clearly defined as might be expected; men as well as women collected plant products even though it was the men alone who hunted and collected honey. The individualistic and complementary labors of a man and his wife led to the self-sufficiency of the nuclear family in subsistence pursuits.

The manufacture most important in food-getting activities was the digging stick, which consisted of a wood or bamboo shaft tipped with an iron point obtained in trade. With this instrument men and women alike loosened the ground in order to remove tubers, which were the dietary staple. Some of these could be harvested throughout the year, while others were available only seasonally. The forms which were always available were collected intensively only when other varieties were scarce.

The tuber-based diet was supplemented with wild berries, fruits, blossoms, and seeds as they became seasonally available. A favored food of the Chenchu was honey, but it was difficult to obtain because the bees' nests often were located along the sides of cliffs. In order to obtain honeycombs from such nests, a man was lowered over the side of the cliff on a stout fiber rope which was paid out by another person. The man carried with him a spatula-shaped instrument, and when he approached a nest, a second line with a toggle bar at the end was lowered by the man above. The honeycomb was skewered with the toggle, and then the spatula-like tool was used to cut it free so that it then could be lifted to the top. When a honeycomb was located in another type of inaccessible place, an arrow with a string attached to it might be shot into the nest; the honey then flowed down the string and was collected in a basket.

Men hunted, but their success was limited, possibly because game had grown increasingly scarce and restrictions had been placed on hunting by governmental authorities. In the recent past the bow and arrow was the most important weapon. The self bow was made from spliced strips of bamboo and was strung with a long, narrow piece of bamboo which was attached to the bow with deer sinew. Arrows were shafted with bamboo and usually feathered with three vanes, which occasionally were twisted in a slight spiral. The socketed metal points were triangular, slender and either pointed or blunted at the tip; they were made by the Chenchu from points of digging sticks by heating the metal to soften it and then hammering it into an acceptable form. The fourth style of arrow was a piece of bamboo flared and blunted at the end to stun birds. The people sometimes employed dogs to aid them in obtaining game, but they did not make traps or snares. The favored technique for hunting large game appears to have been to build a blind of leaves at a spot known to have been frequented by animals. After an unwary animal was killed, it was butchered at the kill site. The hunter then returned to his village to summon other men to the spot. Here they roasted some of the meat, consumed as much as possible, and then returned to the settlement with the balance, which was divided among the represented households.

Chenchu men were unaware of the duration of pregnancy, but a midwife maintained that the period was nine months for a male offspring and ten months for a female, the latter requiring a longer span because it was weaker than a male. As was true of virtually all peoples around the world, they recognized the biological nature of conception. The Chenchu, however, believed that a child conceived in the rain would cry a great deal and one conceived in total darkness would be born blind; therefore, they did not fornicate under these conditions. Once a woman conceived, the couple continued to have intercourse until a few weeks before the anticipated birth. Stillbirths and miscarriages were rare, but those that did occur were explained in supernatural terms. No behavioral or other type of restrictions were observed during pregnancies by the potential father or mother; it was felt, however, that the woman should perform her usual chores in order to insure an easy delivery. When she began her labor, female friends and a midwife gathered before her house. When her pains increased in frequency, the women went inside the house to await the delivery, which was aided by the midwife. In the case of a prolonged or abnormal birth, the power of deities was invoked, and promises might be made to particular gods to insure a successful birth. The umbilical cord of a newborn was cut with a knife and tied with any available piece of string; the afterbirth was buried near the house. The father was not expected to be present during a normal delivery, but he might be summoned for aid and consultation under extraordinary conditions. A day or two after giving birth, a woman was expected to resume her normal routine, and as during the pregnancy, neither she nor her husband were subject to any restrictions. Chenchu women bore many children, but because the infant mortality rate was high, only about two thirds of the persons born reached maturity. When labor was difficult, a fetus was named before birth; since each name could be used for either males or females, the sex of the offspring was unimportant. On the other hand, a neonate might not be named until after several months had passed. Most names were taken from a small group, and within one family the same name might be given to a number of children of the same sex, the words big, middle, or small being added to the name. Alternative means for clarifying a person's identity included the use of nicknames and sib designations with a name.

A neonate was nursed whenever it was hungry, and for the first eight months of life milk was its only food. A baby was washed and groomed daily by its mother, but by the age of four a child washed himself. Food supplements were added gradually after about eight months, but a child was not fully weaned until it was about seven years of age. At about the age of two its head was shaved for the first time, and the trimmings were collected to be thrown into a moving body of water while a short prayer was recited to the water goddess in an effort to gain her further protection for the child. Before a child walked, it was in the almost constant company of its mother, who carried it in her arms or on one hip. Whenever it was necessary for her to perform some task without the child, it was cared for by the father or an older child. Once a young child began to walk and was too heavy to carry, it often was left by its mother, and this it tearfully protested. A father might try to comfort it or an older child might be delegated the task. One technique used by the older one was to try shouting louder than the child could cry.

Once a child began to walk, it became increasingly independent of its mother. During the day a village was largely deserted by adults, and children were left to their own devices. They participated in a few games such as swinging from the vines beneath trees and swimming, but much of their time was devoted to copying adult subsistence activities. In the manner of adults they divided into small groups by sex, and their subsistence pursuits had economic rewards. Little girls five years of age collected tubers which they cooked over small fires and consumed. Small boys climbed trees to knock down nuts which they broke open and ate.

The transition from childhood play to the food-getting activities of adult-hood was gradual in most instances. Children were not excluded from most economic pursuits of adults, and furthermore comparatively little overt instruction was needed in order to produce the necessary skills. A few activities, such as hunting or honey collection, did require training because they could be dangerous, and not until a youth was half-grown was he permitted to accompany men on these ventures.

In terms of child-rearing methods the Chenchu would be labeled as permissive. Reprimands were few, and physical punishments, such as a slap, were rare and not premeditated. If a child disobeyed an older person, the elder was likely to ignore the action after a reprimand. In this lax setting, largely unencumbered with restrictive social norms, girls were free to visit relatives in nearby settlements. When a girl began to menstruate, the fact became widely known, although there was no ritual associated with this or any subsequent menstrual period. On their visits girls became familiar with potential spouses, and premarital sexual experience appears to have been common. So long as a girl did not gain the reputation of being promiscuous, she usually was not rushed into a marriage. If she became pregnant, she might attempt to abort, but if she named her lover, he was obligated to marry her even if he already had a wife. In theory, marriages were arranged by the parents of a couple, but in fact the principals had a voice in accepting or in rejecting a potential spouse.

The primary culturally-imposed restriction on the selection of a spouse, apart from incest prohibitions, stemmed from the unilineal descent system. A person calculated his or her descent along a male line to a presumed common ancestor, and individuals belonging to any one of these units were distributed widely (patrisib). The ten distinct and viable patrilineal groups were named, were nontotemic in nature, and were lumped into four unnamed groups with presumed relationship ties (phratries) which were even more vague than those which existed within a sib. Each phratry had either two or three component sibs and tended to be localized geographically. Perhaps sibs had been restricted to particular areas in the past (they then would have been clans or more technically patriclans), but at the time of the study persons representing different sibs lived in the same locality and apparently had done so for many years. In practical terms the sibs and phratries served above all else to regulate marriage. An individual was prohibited from marrying anyone with the same sib name or anyone belonging to a linked sib (phratry exogamy), in spite of the fact that one might not be able to trace genealogical ties to such a person. When a marriage was being contemplated, a strong tendency existed to seek a partner from another village. The reason given was that one should not marry any person, even in another phratry, with whom one had grown up. A boy's marriage with his mother's brother's daughter or father's sister's daughter was preferred (cross-cousin marriage), but there was no overwhelming obligation for such persons to marry. Another preferential mate for a man was his sister's husband's sister. No formal arrangements existed whereby families exchanged spouses, but there was a tendency to seek mates from those families with which marriages had been negotiated in the past.

Once the social arrangements for a marriage were completed, the groom and his parents began to accumulate enough money to buy a sari for the bride and two sleeveless bodices, one for the bride and one for her mother. After these purchases had been made and food as well as a locally distilled liquor obtained, the day of the wedding was set and relatives invited to attend. Accompanied by the village leader the groom and his relatives traveled to the bride's village, where they were received and the gifts presented. The bride soon was dressed in her new sari and seated beside the groom. The leaders of the respective villages asked the couple whether they accepted each other as husband and wife, and they answered in the affirmative. This brief service culminated when the end of the bride's sari was tied to the groom's breechclout. Afterwards the village leaders and the others blessed the couple and showered them with rice. The assembled guests ate, drank, and danced until they were tired, after which they slept anywhere that was convenient. A couple had the option of living near either set of in-laws (bilocal marital residence). If they were to reside in the settlement of the groom, a second feast was held at his village, when he could afford it, and the close relatives of the bride were invited. The knot-tying ritual was repeated, and then the couple was considered to be married. Seemingly the ceremonial aspects of marriage were borrowed from adjacent Hindus in comparatively recent times.

Parental opposition to a marriage sometimes led to elopements. Under these circumstances the couple lived alone in the jungle or in the household of sympathetic relatives until time weakened the opposition; when they returned to one of their respective villages, the couple was accepted without stigma. If a wife came to dislike her husband, she was free to leave him, provided they had no children, and live with relatives. Once she began to live with another man, her former husband could not force her to return. Only after the death of her first husband could a woman remarry, but no stigma was attached to informal unions. A man might leave his wife or send her away, or he might take a second wife who, in the few reported cases, usually was the sister of his first wife (sororal polygyny). A couple was not likely to separate after they had children since pressure for a reconciliation was brought to bear by their relatives; fleeting instances of adultery were not considered as grounds for divorce.

In the kinship terminology we find that persons of one's sib or a linked sib were termed by words broadly comparable to mother, sister, daughter, father, brother, and son, depending on the relative age and sex of the person. For all other persons the same designations were used with the addition of the words "in-law." To this basic system important refinements were added; for example, one's biological father was distinguished by a distinct term and his brothers called "big" or "little" fathers, depending on whether they were older or younger than one's father. The same categories prevailed for a mother and her sisters. Husband and wife usually spoke of each other as the mother or father of one of their children, whom they then named (teknonymy).

Although women could not inherit property of significant value, they were not otherwise in an inferior position to that of men. A woman's contribution to the maintenance of a household was equal to or greater than that of her husband, and in her daily round of activities she was her own master. Furthermore, a man did not make any important decisions without first consulting his wife, and she was free to participate in virtually all ceremonial activities. Personality differences made some men henpecked and some women docile, but by and large a couple met on equal grounds.

The routine of adult life was punctuated by occasional disruptions which upset the customary village harmony. In general, when a social rupture occurred, the injured party attempted to rectify the injustice himself. If this proved to be impossible, sib elders and village leaders might assemble along with the disputants and a hearing might be held. The accused was obligated to feed the gathering, and should he refuse some of his property was seized and bartered for food. Amidst feasting and drinking the details of the episode were discussed at length and a judgment rendered which reflected prevailing public opinion about the situation. Open discussion of the matter by the assembly usually was sufficient to end the matter, although compensation in terms of property might be required to bring about a settlement. Meetings of this nature were quite uncommon and were held on an average of once a year, if at all, because individuals prided themselves on being able to handle their own affairs. The two most common causes of conflict were disputes over boundaries and over women. If a murder were committed—which was extremely rare—a feud was likely to erupt between the families involved, and neutral parties attempted to settle the conflict. Occasionally the rule of sib exogamy was broken, in which case the transgressing couple were in theory killed or boycotted by all the people. However, even incestuous unions of this nature were in time reluctantly accepted.

In the treatment of disease the Chenchu were able to cope with minor disabilities with a certain degree of success. For lesser complaints they took a twig from a particular tree, bent it double, and heated the looped end over a fire. The skin over the locus of the pain, as on the head for a headache or ankle for a sprain, was burned with the twig in different patterns. The people placed a great deal of confidence in this form of treatment. The milky juice from another plant might be rubbed over the stomach if it ached, and for a fever a combination of plant products was pulverized, mixed with water, and drunk. To treat large cuts, a paste was made from the crushed leaves of a plant and applied to the wound. Serious illnesses were attributed to the angry soul of a dead person or more often, to the action of a deity. In order to determine the god or goddess responsible, they resorted to a particular divining technique. Many families owned a smooth river pebble which was passed down the male line; if one were not owned by a particular family, it was borrowed from another family in the village. The male or female who served as diviner had no special standing with reference to this activity. With the stone placed on top of his head, the diviner sat before the patient, held his hands in front of his face, and named the deities one by one. When the stone fell into the diviner's hands, it was taken as a sign that the deity mentioned was not responsible for the illness; if the stone dropped to the ground, it was assumed that the patient soon would die. When the deity responsible for the illness was finally isolated, it was promised offerings if the patient recovered.

When an individual lapsed into an unconscious state and did not recover, it was presumed that his soul had left his body and would be received by a god named Bhagavantaru. As soon as a person died, the body was washed by a relative, the legs were rubbed with ashes, and the feet coated with saffron. The hair of the deceased was loosened, and the body was dressed in the clothing worn in life. The relatives gathered, usually within a few hours, and the body was buried in a cemetery near where the death had taken place. The corpse was placed face downward in an excavated grave, and the surviving spouse—or in the absence of such a person, the nearest blood relative—threw two handfuls of earth into the grave and recited a traditional statement of farewell. The grave then was filled with earth and covered with stones in order to protect the body from wild animals. Afterwards each of the persons who participated in the burial washed himself with water before returning home. During each evening of the three days to follow, food was placed on the grave, and the soul was said to visit its former dwelling. On the third day prayers were offered, and about seven days later a feast was held if the deceased had been a married person and if the necessary food was obtainable. The relatives and close friends of the deceased gathered for the event, which focused on the placement of three food parcels. One of these was opened for crows and left on the way to the grave; the second was placed at the burial site, and the third was submerged in a body of water. The reasons for distributing the food in this manner were unclear. Ritual bathing by the participants and a feast were the final acts of the ceremony.

These people did not speculate about the origins of man and the creation of the natural world, and neither were they deeply concerned about the fate of human souls. Nevertheless, a firm belief did exist that individuals obtained souls from Bhagavantaru, and it was he who received their souls at death. Occasional offerings of food to souls enlisted their aid in providing for the welfare of the living, a concept which bound the living and the dead in Chenchu thoughts.

When thinking about the ways of ethnics, we often presume that their lives were restricted excessively. Evidence in this regard is found in the observance of innumerable and seemingly irrational taboos and complex ceremonial involvements as well as a host of other culturally determined restrictions on their actions. Some of the peoples described in this volume approach such a stereotype, but the Chenchu are not among them. The expansiveness of freedom among individuals is impressive, as is the absence of involved ceremonial obligations. Equality between the sexes and the continuity of goals from childhood until death are notable indications of an acceptance of individuality. Thus, the Chenchu and many other ethnics must not be considered as bound by a host of restrictions which rigidly limited personal action. Throughout his life each Chenchu maintained a great deal of freedom, even though he would not normally aspire to be very different from anyone else.

Source: Fürer-Haimendorf 1943.

LAPP SOCIAL LIFE

In considering kinship terms and associated behaviors among other peoples, we are likely to assume that the manner in which they think of such persons is similar to our own. This view presumes, however, that our standards are also theirs, which is incorrect more often than correct. Our social norms have arisen as a result of our past cultural experiences, and thus peoples with very different backgrounds might be expected to exhibit different patterns of behavior, which is precisely the case. For instance, we normally identify only one person as "mother"; we treat her in a particular manner and expect certain patterns of response from her in return. But suppose our mother and all of her sisters were called "mother." The fact that some peoples expand on the word "mother" in this manner does not imply that they are unaware of their biological mother's identity; instead, it usually means that under most circumstances they feel no need to distinguish her from their sociological mothers. The concept of mother would have a very different meaning to them than to us. The same would be true if the father term were extended to father's brother. In a somewhat similar vein we would expect a couple to go off on their own after they marry (neolocal marriage residence) or to have certain feelings about seniority among siblings. By presenting the social conventions of the Lapps in Scandinavia, we may illustrate norms that are in some respects quite different from our own. The example should illustrate that behavioral expectations based on relatedness may differ widely around the world.

The Lapps, as the first ethnics to be well described by Europeans, have long attracted attention, probably because they lived so near and yet followed a way of life so very different from that of Europeans. Their colorful clothing is striking, and more important is the romance associated with their lives as reindeer herders. Lapp culture has exhibited a great deal of vitality, and even though these people are subject to the political control of the nations in which they live, their lifeway persists. In the late 1940s the Karesuando Lapps of northern Sweden still traversed nearly 200 miles each year in their herding activities. The primary item in their diet was reindeer meat; most items of winter clothing were made from reindeer skins, and these animals pulled their sleds in the winter or served as beasts of burden in the summer. Furthermore, selling reindeer to Swedish meat buyers provided the cash which the people required to purchase nonlocal materials, manufactures, and food.

In the winter their semidomestic reindeer, which sometimes numbered in the thousands, grazed on lichens in the area around Karesuando, and in the spring the people migrated with their herds to Norway, where they remained for the summer, returning to Sweden in the fall. During migrations life was most difficult, for it was necessary to herd the animals closely in order to prevent them from straying. Occasionally the herds from separate bands mingled, and it was necessary to corral all the animals and separate them on the basis of earmarks, which indicated ownership. Before going to the winter range diverse owners herded their deer together into a permanent corral. Here the calves born in the late spring were marked; cows were milked only at this time, animals were slaughtered or sold, and bulls castrated. At this time, too, meetings were held to establish local herding areas.

These people thought of their relatives as being arranged on a family tree, with the roots, trunk, branches, and crown occupied by persons manifesting different degrees of kinship. The total included all relatives by blood on both sides of the family (kindred). The outer edges of the branches were represented by third or fourth cousins, while the roots were comprised of persons removed farther than two generations. In general terms, persons who were second cousins, or sometimes first cousins, were regarded as "near-blood relatives"; others were "distant blood relatives," while affines were "made relatives."

The most important social group among these Lapps was the band, and its members, all of whom were related in some way, collectively herded their reindeer from one pasturage to another. A man's wealth was calculated in terms of the number of reindeer that he owned, and when he died, his legacy was inherited equally by related males and females. The egalitarian nature of inheritance made it important to be aware of relatives along both lines (bilateral descent). The members of a Lapp band were a coresidence group but not a corporate body since they did not think of themselves as a collectivity in terms of property ownership or in other legalistic contexts. Instead, a band comprised an aggregate of largely autonomous and self-directed families. A further indication of the looseness of band ties was reflected in the fact that an individual might change his band association a number of times during his life. Yet within a band the members were bound to each other by bonds of blood or marriage or by linkages of this nature through a third person. A band gained its greatest internal cohesion through the solidarity exhibited among siblings and other relatives of the same generation; the parent-child relationship was much less important.

The cohesion exhibited at one's own generational level is well reflected in the kinship terminology. The words for "brother" and "sister" were extended in a slightly modified form to include cousins. The word for a male cousin was a contraction of the terms "brother" and "half," and similarly, "half-sister" was the word for a female cousin. In their full form these words referred to "stepbrothers" and "stepsisters." Thus for all practical purposes cousins were equated with siblings. The logic of the terminology is seen in the fact that it was these individuals who cooperated most intensively in herding activities.

The kinship terminology for the first ascending generation above Ego (mother, father, uncles, and aunts) reveals the importance attached to relative age among the members of the parental group. Different words existed for father's brothers or mother's sisters depending on their age in relation to Ego's father and mother. Thus Ego referred to his father's older and younger brothers by different words, and the same was true for his mother's older and younger sisters. In-marrying spouses (father's sister's husband and father's brother's wife or mother's brother's wife and mother's sister's husband) were distinguished only by sex, and the terms were the same for both sides of the family (i.e., "aunt-in-law" or "uncle-in-law"). The most notable characteristic of the first ascending generational terms, apart from this distinction based on relative age, is the fact that while sometimes different, the terms are nonetheless balanced for both sides of the family. The stress on age correlates with the probability that an elder person would assume the leadership of a band. In addition to cohesion between siblings and cousins, integration was achieved through the dominance of one particular parental group within a band. It was from this cluster of persons that band leaders were chosen and that their successors usually were recruited.

By considering the band in which a couple resided immediately following their marriage, it is possible to understand more about the nature of band organization. The people reported that a woman should join her husband's band after marriage, but in actual fact it was just as common for a husband to join his wife's group. An individual was not to marry anyone more closely related than a third cousin, since to have done so was considered incestuous. Beyond this restriction a man was free to seek a mate either within his band or from another band (agamous bands). There were no rigid rules about whom one married, apart from incest prohibitions, or where a couple would reside. This does not mean that these matters were considered unimportant, but that circumstances varied widely for any particular marriage. One major consideration was the relative wealth of the families of the couple involved. A person with few reindeer from a poor family tended to become associated with a spouse from a rich family with many reindeer. In fact, a rich man often felt that it was best for one of his children to marry a poor person. The reasoning behind the decision was that a poor person would contribute additional labor to the band and also his offspring's reindeer would not be taken away. If the siblings or parents of one spouse were of high status, the couple would prefer to take up residence with them. If an individual had several siblings who could adequately care for their reindeer but the opposite were true for a mate, they joined the band where labor was in short supply. The relative age of marriage partners might be relevant. If one were old and the other quite young, they tended to join the band of the older person because he or she probably would have more property. The age of one's siblings might be important, since an oldest son of a wealthy man tended to remain in his parents' band. A rich man's son, however, would be likely to join his wife's band if there were not enough pasturage available to support additional reindeer. Lastly, the youngest son of a widow remained with his band to care for his mother while his siblings worked for other bands. Quite obviously the choice of residence was based on a rather broad set of individualistic variables.

A Lapp family (from Scheffer 1704).

Important qualities of social structure are further revealed by leadership patterns. A factor of initial importance is that small numbers of persons were involved in the make-up of any band. One cluster of Karesuando Lapp bands numbered 193 individuals in 1952; the largest of the five summer bands had fifty-one persons and the smallest nineteen persons. In the winter these bands divided into even smaller units; the ten winter bands ranged in size from seven to twenty-eight persons. Any band was comprised of relatives on both sides of one's family, and the "master of the band," or herding leader, had authority with respect to the people's handling of the reindeer. The people were bound together by the common goal of maintaining their reindeer holdings, and the primary duty of the herding leader was to manage the herd in the most productive manner possible. In general he had no power concerning matters not related to herding, for in group decisions he could be overruled by the other members of the band. He was nonetheless a leader since the band was named after him, the herd was his responsibility, and he was the pivotal figure in dealing with other bands. He also had the authority to determine who might join the band, and he decided when and where to move the herd.

In ideal terms a herding leader was rich and was the oldest son of the previous leader; it was ideal if such a man chose as his wife a woman with many relatives. The leader, if not the oldest son of a leader, was most likely to be chosen from the core of the dominant sibling group within a band. A younger son might become a leader of another band through a strategic marriage. If a man married a girl whose father was a herding leader and if he had only young sons or none at all, the son-in-law was likely to become his successor. Thus, the role of leader could be passed down through either males or females. Other persons moved in or out of the band largely on the basis of marriages and deaths within this core group. At the same time leadership, like marriage residence patterns, was not as rigidly determined as might be presumed. A herding leader actually was selected informally, and he held the office throughout his life, although he might step down as a result of illness or old age. Large sibling groups were likely to endure well since a large herd could not be managed effectively by a core composed of less than three siblings.

With Lapps we share a bilateral descent system, a flexible pattern of marriage residence, and an essentially egalitarian basis for social life. These similarities are not overly significant, however, since they would be found in many other societies of both small and large scale. Likewise, the ways in which they differ from us in their economic activities and kinship terminologies are widely shared. What is important about the Lapp pattern of social organization is the manner in which kinship terms, leadership patterns, and group cooperation are integrated functionally with one another. Each becomes understandable in terms of the others, and an awareness of this cohesion should lead to our greater appreciation for the logic of social behaviors which are foreign to our customary thinking.
Sources: Pehrson 1951, 1954a, 1954b, 1956.

CHUKCHI REINDEER AND WIVES

Often when reading about ethnics we become carried away by the strangeness of their ways. The reasonableness of their actions is obscured by their bizarreness in our eyes. The appeals of ethnics to supernaturals who seem so vague to us, their styles of dress (or lack of it), and the disparity between their social norms and those which we cherish, often are striking points for comparisons. Unjustifiably the things that ethnics do sometimes are characterized as more humanlike than human. Yet one observation above all others is fitting in this context. Those peoples whom we often view as so different survived at least until the beginnings of historic times; their customs and conventions must have served them well for hundreds or more likely for thousands of years. In other words, they had learned to cope with their environment effectively enough to feed themselves and raise children to adulthood. They rarely built roads, dammed streams, or otherwise purposefully modified their physical environment in dramatic ways, but they did aid one another effectively and used their natural setting in a rational and positive manner. The management of reindeer herds by the Chukchi of northeastern Siberia will serve to illustrate the logic of the ecological and social adaptations made by pastoralists.

In recent historic times, specifically around 1900, the Chukchi occupied most of northeastern Siberia; only the Siberian Eskimos stood between them and the gateway to the New World. The Chukchi spoke a language of the Chukotan phylum as did their neighbors the Kamchadal and Koryak to the south and to the west. Chukotan is distantly but clearly related to the Eskimoan linguistic phylum represented by speakers of Eskimo and Aleut. About A.D. 1600 the Chukchi had been confined to a much smaller area near Bering Strait, but they steadily expanded westward, partially because of their effective reindeer management practices. The Chukchi population around 1900 was about 12,000 persons, and of this number nearly 9,000 lived by herding reindeer. The balance of the population consisted of coastal sea mammal hunters, but only the reindeer-herding Chukchi will be considered here. Most of their food consisted of meat from domestic reindeer (henceforth reindeer), although they also hunted wild reindeer or other game, and did some fishing. Their subsistence welfare depended largely on the management of reindeer herds.

A minimal herd for a small family included from 70 to 100 animals. If we assume a herd of 100 animals, the largest segment was about 50 does, who formed the female breeding core. There would have been about seven studs and eight geldings used mainly for pulling sleds or secondarily for hunting. The balance of the herd consisted of buck and doe fawns. A few of these fawns would have been kept to replace adult reindeer that died, ran off, or were barren. Thus, about 30 animals could have been slaughtered each year if all went well, but there were many conditions which could lead to the catastrophic decline of a small herd.

In a very real sense Chukchi reindeer must be considered as semi-domestic animals since they were fully capable of surviving apart from the company of men and could breed freely with the wild reindeer in the area. Wild reindeer sometimes were hunted by using domestic animals as decoys. This was a tempting practice for the owner of a small herd since he could use the meat and skins of the wild animals without depleting his original stock. However, the distinct possibility existed that his tame deer might run off at any time to join wild reindeer. The smaller the herd the more likely that it could not be controlled effectively since the animals could escape rather quickly. A herd also might be reduced in number, sometimes within a matter of days, if the deer contracted one of the diverse diseases which sometimes spread in epidemic proportions. In addition, human predators, wolves, wolverine, and black bears might kill or drive off a man's reindeer. Another possibility was that a herd might wander away during a snowstorm or in a fog when they could not be pursued effectively; this also could occur if wild reindeer were nearby or if insects made them restless. Finally, it was at times difficult to find adequate food for a herd. Thus, the owner of a small herd faced the constant danger that all his animals would vanish or else that the herd would be

A Chukchi camp (Courtesy of the American Museum of Natural History).

reduced to such a small number of animals that he could not maintain himself and his family. The loss of one's herd literally destroyed one's family.

A number of means were open to a man with comparatively few reindeer to increase the size of his herd apart from its natural growth. A small but adequate herd was one that produced enough deer for pulling sleds and for eating without endangering the breeding stock, and at the same time included enough animals so that a catastrophe would not destroy it. By combining their marginal herds cooperating men could decrease the number of vicissitudes to which a small herd was subject. Persons who were likely to join their herds usually were closely related along a male line (patrilineal descent) and occupied adjacent areas. An independent herder, however, had a certain amount of reluctance to consolidating his reindeer with those of another because of the extraordinarily high positive value placed on individual accomplishments and freedom. To succeed alone in the face of great adversity and to become a "strong man" was a theme that ran through the core of Chukchi life.

An aggressive and ambitious man who owned a small herd might drive his animals into the herd of a rich man, especially during the summer when herds were far less likely to be isolated. When the animals were separated, the poor man claimed his own animals as well as some belonging to the other herd. The deception could be accomplished because the rich man could not recognize all of his animals and often had not placed his identifying mark on the ears of all of them, especially the fawns. The size of a small herd might be increased legitimately by contracting to work for a man with a large herd. The worker and his family were fed by the rich man and received from five to ten doe fawns each year. The contract might be terminated when the poorer man felt that he had enough new animals to sustain his herd as an independent unit. By this method a man who had no reindeer of his own could assemble an independent herd of about 300 does in about fifteen years. Thus, a poor person could learn the complexities of herding under a rich man and become rich in turn. Another alternative was for a poor man to attach himself to a rich man's camp permanently through adoption into the unit or by being in actual charge of the herd when the owner died. Another means for acquiring an existing herd was to marry a rich man's daughter.

A young man might acquire deer or establish his place in the herding economy by spending up to three summers serving the father of a girl he hoped to marry. Bride service was difficult because the girl's father was a severe taskmaster, and for the young man to succeed it was essential that he be physically powerful and able to withstand a great deal of abuse. The span of a man's service probably hinged on the rate at which he acquired all the herding skills. If he proved to be incapable, he was forced to leave the camp, and the engagement or marriage was terminated. Once he had demonstrated his abilities as a herder the son-in-law might be permitted to take for his own all of the reindeer that he could mark in a single day. A second possibility was for the groom to become permanently associated with the camp and emerge as a prospective heir to at least part of the herd. A man who took a second wife (polygyny) was obligated to perform only a short period of bride service, if any, because he had herds already and had demonstrated his abilities in reindeer management.

Maintaining a large herd which ranged up to about 5,000 animals required the conjunction of a number of critical factors. A basic requirement was a large area where the lichens and mosses formed a dense cover; it could be grazed over lightly during the winter for about three years and then must be allowed to lie fallow for about five years. An overgrazed locality could not serve as adequate pasturage for at least twenty years after it had been destroyed. A large herd required winter pasturage which extended up to about 150 miles, usually along a river system, within which the animals could range over the years. A critical factor was the adequacy of winter food, and this was largely a function of local temperature, drainage, and precipitation patterns. Summer grazing lands were far less critical since they seldom were inadequate. The larger herds were difficult to control and depleted pasturage rapidly. Diseases could wipe out a herd of any size quickly. In one instance 3,000 diseased animals were killed within three days in an effort to prevent the total destruction of a herd.

The Chukchi were fully aware that a herd of 100 to 300 animals was a minimal size for continuity. It was equally appreciated that maximum herd size was from 3,000 to 5,000 animals, depending on the pasturage and the personnel available for herding. Thus, it was essential for them to have management practices which prevented herds from growing inordinately large. A number of ecological factors tended to reduce the likelihood of reaching maximum levels. A female reindeer usually conceived at the end of her second year of life and bore a fawn each spring for about thirteen years. Some fifteen percent of the calves died soon after birth as a result of adverse weather conditions, but if they survived this period, they were likely to mature. Considering all the customary factors which would reduce the fawn population (e.g., kills for food, lost animals, payments to herders, and so on), it appears that under model conditions the does in a herd numbering 1,000 animals originally would have brought the herd size to the maximum limit in about six years. Thus, herds increased rapidly under ideal conditions, but additional methods could be applied to cut into herd numbers. Pregnant animals sometimes were killed; reindeer were awarded as prizes in contests by rich men, and most importantly reindeer were slaughtered for sacrifices. In actual fact, killing a reindeer at any time was accompanied by ritual practices, but a sacrificed animal was killed for a particular purpose. Small numbers were killed when a winter house was established or at the winter solstice; a single animal was slaughtered on any unusual occasion, such as to insure protection on a trip. The largest number always were sacrificed in the fall when the skins were prime for clothing and for trade. In the fall rich men invited guests from near and far for the occasion. A fawn was slaughtered as a gift to each guest, and over 100 fawns might be killed for guests, for camp use, and for trade pelts. A rich man might even kill over 1,000 animals in order to have a stock of trading skins. Persons of means who received a fawn were expected to present their host with a subsequent gift, but a present was not anticipated from a poor person. Poor herders sacrificed only a few animals at this time. The practice above all else served to reduce the number of surplus animals in large herds.

When a herd reached its maximum limit, the owner had two options; he could divide his holdings and place the excess animals either in the charge of relatives, preferably sons or brothers, or in the charge of a male taken into the camp through marriage or adoption. The former alternative was much preferred because it was felt that close patrilineal relatives were more likely to respect the desires of the legal owner. Yet once a son or brother had ventured to new pasturage with a large portion of such a herd, he was likely to assert his independence and ignore the wishes of the legal owner; this attitude was expected even more from a son-in-law or an adopted son. An old man could complain about the ingratitude of the recipient and talk of taking the herd back, but this was only an idle threat since the conditions which led to the original division would prevail again if the splinter herds were assembled into one large herd.

Chukchi expansion from a small corner of northeastern Siberia seemingly was facilitated by a rise in the mean temperature in the 1800s. This warming increased the number of frost-free days and thus produced more favorable conditions for plant growth than had existed previously, which in turn contributed to the support of greater herds on a given area. In addition the Chukchi were notoriously aggressive people, and they succeeded in seizing the herds of adjoining Koryak, Yukaghir, and other peoples. This made it possible for them to obtain great numbers of animals rapidly. Through territorial expansion they obtained better grazing lands and were able to space their herds widely, which in turn decreased contact between herds and the likelihood of the spread of epidemics. In the same vein it then became easier for the owners of large herds to capture wild reindeer.

The Chukchi population increased at a much slower rate than did the reindeer, and diseases took their toll of the group. The most disastrous example was the smallpox epidemic of 1884 in which one third of the people died. Many losses of Chukchi and reindeer life could not be anticipated, and yet each was adaptive, when not broadly destructive, since herd size ultimately was reduced in either situation. Given Chukchi individualism each man simply set out anew after any disaster to rebuild a herd. Thus, we see that their attitudes, social institutions, and herding practices, as they operated within a particular environmental setting, were in the long run adaptive for their survival as a people; the Chukchi lifeway was a rational system which led to their vitality as a people.

In the name of ethnographic exotica it would be a travesty not to discuss the marriage pattern among the Chukchi. Their attitudes were so different from our own in certain respects that they command attention, not because of their strangeness, but because they illustrate an unusual combination of conjugal possibilities.

For an adult man, life was almost unimaginable without a wife and a dwelling of his own. A young, energetic wife was required to perform not only ordinary household chores but to help care for the reindeer in unusual situations. Most important, a wife was needed to keep a man's clothing in good repair, for the Chukchi lived in one of the coldest areas of the world. A man also sought a wife in order to perpetuate his family line, which was not an unimportant concern among them. In addition bachelors were considered as idlers and as tramps of little worth. Physically strong women were most sought after as brides. They were expected to be sensual as well, but their virginity, or lack of it, was of no concern. For a girl to bear an offspring outside of marriage was no disgrace; she simply lived in her father's camp as any other woman. Another factor which obscured the importance of physiological fatherhood was that divorces were rather common and children might subsequently be identified with either their mother or father. It was unusual and considered wrong to have intercourse with an immature girl or to rape a married woman, but any retaliatory measures were left to the relatives or the husband of the female involved. Infant betrothal between cousins in the same or adjacent camps sometimes took place, and friendly families might agree to intermarry their children even before they were born. Marriages sometimes were arranged in which great age differences separated the couple. A boy of five was, on occasion, known to have been married to a woman of twenty, and she might serve as her husband's nurse. Similarly a young girl might be married to a much older man. Occasionally romantic love drew a couple together, but far more common was an arranged marriage. A father or uncle of the suitor made the overtures to the girl's father; he labored about the camp while attempting to persuade the potential father-in-law that the young man was a capable individual. When the girl's father was reasonably convinced, the young man joined his camp and labored hard. In other instances the suitor pressed his own case from the beginning by supplying the camp with firewood, which was the most distasteful of household chores. He performed bride service for one, two, or sometimes three summers; he was the first to rise in the morning and the last to go to sleep at night. In spite of his labors he was forced to sleep in the cold, and he might not be fed at all. Usually he was told to leave in spite of his diligence, but if he departed he was regarded as a weakling unworthy of the girl. If he persisted in the face of the privations and verbal abuse to which he was subjected, the males of the camp relented somewhat. In time the suitor was permitted to sleep with the girl, and he then regarded her as his wife although his father-in-law often postponed the formal marriage as long as possible in order to take advantage of the young man's labor. The marriage ritual consisted primarily of anointing the couple with the blood of a sacrificed reindeer; they painted their faces with the family mark of the groom (patrilineal symbol) as a ritual means of binding the bride to her husband's family group.

It was considered proper for the couple to remain with the bride's family for two to three years (temporary matrilocal residence) and for her father to give the husband at least some reindeer when they departed for his family's residence (secondary patrilocal residence). In spite of the length of bride service and the ritual nature of marriage ceremonies, divorces were rather common. Soon after the couple arrived at the camp of the groom, his parents might take a dislike to the bride and send her back to her parents. Most men had a single wife, but in some sectors of Chukchi country as many as a third of the men had multiple wives (polygyny). They justified the practice by saying that a man required the services of a woman for each herd; thus the owner of two herds needed two wives. Some men with a single herd had multiple wives, however. A man usually had only one or two wives, but some well-to-do men had four wives at one time. The husband usually attempted to have separate tents for each wife, but sometimes he might sleep between two wives. One wife usually was much younger than the other, and the older one tended to treat the younger one as a maid.

A Chukchi married couple never functioned as an autonomous sexual and conjugal unit but was part of a marital network that included up to ten couples. This arrangement has been termed "group marriage," and among the Chukchi, men of such marriage were termed "companions in wives." These bonds most often were established among men who were neighbors, friends, and rather distant relatives such as second or third cousins, but not brothers. The binding ritual involved the sacrifice of reindeer and anointments with the blood in one camp after another; this joined the males in a fictive patrilateral group. Young men were anxious to create such bonds with persons of standing and might even serve a rich man briefly in the same manner as for bride service. The general feeling was, however, that the persons involved in a group marriage should be about the same age. Young bachelors had difficulties entering into such arrangements because they had no wives to offer in exchange, but the possibility for them to join in a group marriage existed.

It should be noted clearly that group marriage arrangements seldom were made within a single camp, but rather bound together couples living at some distance from each other. Group marriage among the Chukchi was not a game of musical bedrooms. Customarily it was when a man visited the camp of a companion that he slept with the companion's wife. In this instance, the first husband made it a point to sleep elsewhere, but he was likely to return the visit and claim his rights before very long. At times companions-in-marriage exchanged wives for several months, and a wife might even become permanently separated from her original husband in this manner. In most instances women had no voice in such exchanges and might even be beaten if they refused to participate when called on to do so. The persons in a group marriage were friends and protected one another in times of need; they were regarded as even closer to one another than relatives, although distant blood ties also may have linked them. In theory a group marriage could have been terminated, but specific instances of this nature were not recorded. The same form of bonds were established with foreign traders such as Russians and Tungus, and quite possibly economic considerations between Chukchi companions-in-marriage were more important than is suggested in the literature. A further indication of the group's solidarity is the fact that children born of such unions considered each other as cousins or even as brothers and sisters and could not marry one another.

The ethnographic details about Chukchi life were recorded mainly by Waldemar Bogoras, who lived among these people as a Russian political exile to Siberia for about a decade just before the turn of the present century. The account by Bogoras approaches being an ethnographic classic. Yet, as surprising as it may seem, most of the information about reindeer in the foregoing descriptions was not taken directly from the study by Bogoras. Instead it was drawn almost entirely from an article by Anthony Leeds. The report by Bogoras is extraordinarily comprehensive, but Leeds was concerned only with the ecological adaptations of Chukchi reindeer management practices. From the work by Bogoras, he compiled an integrated report clearly demonstrating the rationality of Chukchi herding norms. Leeds' study is a fine illustration of how old ethnographies may be evaluated in new ways for a superior understanding of a particular aspect of a people's culture, one which is not obvious in the original study.

The information about Chukchi group marriage has been introduced largely to illustrate that social institutions may arise and become extremely viable entities because they come to serve specific needs in spite of the fact that they may be very different from those found among other peoples.

Sources: Bogoras 1904–1909; Leeds 1965.

YAKUT EPOS

Epos is a body of poetry expressing the traditions of a people, and it is much more often ignored by ethnographers than listened to and recorded. Yet it is in the area of literary achievements that we may perhaps come to realize how ill-conceived such terms as "savage," "barbarian," or even "primitive" are when referring to the accomplishments of ethnics.

The Yakut numbered about 235,000 in 1926 and belonged to the Turkic linguistic phylum; in recent historical times their language was without dialects or even significant regional differences, which suggests that their wide dispersal had occurred only a short time earlier. In the not-too-distant past they occupied the Lena River drainage system in eastern Siberia. This is an area of mountains and lowlands with a taiga environment and continental climate, where there are extremely cold winters and hot but short summers. In the tenth century A.D. they began to wander here from the Lake Baikal region. As pastoralists, they settled among already established hunting and fishing peoples and soon began to assimilate them. By about 1620, when contacted by the Russians, they were grouped into diverse, independent subethnics, each of which included persons who were rich and poor. Powerful men were termed *toyons*, and it was through these persons that the Russians came to control the people and the area.

In early historic times the more southerly Yakut raised horses and cattle as their most important domestic animals, whereas in the extreme north they herded reindeer. In general their winter settlements were widely scattered and small, consisting of from one to three dwellings. A structure usually was occupied by a man, his wife, and their children (nuclear family), but sometimes the residence unit included other relatives as well. Some rich men had more than one wife (polygyny), in which case a separate household was maintained for each woman and her children. Related families in adjacent households of a hamlet traced their kin ties through the male line (patrilineal descent). Segments of a subethnic apparently became localized and formed clans (unilineal descent groups with a presumed common ancestor, in this instance patrilineal, who occupied a particular area), and marriage was with persons from other clans (clan exogamy). Marriage residence was near the husband's family (patrilocal residence).

The winter houses were square, pole-framed structures with low pyramidal roofs. They were covered on the outside with first a layer of bark, then earth, and finally a cow dung and clay plaster. To one side of the house an adjoining structure of the same form was built for cattle, and this could be entered from the house. The major furnishing inside a house was a large clay hearth with a chimney built of poles and covered with clay. It was built a short distance from the center in one quadrant and was tended only by the female household head; the hearth was considered as the protector of a family and received ritual attention. Around the walls were benches where people lounged and slept, and each bench was associated with given members of the household. In the summer the people lived in cone-shaped houses made of pole frameworks covered with sewn strips of birch bark. These dwellings also had benches around the walls, and there was a central fireplace. The clothing of these people was made from fur and hides, with a knee-length fur coat the accepted outer garment. Beneath it men and women alike wore shorts and leggings of leather as well as a fur stomach-warmer. Relatively short leather boots were worn along with a fur hat of a wide variety of styles and fur mittens. The most important and specialized craft skill was ironmaking. The raw ore was mined, smelted, and forged into a wide variety of weapons, implements, and utensils.

Yakut subsistence welfare was based on domestic animals as well as fishing and hunting, but the latter pursuits were of secondary importance except among poor people. Their horses were used for riding and as draft and pack animals; they also were milked. In the winter and summer alike the horses grazed freely; grass might sometimes be cut as fodder, but during most of the winter horses were forced to dig through the snow to find food. One important food, consumed in large quantities, was koumiss, made from mare's milk. Cattle were ridden occasionally and were used as draft animals to pull sleds during both the summer and winter; the Yakut did not have wheeled vehicles. The fresh milk of cows seldom was consumed, but a wide variety of sour milk products were important in their diet. Cattle were slaughtered for meat more often than were horses, yet horse meat was much preferred to beef.

The Yakut honored persons who were eloquent, and this quality was most apparent in their recitals of great epic poems. Narrative poetry was their highest form of artistic achievement, and in comparison to it their folklore, dance and music paled. A person who recited poetry well was highly respected and was assured of a hospitable reception wherever he traveled. An epic poem or *olonkho* might be extraordinarily long and require days to narrate in full. Sometimes a number of storytellers co-operated in order to dramatize a tale. One man might assume the role of the main character, another his adversary, and a third person present the accompanying narration. The text of an olonkho often included archaic words and obscure expressions, but it was rich in verbal imagery and filled with dramatic episodes. A typical olonkho described the amazing adventures of a mythological warrior.

As in the following example a typical olonkho opened with a description of the setting as a general background (Okladnikov 1970:264–265).

> To the north of the dwelling,
> As it were nine hundred
> Dignified elders bunched together,
> Stood with peaks projecting
> Tall-trunked larches.
> To the east of the dwelling,
> Like yet strong old women

Gathered in a bunch,
Dancing together,
Appeared the pine-grove.
To tell further,
To the left of the house,
Like princesses
In festive attire,
Hand in hand
And walking in rows,
Were seen the clumps
Of dense-leaved birches.
In the high heavens
The wingéd creature
The snow-white crane,
Seven days and nights
Without rest,
Cutting the air with its wings
Would not reach that border,
Such broad steppes,
Dry and well-drained
Stretch out there.
The black crow,
Child of the frosty sky,
In three days and three nights
Would never cross
From border to border
The dense depths of the taiga,
With chasms, with ravines.
But there amidst the forests
The many-branched,
Tender herb
Cleared a path for itself.
Here and there on the drifted
Red sand,
On the settled
Greenish silt,
The nine-branched
Herb, the horse-tail,
Grew up.
As it were spread
With the skins of light-bay horses,
The bright-misted meadows
Could be seen,
Gay with flowers.
As if covered
With the skins of grey horses,

> The vertical peaks
> Projected forth
> From the dark border
> Of the larch-forest.
> The trees were adorned
> With hanging branches;
> The fine stems
> Were intertwined,
> Thickening the pattern.
> The dark-streaming river
> Flowed between steep banks.

In Yakut cosmology the universe was comprised of three worlds which were united by a sacred tree. The tree's uppermost branches reached the heavens, and from lower limbs dropped a life-giving dew. At the base of the tree spread a milk-like lake, and the tree's roots reached into a nether world. This magnificent tree grew at the center of the universe. The world-tree's form was described in poetry (Okladnikov 1970:268–270).

> At the very top of the cape,
> High, facing the waters
> And consorting
> With black whirlwinds—
> The souls of sacrificed beasts,
> Lonely grew the many-branched
> Holy tree of happiness—
> With raised roots,
> With slightly rubbed bark,
> With bare branches
> And top bent askew.
> Bottoms upward,
> Kumiss cups with crest
> Like silvered cones
> Hanging.
> To the eastern hill
> From the end of a cone
> With a willow ptarmigan
> Flew to earth
> A foamy moisture.
> Like wisps of hair
> From the tail and mane
> Of horses,
> Gathered in a bunch,
> Trailed far-flung
> Silken

The World-tree of the Yakut (from the drawing of I. V. Popov, Tattinsk *rayon* [from Okladnikov 1970]).

Green needles,
The foam by drops
(as large as) a ptarmigan-cock
Flowed forever.
From the westward points
Of its branches
In an endless stream
Foam oozed
On the holy earth.
This stream,
Three hand-spans deep,
Dug deep in earth-mother.
And of pure milk
Formed a lake.
Nourished with the juices of this tree,
Bathing in its enlivening flow,
The weak grow strong,
They grow, the small filled out,

The sickly were made whole.
Such was the purpose
Of that, for the happiness of the living,
Created blesséd
Regal tree.

Between the heavens and a lower world of reality was a wondrous middle realm, a land of eternal summer which existed when the world was young (Okladnikov 1970:271–272).

In this sacred land,
When the first men
Knew not the heaviness of sins,
They knew no evil crimes . . .
The radiant sun-god's
Wrathful thunder fires
Constantly played,
Rolling thunder passed by,
Flashing lightning flared.
Then divine fire cleansed,
Since in those times
Disease, frailty, and illness
Hindered people not.
Of death they knew nothing at all.
Cough, contagion did not touch them,
In the cattle yard at the stake
The calves did not drop from hunger,
And in the horse shed, sores
Did not ruin the young stallion then.

Descriptions such as these served to introduce long and extremely complex tales with plots and counterplots coupled with extended tangential episodes. The central theme of a poem was likely to be the courageous ventures of a culture hero. In one such poem the hero had no parents and knew nothing of his origins. He yearned to establish his identity and asked the spirits (Okladnikov 1970:273), "Of whose blood am I, and from whose womb? By what deity was I created? Is there not a commandment of fate on me? He who lives on the milky lake by the foothills of milk-like stone, the White Creator-Lord, did I not spring from him?" The spirits to which he appealed could not answer his questions, but then it thundered unexpectedly and the sky opened, revealing three youths riding milk-white horses. These were messengers dispatched from the White Creator-Lord, his grandfather, to convey his will. The hero must receive from the father of nine smiths, armor made of seven layers of iron, and from the trees of a particular winding valley he was to receive a bow and burning arrows which were feathered, as well as a mace of great weight. In exchange for this weaponry he must offer the blacksmith the daughter of the lord of the underworld. After performing this herculean task his true adventures began. Thus, the hero was a special creation of the gods singled out to perform their will and ultimately to become the father of mankind and the originator of a pastoral way of life.

Sources: Jochelson 1933; Okladnikov 1970; Tokarev and Gurvich 1964.

TODA CUSTOMS

When reading about the customs of other peoples, much of what we learn is in one way or another familiar, and even though particular activities among ethnics may seem quite out of the ordinary, if the sources are judged as reliable, we accept them and read on. Occasionally one exotic fact repeatedly follows another, and then we are likely to query, "Can this really be?" Often the answer is a clear "no" as further investigation reveals the unreliability of the source, and sometimes a "perhaps," which results from putting the behavior in its correct context, thus making it much less startling. But in certain instances the response is "yes" without qualifications. There is a society where dairies were temples, the people never participated in war nor recognized crimes in the ordinary sense, sexual behavior was in certain contexts quite permissive, and a man could legally father a child after his death. The Toda, who without question followed each of these behavior patterns, represent an orientation to life decidedly different from that which we have come to consider normal.

The Toda had been influenced by other peoples of India and by Europeans long before they were studied by William H. R. Rivers in 1901–1902. Yet at this time the effects of Christian and Hindu missionaries were negligible, and in some sectors of their country the Toda had continued their institutions in all of their aboriginal vitality. Their sector of southern India is called the Nilgiri Hills, and the upland plateaus which form the hills are about 6,500 feet in elevation. Situated near the equator, the region is approached through a dense jungle filled with malaria-carrying mosquitoes, but the climate of the plateau itself is pleasant. The lasting quality of Toda ways is in a large part explained by this inaccessibility of their region, but these people were not the only occupants of the hills nor were they sufficient unto themselves. They were almost exclusively herders of water buffalo, but their neighbors the Badaga were farmers, and the nearby Kota were artisans. These three peoples were integrated by important economic ties, and overt hostilities among them were unknown.

The Toda numbered about 800 persons at the turn of the present century, and in physical terms they stood somewhat apart from other persons of southern India. In contrast to the latter, the Toda were of light complexion and comparatively great stature; in addition, the men had heavy beards and extensive body hair. A cloth pubic covering was worn by each man, while men and women alike wore a cloth cloak and a skirt-like garment which reached below the knees. The cloak most commonly was worn so that it covered both shoulders and both arms. These people lived in small, scattered hamlets built on raised plots of ground near wooded areas with at least one stream nearby. Their houses were elongated domes framed with bamboo, and they were covered with thatch in such a way that there was no break between the roof and the sides. The walls at each end were vertical and were made from planks; in one of these was a small entrance. The interior was divided into a rear portion, where residents slept and women worked, and a forward portion, where men performed certain tasks associated with dairying. In the middle of a house floor was a hole which served as the mortar in which women ground grain, one of their most important tasks. The one to six houses of a hamlet were surrounded by a low stone wall in which there were openings wide enough to accommodate people but not buffalo. A short distance away were dairies, which had the general appearance of ordinary houses but were surrounded by high stone walls.

Their herds of buffalo were the most important interest of Toda men, and much of their lives was spent in tending them and in associated activities. The buffalo of their region was a semidomestic variety of the Indian water buffalo, and ordinary animals were tended largely by boys and younger men under the general supervision of an elder. The animals were milked in the morning and then driven out to pasture; in the afternoon the buffalo returned to be milked again, and then were driven into a nearby enclosure where they spent the night. Their milk was churned into butter and whey, which were important food staples. Among the Toda group called the Tarthar, some of the buffalo were sacred in three different degrees; each level of sacred buffalo was cared for by specially trained priests, with their ritual involvements differing by level. The second segment of the Toda, the Teivali, had only one class of sacred buffalo. Some Tarthar herds were so much honored that they were maintained away from any settlement by priests devoted to their welfare. The most revered of all dairies were the cone-shaped structures where milk products of the most sacred Tarthar buffalo were processed; at the time of the study only three such structures existed. Ordinary and most of the extraordinary buffalo were owned by individuals or by family groups; some of the most sacred herds were held collectively by the members of particular sibs. A sib also was the unit of ownership for a village as well as for its land.

In economic terms the most important food products derived daily from the herds were whey and a form of butter to which grain or rice had been added during the processing. The Toda raised no crops themselves, but they received a portion of their grain supply from the Badaga as a form of tribute. The land which the Badaga tilled was presumed by both peoples to have belonged originally to the Toda, and the Badaga feared the effects of Toda sorcery if they did not pay in grain for its use. The tribute received was not enough to sustain the Toda, and they obtained additional grain and rice by exchanging their milk products in the markets. The Toda considered the Badaga essentially as social equals, but the Kota were considered inferior. A Toda would not normally touch a Kota nor would he eat with one or spend the night in a Kota village. The linkage between these peoples was economic and ceremonial; the Kota supplied the Toda with iron products and with pottery vessels used in ordinary dairying. The members of each Kota settlement were responsible for supplying these goods to a particular segment of the Toda population. They also made other utensils, were the musicians at Toda funerals, and provided cloaks for the dead. In return they received buffalo killed during the funerals.

Compared with most other peoples Toda life was unusual in many dimensions. The fact that much of their food and many of their material goods were produced by adjacent ethnics is out of the ordinary. In their food consumption, dairy products were most important, followed by wild or domestic plant foods; only under very special ceremonial circumstances did they eat buffalo meat. These people made no intoxicants nor did they hunt and fish. They did not fight as individuals or as groups against other peoples, and the only weapons which they possessed were the club which figured in their funeral rites, and the bow and arrow which had legal significance only. The Toda very literally considered their sacred dairies to be temples; if a person were guilty of a sacrilegious act associated with one of these dairies, it was not a crime to be punished by men, but a sin to be rectified by the gods. Unwanted infants were killed (infanticide), but this was a practical matter and of concern only to the family involved, not a crime against society. In the text of one legend a murder is described, yet historic examples of any violence were extraordinarily rare. Occasionally a man seized a woman and forcefully carried her off, but he did so only if a legal judgment in his favor had been reached and was supported by the people.

In their network of social relationships, relatives were traced through the male line (patrilineal descent) and were divided into two groups, called the Tarthar and Teivali; it was obligatory for an individual to marry within his or her group (moiety endogamy). Within each moiety were other clusters of related individuals, and mates had to be sought outside of these. Members of each of these clusters, or sibs, were distributed among various settlements (sib exogamy). The Tarthar had twelve sibs, and the Teivali formed six sibs; furthermore, within each sib were two additional groupings, one of ceremonial importance and the other of economic significance. Sibs were the most important corporate groups, and the leading lineages within particular sibs contributed the political office holders. The only formal governing body was the *naim* or council. Three of its members were from the Tarthar moiety, and one from the Teivali. A fifth member, who was a Badaga, usually was present only when a dispute under consideration involved a member of his ethnic group and a Toda. The naim most often met to settle disputes resulting from the transfer of a wife from one man to another. When such cases were heard, representatives of the contestants were present to offer evidence; if a judgment could not be reached in one day, the council met again and again until a decision was reached.

The arrangements surrounding marriage were rather complex, but they were spelled out with great clarity by the people. A man ideally married either the daughter of his father's sister or of his mother's brother (cross-cousin marriage), and, furthermore, any individual who was a cross-cousin was addressed as "husband" or "wife" because he was a potential marriage partner. If an ideal mate did not exist, a spouse was found from another sib within the moiety. Under no conditions was marriage permitted with a non-Toda. Marriages usually were arranged by parents when the principals were a few years of age (infant betrothal), and sometimes a small girl was raised in her husband's household. More commonly, however, she remained with her parents until about fifteen years of age. Just before a girl reached the age of puberty she had intercourse with a strong man for a single night; the only restriction in selecting him was that he could not be from her sib. If this ritual deflowering did not take place before her puberty, it was a lifelong disgrace for the female. When a girl married a particular man, she automatically became the wife of his brothers who were living or yet unborn (fraternal polyandry). A wife joined the household of her husband (patrilocal residence), and the Toda considered it ridiculous that one cohusband could be jealous of another. A husband who planned to spend the night with his wife left his cloak outside the door as a sign to her cohusbands that they should sleep elsewhere. When a wife became pregnant for the first time, the oldest brother performed a ceremony in order to establish his legal paternity. This was achieved by presenting the woman with a bow and arrow late during her pregnancy. The other cohusbands were "fathers" to the offspring in a sociological context but not in legalistic terms; identification of the biological father was not considered as important. Once a man presented a bow and arrow ceremonially to a pregnant wife, he was the legal father of any offspring by her until another husband performed the ceremony. A man might die before another performed the ceremony, and thus the dead man would be the legal father, even of an offspring conceived after his death.

Polyandry probably arose among the Toda as a result of the scarcity of women brought about by their practice of female infanticide. Among most ethnics the barrenness or adultery of a wife were grounds for divorce, but this was not so among the Toda. A man usually divorced his wife for only one of two causes: because she was lazy or a "fool." The wife's relatives might attempt to have the marriage continue by appealing to the naim. Even when their judgment was in favor of the woman, however, there was no mechanism by which to force the man to take his wife back. After divorcing a woman, a man was obliged to pay a fine of one buffalo to her relatives. "Adultery" could not be grounds for divorce because it was institutionalized under the term *mokhthoditi*. The arrangement usually was between a Tarthar man and a Teivali woman or vice versa, and a woman might have as many as three such networks of sexual ties. Two arrangements for carrying out these ties were possible. A woman might live with a man in terms of the mokhthoditi and be fully his wife except that any children produced belonged to the most recent husband to perform the bow and arrow ceremony. The other alternative was for the male partner to visit the woman at her house. In this case he apparently put his cloak outside the door as would one of her husbands.

Obviously many important Toda behavioral patterns are rather different from those most often reported among ethnics. The virtual absence of physical violence within the society and the complete absence of hostilities against neighboring peoples would seem to be desirable universal human goals. The permissiveness of their sexual life produced comparatively few strains in a domain which often is a focal point of stress in many societies. Yet their total way of life was not idyllic by any means. They were racists who believed firmly in their own superiority, and members of the Tarthar moiety looked down on those who were identified as Teivali. Their religious system with its extreme emphasis on the importance of buffalo resulted in many complex ceremonial involvements which consumed a great deal of time and effort and over which they had no control. There were disputes over women, which led to ill feelings between the persons and families involved. Finally, and of considerable importance, the ever-present possibility that sorcery would be employed against one resulted in many anxieties which could not be dismissed throughout one's life.

Sources: Rivers 1906.

AINU BELIEFS AND RITUALS

In many respects ethnics are much alike: They usually subsisted by gathering, small-scale farming, or herding; they dealt with each other more often as relatives and kinsmen than as strangers, and they possessed comparatively few, rather simple artifacts. The differences between peoples were more a matter of degree than of kind. The contrasts seem greater among belief systems than for most other aspects of culture. The ways in which to fashion a knife or to till a garden clearly are limited by raw materials, technological norms, and the physical environment. The formulation of views about supernaturals is at least superficially more expansive and potentially more variable than is the patterning for most other forms of behavior. Simple peoples sometimes had one supreme deity, while some more complex societies had a host of gods, but the reverse might also be true. Spirits loomed large and important or were of negligible significance among various peoples at the same general level of cultural complexity, and so it was with prayers or the use of sacred masks. At the same time there appears to have been a common basis for religious behavior; it is the belief, called animism, that spirit beings dwell in objects. Among the Ainu of Japan animistic beliefs were elaborated to an exceptional degree and became a focal point in life.

The Ainu long have attracted the attention of anthropologists, in large part because they stand as racially distinct from the Mongoloid peoples of northeastern Asia. The Ainu were short in stature, their skin was light in color, and most notably they were very hirsute—so much so that they have been called the "hairy" Ainu. Their hair was dark brown and wavy; adult males had heavy beards and an abundance of body hair. Possibly they were the original inhabitants of the Japanese islands and represent an archaic Caucasoid racial stock. The Japanese virtually exterminated the Ainu of Honshu in the ninth century, but on the northern island of Hokkaido they remained largely independent until Japanese trading interests encroached on one sector of the island in 1599. Two hundred years passed before more intensive contacts occurred, this time with Japanese military forces. By 1854 the impact of colonialism was intensive, and in 1868 when the island of Hokkaido became a part of Japan, the long-standing efforts to destroy the Ainu were greatly intensified. In 1923 it was reported that the Ainu numbered about 15,500, but another source states that in 1939 on the islands of Hokkaido and Sakhalin and the Kuriles, the population was about 170,000. The latter figures must refer to persons of partial Ainu ancestry, for it appears that the remnants of Ainu culture have been fading rapidly.

Traditionally, the Ainu lived in long-established, permanent settlements, which were located most often on the edges of river terraces or along the seashore. These communities rarely contained more than twenty houses and more often consisted of ten or fewer residences. A settlement was permanent as long as local resources were abundant. As food stresses were felt, the pattern seems to have been for a few families to take up residence on nearby unoccupied lands which belonged to their community. The people subsisted mainly on salmon, which were harpooned, speared, and netted. The basic fish diet was supplemented with deer meat obtained by men who hunted in the hills during the early winter. Game was taken with bows and arrows, the set bow, and in snares. The arrow-points might be tipped with poison made from aconite, and dogs were used to bring deer to bay in order that they might be killed. Vegetable foods were collected but were of secondary importance in the total diet. Judging from the long-term occupancy of many settlements, it appears that food was plentiful and even abundant.

Men and women alike wore their hair shoulder length, and wavy hair was much admired. The tattoos of women were the most distinctive form of bodily decoration, and they were made in order to beautify and strengthen a woman. The area around a woman's lips was tattooed so that from a distance she appeared to have inordinately large lips. Their arms and the backs of their hands likewise were covered with bands of lines, which sometimes crossed. The designs were made by cutting the skin with a knife, and the incisions were rubbed with soot. The first incisions were made when a girl was young, but the designs apparently were not completed until just before she married. The primary garment of a man or woman was woven from thread made from the inner bark of mountain elm trees. This cloak was nearly ankle-length, had wide sleeves, and was belted at the waist. In the winter the same style of garment was worn, but it was made of animal skins sewn on a cloth base. Sandals and leggings of cloth were worn in the summer, whereas winter leggings were made from skin and were worn with skin boots interlined with dried grass.

It appears that each male family head was largely responsible for the behavior of persons in his residence unit, and since small hamlets were composed of closely related persons, social control was a family affair. Even large settlements were comprised primarily of persons related through the male line (patrilineages). A hamlet or village leader was responsible for officiating at marriage and death ceremonies, settling disputes between families or with outsiders, and leading trading or warring ventures. The office usually was passed from father to son, but if there were a question of succession, a council of village elders chose the next leader. The members of a patrilineage lived in one or more settlements and held exclusive rights to exploit a given territory. A village leader's effective sphere of influence sometimes extended to a number of communities of the same lineage, but his power was greatest within his own settlement. Disputes within a village often were settled by having the principals debate the issue before the assembled villagers. A winner was declared if one contestant gave up or collapsed, or if one speaker was judged the victor by the village leader. A person accused of wrongdoing could be forced to submit to an ordeal to test his innocence. For example, a stone might be heated and the accused be asked to hold it; a refusal constituted an admission of guilt whereas holding it with no ill effects indicated innocence. A murderer seldom was killed, for death was not regarded as effective punishment. Instead his eyes might be pierced with needles, or the ligaments of his heels cut to render him a cripple. A thief was beaten the first time he was caught, but a habitual thief might have the tip of his nose, a finger, or his earlobes cut off.

Considerable stress was placed on ancestral lines, and some Ainu could trace their patrilineal ties through fifteen generations. Identity with a particular patrilineage was recorded by designs on libation wands (often called "moustache-lifters"). During ceremonies these wands were used to sprinkle sacred beer into the air in honor of deities and ancestors. Each Ainu woman was identified with a patrilineage as well as with a hereditary line of females. The bonds among women were recorded on a belt worn beneath a woman's clothing and called a *kut*. Its form as well as the designs on it were inherited from the woman's mother. Men were not permitted to see these belts nor were they supposed to know of their existence. The belts were considered to have magical power in times of great disaster. In a social context, the old women who arranged marriages were the ones to establish the kuts of the couple since a rule of exogamy prevailed; a prospective bride could not marry a man whose mother had the same kut as her own. Before marriages became monogamous in recent times, a man's wives could not be sisters since they had the same kut and were considered as one person.

Among the Ainu, during ordinary and extraordinary activities alike, religious rituals were performed in order to supplicate a host of spirit beings. Their supernatural system and derived dogma were based on the concept of *ramat*. In the language of the Ainu, ramat literally meant "heart," but figuratively it was the invisible, spiritual essence of every living form. It was present in different proportions in various species; mosses had little ramat, but the wood from living trees had a great deal, as did men. Ramat was everywhere, and without it a form was nothing. When living things were broken, burnt, or died, their spirit abandoned them and went elsewhere. Furthermore, when a man slept or was otherwise unconscious, his spirit left his body, and there was always a fear that it might not return.

A *kamui* was a god, deity, or perhaps more correctly a concentrated supernatural force which ranged in power from a god to a lesser spirit. These beings were good and beautiful, bad and hostile, mischievous, or largely neutral in the affairs of men. Kamui were of unequal power and were not generally ranked with one another although one tended to be superior to all others. Collectively they lived in a land of their own where they assumed human form and lived in a manner similar to that of the Ainu. The sun and a being who was a teacher and culture hero lived in the sky, were remote, and were largely unimportant in human affairs. Another group of kamui were helpful, and these could be influenced through the performance of rituals. Most important among these was the Goddess of the Hearth (Supreme Ancestress or Supreme Grandmother) who controlled the spirits of the dead and was embodied in the sacred fire of the family hearth. The hearth fire was sacred, because it was through it that the souls of the dead could be reached. These fires were not permitted to die; at night the embers were covered with ashes in order to sustain them. The Goddess of the Hearth was wrathful, and ill fortune would follow if people did not live up to their ritual obligations to her. She was important too because no other kamui could be invoked without a preliminary prayer to her. The sister of this deity was responsible for the sustenance of the Ainu. Another kamui of this class was associated with snakes, and a host of others were embodied in various configurations of water, such as undercurrents, rapids, waterfalls, and the surf.

Kamui of lesser but nonetheless important standing dwelt in the black fox, wolves, bears, and eagle owl. The skulls of mammals and turtles served as spirit protectors after they had been cleaned, smoked, and stuffed with shavings from living willows. The skulls were wrapped in shavings and then were hung along the north wall of a house, stored in boxes, or carried by travelers; in each instance they served to protect their possessors. Certain kamui who lived in wild places, such as crags, marshes, and river eddies, could be dangerous or at least unpredictable in their behavior. A water nymph could be helpful, but it also demanded that a person be drowned each year. Two additional classes of deities clearly were associated with evil; one type brought diseases such as smallpox and was so much feared that even though it was extraordinarily evil it could not be spoken of as such. Some bears killed men and were evil, as was a large bird who lived in a cave and ate human flesh. Finally, a certain form of caterpillar, which was associated with the Japanese, was regarded with the utmost fear and horror.

Ramat, the spirit force of living things, was expressed in different kamui, and in order to solicit the aid of the most helpful of the kamui, *inau* were prepared. Inau were branches carved into schematic representations of human beings or left plain, but both usually were decorated with curled wood shavings. The shavings were attached in different patterns; also the bark might be removed or slit vertically to form narrow projections or wings. They might best be termed messenger sticks since their primary purpose was to convey the hopes and prayers of the Ainu to their gods. While most inau served this purpose, others warded off the spirits which brought disease and bad luck. Certain types were burnt in the fireplace as appeals to the Goddess of the Hearth to carry a message to ancestral spirits. Some types were thought to contain the spirit force of ancestors. The different varieties of inau were placed at propitious places within a house, and at a short distance outside a sacred opening in the east wall, clusters of inau were set on supports or stuck into the ground. These supernatural aids, to which offerings were made, were always near at hand to protect and help the residents of each household. Furthermore, other groups of messenger sticks were erected, and their number added to periodically, at widely scattered localities deemed propitious for reaching their gods.

The Ainu fashioned a wide variety of other forms which aided them in their quest for rapport with ancestors and deities. Wooden effigies were important helpers, curled wood shavings alone were aids, bracelets made of twisted shavings were worn by women performing certain ritual acts, and a pillow stuffed with curled shavings protected one while sleeping. In addition, libation wands, which were rectangular pieces of wood decorated with symbols of the owner's patrilineage, were used to gain supernatural aid.

An Ainu house was not only a dwelling but a place of family worship. The home of a village leader was, in addition to these purposes, the setting for certain community ceremonies. The most important ceremonies, such as those surrounding bears and salmon, were likely to be held in a village leader's home. The rectangular houses of the Ainu were framed with poles and covered with bundles of grass; the roofs were steep, gabled, and thatched. A house was entered through a shed or lean-

The inside of an Ainu house facing the sacred northeast corner (Courtesy of Columbia University Press; from Munro 1962).

to on the west side. In the opposite wall was the sacred opening, beyond which rows of inau were arranged. At the center of the room was a large rectangular fireplace with a wood frame surrounding it. The section of fire in the hearth which was nearest to the opening in the eastern wall was extraordinarily sacred. In this fire lived the Goddess of the Hearth for the home, and each night the embers were covered with ashes so that the Goddess could sleep. It was a grievous sin and grounds for a divorce for a woman to permit this fire to go out. In order not to contaminate the sacred fire, another part of the hearth fire served ordinary household purposes. Seating arrangements around the fire were rigidly defined by custom: The homeowner sat at the northeast corner; his wife sat beside him toward the door; children sat opposite their parents, and honored guests sat at the head of the hearth, between it and the sacred opening. Within a house were the diverse kamui representations and inau who served to protect the dwelling and its residents. On the northeast side were treasured lacquered vessels for sacred beer as well as other containers and associated utensils for ceremonial use. Attached to the wall behind these items were swords and imitation swords as well as wooden tablets and other honored objects. The weapons were used on ceremonial occasions to drive away evil spirits.

The House-Warming Ceremony is one type of religious performance, and its general patterning may serve as an example of Ainu liturgies. It was necessary to perform this ceremony before a new house could be occupied or before new occupants could take up residence in an old house. The House God (a kamui) was honored, and his effigy was placed in the sacred northeast corner of a dwelling. Further preliminaries included shooting a particular form of arrow into the roof to ward off any evil spirits that might be lurking about, and brewing a sacred millet-based beer. All important kamui were summoned as honored guests, and invitations were extended to friends and relatives. A sacred mat was laid out near the hearth, cups were placed on it with a libation wand resting across the rim of each, and a large container of sacred beer was placed nearby. Each male guest entered slowly and respectfully offered a salutation by raising his arms once or twice, first to a fickle spirit and then to the House God. He seated himself at a designated place near one of the longer walls and saluted the Household Goddess. Other persons entered and were seated on the basis of age and sex along the long sides of the house. The woman of the house then stirred the beer and ladled it back and forth between two vessels in a precisely defined manner. Next two village elders, who wore special protective headbands, were asked to honor first the House God and then an Ancestral Goddess whose inau had been placed on the sacred fence outside the house. This goddess was the sister of the Goddess of the Hearth and was responsible for feeding the people. The household head and the elder who honored the House God each wore a sacred sword and sprinkled sacred beer with a libation wand on inau placed in the ashes of the hearth as well as on the fire itself. Salutations and prayers were offered to the Goddess of the Hearth, who was asked to grant prosperity to the household. One of the selected elders made offerings of beer to the House God, and the second went outdoors to perform similar rituals before the sacred fence on which was a representation of the Ancestral Goddess. In most ceremonies the sacred artifacts and beer were taken outside by passing them through the sacred wall opening, but in this instance the elder carried a cup of beer and libation wand with him. Animal heads filled with shavings were placed by the hearth and were offered a few drops from the bottom of a cup of sacred beer as their reward for protecting the beer as it brewed. After the elders had completed their ritual tasks, guests were free to offer libations to the House God or to the kamui on the sacred fence. All of these activities were carried out in a solemn and respectful atmosphere. Outside the house, near the end of the formal ceremonies, a ritual salutation was made by the host, and he was joined by men who purportedly were from the same common ancestor. Some beer was drunk quietly until after the All Souls Ceremony was performed. It involved ritual offerings of food to the Goddess of the Hearth as the representative of ancestral spirits, and then the graves of respected elders, which were at the northwest corner beyond the house, were honored by the assembled women in the company of the household head. Inau were erected, libations made, and food offered to the ancestral spirits, who were asked through prayer to protect the new house and to watch over its children.

After these observances were completed, the atmosphere among the assembled group changed from one of reverence to gaiety. After the sacred artifacts were returned to their places, a large container of beer was placed near the sacred wall opening, and the household head or his delegate sat near the beer container and controlled the drinking. The guests were reseated, speeches were made, and prayers offered; the men began to drink heavily, although the beer still was handled in a ritual manner. At this point songs and chants were sung as some persons danced. Women drank little but grouped around the circular lid of a large beer container to sing. They later danced around the lid and eventually around the hearth. As the night wore on, most guests left, but some lingered for the farewell dance and the telling of ancient tales by a few persons who clustered around the sacred hearth.

The most famous ritual set of the Ainu and one of the most sacred was the Bear Ceremony. A cub was captured and housed in a wooden cage, where it was fed and honored, for up to three years; only one bear at a time was raised in any particular village. As the time for the ceremony approached, invitations were extended to persons in the surrounding area to attend. The message was couched in the following terms: "I . . . am about to send away the dear little divine one whose home is among the mountains. My friends and masters, come ye to the feast and we will unite in the great joy of sending him off. Come!" (Batchelor 1927:205–206). The guests wore their finest garments and ornaments to the event, and in preparation for it the women refurbished each other's tattoos. The hosts and guests alike prepared special foods, and the festivities were centered in the house of the village leader. Offerings were made to the Goddess of the Hearth and other deities represented both inside and outside the house. After these preliminaries the men told the bear that they were going to send him to his ancestors but that he should not be angry. Ropes were attached around the bear's neck, and he was taken from the cage to be paraded before the assembled throng as traditional songs were sung. The animal then was shot with blunt arrows which did not penetrate his skin, and after being tied to a special post, he was shot with additional blunt arrows. Daring young men rushed toward the bear and seized it by the head as other persons held on to its hindquarters; as the bear opened its mouth to snap at someone, a block of wood was wedged between its jaws. It was dragged to a spot where two poles had been placed and apparently tied together at one end. The bear's neck was placed between the poles, and the upper one was pressed downward to strangle it. The dying animal was shot with a sharp bamboo-pointed arrow or stabbed through the heart, and the blood that gushed out was carefully caught in a container so that not a single drop touched the ground. The warm blood was drunk as divine medicine by the participants. The dead bear was taken into the leader's house after the sacred opening in the east wall was enlarged, and the body was skinned immediately. The head was severed and placed facing the hearth, with food set before it. The men then danced as the bear meat cooked, and some of it was offered to the head. A feast was made of the bear meat, and later the skull was placed on an inau fence as a spirit fetish.

The most pervasive characteristic of Ainu life is the extent of their ceremonial involvement. To cut down a tree necessitated ritual observances to the kamui associated with the species. Hunting, fishing, eating, and even sleeping were accompanied by ritual actions or restrictions designed to gain the cooperation of the associated deities. As is so often the case among ethnics and others, rituals were performed in a particular manner because of the dictates of tradition. Undoubtedly even the best-informed Ainu elder could not have explained the meaning of many procedures and acts, and yet their religious significance was beyond question and served above all else to give purpose and order to their lives.

Much of the systematic information about the Ainu was collected by the Christian missionary John Batchelor and the Scottish physician Neil G. Munro. Both men spent many years among the Ainu around the turn of the present century, and although they were not trained ethnographers, each was a capable observer. The contrasts between their accounts is notable. Batchelor's descriptions are far-ranging, presented in a chatty style, overly generalized, and sometimes demonstrably false. Munro's information was recorded methodically, with care taken to designate precisely which subgroup of people he was discussing, but the material is limited in scope. These accounts supplement each other admirably and demonstrate that within recent times nonprofessionals may prove rewarding sources for ethnographic information. In a sense, long exposure to ethnics and an ability to observe with care may serve ethnography as well as would more extensive training in the discipline.

Sources: Batchelor 1927; Munro 1962; Shinichiro 1960; Watanabe 1968.

FIVE

SOUTH PACIFIC

In terms of both environment and ethnics, nowhere in the world were the contrasts greater than in the South Pacific basin. The island habitats ranged in size from the continental dimensions of Australia to tiny coral atolls in Micronesia. The virtually uninhabited deserts of Western Australia contrast sharply with the lush and densely populated islands in some sectors of Polynesia. Possibly the least complex lifeway of any people throughout the world that survived into early historic times was one reported for Tasmania, and as such it stands poles apart from the great social and cultural elaborations recorded for Tahiti or Hawaii. Furthermore, while man has lived for hundreds of thousands of years in sections of Indonesia, some Pacific islands had not been occupied by man until within the Christian era. By and large, aboriginal baseline information about peoples of the South Pacific is far superior to reports for Africa and Asia. One reason is that effective historic contact was comparatively late on most Pacific islands. Although an island cluster might have been occupied by traders or missionaries, the local peoples remained out of contact with most outsiders because of the vast expanses of water which surrounded them. In Australia the environment of the interior was such that permanent settlement was difficult and thus delayed, which permitted some aboriginal peoples to follow their ways without dramatic change until essentially contemporary times. However, along all the coasts of Australia except the northern one, European colonists soon exterminated or displaced the indigenous peoples. Sectors of the New Guinea highlands, which again are interior regions, have remained fertile areas for aboriginal studies down to the present.

Among the culture areas of the South Pacific—and even among those of the world—Australia is unique in a number of respects. It is the largest region, nearly three million square miles, in which ethnic living was homogeneous enough for a continent to qualify as a culture area. The population at early historic contact is estimated at 300,000; the people were divided into about 500 distinct groups, with an average of about 500 persons per ethnic. The basic similarity among aboriginal Australians is reflected in their linguistic unity on a continentwide basis. The grammar, syntax, and certain morphemes were similar everywhere, yet linguistic differences of enough magnitude existed to distinguish five subfamilies. All aboriginal Australians had economies based on gathering, and the collection of plant foods often was more important than the sustenance gained by hunting, with fishing on the whole even less important. The only domestic animal was the dingo, and the technology was simple in comparison to that of other ethnics. Australians tended to range over extensive areas in search of food; thus it is not surprising that their homes usually were rude shelters and that their artifacts were highly portable. Among the most widespread manufactures were the spear-thrower used to propel a wood- or stone-pointed spear, the throwing stick, digging stick, trough-shaped wooden carrying container, stone ax, and stone knife. Another notable characteristic was that raw materials and manufactured forms might be traded over great distances. Circumcision was practiced widely, and complex initiation ceremonies were held for young adult males. Within an ethnic there often were two, four, or eight social groups which were important in marital arrangements, and identity with a totemic form was the norm. In many respects indigenous Australian culture was impoverished, but it was elaborated in some rather unexpected dimensions. The mythology was rich and varied; rock art sometimes was sophisticated, and ritual life often was well developed.

Contrasting with the landmass of Australia, the remaining land areas of the South Pacific basin were comparatively small. Although the island of New Guinea is about 312,000 square miles and the Indonesian culture area encompasses about 1,004,000 square miles of land, the total land area elsewhere is only about 50,000 square miles. Ethnographers find the insularity of many Pacific peoples to be an attractive feature for a number of reasons. On islands the problem of ethnic boundaries is simplified, and it usually is less difficult to distinguish between local developments and borrowings. Furthermore, the population of a small island was likely to be socially integrated and relatively stable, although trade and political ties among islands sometimes were of great importance.

The Pacific basin includes about 25,000 islands, which vary a great deal in physical form. New Guinea is a "high" island, with lofty mountains along its central length; away from the mountains are high central plateaus, fringed on the north and south by swampy lowlands. The

Philippines and New Zealand also are examples of high, continental-type islands with varied landforms and climates. Other high islands, such as those in the Hawaiian group, are of volcanic origins and are characterized by deep valleys and precipitous cliffs; Tahiti, Truk, and Yap are of this type. Some "low" islands are coral atolls which rise only a few feet above high tide, while others are higher landmasses with coral reefs attached.

Melanesia, named the "black islands" after the Negroid occupants, is a culture area of striking contrasts. The island habitats range in size from the extensiveness of New Guinea to small reefs. High mountain environments, humid swamps, dense jungles, treeless plains, and palm-lined strands all are to be found there. The inhabitants of this area came from Southeast Asia at different times, represent different racial strains, and expanded as far as Fiji. The early migrants probably were hunters and fishermen, but by the time of European penetration they had become relatively sedentary cultivators. Their most important crops were bananas, breadfruit, coconuts, taro, and yams, each of which was derived from Asia. However, the sweet potato also was raised; this was the only cultigen from the New World. We find also that these peoples made tools of polished stone, fashioned pottery, and raised pigs as well as fowl. Throughout many parts of Melanesia significant differences existed between the peoples living along the beaches and those inhabiting the "bush," with the former possessing a richer technology and a more varied diet. The cultural ways of New Guinea ethnics lead some persons to regard these islanders as a distinct and separate cluster (Papua), but in the present culture area classification they have been considered a part of Melanesia. Yet the peoples of New Guinea do stand apart in certain respects. Most of them cultivated with digging sticks, fought with bows and arrows, took human heads, had huge festivals in which the consumption of pigs was important, maintained separate residences for men and women, and were dominated by "big men," who were self-made rather than hereditary political leaders.

The peoples of the "tiny islands," or Micronesia, were scattered over an immense expanse of ocean, but the land area which they occupied included fewer than 1,300 square miles. Among these ethnics, those who lived on high islands cultivated gardens in which they raised taro, breadfruit, or yams as their most important crop but added coconuts and pandanus; on atolls, fishing was important and gardening of more varied significance. The digging stick was the most important implement for cultivation. These people occupied scattered homesteads and hamlets more often than large villages. The basic residence and subsistence unit was either the extended family or a group of individuals who traced their descent through related females. The descent ties of an individual were extremely important for determining social standing, which ranged from commoner to nobility.

Polynesia or "many islands," with its handsome men and alluring women, is a more romantic region than the fabled East to Westerners. Polynesians were derived from Southeast Asia, the earliest migrants to the islands venturing forth in the early Christian centuries. Some appear to have traveled through Micronesia and others through Melanesia on their far-flung voyages. Later migrants appear to have arrived via Micronesia from Malaysia. For some of these movements we have legendary accounts of dramatic voyages, which mention that peoples already were established on many islands. The ethnics of this culture area raised bananas, taro, yams, and sweet potatoes in their gardens; fish also were an important item in the diet. Their technology included grinding and polishing stone and shell into cutting blades, and fashioning knives from pieces of bamboo. Their effective weapons were spears, axes, and clubs, but not the bow and arrow even though the form was known. The most important social grouping was that of persons living in a particular geographical area who were interrelated along both sides of the family and often married distant relatives within the unit. These "clans" tended to be self-sufficient and at times fought with one another. The important activities of a clan were directed by a leader who acquired his position by being the firstborn male in the most important clan segment. He traced his descent back to a supernatural founder of his group, and through this association he had a great deal of *mana*, or supernatural power. Mana often has been considered analogous to electrical power; it was amenable to control but only by persons skilled in handling it. The idea of taboo also was important in religious life; it meant that certain persons or objects, those with a great deal of mana, were dangerous to those who had very little mana. As full-time specialists in supernatural matters, priests were highly charged with mana, and they manipulated nonnatural forces, often through ceremonies, to further human welfare and the religious system itself.

The islands adjacent to the southern and eastern coasts of the Malay Peninsula comprise the Indonesian culture area. Most of the peoples represented large-scale societies with complex ways of life. This culture area is in most respects an extension of and is similar to the "Indian-Southeast Ethnic Enclave" area defined for Asia, and like the latter grouping it has little integrity as a culture area. Indonesia or Malaysia was for thousands of years strongly influenced and often controlled by Indian, Chinese, and Islamic expansionists. The ethnics found in this region at historic contact usually were in relatively inaccessible areas and are represented by such peoples as the Ifugao and the Negrito peoples of the Philippines.

Sources: Elkin 1964; Honigmann 1959; Kroeber 1948; Oliver 1952; Spencer and Johnson 1968.

THE TASMANIANS: A CULTURE OF MATERIAL POVERTY

It sometimes is said that the imagination of man knows no bounds and that men are capable of solving any problem if they diligently set their minds to the task. These phrases seem reasonable and might be numbered among the host of commonsense truisms known to Everyman. And yet anthropological experience leads us to suspect that both statements are more nonsense than sense. Why? First, men are capable of imagining only within the context of their culture and society. Imagination is but expansive thinking in terms of what we already know, and even the most creative persons, those who are capable of approaching the horizons of their culture's knowledge, are unable to project beyond its potential. Likewise, problems can be solved only when existing ideas are combined successfully in a unique manner. For example, there was a time when men did not know how to make bows and arrows. The question is, how did the bow and arrow come into being? Some persons might suggest divine inspiration, but it seems far more likely that the weapon was originated as a recombination of ideas already existing in some prehistoric culture. Possibly a person was playing with a stick which had a string attached at one end, and for some reason he bent the stick and tied the string to the other end of the stick. When the taut string was plucked with one's fingers, it gave off a pleasing sound, and thus the bow used as a string instrument originated. The form may have existed for a few years or perhaps for generations as a musical toy before someone placed a stick across the string and pulled on the bow to project the stick when the string was released. Now we have a new toy, but not yet a weapon. The bow-stick combination had the potential, however, of becoming a powerful weapon, and in time this is precisely what happened. Thus it should be realized that "needs" in themselves do not lead to the creation of new forms; the technology will produce new forms only insofar as recombinations and alterations are possible within it.

This ambulatory introduction leads to an isolated island called Tasmania, which is south of Australia. It was here that one of the world's most primitive people lived at the time of historic contact. Why were their cultural ways so backward? There is no reason to think that it was because they were dull and unimaginative creatures; it is rather because they were removed from the mainstream of worldwide culture at a critical time in human prehistory and were obliged to build on only a small inventory

Table 3.   CULTURE AREAS OF THE SOUTH PACIFIC

Australia: Malayo-Polynesian (Austronesian) languages; collecting, hunting; patrilateral emphasis, male initiations, totemic groups; band organization; fertility ceremonies to increase food production; chipped stone tools and weapon points, simple brush shelters, no clothing; spear with spear-thrower and the throwing stick as the most important weapons.

Melanesia: Malayo-Polynesian languages; yam and taro cultivation, domestic pigs, hunting and fishing secondary; most important social group was a male or female line of relatives; politically autonomous settlements; animistic religious focus; elaborate men's houses; cannibalism.

Micronesia: Malayo-Polynesian languages; coconuts, breadfruit, pandanus and taro cultivation, pig and fowl raising, fishing; monogamy, relatives often traced along the female line, social groups ranked on basis of descent; chiefdoms; animistic religion; rectangular houses of wood and thatch, grass skirts; skillful navigation of outrigger canoes, tattooing.

Polynesian: Malayo-Polynesian languages; cultivation of yams, taro, and breadfruit, raising of domestic chickens and pigs, fishing important; stress on birth order and social rank; hereditary chiefdoms; mana and taboo focus of supernaturalism; bark cloth clothing; kava important beverage, skillful navigators.

Indonesia: Malayo-Polynesian languages; rice primary crop, chickens and pigs important domestic animals (enclaves of gatherers); social norms highly variable; villages tended to be maximal political units; Islam widespread; village and regional specialization in manufactures; water buffalo as draft animal, blowgun (peoples of Madagascar belong to Malay-Polynesian language family, but their culture reflects African developments as well as Indonesian features).

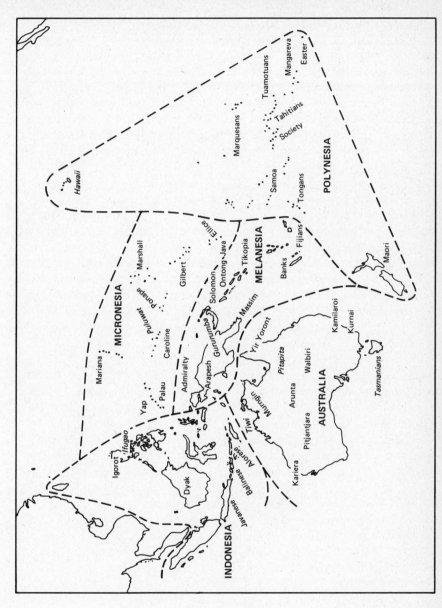

Map 3. Culture Areas and Select Ethnics of the South Pacific.

of existing ideas. It is probable that Australia first was occupied at least 25,000 years ago, at a time when the sea level throughout the world was much lower than at present, resulting in a greater land connection between Australia and the Malay Peninsula than exists at present. No one knows for certain when the first men arrived on Tasmania, but it is likely that they went there from Australia more than 10,000 years ago. Once the sea levels rose, Australia and Tasmania were isolated from the remainder of the world until the European expansions of historic times. The culture that the early migrants had taken with them apparently changed comparatively little for thousands of years.

It often is reckless to cite what a people did not have; in the case of the Tasmanians, however, the inventory seems to be reasonably complete. They did not have a central banking system nor did they manufacture latex girdles, which should be obvious. Yet also absent are many material objects and other forms which we would expect to find among them because they exist so widely among gathering peoples elsewhere in the world. Like most aboriginal Australians the Tasmanians did not know of the bow and arrow, make pottery, or work metal. Unlike the Australians the Tasmanians did not have the boomerang, spear-thrower, or spears with separately attached points. In fact, they made no composite tools or weapons. Thus, all Tasmanian knives were without handles, and spears consisted of simple shafts of wood. These islanders had no domestic animals, not even the dog. Although diverse species of fish were available along the coast and in interior rivers, they did not fish for food. Neither did they know how to kindle fires; if a fire went out, an ember was borrowed from a neighbor.

Unlike much of Australia, Tasmania is a temperate setting in which indigenous food sources were plentiful, even abundant. Given this general environment, it cannot be reasoned that these islanders were reduced to making very few things because of the scarcity of resources. Estimates vary widely concerning the number of Tasmanians when the British first settled the island in 1803. Possibly there were 4,000 occupants, and they were divided into localized subethnics comprised of a small number of families. Groups such as these were allied with each other, and the activities of each appear to have been guided by a leading warrior. In the event of conflicts between groups, the differences were settled most often by fights between individuals who were selected to represent their kinsmen. Each Tasmanian male was a warrior and a hunter, and he ranged widely around an area which he and his associates defended against intruders. These people usually have been described as having reddish-brown skin and negroid features. The men were a few inches more than five feet in height, and the women were somewhat shorter than the men. The most

A Tasmanian man (from Bonwick 1870).

striking aspect of their appearance was the hair of the men; covered with grease and red ocher, the hair was formed into coiled spirals, which hung down to their shoulders. The bodies of both men and women often were scarified with short lines or with circles to represent the sun or crescents to represent the moon. The distinctive scars were made by cutting the skin and then rubbing powdered charcoal and ocher into the incisions. The heads of the women were shaved, although there were local variations in hairstyles. Their dwellings were simple windbreaks built of brush and bark at the sides of a hearth. They usually went about naked, but in cold weather they wrapped themselves in skin cloaks and sometimes wore moccasins of skin on their feet. It would be desirable to discuss the artifacts and subsistence activities of a single band of Tasmanians to gain an accurate view of the lifeway of one population segment, but this approach is impossible because the people were destroyed by British settlers and sealers before any adequate record could be made about the activities of any small group. The information which follows is a composite description for the islanders recorded early in their history and drawn almost entirely from the excellent journals of George A. Robinson.

The primary food staples probably were the kangaroo and wallaby taken by men and shellfish and crayfish collected by women. At certain times of the year ducks and swans were plentiful and served as important food in some localities, and seals were important in others. In addition, diverse plant products such as roots and fruits were collected; these edibles were detached by hand and consumed without processing. In this context the Tasmanians are reported to have removed edible fungus and gum from trees, and these were eaten without any further preparations. The same apparently was true of toadstools. Similarly without equipment, they might catch a platypus by swimming after it in a stream and grabbing it in their hands.

The hand procurement of foods is the simplest known means for gaining sustenance. It is a somewhat more complex process to use forms which occur naturally but which are not modified in any manner before they are brought into play; these items are "naturefacts." For example, the Tasmanians killed ducks, swans, and snakes by throwing natural stones at them. To remove a material from its natural setting and then modify it in a simple or complex manner is to produce an artifact. The most important artifactual weapon among the Tasmanians was a spear made from a shaft of wood some ten or more feet in length. This shaft was straightened by heating it near a fire and then biting it into shape with their teeth. The tip of the shaft was sharpened to a point with a piece of flaked stone. A second weapon, and the only other one of note, was the throwing stick, or waddy as it sometimes is termed. It was a shaft of wood about eighteen inches in length and about an inch and a half in diameter. It was made from hardwood and was hurled with great accuracy at game as well as enemies. Hand-held, this type of stick functioned as a club. The throwing stick must not be confused with the spearthrower (throwing-board, atlatl), which is an aid in hurling a spear, and as already mentioned is unknown among these people.

Artifacts also might be used with naturefacts. In Tasmania opossums lived in holes in very tall trees. In order to obtain an opossum, a man fashioned a grass rope in a single loop around his legs and the tree. By bruising the tree's bark with a stone he made footholds, and he climbed upward by forcing his legs backward against the rope. In this manner an opossum hole was reached, and the animals could be pulled out, presumably to be killed by striking their heads against the tree.

Possibly the most reliable way to take game is to set traps, since a hunter who approaches his quarry must launch a weapon at precisely the proper moment, whereas traps work in the absence of the person who set them. The aboriginal Tasmanians had few such devices. It is reported that short sticks were forced into the ground with their exposed ends sharpened to points; these were designed to wound or kill animals that fell onto them. Likewise, along game trails crossed spears were placed in the ground with their points upward to impale unwary kangaroos and wallabies. A less efficient device, because it required the presence of a man, was employed by the occupants of the southwestern sector of the island. A small cone-shaped shelter was built and covered with grass. A man hid inside, and a fish was fastened as bait to a nearby stone. When a crow flew by and saw the fish, he landed and then was grabbed by the man. Similar blinds were constructed to take ducks, but the bait employed for them was worms.

There appear to have been a few methods of obtaining food complex enough to involve the use of more than a single artifact, the cooperation of a number of persons, or the two conditions in combination. A group of Tasmanian men sometimes cooperated in setting wooded areas on fire in order that game would flee into the open, where other hunters attacked the animals with spears and throwing sticks. One clever combination was employed in taking kangaroo. Prior to a hunt, men tied adjacent tufts of grass together at scattered localities. The pursued animals tripped across these barriers and were more easily taken with spears. An important item in the diet of some coastal dwellers was the ear shellfish, a species of *Haliotis*. When a woman dove to collect them, she carried a reed basket suspended over her shoulders with a strap. On reaching the shellfish, which were attached to rocks on the ocean floor, she pried them free with a stick which had been pointed and fire-hardened at one end.

The reports of the earliest competent observers indicate that the Tasmanians relied primarily on their skill and speed in order to harvest game animals since their weapons were limited to two shafted forms, the spear and throwing stick. Their entire food-getting inventory of instruments, facilities, and weapons was minimal as was their total usage of material objects. Mollusk shells served as cups; awls were fashioned from bones; baskets were woven of grass or reeds; knives, chisels, and borers were percussion-flaked pieces of stone; and water containers were made from pieces of kelp held together with wood skewers. Some groups made boats by binding together bundles of reeds or bark; these vessels were propelled with the aid of poles. It might be added that ceremonial life was poorly developed, and there appear to have been neither group rituals nor initiation ceremonies. At the same time dances, which appear to have been largely social events, often were held.

To return to the influence of imagination on technology and the reasons for the paucity of Tasmanian manufactures, a number of ideas seem pertinent. If the aborigines who entered Tasmania were in possession of only a few artifacts of simple design, no matter how imaginative any individual might have been he was in a poor position to originate many new forms. Innovations must arise from old forms, and if very few models are available to begin with, the likelihood that something new will be conceived is comparatively small. By contrast, among peoples with hundreds or thousands of artifacts, innovative achievement is much more probable because a large number of new combinations are possible. It is true that the Tasmanians probably developed moccasins, and they formulated the idea for bird blinds. These new forms must have resulted from creative adaptations of extremely simple models and indicate that imagination can function to a certain extent in even the simplest cultures. However, if men were indeed imaginative to the ultimate of the environmental potential rather than the cultural potential, we would expect the Tasmanians to have developed many new artifacts in spite of their isolation. Since this was not the case, it might be assumed that imagination without an expanding cultural base originates very little in the course of human events.

Source: Robinson 1966.

DISEASE AND DEATH AMONG THE PITAPITA

Ethnographers manifest differing degrees of diligence in assembling accounts of the peoples they study. It is acknowledged implicitly that an ethnography should deal with a broad range of subjects and have at least some discussion of all the major behavioral involvements of a people. Thus chapters are devoted to material culture, religion, property, and so on through the range of cultural universals. At the same time investigators, by temperament and training, find certain subjects of more intense interest, and on these they tend to elaborate. In one sense it is laudable to stress topics of personal concern because one tends to record those matters better than others. Thus, we find that particular investigators will devote an inordinate amount of attention to basketry, child training, plant foods, or similar subjects. If an ethnographer not only has an interest in a particular topic, but also possesses a sophisticated knowledge of it in terms of his own culture, he then is more likely to be able to probe the subject effectively with informants from another culture. An ethnographer who had been trained as a psychoanalyst in a Western country would be the ideal person to work with a shaman from another culture in which psychological curing methods were important. Professional ethnographers seldom have training of this nature on which to draw since they usually are anthropologists above all else. However, the ability to apply ethnographic investigative techniques tends to offset this limited knowledge about particular topics. Quite often, too, an amateur ethnographer is able, because of his specialized training in another field, to derive valuable information from ethnics. An example of such a person is Walter E. Roth (1861–1933), who received a B.A. degree in biology at Oxford and later was trained as a medical doctor. He practiced medicine in the Boulia district of Queensland, Australia, from 1894 to 1897, at a time when the aboriginal people were just beginning to acquire material goods and other offerings from white Australians. In a study of western Queensland area peoples, Roth assembled most of his information about the Pitapita, whose language he learned to speak.

There is a tendency to regard all aboriginal mainland Australians as having barely managed to survive in desert wastelands, but actually some localities, including that of the Pitapita, were relatively rich in food resources. Peoples living in these areas often reflected greater cultural elaborations and had more economic security than was found over much of the continent. The success of food-getting practices and the environmental potential are factors which often may be judged from dwelling forms; for example, peoples who built flimsy shelters usually moved often and had unreliable food sources. Although the Pitapita made rude brush shelters, which would be expected in Australia, these were only temporary structures built by persons caught in rainstorms. Their much more permanent winter dwelling was constructed in an elliptical excavation a foot and a half or more in depth. At each end of the depression a pole with a forked top was forced into the ground; these poles were bent inward and interlocked at the center. From the edges of the excavation to the arched poles were leaned other poles; between these brush and grass was wedged, and then the entire structure was covered with mud. A dwelling of this nature was entered through a doorway at one end; in front of this opening, a brush shelter was made to protect the entrance from the elements and to enclose a campfire. Another dwelling form, the standard summer house, was similar to the type just described, but it was built on the surface of a small knoll.

The Pitapita consumed an impressive variety of food products, and these were harvested by diverse techniques. Plant foods included some species of grass seeds which were separated from their hulls, ground between stones, mixed with water, and roasted in a fire, and others which were ground and eaten raw. Edible roots were roasted or ground and eaten raw. Wild fruits were gathered, the blossoms of particular flowers sucked for their honey, and the honeycombs of bees were removed from trees. Fishing does not appear to have been important, but some species were taken in small, hand-held nets. A net usually was handled by a number of individuals while others attempted to frighten the fish into the mesh. Another fishing technique was to build a weir of stones across an area of receding floodwater. The weir was broken at intervals by lower stone platforms topped with grass, and fish became stranded on these in their efforts to go beyond the obstruction. Hunting techniques included driving emus into set nets, which sometimes were supplemented with brush fence guides. The trapped birds then were killed with boomerangs or throwing sticks. Although the boomerang was used widely in Australia, the self-returning variety was not common; where it did occur, as among the Pitapita, the form was a toy. A throwing stick is, as the name implies, a stick that was hurled at an animal; these sticks were shorter than spears and did not have a separate point. Kangaroos were tracked and killed with spears with or without the aid of semidomestic dingos. Pitfalls were dug in localities where emus searched for food, and these were covered with boughs to trap unsuspecting birds. Bustards, which are game birds related to cranes, were snared or encircled by grass fires and then were killed with boomerangs and throwing sticks. Small birds such as pigeons were netted, and other birds were killed on the wing with boomerangs.

Pitapita artifacts are reasonably typical of the forms reported widely in Australia. The multipurpose container was an elongated wooden tray made by cutting a section from the trunk or limb of a living tree and charring the inner surface so that a concavity could easily be hollowed out with an adz. A woman carried this type of tray either on her head or slung under one arm with a supporting cord passed over the opposite shoulder and beneath the tray. Trays were used mainly to carry water from a nearby source or to hold plant products after they had been reaped. The trough-shaped tray and a digging stick, some four feet in length, were the two key artifacts employed in the collecting activities of women. A multipurpose container carried by women, often referred to as a dilly bag, was woven from plant fibers or string made of opossum and human hairs combined. These bags were suspended from a shoulder by an attachment cord. The bag for carrying water over long distances was made of skin, usually that of a kangaroo or an opossum. The animal's head was removed and the carcass extracted intact. The front legs and the tail were cut off, and these openings, as well as all others except the one at the neck were closed with bone pins, which sometimes were bound in place with sinew. The neck opening served as the spout, and it was closed with a cord when not in use. The lower portions of the hind limbs were bound together and served as a carrying loop.

Among the very few tools for processing materials was an adz; it was made from a slightly curved piece of wood, up to two feet in length, and a piece of chipped stone which was attached at one end with a lump of plant resin. The knife in everyday use had a triangular blade made from chipped stone, and the handle end was covered with a coating of plant resin. The only heavy, woodworking tool was an ax. The oblong head was made from stone that had been chipped and then polished. The handle was fashioned from a single piece of wood bent around one end of the ax head and bound together with cord; the head was prevented from slipping by forcing plant resin between it and the handle.

Food processing equipment again was quite simple. Newly collected seeds were placed in a hole in the ground, and they were hulled by the rotary motion of the bare feet of a woman. The seeds then were ground between a flat, oblong milling stone and a smaller, hand-held grinding stone. An artificially smoothed oblong stone was used to crack one species of hard-shelled nut, and this seems to exhaust the list of artifacts associated with the processing of food for cooking or direct consumption.

Fire was kindled either by sawing one piece of dry wood against another at right angles until the nearby grass tinder caught fire or by rotating a wood shaft rapidly between the palms until it lit the tinder placed on a flat stick used as a base.

In comparison with other manufactures, weapons were both numerous and varied in form. The boomerangs made for fighting either had a gentle curve toward each end or were hooked at one end. In order to ward off a boomerang blow during a fight an opponent carried a stick, spear, or shield. The hook-ended boomerang was designed to strike an upright defensive weapon of an enemy and then to swing around and hit him on the head. In hand-to-hand combat wooden swords, some four feet in length, were manipulated with both hands. Some spears were hurled by hand, and others were propelled with the aid of spear-throwers. Light, oblong wooden shields were carried, and short poles, pointed at each end, were employed both as defensive and offensive weapons. Finally, throwing sticks were hurled at enemies who were nearby.

This inventory of those Pitapita manufactures associated most intimately with procuring and processing foods, carrying materials, and making things, or defending oneself against human enemies, is brief, but included are most of the basic forms that would be found among any people. All ethnics made and used containers since the human digestive system has a very limited and short-term carrying capacity and since everywhere in the world sustenance is irregularly distributed over the landscape. Similarly all peoples made knives, which cut more efficiently than human teeth, and pounders or grinders that were stronger than human fists. The sticks and spears which were thrown extended the reach of human arms, traveled faster than human legs, and cut or penetrated more effectively than human fingernails. In a very real sense the most basic and widespread artifacts are largely effective elaborations on human anatomy.

Ethnics the world over developed certain methods and techniques designed to cure illness and to prevent death. A ready, and seemingly reasonable, explanation for the innumerable curing means reported is that, in the absence of scientific medical knowledge, disease was a great unknown quality enveloped with fear and danger. The tendency among ethnics, as among ourselves, was to try both natural and supernatural cures in the hope that at least one technique would be effective. Naturally-derived aids were enlisted when the illness was of a known and curable nature, but for maladies with nonlocalized or vaguely manifest symptoms, it was common to seek a supernatural cause and treatment. A person who employed his knowledge to help individuals who were ill is termed a shaman. The word "shaman" was used among a Siberian people, the Tungus, to mean a person who is a specialist in supernatural matters and derives his, or her, power from nonnatural beings. A shaman cures, foresees, predicts, and aids, whereas a sorcerer employs his supernatural powers to cause illness, disease, and death. An individual might be a shaman and also a sorcerer, depending on the manner in which he employed his power in any particular set of circumstances; in such a case the person generally has been termed a shaman.

A shaman among the Pitapita was always a male, and he obtained supernatural powers by one of a number of means. One avenue to this power was through a magical snake. Unknowingly a man who was fishing might have a bone pointed at him by a huge, supernatural water snake. Later, as evening approached and the man continued to fish, he would see what he thought to be the snake coming across the water, and he would run away as quickly as possible. The following morning he would feel ill, and his condition would worsen until some four or five days later when a shaman would be called in to remove a foreign object by sucking it from his body. The substance removed was said to have been a piece of bone, a pebble, or a stone flake which had been magically inserted into his body by the water snake. The patient was thus cured and in turn became a shaman himself. Shamanistic power might also be gained as the result of a revisitation from the soul of a deceased person, or a child might have a piece of bone magically inserted into him by a shaman and in later years become a practitioner. The most common means to become a shaman, however, was for a person to wander about until he was exhausted, at which time a supernatural object would be placed in his body by *Mulkari*, a beneficent supernatural. Each shaman, irrespective of how he gained his power, was in theory an equal to all others for doing social good or evil, and on occasion they aided one another in the performance of their tasks. Shamans participated in the same daily routine as ordinary persons, and were distinguished from others only in their possession of certain objects which were tangible representations of their extraordinary powers. The objects possessed included small pieces of bone, strangely shaped stones, crystals, pebbles, and other unusual forms derived from Mulkari or from the water snake.

Among the Pitapita objectively derived means for prolonging life are clearly set forth and relatively few in number, whereas supernatural curing methods were much more complex and more frequently used since most illness was thought to be of supernatural origin. If a disease or discomfort were considered of secular origin, the cures tended to be straightforward. A broken limb was bound with splints for a month or two, small balls of mud or clay were swallowed in order to cure diarrhea, and a plant was steeped to produce a tea for curing colds and coughs. Any grass or shrub growing near the water was less reasonably used to relieve pain associated with urinating. Rational and supernatural techniques seem to have been combined in a single method of treatment for a nonfatal snakebite. After being bitten, the victim watched the snake re-enter its hole, and he then covered the entrance. Using his belt of hair or any other piece of cord that was convenient, he bound the limb above and below the bite and then sucked the wound. The man's wife or anyone else near at hand rushed off to consult the nearest shaman and then returned to dig a large pit close to the site of the accident. A fire was built in the hole, and stones were heated in it. As the flames died they were sprinkled with water, and newly cut boughs and branches were placed on the embers. The afflicted person lay down on this warm bed for two to three hours. Full recovery occurred only after the consulted shaman came to the area and completed the treatment. He dug out the snake and hit it with stones, which are said to have made it decrease in physical size. After the snake was inert, the shaman peeled half of its skin back; filling this skin sheath with water ended the curing process. It would appear that the binding and sucking of the wound were fully rational techniques to remove the venom, and steaming the victim might also have been efficacious physically. The activities of the shaman, however, could only have rendered psychological service.

If a person drowned, the death usually was attributed to a supernatural water snake; if an individual disappeared forever, another supernatural was held responsible. Men had little or no control over events such as these, but they were directly responsible for other types of death and for most serious illnesses. If a person became ill and could not explain his affliction in ordinary terms, he sooner or later concluded that a death bone had been pointed at him. "Bone-pointing" was a ritual performed by a sorcerer acting either on his own behalf or, more likely, on behalf of a client who wanted an enemy killed or injured. A death bone was fashioned from a human forearm or from an emu bone and was ground to a point at one end. Attached to the opposite end was a piece of string, from four to fourteen feet in length, which was extended through a short, hollowed-out section of human arm or leg bone and cemented to the pitch used to seal the end. When the victim was a short distance away, a sorcerer secretly placed the bone cylinder upright in the ground, and sitting on the ground, he placed one foot in the direction of the victim. Using his big toe and the one next to it, he held the pointer facing the potential sufferer. By magical means the sorcerer sent a foreign material into the body of the victim, and the victim's blood flowed magically into the pointer and then along the string to the bone cylinder.

The bone-pointing ritual was employed by men in order to produce either the illness or death of another person. It is reported that occasionally a person who learned a bone had been pointed at him abandoned his will to live and soon died. If he did not abandon hope, he sought the aid of a friend or relative to find out who had plotted his downfall. If the victim's friends and relatives could not help him, he might dream of the identity of the person or sorcerer. The final means for determining the cause of one's illness, if all else had failed, was to consult a friendly shaman for treatment and to request that he learn the identity of the enemy. The shaman usually worked over the patient and appeared to remove a foreign substance from his body by massaging the afflicted area, blowing on the patient's chest, and finally sucking out the material magically without breaking the surface of the skin. He examined the foreign body that he had removed, and after consulting his fellow curers in secret, he determined the guilty individual. Even when in possession of this knowledge, the half-well victim acted with caution. He might cripple the enemy and his agent, the shaman, with a weapon, but he would be careful not to kill them because they still had his blood in their bone-pointer case, and if they died the murderer would surely die as well. His more likely recourse was to enlist the services of another shaman to point a bone at his opponent and the opponent's shaman in retaliation. After obtaining the opponent's blood, they went off alone and built a fire over which they heated the bone cylinder containing the blood. This done, the original victim went off and talked with his opponent, and if the latter admitted that he did not feel well, this was taken as evidence that the pointing had succeeded. If no sign of his illness could be detected, the shaman washed out the container with water, and the bone-pointing ritual began again. If it succeeded this time, the enemy came under the power of his intended victim and might be made ill by heating the blood or killed by burning the blood-filled container. If neither man died during these procedures, they would sooner or later confront one another, and their differences were then brought out in the open. Mutual exposure tended to resolve the problems, and the vessels said to contain their blood then were washed with water, and the episode was concluded.

The bone-pointing complex among the Pitapita raises a number of meaningful questions about the honesty of shamans. Did a typical shaman really believe in his power? The answer seems to be clearly that he did. There were no doubt a few charlatans in the fraternity of shamans, but it appears that most often these men genuinely believed in their supernatural powers. How could this be? Imagination, personal conviction, the powers of suggestion, and above all else, the need for a method of handling that which was unknown, the nature of certain diseases. Did a shaman really believe that he could capture the blood of an enemy in a bone container? Probably not, since he could actually see into the container, but he probably did believe that he could gain and control some magical essence of a person's blood. Did a shaman deceive his clientele? Yes, in some respects he tricked them, but in this capacity he was more a magician than a trickster. Thus, the Pitapita shamans were extraordinary persons who served genuinely important functions: they were able to explain in absolute terms that which was otherwise unexplainable. Their actions brought the people a sense of confidence and knowing which better enabled them to deal with the world in which they found themselves.

Source: Roth 1897.

TIWI MARRIAGE AND BROTHERS

For us to judge the ways of other peoples in terms of our own way of life is not surprising, since our system is the only one that we know well. Yet this is an ethnocentric perspective, and it seems to have been the norm for earlier Euro-Americans and for most other peoples, as should be evident from the introductory chapters. Even when we assume an anthropological outlook and leave behind our most crass biases, it remains difficult to accept as normal behaviors which are vastly different from our own. Obviously one of the aims of this book is to convey a greater appreciation of variability as it is evidenced among ethnics. There are no inherent reasons why what we regard as the social role of a father cannot be filled by a woman, why a female cannot be a functioning wife before she reaches puberty, why a person cannot be considered as sociologically dead before his physiological death, or why all political decisions cannot be unanimous. Each of these behaviors is accepted by some people but seems quite bizarre in our terms. So it is with the Tiwi marital system.

Another justification for describing the Tiwi is to convey the fact that the members of a small-scale society need not all behave in a similar manner. A typical ethnographic account is based on the presumption that one individual acts and reacts in much the same way as another. Observers admit freely that some persons are intelligent while others are dull, but by and large the behavior of normal adults is assumed to be much the same. When thoughts about the personalities of ethnics are cast within this framework, it becomes possible to write of a homogeneity of personality type for a particular group. Any observed variability usually is considered to result from unique personal experiences or minute and vaguely conceived genetic differences. Thus, the normative ethnography, while not a mirror image of individuals and their behaviors, is assumed to be an accurate composite of reality. If suppositions such as these are correct, then we would anticipate that among ethnics at a comparatively simple organizational level the behavior of the children of one mother would exhibit a general homogeneity. Biographical sketches of the five sons of a Tiwi woman named Bongdadu, which were collected by Charles W. M. Hart, are instructive concerning personality differences manifest among one particular group of ethnics.

The Tiwi lived, and continue to live, on Melville and Bathurst islands off the coast of northern Australia. The continental coastline could be discerned in the distance, but these people maintained that before the arrival of whites they had no direct contact with the mainland and thought of it only as the home of Tiwi souls. The Tiwi were like the mainland Australians in most respects, but they did not make spear-throwers nor did they perform the circumcision or subincision operations on initiates that were practiced by some mainlanders. Unlike the mainlanders these islanders made elaborately carved and painted grave posts, and some of their social norms, such as the extent of plural marriages and the fact that a female of any age could not be unmarried, were unique. Likewise the Tiwi homeland differed from much of Australia because the islands, comprising about 3,000 square miles and supporting about 1,000 persons in 1928, were a favorable setting for people with a gathering economy.

The nine Tiwi bands, or territorial units, numbered from 100 to 300 persons each, and a single band exploited about 200 square miles of country. Men tended to be identified with a particular band, but women changed their band affiliation rather often during their lives. The bands were primarily the land-holding units with which one was associated, but it was a person's immediate family which loomed as most important in daily life. All the members of a band lived together only briefly during the year, and the component families dispersed widely in order to pursue their hunting and collecting activities most effectively. The family, or household unit, consisted of a nuclear family (a man, his wife, and their children by birth or remarriage) with the addition of multiple wives for an older man and a few other relatives such as bachelor uncles, cousins, or old widowers. During a typical day in a Tiwi camp the women, with some of their children, ranged widely in search of food. They collected anything edible, but vegetable products such as palm nuts and wild yams were found more often than grubs or worms. If a husband was not aged, he hunted, but if he was old his sons and stepsons spent their days tracking and killing wallabies. In the evening after the hunters and collectors had returned, the main meal of the day was prepared. The primary staples were collected by women; thus the more wives a man had, the greater the likelihood that he would be well fed. Each family was self-sufficient, but since the large family groups produced the most food, smaller ones tended to occupy localities at the fringes of larger groups and might appear at the fire of a large household at mealtime. Two brothers with large families might camp together for weeks on end, and with the addition of small fringe families a total of up to fifty persons might be clustered for a relatively long period of time, which suggests the abundance of vegetable products in relatively restricted localities.

Unquestionably the most notable facet of Tiwi life concerned their conventions surrounding marriage. As strange as it may seem, they had a marital system in which all females must be married, irrespective of their age or inclinations. In terms of this ideal an unmarried female could not be accommodated. In Tiwi thinking, the arrangement was eminently reasonable because they believed that a woman became pregnant when a spirit entered her body and therefore the only way in which to insure that the offspring would have a sociological father was to make certain that each female was married at all times. Thus, a neonate, or even an embryo, was betrothed, and a widow was remarried at the grave of her former husband irrespective of her age. Prenatal and immediate postnatal marriage and the immediate remarriage of a widow negated the possibility of the unmarried status for females; in fact, no word existed for an unmarried female. As Hart and Arnold R. Pilling noted, the Tiwi probably were unique among the world's peoples in reducing the nonlegitimacy rate to zero.

Obviously the key figures in the marital system were those individuals who had the right to allot wives. This prerogative belonged to the male family head, the husband of a woman at the time of a female birth. A man bestowed a wife on the basis of the greatest potential for himself, except that certain factors over which he had little or no direct control entered in the decision. He was forced to abide by marriage restrictions within the kinship system and to honor an often complex set of prior promises that he had made to other men. Ideally a husband was selected from among friends, allies, and men who potentially fit these categories. A further characteristic of the system was that it did not involve newborn or young males; infant daughters were given only to adult males, preferably those who were mature and in all likelihood about the same age as the father. A man offered his young daughters to men from whom he was likely to receive daughters. One variation was for a man to offer a neonatal daughter to a younger man, one in his early thirties, because he calculated that this individual would become an important person in later years. In this situation the father was assuming that he could later depend on the younger man for aid because of the obvious favor that he had received. Under ordinary circumstances no man could anticipate obtaining his betrothed wife until he was in his thirties, the girl involved then being about fourteen years old. At this age, if the man had been judged previously as a person of great potential importance, he would receive as many as six wives as a result of earlier betrothals. Men of great social stature sometimes had a cumulative total of about twenty-five wives during a lifetime, but at any one time some of these wives would be infants, girls, or deceased.

In order to become an important male in Tiwi society, it was essential to have been judged as a prestigious person early in life and to have had a life span long enough to actually obtain a large number of wives. Many Tiwi males were not "big men"; in fact, some were so poorly regarded as young adults that no father was willing to commit an infant daughter to them. These males were not doomed to permanent bachelorhood, however, since they could marry a widow. A big man could largely control the dispersal of his daughters, but he could not influence the reallotment of his wives when he died. Since a Tiwi man was always senior to a bestowed wife, he usually died before she did. Such a widow was likely to pass into the hands of another older man, but as she grew very old, she had some voice, through her sons, in the decision about whom she would marry next. Her choice often was to marry someone of no standing who was much younger than she and a friend or age-mate of her sons. The tendency was for sons to exchange each other's mothers in widow remarriages.

In this marital system the pattern was for fathers to arrange the marriages of daughters; if the father were dead, the female's brothers made the decisions, and in their absence the female's sons were the decision makers. However, by a complex renaming system, when a man died his children were renamed by their new stepfather, and this act gave him some influence in deciding whom the females involved might marry. Furthermore, in the marriage theories of the Tiwi a man's mother's brother's daughter was an ideal wife (matrilateral cross-cousin marriage), but this norm was tempered by all of the other intricacies of the marital system. Final marriage customs of note are that sometimes sisters married the same man (sororal polygyny), because the girls' father had committed all of them to a particular individual; such wives who were sisters might be passed on to the same new husband (modified sororate).

Now to return to the Tiwi mother named Bongdadu and her five sons. Among the Tiwi of southern Bathurst Island lived an important man named Turimpi. An indication of his local stature is that before he died in the late 1890s he had married twenty-five women, one of whom was Bongdadu. She bore him three sons who lived to adulthood; their names in English were Antonio, born c. 1883; Mariano, c. 1886; and Louis, c. 1893. Following Turimpi's death Bongdadu remarried and had two additional sons, Tipperary, c. 1900, and Bob, c. 1901. When Hart arrived to study the Tiwi in 1928, the people were no longer following a fully aboriginal way of life, but the impact of dramatic changes was just beginning to be felt.

Initial direct contact with Europeans probably was in 1705 when a party surveyed the island area by ship. The Portuguese raided the islands for slaves for the next hundred years, and this temporarily crystallized Tiwi opposition to all intruders. In 1824 the British founded a fort on Melville Island and abandoned it in 1829; Tiwi-British contacts during the interim were hostile. An occasional shipwrecked crew as well as exploring or other types of parties of Europeans who landed on the islands were speared, robbed, and killed if at all possible. As opposed as the Tiwi were to the intrusions of foreigners, at the same time they nonetheless coveted iron axes and knives and the metal from which these items could be made. In time the Tiwi were not satisfied with receiving iron goods sporadically, and by the turn of the present century they had decided that they would not oppose the establishment of a European settlement in their midst so long as they were assured a continuing source of iron. About this time Malays and others ranged by ship to the islands in search of mother-of-pearl shells, and satisfactory contacts were made with these intruders. In 1911 a Roman Catholic mission was established on Bathurst Island; five years later it was a thriving enterprise. A different avenue of change was represented by Japanese pearlers, who arrived in the mid-1920s and carried on trade with the people as a sideline. From the pearlers the Tiwi received iron tools, tobacco, and European foods in exchange for a single local commodity: sexual access to young women. It is not difficult to imagine the Roman Catholic view of the Japanese pearlers, infant betrothal, and plural marriages; the missionaries did their best to destroy the aboriginal system among the younger generation. The Japanese, however, gave more goods than the mission and asked for less in return; this had pitted the mission against the pearlers at the time Hart arrived. Under these circumstances of change he recorded the biographical sketches of Bongdadu's sons.

The Tiwi expected the eldest son, Antonio, to replace his deceased father, Turimpi, as a person of authority, on whom they could depend for guidance and effective leadership. It was anticipated that he would mold public opinion at meetings, express ideas with conviction, and be a fierce contestant in tribal fights. However, he was not that kind of man. He is described by Hart as being insecure, vacillating, and uncomfortable in public life. His position in the controversy between the Roman Catholic mission and the Japanese pearlers illustrates the point. The Japanese favored men with many wives, while the missionaries deplored such individuals. Antonio had a number of wives, but the locality in which he lived was not one with Japanese contacts. Although he had no opportunity to offer any of his wives to the Japanese, he profited from the material rewards of others who had, and he contemplated a trip to the area where the Japanese were working to see what was happening for himself. On the other hand, Antonio apologized to the missionaries for his many wives. He spent a great deal of time at the mission and was sycophantic toward the missionaries, yet he was deplored by them. Antonio was expected to be a leader, but he did not have the personal qualifications to become one in spite of his high social position by birth. He was most content when at an isolated camp where he could hunt with his dogs and play with his children.

The second son, Mariano, was a relatively young man when the

mission was founded, and soon he became the go-between for missionaries and Tiwi. In the eyes of the missionaries he was an almost ideal
person to fill this role. He came from an important family, was from the
immediate locality, was young enough to be flexible, and was willing to
work for the mission. During the founding days of the mission he performed his obligations well enough to become a trusted interpreter and a
steady worker. By 1928 Mariano's position had eroded considerably at
the mission because he had rather frequent quarrels with the missionaries.
After such an episode he would go to Port Darwin, where he always was
able to obtain good jobs with prestigious whites. In spite of the fact that
he was the Tiwi most familiar with the ways of whites, he was respected
by the tradition-oriented men because he was both forceful and articulate
in expressing his views. What was his position in the mission-Japanese
dispute? He fully supported the stand of the mission, reasoning that if a
man had only one wife he would not consider lending her to the Japanese.
Hart's characterization of Mariano includes such words as determined,
aggressive, and bumptious, and conveys that he had a sincere but exaggerated idea of his own self-importance. The people listened to him, but
because they did not really like him, he enlisted no following.

Louis and his older brother Mariano were similar in a number of
respects; each tended to be a loner who was severe, dedicated, and un-
friendly. The world of the white man was the center of Mariano's greatest
attention, whereas Louis apparently focused much of his life on sex and
seductions. Among the other Tiwi, Louis was famous for his conquests,
but whether he fully deserved his reputation is not clear. He was accused
vehemently and often, but since he did not verbally respond, it is difficult
to establish whether the accusations were justified. The opportunities for
seductions were frequent since women sought vegetable foods alone and
in the brush where young men often hunted. Old men made almost constant accusations against young men about seduction episodes, and no
young man could be expected to be above suspicion for more than a few
months at a time. Louis, however, was singled out for criticism much
more often than his age-mates, and contrary to the established norms, he
did not attempt to deny his participation. He simply said nothing, remaining silent and withdrawn even when faced with the most heated accusations. Furthermore, he took no part in formal or informal decision making; in fact, he was reluctant to express his views about any subject. Apart
from his reputation for seduction, he had one other outstanding quality,
which was that he fought well. Even this he did alone, and he did not
allow himself to be drawn into the disputes of others. In general he
appears to have been a highly successful person with respect to the few
activities in which he participated wholeheartedly.

Tipperary, better known by his diminutive of Tip, was nearly ten years younger than his youngest stepbrother. When he was first seen by Hart, Tip was just approaching the age at which he might be expected to offer his opinions cautiously after his elders had spoken. Although he often spoke out of turn, just like his stepbrother Mariano, Tip was not considered to be brazen in doing so; in fact, people seldom seemed aware that he was ignoring proper decorum. The reason was the quality of his humor. He was a genuinely funny person, without malice in his humor and without being a clown or buffoon. He lacked the self-consciousness of his brothers, and Hart states that he "was a person whose whole life was devoted to laughter." Once in the middle of the night it was thought that a ghost was about, and the persons in the camp huddled fearfully around their fires. Finally when it seemed to have left, Tip remarked in a loud voice, "Perhaps it's gone to Port Darwin to see a movie," which dispelled the tension immediately. Thus, his humor was not necessarily frivolous; often it seemed to be a catalyst for some new form of action. His fun-filled mind probably carried over into his mature years because humor was not limited to youth among the Tiwi. Tip had many friends, but his brothers were not numbered among them.

The youngest of the brothers, Bob, was a "complete nonentity"; he did not express himself in either a positive or negative manner. Although youthful and not expected to be generally assertive, even when a situation arose in which he should have taken a stand, he said little and was uncomfortable in his actions. Thus, about all that can be said about Bob is that he was colorless and bland.

As Hart points out in his article about the sons of Bongdadu, no firm conclusions may be drawn about the personality differences among ethnics based on these data. The biographical sketches of the brothers nonetheless suggest clearly that rather striking behavioral differences do in fact exist among ethnics who so often have been characterized as homogeneous in personality type. Without recourse to psychological tests it appears as though the spectrum of Tiwi personality types is as broad as might be expected in much more complex societies. It is doubtful that Tiwi contacts with Roman Catholic missionaries and Japanese pearlers had modified their personalities in any basic manner, but the acculturative setting did provide a broader base on which behaviors could be expressed.

Sources: Hart 1954; Hart and Pilling 1960.

THE GURURUMBA'S RED MAN

It is a long-established tradition for professional ethnographers to be essentially self-trained in their appointed task. In the classroom and library a student learns a vast amount about ethnics and seeks to fathom the implications of their behaviors, and yet typically he is given little if any methodological preparation for collecting ethnographic data. The usual procedure has been for a museum curator or senior professor to suggest, or insist, that a student work among a particular people or in a specific area. The tyro then attempts to become familiar with the language, read about the area, and talk with others who have been there or at nearby localities. After being offered general advice about dealing with the "natives" by his superior and provided with usually inadequate funding, he is sent off for a year or more. Following his field experience he hopefully publishes a satisfactory account of the people studied. As surprising as it may seem, ethnographers seldom have provided their readers with insightful discussions of their actual field experience. They write chapter after chapter about esoteric particulars but usually offer only cursory remarks about their actual methods for obtaining the data. These are noted in the introduction, if they are mentioned at all. Thus, in spite of the fact that thousands of ethnographies have been written, surprisingly little has been recorded concerning how ethnographers actually go about their business. The net result is that each generation of students faces essentially the same uncertainties concerning successful field methods as those which had confronted their teachers. Given this general scene, it is refreshing to find an ethnographic account dating from the late 1950s which is developed around an ethnographer's methods and techniques for coming to understand the people whom he studied.

In recent years New Guinea has attracted more ethnographers than any area of comparable size in the world. The reason is that the last bastion of pristine ethnics exists in the highlands. In the eastern sector of this great island are the towering Bismark Mountains, and from them the plunging streams of the Asaro River drainage cut a series of steep-sided gorges to separate upland areas some 5,500 feet in elevation. These cool and damp expanses are covered with lush vegetation and are separated from one another by precipitous slopes. In one such sector live the Gururumba, who like other highlanders, cultivate sweet potatoes as their primary staple and own pigs as their most important domestic animals. They occupy scattered villages which are associated in autonomous territorial and political units based on a common dialect.

By 1959 the Gururumba had been under the loose control of the Australian government for about ten years, a road had been built into the area, and government officials occasionally visited for a few days at a time. The only whites living in the general vicinity were a missionary and a coffee planter. In 1959 the ethnographer Philip L. Newman arrived with his wife and two children at the road's end, prepared to stay temporarily at a government house near the Gururumba community of Miruma. They found to their surprise that over 300 persons were gathered in the vicinity. A partial explanation for so many people being assembled at Miruma was that an Australian medical doctor was there to see and treat them. This official also took the opportunity to summon the people together to explain that the Newmans were not government representatives or missionaries, but had come to study the "fashions" of the people. The medical doctor soon left, and only then did the Newmans realize that another reason so many people had gathered was in order to attend a betrothal ceremony. The Gururumba previously had had white visitors arrive to view an occasion such as this one, and they assumed that the newcomers would follow the pattern of other whites and leave within a short time. The Newmans and their extensive amount of goods were examined with intense curiosity by great numbers of visitors. Older women in particular were curious about the bodies of these novel whites and took the unprecedented opportunity to examine their skin and hair with care. One man removed the ethnographer's boots and socks in order to study them as well as his feet. Within a short time bundles of food were placed at their door, and by accepting these presentations, they unknowingly became involved in a host of exchanges with diverse people.

"Red men," as whites were perceived and termed, appear to have been regarded originally as "ghosts," and while the anthropologist clearly was not a ghost, he did possess great quantities of material goods, which to these people indicated unknown and therefore magical resources. Thus, like other whites Newman was an important person since among the Gururumba wealth and material goods were prized and greatly desired. When the people came to realize that these whites planned to stay with them for an extended period of time, they were pleased at the prospect. Not only were they the only local people to have their own red man, which was an honor to them, but much more importantly, he appeared to be an obvious avenue to material goods. Rumor had it that he would open a store with extremely low priced items for sale. With a minimum of bargaining a house was built for the visitors and the study was begun.

After settling in, the ethnographer's first observations focused on those visual characteristics of the people most novel from a United Statesian viewpoint. It was noted that men walked in front of women, that persons either sitting or standing in groups sought close body contact with individuals nearby, and that when people counted on their fingers, they began with a little finger and held the added digits close together. At first it appeared that everyone dressed alike, but it soon became obvious that there was variability, especially in the clothing styles of men. The most common male apparel was a belt; at the front a piece of cloth or netting was attached and at the rear was a bundle of leaves or grass. Other males wore tight-fitting G-strings of bark cloth or the shorts of red men. On their heads men wore crescent-shaped headdresses of wickerwork, a headpiece of fern leaves, or a knit cap. In a man's nose was an ornament made from shell, wood, or bird quill, and around his arms and legs were bands of diverse materials. Women had facial tattooes, and their dress was more homogeneous. From a belt hung string aprons; the one in front nearly reached the knees, and a shorter one was fastened to the belt in back. A woman always carried a netted bag which covered her back, whether or not the bag contained anything. These were observations that any traveler might have made, but an ethnographer goes on to make more important observations, whereas most travelers pass to another exotic scene inhabited by another strange people.

It is in a sense reasonable to liken the learning of an ethnographer during a field study to that of a child acquiring his cultural perspective. The major disadvantage for the ethnographer is that although he is past the stage of childhood he does not know many childish things. Thus, he must acquire ordinary childhood knowledge rapidly. The Gururumba had a minor ceremony during which young boys were taken to a vantage point from which most of the upper Asaro valley could be seen. Here the features of the landscape which were essential to an adult's perspective were pointed out to them. The ceremony was held for Newman, and in this manner, as well as from his general observations, he learned to see the country through Gururumba eyes. He was told which sectors harbored friends or enemies, that ridges bounded human groups, and that directions were organized in terms of up- or downhill, up- or downstream, or toward or away from a particular place.

Once he began to assimilate geographical knowledge, Newman drafted a map of the region, and it became obvious that habitation clusters existed in a number of different settings and served distinct purposes. Isolated houses were built near those gardens which were so far from a man's village that he needed to live near his crops during the period when farming activities occupied most of his time; it was here too that he usually kept his pigs. In an ordinary village about twenty-five houses were arranged in a single line along a comparatively narrow ridge-top. The circular walls of a house were constructed from upright poles between which grass was stuffed and held in place with strips of bark; the roof was conical, with a long vertical pole at the apex. The single door of a house opened on a path that ran the length of the village. In the front portion of a dwelling was a hearth, and behind it was a sleeping area, sometimes separated by a low partition. On the opposite side of the village path from the houses were one or two structures, men's houses, where adult males lived. Around particular clusters of houses or wards, as well as around the entire village, fences were built. Other smaller communities were ceremonial centers, and here the houses were arranged in a rectangular plan. Along three sides were circular houses, and on the fourth side was a shed-like structure built to accommodate visitors attending ceremonies. The ceremonial center itself was surrounded by a fence, and within it another fence enclosed an area where rituals often were focused.

The contacts with Australian government representatives led to a change in the size and location of settlements. When warfare had been suppressed and at the government's encouragement, most people abandoned their defensible ridge-top settlements and moved to lower elevations where farmland was more productive. Some conservative people, however, still feared the open grasslands for supernatural reasons as well as because enemies had been encountered here in the recent past. They refused to settle in the new communities, and this led to the continued occupation of some old-style villages. The new settlements were larger than the old villages, a pattern encouraged by the Australian government in order to make local administration less difficult. In the large new villages the families from each of the old settlements lived in fenced-in wards, each with its own men's house.

A more intensive investigation was required to establish the exploitation patterns for diverse ecological zones. The highest zone, from about 8,200 feet to the tops of the divides, was a humid forest with moss-laden vegetation. No one lived there, but it was utilized as a source for wild animals and plant products. Below this zone and extending down to 7,500 feet was the land farmed most intensively in aboriginal times, but the steepness of the hillsides made cultivation difficult. When fear from attacks by enemies was past, the people were able to utilize a lower level, 6,000 to 7,500 feet, for their gardens, and it was here that all of the new villages were situated. In this zone, garden plots bounded by fences were cultivated by a number of families. From here to the valley floor the dominant vegetation was a tall, reed-like grass which was important as a manufacturing material. Game could be hunted here, but fear of the area lingered, since enemies had lurked here in the recent past. The ethnographer finds it most helpful to map the pattern of physical settlements and relate these to economic units as well as to the landscape. With this task completed, the time had arrived to consider the social lives of the people in detail.

The well-established technique for isolating social units initially is to collect genealogies, and Newman began to gather this information for the residents of Miruma. The task was tedious since it required interviewing all adults and asking each innumerable questions. The standard list of queries includes information about an informant's relatives by blood and marriage in terms of their names, birth order, kinship status, whether such individuals are living or dead, and, if they are alive, where they reside. This corpus of data provides essential information about social life, and through it many sociofacts are revealed. For example, it was found that in Gururumba kinship terminology close relatives often were grouped by the use of comparatively few terms (e.g., the word for "father" was also used for father's elder brother, father's father, and mother's father); spinsters did not exist, but about 4 percent of the men were bachelors; about 10 percent of all marriages were polygynous; and a man's first wife often left him because of her own discontent or because she was forced out by the man. Thus, the genealogical statistics were not only important in themselves but served the added purpose of offering clues and insights into more complex social involvements.

The genealogies revealed the kinship basis for social life as well as the composition of household units. The next problem was to determine the nature of other social clusters, and this could be learned only by becoming familiar with adults, plotting their activity patterns, and discussing attitudes of villagers toward one another. The Gururumba, who numbered 1,121 persons, maintained six villages over a thirty-square-mile area. Although they were allied closely with some adjacent peoples, they were the enemies of others. The Gururumba considered themselves to be of common descent and were joined into a number of patrisibs (groups of persons presumed to have been descended from a common ancestor in the male line). These patrisibs united in the defense of their area and cooperated with each other in rituals and in hunting. In the routine of living, members of one's patrisib were most important since it was these individuals who most closely cooperated as hosts or guests and who united in warfare. Sib unity is well reflected in the kinship terms employed by the members. For example, any elderly person of ego's sib was addressed as "father" or as "mother," while persons nearer ego's age were "elder brother" or "elder sister." In addition, if a man killed a person from another sib, irrespective of the reason, he could expect his sib mates to rally to his defense in the event of retaliation. If a man killed a person from his own sib, he was forced to defend himself alone against the near relatives of the deceased. A sib's importance was further indicated by the fact that it was the exogamous unit (i.e., a man must find a wife from another sib).

The patrisibs were in turn comprised of patrilineages (persons who traced actual genealogical ties along a male line, as from father to son and to grandson), and from six to fifteen patrilineages were represented in a village. However, the members of a community did not address or refer to fellow villagers by kinship terms irrespective of their lineage affinities. Instead they used personal names and teknonymous designations (an individual was addressed or referred to as the parent of a child, e.g., the father of John). In day-to-day village life, sib and lineage ties were not overwhelmingly important; the persons of a settlement were united by virtue of the fact that they lived together. It was at the village level that disputes were adjudicated between members, that certain rituals were performed, and arrangements were made concerning bridewealth at the time of marriages.

Once the organization of kinship and settlement groups had been determined, it was possible for Newman to study the activities of individuals. Personal behaviors were categorized in terms of roles or Gururumba expectations based on age, sex, and abilities. Role expectations governed most behavior and provided the guidelines for interactions between all persons. The distinct roles were recognized by observing what people did, listening to informants as they described what people should do, and attending meetings at which disputes were resolved. Certain duties were the obligations of men and others of women, and only rarely was there an overlap. Men prepared the ground for gardens, built the fences, and dug drainage ditches when necessary. Women cultivated the ground further, planted sweet potatoes and the other vegetables which were staples, and did most of the weeding. Men planted and cared for sugar cane, bananas, taro, and yams, which were foods for special occasions. Meals were prepared by both men and women, but men alone cooked the large amounts of food for festivities. The routine care of pigs was woman's work, but these animals were owned, killed, traded, or given away by men. In general it was found that women exercised little control over property apart from objects of personal use and spells associated with gardening magic.

The division of economic labors and the norms of property control were important, but in a sense they were a comparatively minor aspect of the male-female distinctions. The dichotomy ran much deeper and was in part based on the physiological differences between men and women. Menstrual blood and exposure to menstruating women was thought to weaken a man, lead to his illness, and even cause death. Thus, male well-being was contingent in part on the avoidance of all contact with this contaminant. Then, too, certain key roles were closed to females; only a man could become a shaman, warrior, or person of renown. Men played flutes in the gardens and forests in order to promote the growth of plants, yet women were prohibited from seeing the flutes and were led to believe that their music was the call of a magic bird. Summarily, recognition of the male-female role distinctions led to the viability of the Gururumba as a people.

Much of the time adults were involved in gardening and the other activities expected of them because of their age and sex. Some persons, however, emerged as notably different from others because of unique personal attributes. They were isolated with clarity only after intensive study, since they dressed like other persons, bore no special badges of office, and lived in the manner of other villagers. Foremost among these individuals were "big men," who usually were in their forties and were renowned for their strength, abilities as warriors, oratorical skills, and aggressive manner. Such persons were skilled at manipulating economic exchanges, articulating an acceptable compromise view in disputes, and participating in certain rituals. As the reputation of a big man grew, he attracted a larger and larger following, but only rarely was such a person able to extend his influence over more than several villages. The second major cluster of extraordinary persons was that of shamans, who summoned their skills to cure, anticipate the future, bring lovers together, and control the weather. Shamans were older men, and because they were few in number, they sometimes traveled considerable distances in their practice. Curing techniques included divining the cause of illness, which usually was diagnosed as supernatural. It often was established that a sorcerer had placed a foreign substance in the victim's body, and it was extracted by magical means. The victim appeared usually to have been cured, or his malady relieved, through faith in a shaman's abilities.

After individuals had been identified and characterized socially, the next problem was to establish the manner in which persons who occupied different roles interacted with one another. Observations centered on the persons involved and on the course of a paramount activity in Gururumba life. The focal area in which to establish the quality of social integration became obvious: it was that of property exchanges. The compelling interest of these people in property found expression in an avid desire for material wealth, in conversations about worldly goods, in their enjoyment of taking stock of what they owned, and in fondling wealth. Men even carried small sticks on which were marks to indicate the thickness of the fat layers on their pigs. It was normal and ordinary for a person to demand a puff on a cigarette, a bit of food, or an item on loan. The owner resisted, but if he finally submitted, he did so shouting "take." Activities and behaviors such as these found more formal and important expression in the exchange of food and material goods; the manipulation of property gave them greater satisfaction than actual ownership. Individuals frequently were involved in carrying out exchanges, because at each major transition and many minor ones in the life of a person property exchanges were necessary. Exchanges honored births, namings, the first time an infant walked, and a host of other personal occasions as well as more momentous events such as making peace with an enemy group. Before the actual exchange took place, the food and goods offered, at times including tons of property, were arranged in elaborate displays.

Food production and gift-giving activities were intimately linked and were functions of the male role. Men raised bananas, sugar cane, and taro, which were the most appropriate cultigens for food exchanges and feasts. In order to have desirable foods available at the proper times, they were planted at staggered intervals. For major celebrations, such as the initiation of a son or the marriage of a daughter, special plantings were made as much as a year in advance of the anticipated event. In a like manner an individual's herd of pigs was managed so that he would have animals available for any anticipated or unexpected exchange. Quite obviously a big man was deeply involved in the production of pigs and foods for feasts. The activities of one big man, who was the leader of a particular men's house in Miruma, were plotted by Newman. He found that this big man's lineage was the largest in the sector of the community in which he lived; thus he had many relatives on whose aid he could depend. A man of note as a warrior, he had four wives at the time of the study, and had had a total of twelve wives. He attracted others to the village because of his leadership abilities, and had even introduced an important change in the pig festival. More careful examination revealed that this man had greater economic resources at his command than any other villager. Of greatest importance many persons were bound to him by economic debt and dependence. Through the economic activities of these dependents as well as his own highly successful property manipulations, this big man was able to function not only as a notable provider, but also as an influential leader.

The activities involving the sacred side of living came under scrutiny following the study of secular life because such behaviors, while sometimes readily observable, often are difficult to understand. For example, in one garden of each man was a fenced area enclosing a small, dome-shaped structure with an entrance and a miniature oven in front of it. These complexes were obvious to even a casual observer and seemingly served no objective purpose, but in time their place in the supernatural system was realized. The Gururumba felt that there were two classes of transparent, male spirits manifest in semihuman form but capable of assuming fully human countenance. In one group were forest spirits; the others were spirits of the lowlands. They lived in clearly recognized spots, and if a person wandered near, a spirit might attack and cause his illness

A "big man" holding forth before a pile of food and material goods assembled for a redistribution celebration (Courtesy of Philip Newman).

or even death, not from malice but for self-protection. In order to guard himself, his family, and his resources, a man provided quarters for a spirit who would aid him. This spirit lived in the dome-shaped structure in the man's garden, and bits of meat were offered it as food in return for protection of the gardens and pigs. An entire family spoke to its spirit protector when meals were prepared; this was the only time that a family functioned as a separate unit in a ritual task. Other more diverse rituals were associated with many points regarded as critical in the life cycle of an individual. A birth was surrounded by restrictions for the father in order to prevent his loss of health through contamination with the after-birth and blood. For a short time after a birth the father refrained from any activity which involved pounding, since it was thought to be danger-ous to the neonate and would break his bones. Rituals were conducted to name an offspring and to prevent sibling rivalry. These and many other observances protected an offspring and stressed his lineage ties. A cere-monial set was focused in the men's house of a ward, and thus involved a number of lineages whose members lived near each other. When boys reached ten to fifteen years of age, they took up residence in the men's house, where they were hazed and instructed in behavior fitting for adult males. The existence of the sacred flutes was revealed to them, and they were taught to play the music which was associated with fertility, growth, and strength. Thus, the activities in the men's house integrated the men with one another in yet another set of social ties which focused on sacred activities.

The most momentous ceremony was the pig festival held at intervals of five or more years by a sib as a unit. The host sib invited guests from one or more neighboring sibs and persons from distant but friendly eth-nics. The festivities were announced by blowing "pig flutes," and after the guests had assembled, great quantities of food and property were placed on exhibit. Planks which were from a few inches to several feet in height were decorated with elaborate, multicolored geometric designs for such an occasion and were paraded by boys and youths. The designs symbol-ized the prosperity and growth of the sib. These often are referred to as gerua boards in the literature and were made to honor the ghosts of the dead. The climax of a pig festival came when hundreds of pigs were butchered, and the number and size of the rows of cooked pigs would long be remembered by guests and hosts alike. Later the gerua boards were placed on display in the fenced area near the center of a village as symbols of sib vitality.

Fertility, growth, and strength were abstract conceptual foci of the Gururumba, and these were manifest in physical well-being as well as in economic productivity. Late in the field study the supernatural dimensions of these qualities came to be understood as an abstract system which was not verbalized by the people but which integrated the culture as a whole. Songs were sung about plant growth, spells were invoked to make gardening tools productive, amulets and charms were employed to ward off evil and to attract good, and rituals were performed to increase the productivity of plants. The overall purposes of these and other forms of magic were pieced together by the ethnographer only after intensive fieldwork led to the broadest understanding of the Gururumba.

The step-by-step discussion of his ethnographic methodology, accompanied by the actual findings, makes Newman's account a highly useful guide for a prospective fieldworker. Furthermore, he offers the reader a broad account of one of the diminishing number of ethnics to survive into our times. Without recourse to a study of this nature, ethnographers who are tyros might obtain certain classes of information in the sequence offered in this work. It is doubtful, however, that they would accomplish their task as efficiently or as effectively without reading it, even though the people they are concerned with would not have the same key sociocultural characteristics. This work is valuable because it emphasizes that there is a logical and orderly sequence in which one's ethnographic knowledge about a people expands. Learning adequately about another culture is not a haphazard process, and the beginner might conduct his research more effectively after studying a presentation such as this.

Source: Newman 1965.

IFUGAO LAW

Roy F. Barton, the author of a widely respected work about the legal system of the Ifugao, observed that, "There is no law so strong as custom." He was explaining that the social norms which pilot our lives are less likely to be disregarded than written rules, regulations, and laws. The gradual changes which do occur in customs may be almost imperceptible, for there are no rigid codes against which to plot shifts in conventions. By describing the manner in which the Ifugao adjudicated disputes in the absence of written laws, formal courts, or meaningful political organization, we learn not only about the operation of a complex judicial system, but also about the validity of conventions serving as a firm basis for legal actions.

The Ifugao lived in the north-central area of Luzon in the Philippine Islands and numbered about 120,000 in the early decades of the century. Many other peoples of Luzon had extended exposure to Islamic and

Christian intruders long before the turn of the present century. However, living as they did in the island's interior and surrounded by other aboriginal peoples, the Ifugao were largely unaffected by the Spanish, and they were only loosely controlled by American authorities at the time Barton worked among them soon after the turn of the present century.

The Ifugao occupied about 750 square miles of rugged mountainous terrain. The occupants of each valley were friendly toward one another but usually were hostile to settlers of other valleys. Precipitation was heavy throughout most of the year, and the steepness of the mountain slopes led to erosion of the rich soil, leaving a fine clay base. In some localities deer, wild carabao (buffalo), and wild pigs were an important source of food, and usually they were hunted with spears. A small number of fish were captured in lakes after the beginning of the rainy season. These fish bred and matured rapidly and were "planted" in large rice fields, only to be harvested later in significant quantities. Wild plant products were collected, but it was from cultivated plant species that most food was obtained. In order to raise sweet potatoes, the primary staple, mountain slopes were cleared and burned over, after which the soil was loosened with digging sticks. A few weeks later small pockets were scooped out of the soil, and slips from the ends of sweet potato vines were planted. Although these plants would grow nearly anywhere, new plots were cleared each two or three years for the best production. The second staple, rice, required more careful cultivation. In order to create flat plots where rice plants could be irrigated, great networks of terraces were constructed. In general, the terrain was so steep that it was necessary to build retaining walls; on some occasions these were over twenty feet in height in order to create a plot eleven feet in width. Along the mountainsides in many sectors the terraces extended from elevations of about 1,500 to 4,500 feet. Before the annual planting, the flow of water was stopped, the terraces repaired, and the soil turned over and piled into mounds to aerate. After the seeds planted in special beds had sprouted, the water was turned on in the irrigated plots, and the soil was leveled in order that the women might plant the seedlings. At three different times during the next two months women pushed the weeds that had grown and the scum that had formed into the soil in order to enrich it. The individual rice plants were pruned for optimum growth, and any diseased sections of a plant were removed and burned. At harvest time the stalks were cut individually and bound into bundles, after which they were carried to a granary and stored beneath it in order to dry. Harvesting rice involved a great deal of physical work for adults and youths alike, but it was also a happy time of feasting and drinking.

The Ifugao house was built on an elevated wooden platform supported by four posts. The wall posts, plates, and supports for the low, conical roof were mortised, and the house frame was covered with mats. A dwelling of this nature served a family for many years. In this area with a warm climate the clothing styles of the men and women were simple. Men and women did not normally wear a garment on the upper part of their bodies. The men wore cloth breechclouts, and the women wore knee-length skirts of cloth. Both sexes favored a wide variety of adornments, which included necklaces, bracelets, and ear ornaments. These people were divided into three distinct social classes. In order to establish one's self as a wealthy man it was necessary for an individual to enlist the aid of his fellow villagers in building a lounging bench of wood. In conjunction with this enterprise he gave an expensive feast honoring the occasion. However, a man born into a wealthy family was not required to validate his position in this manner. A wealthy man did not have any political power, but he did have considerable social influence as a result of his riches. Persons who had very small rice fields or none at all were considered poor, and they either became servants or lived as tenants on the lands of others. Between the rich and the poor were those families who were able to support themselves most of the year but had to borrow rice just before harvest time. They were obligated to repay this rice two or threefold from their crop. The Ifugao were customarily involved in a great deal of borrowing and lending, especially in times of crises. Paying debts and collecting on loans led to many legal actions.

Breaches of behavioral expectations were either violations of taboos, which often had magical implications, or violations of customs, which involved other persons. To ignore a taboo was an "evil way," but because it did not affect other people, it was considered a matter of individual concern only. For example, it was taboo for a pregnant woman to wear an encircling string of beads because this would make childbirth difficult. Somewhat similarly, for a man to defecate when his brother was near could bring harm, but the matter was of concern only to the individuals involved. Breaking a taboo was acting beyond the bounds of propriety, but it was far more serious when the customary rights concerning property, resources, or the behavior of unrelated persons were infringed on. Legal action was taken only when a person from one family in some way injured or jeopardized the position of an individual from an unrelated family. Given this ground rule, all disputes between the members of a single family were their personal concern and were not a matter for extrafamilial attention except in very unusual circumstances. If a murder took place within a family or incest occurred, these were family matters. Even distant relatives involved in crimes would be excused or only light fines imposed because of the kinship bond.

The major crimes against other people were murder, sorcery, adultery, and theft; punishment was in terms of fines or execution. Entire families became involved in litigations as a result of actions by individual members. Not only was the person who committed a wrong against another family responsible for his act, but his relatives were nearly as liable, their degree of liability depending on how closely related they were to the offender. Familial unity was to be preserved above all else, and families were guided by the principle of pressing their demands as forcefully as possible while at the same time resisting the pressures of other families with the greatest possible agility. Given these circumstances, the degree of fine or punishment depended on the strength and social solidarity of the family. The vigor with which an individual supported his family's interests depended on the closeness of his kin ties with the accused and any other persons involved, his general loyalty to the family group, and the evidence bearing on the case. When a claim was pressed, the punishment or fine was levied preferably against the guilty party, but if this course of action was impossible, a near relative, such as a brother, was held in account. A cousin could be held accountable only if the culprit had no closer male relatives. A total fine was divided into either six or ten units of unequal proportions, and it was rendered in units of rice. The amount of a fine depended partially on the type of crime committed and partially on whether the culprit involved was rich, poor, or average in terms of wealth. For example, a certain form of adultery required payment equal to eighteen pesos for a rich person, nearly five pesos for a poor person, and about nine pesos for someone of moderate wealth. The first unit of a fine total was of the greatest value and went to the injured party. The second portion was smaller and went to an intermediary or negotiator, and the others went to the relatives of the offended party according to the efforts that they had exerted in his behalf. Sometimes the negotiator's fee was calculated outside of the actual settlement, in which case the relatives of the injured person received all but the first payment.

If a person had conceived or planned a crime, whether or not he actually participated, he was considered directly responsible and was the person most likely to be punished. Assume that a man planned a murder and enlisted the aid of others in carrying it out. If a shaman were consulted and divined that the venture would be a success, it was begun. Even though the organizer might not be able to participate because of some sorcery on the part of an enemy, he still bore the primary responsibility for any murder that his helpers committed during the venture. If a spear thrown at an enemy killed him, the "thrower" was next in line after the "principal" in terms of responsibility. Of lesser responsibility were the accomplices, persons who helped to plan or carry out the offense. Finally, there was a separate category for the "informer," who was anyone aiding the party in locating the victim. The revenging relatives of the victim would make every effort to kill the principal and the thrower as well as one or two others who were involved. If only the principal could be killed, it was incumbent on the thrower to be cautious, for he would be the next intended victim. However, if the principal died a natural death, then the thrower became the primary target for vengeance. If it became impossible to take vengeance on either the principal or the thrower, then the other members of the party were singled out for death.

The decision of a man to purposefully murder another was made after a serious discussion of the matter with family members; thus, it was quite reasonable that the entire family should share in the guilt. With a few notable exceptions which will be discussed later, when a life was taken, at least one other was demanded in return. Even though a settlement might be made by a retaliatory murder, animosity continued to exist between the families involved because total retribution, meaning the return of the dead, was impossible. This condition led to feuds, or murders being committed in revenge for other killings. Feuds within a district were settled, if at all possible, through the influence of locally important persons. If feuds were between families of different local districts, they did not pit all the inhabitants of one district against those of another. Feuds between districts were not likely to stop until there was intermarriage between the contesting families or until some outstanding member of the families involved contracted a particular disease, such as tuberculosis, which was taken as a sign that certain deities desired to have a peace ceremony performed.

A less personalized type of conflict also existed; it grouped the population of one district against those of a distant district in warfare. The method of warfare was for a small party to attack from ambush and without warning. The goal was to take as many heads of men and women as possible and then escape. In the event that a misdeed was performed without malice, it was excused as accidental. For example, a man might be killed by a spear during a wild pig hunt. If the man had jumped in the spear's trajectory by accident, no revenge could be taken. In the same vein, if a drunk person performed a criminal act short of murder, did so without malice, and repented his actions when sober, the penalty was far less severe than if the act had been committed under normal circumstances. Cases in which the killing of a person clearly was accidental were settled with the payment of a fine, the amount being calculated on the basis of the class standing of the deceased person. A man who was unable to pay his fine immediately assumed the balance of the payment as a debt; if he died without paying the full amount, the responsibility to do so fell to his children.

The most common crime was for sorcery to be used against someone, and the most dangerous form of sorcery was soul stealing. A shaman performed a series of rituals in secret in order to summon the ancestral spirits of the person whom he was hired to kill. With the aid of evil spirits he assembled at the same time, the shaman was able to place the man's soul into a blue-bottle fly, a dragonfly, or a bee. Then when one of these insects came to drink from a container of rice wine the shaman set before himself, it was caught in the container and the vessel was tightly closed. The victim's soul thus was held captive, and he was expected to die soon. If a shaman performed this ritual against a member of his own family and was discovered, he was killed; this is the only instance of a family acting against one of its members. Some persons, either innocently or intentionally, had the "evil eye" and could bring disaster to others. Likewise, words might bring harm to someone or to his property, even though they were spoken without evil intent. For example, one man might comment on the superior quality of another man's litter of pigs and the piglets subsequently would die. Accusations that sorcery was employed through looks or words were made only if strong grounds for suspicion existed; if a man had been accused of sorcery in the past, he was likely to be especially suspect. If someone could prove that another had employed a shaman to perform the soul-stealing ceremony, this was grounds for murdering the planner; for lesser offenses fines were levied.

Two different forms of adultery were recognized as crimes against convention. In the first form a spouse had intercourse out of wedlock but in an affair which was not flaunted before others. The second form was aggravated; the guilty party might openly carry on the relationship or act in a blatantly discourteous or insulting manner toward a marriage partner. In either situation both the man and woman involved were considered as equally liable for punishment. On occasion, a person might forgive his spouse without forgiving the other party. Acceptable proof of adultery was confession by one of the parties or circumstantial evidence such as the couple's sleeping together at night. In theory all cases of adultery required the payment of a fine, but if a couple were caught in the act, the adulterer could be killed. The relatives of the deceased might complain that the dead person should have been given the opportunity to pay the fine and killed only if he did not do so. When a case was brought to light, the standard rule was for each guilty party to pay a fine to his or her spouse and to the offended spouse of the partner. Women were more likely to be accused than men. If a case were not generally known to have existed, a knowing and offended spouse was not likely to take action. However, if the case were common knowledge, then self-respect was at stake, and this required a judgment.

Certain rules of conduct guided the internal legal activities of a family. The principal guideline was that a family could not act against its own members except in very unusual circumstances. Brothers naturally were allied. Cousins and half-brothers seldom acted against each other, and if they did so, mutual relatives intervened to bring about a settlement. It sometimes happened that a relative to whom one clearly owed support was in the wrong. In this situation, the offender secretly was advised by his family to compromise. Distant kin could be litigated against, but to do so was in poor taste. If it became necessary for a man to take sides between two relatives, he supported the individual who was more closely related.

When normal social relations between families were disrupted by a dispute, the members broke off all contacts with each other. They interacted through a go-between whose duty it was to bring about a peaceful settlement. His role was extremely important in Ifugao society, and the only qualification was that he not be a close relative of any contestant. As Barton (1919:94) has written, "He wheedles, coaxes, flatters, threatens, drives, scolds, insinuates. He beats down the demands of the plaintiffs or prosecution, and bolsters up the proposals of the defendants until a point be reached at which the two parties may compromise." The go-between listened to the testimony of each side and presented its view to the other. He made every effort to bring about a successful settlement so that he would receive a sizable fee and gain a reputation as a successful mediator. If one of the parties refused to listen to the reasoning of the mediator, the latter followed him into his house with a war knife in hand to force him to listen. Invariably the accused held out as long as possible, but if he overextended this right, he could lose respect and possibly his life.

Under certain circumstances, when an individual consistently denied that he was guilty or when others doubted his guilt, he might be challenged by the accuser to an ordeal. If the accused withstood the ordeal with no ill effects, he in turn faced his challenger with a fine for false accusation. In one form of ordeal a pebble was dropped to the bottom of a pot of vigorously boiling water. The person challenged was obligated to reach into the boiling water, pick up the pebble, and return it without undue haste. If an individual removed and returned the stone too quickly, his action was interpreted as an indication of guilt.

If a person had not paid a just fine for a crime such as adultery or manslaughter after a reasonable length of time, he was likely to be killed. If a lesser crime were involved, property of a value equal to the fine was taken from the accused by the claimant. In the event that a go-between was unsuccessful in arranging a settlement, he might at least negotiate a truce to prevent either side from taking any ill-advised action. This was a temporary or delaying action only. Another type of settlement which

Ifugao hot-water ordeal (from Barton 1919).

brought an end to conflicts between families was a peace-making ceremony. If the gods indicated by inflicting a particular illness on a family member that they desired peace, then a performance of the proper rituals would establish a permanent end to the conflict. The peace-making ceremony brought together a representative of each side, and after rituals which involved prayers, each participant received spears. These weapons were to be used to kill the first person on either side who reopened the conflict.

Sources: Barton 1919, 1922.

PULUWAT NAVIGATION

Any number of ethnographic facts captivate Westerners because they are remote even in our imaginative fancies. The ability of Eskimos to survive in the high arctic, the bravery of Indian warriors on the American Plains, and the sexual freedom associated with Polynesians are focal points of abiding interest. Furthermore, the ability of some Pacific islanders to voyage in small canoes from one island dot to another fills some of us with respect that borders on awe. The capacity of a canoe navigator in the South Pacific to interpret the wind, the waves, and the stars in order to arrive at a particular island far beyond the horizon is indeed an impressive conjunction of science and art.

Puluwat is a tiny atoll among the Caroline Islands in central Melanesia, or as Thomas Gladwin (1970:1) writes, "Puluwat is an island of green, edged in white and set in a tropic sea." It is one among many low coral island formations, and in the recent past its inhabitants have remained culturally isolated in spite of the fact that the Carolines have been controlled by a varied succession of nations. The five islands of the Puluwat Atoll extend about two miles in their longest direction, and among them a single atoll, Puluwat, was occupied. The two larger islands supported taro swamps and a thick cover of useful trees such as breadfruit, coconut, and pandanus. The nearly 400 residents lived near the lagoon's edge and stored their canoes in thatched structures only a short distance from the water. These shelters, with their high gabled roofs, were not storage sheds but figuratively were "homes" for canoes. These vessels were much more than items of material culture; canoes in their many contexts symbolized the essence of the Puluwatan lifeway. As Gladwin, the authority on Puluwat sailing, has emphasized, these people thought of using their canoes in much the same manner as some people do their automobiles, or perhaps in an even more irrational way. For example, they might voyage 130 miles to another island in the west or make a trip of 150 miles to the east simply to obtain different varieties of tobacco. Admittedly, visiting might be an underlying purpose, but the stated reason was for tobacco. Since tobacco could be obtained via a ship which serviced the islands, quite clearly such ocean voyages were undertaken as ends in themselves, and their frequency as well as their popularity shows no signs of diminishing.

Trolling for fish from a large sailing canoe above the outer reef was an uncertain means for obtaining food, but of greater importance it was an exciting test of an outrigger's capabilities and the skills of its crew. Coursing at high speed over turbulent waters to a spot where seabirds hovered above schools of fish required not only a sound craft but a sense of daring as well. Voyages to other islands were more sustained adventures with broader purposes. Travels such as these offered exposure to new ideas, opportunities to select from a broad range of potential spouses, the chance to barter for exotic goods, and an occasion to further political ties. But above all else, trips to near or distant islands were pleasurable and exciting. During a sixteen-month span in 1966–1967 the fifteen large sailing canoes on Puluwat made a total of seventy-three trips to other islands, and many of these voyages required two or more weeks to complete.

A Puluwat canoe under sail (Thomas Gladwin, photographer: Courtesy of Harvard University Press; from Gladwin 1970).

All of the vessels used on long trips were built locally, and their makers were such accomplished craftsmen that they sold large outriggers to persons from other islands. Of the eighty-one local men, only thirteen had constructed one or more large canoes. These men acquired the necessary skills from their fathers or from other older men, usually relatives, and no man became a master builder before reaching his forties. In the not-too-distant past the apprenticeship program was quite formalized and involved the use of magic and observance of taboos. These features largely have disappeared in more recent times, but the skills necessary to build a fine, large canoe still required several years of practice. The hull lengths, which were V-shaped in cross-section, were about twenty-six feet, and the lower portion was hewn from a single breadfruit tree. Above this lower hull, planks were fitted and lashed to give a greater depth. Thus a hull was deep and narrow, and great skill was required to contour the outer portions. For optimum speed and ease of handling, the master craftsman must be able to calculate at an early stage of construction how the water will flow along the hull. This was the most critical technological step, and a man who could perform it well was presumed to have the capacity for constructing the remainder of the canoe with skill. The basic dimensions of the hull and the breaks in its design were calculated with a length of cord. The construction of the outrigger, a platform on the lee side, and the rigging were likewise standardized; only the contour of the hull was variable and would depend for maximum performance on the builder's craftsmanship. Although master builders and skilled navigators were few, all men could be and usually were involved in sailing activities. Those who were unable to build a large outrigger could help others do so or could make smaller canoes. Men without a navigator's knowledge could join the crews of sailing vessels and thus share in the excitement of a journey. Men also helped one another in launching, hauling up, repairing and maintaining canoes.

The knowledge required of a navigator went beyond plotting a reliable course at sea. His success as a sailing guide depended in part on an ability to anticipate the weather conditions which might be encountered. It was important, if not critical, to know when winds would be most likely to propel an outrigger in a particular direction and when they were most likely to shift and carry the travelers homeward with the least danger. Navigators knew too that it was foolish to attempt trips during periods when storms, unpredictable or high winds, or typhoons were likely to occur. Thus, there were sailing seasons, and between them the people talked about past travels and anticipated future voyages. In general, if a long trip was to be undertaken, several weeks were devoted to preparations; the actual date of departure depended on the forecast of the local weather, which could not reliably be made more than a few days in advance. If sky conditions appeared to be favorable on the anticipated departure date, the outrigger set sail.

The four to six men of a typical crew often were related to the captain-navigator, were co-owners of the vessel, or fit both of these categories. The same persons tended to sail together repeatedly even though there was no rigidity in the membership of a crew and the knowledge required of sailing companions was shared widely among men. As a precaution, an attempt was made to recruit one person other than the navigator who had the capacity to guide a vessel in an emergency. If a voyage was to be long or if women or children accompanied the crew, a small cabin was built over the lee platform. Here the passengers were sheltered, cargo was stored, or crew members slept in disagreeable weather. It was almost obligatory that a woman's husband accompany her on a trip to save her from embarrassments in performing bodily functions. A small child was accompanied by two male relatives so that one of them could watch the child at all times. It might be wondered why small children were taken on voyages since their presence led to a great deal of extra work for the crew. The reason was that the Puluwat sought to instill a love of the sea into their children, and this could be accomplished best by exposing them to the joys of sailing at a tender age.

After an outrigger was loaded with passengers, crew, and cargo, the vessel departed without any formal farewells. One or two men began to paddle across the lagoon as the others began to hoist the sail. As soon as the sheltered water of the lagoon was traversed, the canoe abruptly began to thrust through the powerful currents just beyond the reef, and then it settled down to furrow the ocean's massive waves. It was at this point that the navigator began to plot the first phase of a voyage. Like good sailors the world over he attempted to obtain the best performance from his vessel, which meant minor adjustments of the sailing rig or attaining better balance by having someone change position. It was the navigator himself who usually manned the sheet which trimmed the sail. Most trips were begun about noon, the most difficult time to establish a course. An initial heading was taken after a backsight on the atoll, for the navigator had come to know the direction in which a canoe should be headed when setting off for any particular island. If greater precision was required, as when sailing for a distant island, to have noted the general configuration of the Puluwat Atoll was not enough. Instead he lined up two particular points of land and set his course accordingly. An initial heading also might be established on some voyages by noting the outlines of particular portions of the underwater reefs over which they were sailing. Reef configurations were visible even though they might be from 60 to 120 feet beneath the surface, and their outlines were well known to navigators. After making these observations the navigator was able to calculate the speed and direction of the prevailing current. This calculation was very important, for after the familiar land and reefs had slipped from view, it was impossible to judge effectively the amount of drift produced by the current.

The sun, the waves, and the stars were the directional guides relied on after a course had been set, and each had its limitations. In recent times the Puluwat have supplemented these navigational methods with the mariner's compass. In the morning and afternoon when the sun was low, it served as a guide if not hidden by clouds. In the vicinity of Puluwat, located near the equator, the sun rises and sets in a nearly straight line, and a desired sailing angle was established by positioning the sun over a particular part of the canoe. In certain respects waves were better guides, for they were present regardless of cloud conditions. Three distinct types of waves were recognized. From out of the east was the Big Wave, which was steep and short; the North Wave came from the northeast and was most similar to a ground swell; the South Wave was weaker and less regular than the other two and coursed from the southeast. A navigator saw these forms of waves, but more important by far he could feel them night and day as they rolled beneath a canoe. Wave types were of limited direction-finding value, however; for some headings, such as those which were diagonal to a wave pattern, their impact on a canoe was more confusing than helpful to the navigator.

The stars shape the night, and for a Puluwatan mariner brightly shining stars were unfailing guides. Unlike the sun there were many stars, and unlike the waves they made it possible to steer an exacting course. The stars, as the sun, seemed to rise and set in a vertical pattern except that this movement was less evident for stars in the distant northern or southern skies. Particular stars came and went with the seasons, and these were the most reliable guides, particularly as they rose and set. Like the mariner's compass in the Western world, the Puluwatan compass had thirty-two points, which were stars. Unlike the Western system, however, the star points on a Puluwatan compass were not equidistant from one another. The cardinal direction was east and was marked by the rising position of the most important navigational star, the Big Bird, which is Altair in our system. At about the same latitude but on the other side of the night sky were Procyon and Bellatrix, and one of these stars provided east-west bearings at nearly any season or time of the night. Although the North Star often was obscured by clouds, it was important because it appeared to be stationary and thus was a good reference point. The Southern Cross was somewhat too high in the sky for a satisfactory bearing, but it was a clear marker of the south. Although these were the key guiding stars, others nearby could be substituted. Furthermore, a star to sail by could be aft of a canoe as well as forward since alignment of the vessel with a reference star was the primary basis for a sailing direction. The star compass in the mind of a Puluwatan navigator was most accurate in an east-west line, the direction they most often sailed; they followed no long north-south courses.

To a navigator the ocean that surrounded his island home was broken not only by islands but by innumerable pathways between islands. Navigators not only knew the courses to set for reaching nearby islands, but they had learned the sailing pattern to follow to reach islands familiar only by name. To known or unknown islands the courses were plotted by dead reckoning, meaning that the canoe's position at any time was established by the distance and direction from the last known location. The navigational system of these men, although it was broadly accurate, was not precise because deviations might be brought about by currents, which might be strong at one point during a voyage and slack at another time. Allowance could be made for the effect of a current only by estimating its rate and direction while within sight of an island or a reef which provided a fixed point for reckoning. On a journey reefs which were passed over were useful to verify the accuracy of a course. Since the distinct outline of each reef was known to a navigator, it might be followed to aid in establishing one's position. Islands which were visible but off the direct course served the same guiding purpose as reefs.

One technique above all others led the sailors as they approached their unseen destination. This was to follow the flight of seabirds, especially noddies, sooty terns, white terns, and one kind of booby. These birds shared a number of behavior patterns important to Puluwatan sailors. They all flew in a fairly direct line toward an island at dusk, slept on land at night, and flew away from land at dawn. Thus these birds defined a safety zone surrounding each island, and this was the most forthright of all guides at the end of a voyage.

Contrary to what might be expected, most voyages were undertaken by a lone canoe. One distinct disadvantage of traveling in the company of other canoes was that since each vessel performed differently, they could not maintain the same rate of speed; this led to delays if a group attempted to sail together. Then too if a canoe became separated from the others, it seldom was able to relocate the convoy. Yet if a mishap occurred when canoes sailed together (and this rarely meant more than four), others could come to the aid of the impaired vessel. Canoes sailing in convoys kept in contact at night by blowing conch shells periodically; a distress signal was made by placing a little water in the shell to produce a distinctly different sound. In recent times flashlights have in part displaced the signaling function of the shells. The greatest hazard at sea was for a sudden squall to capsize a canoe at night. Although a vessel could be righted by its crew, the task was difficult. Under normal circumstances the longest unbroken span of sailing time was about five days, and the greatest distance traveled was 400 miles to the east or west. On all extended trips numerous stops were made at intermediate islands. In spite of the frequency of their voyaging, the distances involved, and the physical hazards, no one had died at sea since a typhoon in 1945.

To us the thought of Pacific islanders setting off in small canoes for tiny, distant islands seems dangerous to the point of being foolhardy. Yet when each particular aspect of the Puluwatan navigational complex is considered, their voyaging becomes understandable in terms of a given set of skills. So it is with most of the cultural accomplishments which do not readily fit into our system of knowledge. The mysterious ways of other peoples usually turn out to be very reasonable, and even quite unexciting, within the configuration of their cultural system. Only our lack of understanding makes it sometimes difficult to realize that the ways of exotic peoples are not after all so unrelevant.

Source: Gladwin 1970.

HAWAIIAN ICONOCLASTS

In our times and because ours is a period of dramatic cultural changes, we have come to accept and even to expect iconoclastic beliefs and actions. For ethnics to have challenged the validity of their established religious systems, however, seems at the very margins of credibility. One reason is that religious dogma provided the primary guidelines among some aboriginal peoples for the norms of social life. For other indigenous populations religious beliefs were held as so sacred that to challenge them would have been regarded as madness. Among still other peoples religious systems were accepted as timeless and immutable, so much so that to change them would be more preposterous than mad. No matter what the beliefs for any particular group of ethnics might have been or where the emphasis was placed, they seldom are known to have been destroyed or abandoned without direct outside influence. At the same time challenges to the methods and goals of religious systems must have occurred, especially in aboriginal societies undergoing major cultural adjustments. In this respect it is inviting to consider events in Hawaii during the year 1819.

The aboriginal occupants of the Hawaiian Islands were the most northeasterly people identified as Polynesians. The handsomeness of Polynesians, the beauty of their islands, and their seemingly carefree way of life have had a great deal of romantic appeal for outsiders, and as indigenous peoples, they have been cast into an almost mystical mould by Euro-Americans. For example, some writers of fanciful prehistory have conjectured that they came from a lost continent in the Pacific even though there is not a shred of evidence, geological or otherwise, to support this contention. Others have romanticized the fact that peoples from South America ventured to the islands of the Pacific. Anthropologists long have accepted the probability of such a population spread but have likewise maintained that such voyages, as daring as they probably were, would have had a minor impact on the development of Polynesian culture. Ersatz romance need not be invoked for the origins of the Hawaiians, for the probable truth is remarkable enough. The weight of evidence is that they sailed all the way from Tahiti some time before A.D. 800, which is in itself as remarkable a venture as those made by their contemporaries, the Vikings of Scandinavia. One important reason for suggesting the Tahitian origin of the Hawaiians is that in their tales they single out this island as their place of departure. A statement of this nature might mean very little if recounted among some aboriginal peoples, but in this instance it is worthy of consideration because the Hawaiians were historically oriented. For example, the genealogies of some chiefs could be traced back as many as forty generations prior to A.D. 1900. Another important body of evidence relevant to their origins is linguistic. The language of the Hawaiians is most closely related to the languages of other peoples in eastern Polynesia, indicating the general affinity of this widespread population. In a basic vocabulary of about 200 words the Hawaiians share 76 percent with Tahiti, but only 71 percent with the Maori of New Zealand, and 59 percent with the people of Samoa. These percentages suggest the degree of commonality of background for the peoples involved. Thus, for the present time at least, it is most reasonable to assume that the Hawaiians probably came from Tahiti and furthermore, again on the basis of vocabulary comparisons, that the Polynesians in general originated from Indonesia.

The aboriginal Hawaiians occupied islands of plenty; abundant harvests from the sea and land facilitated the development of a culture characterized by great material wealth and complex social elaborations. They lived in rectangular houses which were framed with posts, had steeply gabled roofs, and were covered with grass or leaves. Each new dwelling was consecrated, and families were expected to have more than one structure at their place of residence. There were separate houses in which men and women ate, since they were forbidden to eat together. In another structure women performed domestic tasks, yet another served as a menstrual hut. In the family house, men and women mingled freely during the day and slept at night. These buildings were furnished with a wide variety of artifacts, some of them for general purposes and some serving special functions. For example, fans were made of coconut leaves, hafted shark-tooth knives were used for cutting hair, and mirrors were made from polished pieces of stone or wood which were moistened when they were used.

When the Hawaiians came to their new homeland, they brought along dogs, pigs, and rats, the latter probably being unwelcome passengers. The pigs and dogs, which were the most important animal domestics, were prized as food items. A wide variety of wild birds of both terrestrial and maritime species were taken for their feathers or meat, or for both qualities. Diverse species of fish, which abounded along the shores and in deep waters, were yet another important source of food. The primary staple was taro, a starchy tuber, of which many varieties were cultivated. Other plant domestics included sweet potatoes, yams, and the semicultivated breadfruit. The availability of varied and rich food sources would lead to the expectation that food would not be a focal point of social regulations, yet as already mentioned, men and women could not eat in each other's presence. This type of restriction is known by the term taboo, a Polynesian word which means a prohibition against a particular act or activity backed by supernatural sanctions. Thus, it is a firm negative rule. The nature of such prohibitions in Hawaii may be illustrated with reference to the taboos surrounding food. Although he could not eat with women, a man was obligated to cook for himself and his wife, but he did so in separate cookhouses and did not mingle the items prepared. Tabooed foods for women included coconuts, pork, certain fish, and whales. Examples of taboos from other aspects of living are legion. High chiefs were prohibited from walking over private land because if they did so it could no longer be touched by ordinary persons; therefore, chiefs were carried about. The shadow of an ordinary person could not fall on the house of a chief, on a chief's back, or on any of his possessions. When a high chief ate, the persons who were in his presence kneeled and dared not raise even a knee from the ground. The violators of these taboos could be in theory and were in fact killed. Thus in spite of plentiful resources, social conventions had developed which were in many respects repressive to commoner and king alike.

The Hawaiian drama of change began to unfold in May of 1819 with the death of the great king Kamehameha I, who had united the islands by conquest. In the face of some opposition from certain high chiefs, he was succeeded by his son, who assumed the title of Kamehameha II. Among the most powerful persons at this time was the dead king's favorite wife who assumed the unprecedented office of "chancellor" in keeping with what was said to have been a dying wish of the old king. Other key figures were the queen mother and two men, the "prime minister" and the "high priest." Dramatic changes in the religious system were most strongly advocated by the two women of royalty mentioned. The test came in November of 1819 when a feast was held at which men and women were seated at separate tables. Ralph S. Kuykendall (1947: 68) reports what happened next from a contemporary account. "After the guests were seated and had begun to eat, the king took two or three turns around each table, as if to see what passed at each. Then suddenly and without any previous warning to any but those in the secret, he seated himself in a vacant chair at the women's table and began to eat voraciously, but was evidently much perturbed. The guests, astonished at this act, clapped their hands, and cried out, 'Ai noa,—the eating tabu is broken.'" Since no supernatural punishments followed this extreme disobedience, orders were issued shortly thereafter to topple the idols and to ignore the taboos. These changes were supported by the high priest, but his potential successor opposed them. This man, who was of a rank nearly equal to that of a king and was an outspoken opponent to the succession of the current king, found supporters among the traditional chiefs of middle rank. This faction soon was quelled, however, in part because of the effectiveness of the weaponry received by the king from Western traders.

The confining nature of the religious system, the successful challenge of it, and its abrupt abandonment are clear and undisputed historical events. The intriguing anthropological question is why this chain of happenings transpired. We are indebted to Malcolm C. Webb (1965) for the most illuminating overall discussion of the episode and its multiple interpretations.

The explanation offered by Kroeber (1948:403–405) was that "cultural fatigue" had enveloped the Hawaiian religious system. The condition of cultural fatigue is not defined clearly, but he apparently meant that people over-elaborated a particular pattern to the point that they found it unbearable and subsequently abandoned it. Culture change of this type was in terms of prior cultural conditions only. This explanation, as logical as it may seem, is inadequate with respect to the Hawaiian situation because it denies the significance of the broader environmental conditions in which the change took place. By way of analogy, biological changes occur in organisms as a result of their existing genetic qualities, but they also are responsive, at least partially, to the physical environment in which the organisms find themselves.

Historians, both academic and aboriginal, sought another prime reason for the changes. Their explanation focuses on the importance of the dissatisfactions of the two high-ranking women involved. Superficially this is a beguiling lure, but it fails to explain why the changes also were embraced with enthusiasm by the king and high priest. Furthermore, by abandoning the system all of these persons stood to lose their extraordinarily high standing, as irksome as it might have been in some respects. Most anthropologists who have commented on the scene have tended to consider the shift a result of Western influences. In general their reasoning is that the changes resulted from the impact of explorers and traders on the local social structure. The exotic goods which had been brought into their lives and the exposure to foreign ideas, including the fact that Europeans disregarded local taboos with no ill effects, placed such a strain on the traditional system that it was abandoned suddenly. These influences cannot be denied, but in themselves they do not appear to have functioned as the basic cause of change.

A brief description of certain key characteristics of Hawaiian life at the time of early historic contact serves to introduce what seems to be the most reasonable explanation for the iconoclasm. In the aboriginal status system a great deal of prestige and authority was based on social rank. High social position in turn carried with it diverse duties and obligations of a religious and political nature. It also is extremely important to note that the gradations in rank which separated a leader from the next person in line for any particular office were very subtle. Thus, leaders and potential leaders were of virtually the same rank, and this inevitably led to almost constant intrigues and struggles for power among those at or near the top. Given these conditions anyone in a position of great authority was obligated to maintain a precise set of religious and political patterns or he would find his power deftly usurped by a potential sucessor. Furthermore, although the nobility had great wealth, much of it was consumed in lavish harvest feasts held because of the dictates of tradition. Contact with Westerners had brought an awareness of a very different way of life, and the Hawaiians were impressed by certain of its aspects. However, in order for the state type of social organization to replace their current pattern, a leader must somehow free himself from the onus of obligatory ritual commitments which drained him of his possessions and employ the accumulated wealth in his own behalf. He must also have available a military force loyal to him alone and be accorded freedom of action unburdened by stifling traditions. By destroying the taboo system and the idols, the dominant ways of the past were discarded, and new orientations in social, political, and religious life were prepared for in one fell swoop.

The Hawaiian variety of a chiefdom rather clearly was in the process of changing to a state form of organization at the time of historic contact. The consolidation of the islands under Kamehameha I and the clear power struggles among the nobility are evidences of such change, and the introduction of foreign ideas and firearms accelerated the process. In order for a state to develop it is essential for a leader to consolidate his position, to possess clear central control backed by legitimate power, and to have access to sufficient resources for achieving these ends. Efforts to move in these directions were made by Kamehameha I and his immediate predecessors. His successor and those who supported him appear to have realized that consolidation could not be achieved permanently within the structure of the existing system and therefore they were prepared to make drastic changes. Possibly a catalyst, but not the deep-seated cause, was the information received by Kamehameha II that the people of Tahiti had successfully abandoned their taboo system in favor of Christianity.

In the recorded histories of ethnics it rarely is possible to discern great steps in culture change. The reasons are that these occur infrequently and that most have been confused so much by the intervention of

Europeans or Americans that it is difficult to determine whether the profound change was really of aboriginal inspiration. The general chain of events which transpired in Hawaii leading from a chiefdom to a state organization took place elsewhere in Polynesia following direct and rather intensive contact with Christian missionaries. In Hawaii, however, historic contact did not occur until 1778, and the iconoclasm had been completed a year before Christians brought their ideas directly to bear on the Hawaiian island sphere.

Sources: Emory 1959; Kroeber 1948; Kuykendall 1947; Malo 1951; Webb 1965.

SIX

NORTH AMERICA

When and how the Americas came to be populated by ethnics are questions debated with considerable interest and often with more controversy than the subject seems to merit. Man clearly could not have evolved from primates indigenous in the New World, since all of the local primates are offshoots from specialized evolutionary lines which are only tangential to human developments. The South American monkeys are very, very distant relatives of man. In contrast the Old World had surviving chimpanzees and gorillas as well as extensive fossil remains of humans and protohumans, both factors which point to an African center for the major developments in human evolution. Thus man must have entered the Americas from elsewhere.

Current evidence, although far from adequate, suggests that people may have entered the New World about 40,000 years ago. By this point in time in the Old World, man was essentially modern in his physical form, and all of the human bones found in the Americas are of this type. The next question concerns the path of entry; this almost certainly was a land bridge which would have existed in the vicinity of Bering Strait during a glacial period when the world-wide sea levels were considerably lower than at present. If, as is presumed, man arrived in the New World about 40,000 years ago, this was long before the development of seaworthy boats, and therefore, any suggestion of trans-Atlantic or trans-Pacific routes of entry appears to be out of the question. Another factor indicating an overland migration is that modern terrestrial mammals, such as caribou, wolves, and wolverine, are found in northern sectors of both Asia and North America; since they must have walked from the Old into the New World, it seems reasonable that men did the same. The first migrants probably hunted large land mammals along the Pacific fringe of

245

Siberia and continued the same hunting practices as they spread into Alaska. Here they may have remained for a considerable length of time, hunting a now-extinct form of bison, horses, mammoth and other large game animals until an ice-free corridor was exposed along the mountainous spine of western America.

It sometimes is stated that men "entered" the New World when the continents split and "drifted" apart; this theory, however, ignores the fact that continental drift was nearly complete long, long before men ever existed on earth. In the same fanciful vein some persons have vigorously maintained that persons from the Mediterranean area sailed to a now-lost continent of "Atlantis" and that when it submerged, they journeyed on to populate the Americas. No geological or cultural evidence exists to support the idea that a continental landmass ever was present in the Atlantic Ocean. Similarly no evidence suggests the presence at any time of a continent of "Mu" in the Pacific Ocean, where sea voyagers might have paused in their travels to the New World. One of the most persistent of the ill-grounded theories about the origins of the first Americans is that they represent survivors of the "Lost Tribes of Israel," who either crossed Asia to the New World or ventured by boat across the Atlantic Ocean. On the basis of man's antiquity in the Americas alone, this theory must be rejected. Furthermore, all attempts to demonstrate linguistic or cultural affinities between American Indians and Semitic peoples have failed.

The Bering Strait avenue of entry is the most appealing for a number of reasons. First, geological evidence supports the likelihood of a former land bridge across Bering Strait; second, some early artifacts recovered from the New World are most similar to those types found in adjacent areas of Asia, although this evidence is not presently as clear as would be hoped; third, there is no evidence of great antiquity for any oceangoing boats, a prerequisite for overseas voyages; fourth, linguistic ties between the Old and New Worlds exist only in the Bering Strait area, between the Eskimoan and Na-Dene of the New World and certain Paleo-Siberian and Sino-Tibetan languages of the Old World; fifth, the Bering Strait land bridge hypothesis is the least encumbered explanation for man's movement into the Americas.

None of the propositions just advanced deny the fact that contacts were made between the Old and New Worlds by oceangoing travelers before the voyages of Columbus. Vikings from Greenland unquestionably visited northeastern Canada. Aboriginal South Americans unquestionably sailed across the Pacific to islands in the South Pacific basin. In all likelihood sea voyagers from Asia had reached Middle America, and possibly the same was true of Japanese traveling to northwestern South America. It is not farfetched that unrecorded trans-Atlantic trips were made as well. However, in most instances the travels were within comparatively recent times, and they contributed little to aboriginal life as it developed in the New World.

Turning to an overview of North American Indian cultures, we find considerable variability in subsistence orientations. One economic tradition was based on hunting big game and had been introduced by the continent's earliest inhabitants. The early historic bison hunters of the Plains typified this tradition as did the caribou hunters of the Subarctic. Other peoples, particularly those who lived in the very arid sectors of western North America, were diversified gatherers, meaning that they hunted game, which often was small, but also relied heavily on plant products for food. Quite possibly this food-getting focus is nearly as old in North America as the great hunter tradition. On the Pacific coasts from northern California to the Yukon River mouth, salmon fishing was the major economic focus; it possibly had originated in the southern sector at least 8,000 years ago. Elsewhere the indigenous peoples were farmers who raised maize, beans, and squash as their most important crops. Farming techniques varied regionally, however. In the eastern United States and over much of Middle America, the pattern was to kill trees and brush in forested areas, permit the vegetation to dry, burn it, and plant seeds with the aid of digging sticks. New lands were cleared as the productivity of established plots declined, which was within either a few years or many, depending on the locality. Hunting and fishing were secondary means for obtaining food, and settlements tended to be small and scattered. In the Southwest and in adjacent sectors of Mexico, the techniques of cultivation were different, although the crops were the same, and peoples tended to occupy larger, more permanent villages. Sectors near flooded riverbeds, plots watered by underground seepages, and artificially irrigated areas near springs and rivers were under the most intensive cultivation.

A conservative estimate of the aboriginal population of North America is about 10,000,000, of whom about 1,000,000 lived north of Mexico. The number of distinctive peoples was about 400. Population density was greatest from central Mexico to the Isthmus of Panama and lowest in northern Canada and central Alaska. In general terms more people lived in the south than in the north; more were concentrated on the coasts than in the interior, and the Pacific coast had a greater density than the Atlantic coast. The salmon-fishing peoples on the Northwest Pacific coast had even denser populations than did farmers in the eastern United States.

The three types of aboriginal North Americans usually identified are the Aleuts, Eskimos, and Indians. The Aleuts lived on the Aleutian Islands, and the Eskimos along the northern fringes of the continent, the northern Canadian islands, and Greenland; all the other peoples are identified as Indians. In terms of population shifts the Aleuts and Eskimos entered North America at a later date than did the other native Americans. Their linguistic ties with Northeast Asian peoples already have been cited, and furthermore, they are more closely related physically to Mongoloid peoples of the Old World than to Indians. However, the extent of the differences between Eskimo-Aleuts and Indians is in most dimensions no greater than the distinctions among different groups of Indians. Thus, it is not overly important to separate Eskimos and Aleuts from other indigenous Americans.

The number of detailed ethnographic reports for aboriginal North America probably is greater than for any other large geographical area. Yet most of these have been reconstructions rather than aboriginal baseline studies. Apart from scattered, but sometimes notable, accounts by early Spanish observers in Middle America and Jesuit reports from the St. Lawrence River region, the best baseline aboriginal data are for the more westerly and northern sectors of the continent.

Sources: Driver 1961; Honigmann 1959; Spencer and Johnson 1968.

THE CARIBOU ESKIMO: HUNTERS OF THE TUNDRA

Without fear of exaggeration it may be said that the Barren Grounds of northern Canada were one of the most forbidding of earthly habitats for aboriginal man. The Eskimos who lived there encountered long and cold winters relieved only by summers which were short and cool. These climatic conditions pose survival problems, but they are by no means especially noteworthy within northern regions. The most striking negative characteristic of the Caribou Eskimo homeland is the narrowness of the potential subsistence base, since all food products were scarce during most of the year. The Barren Grounds are a vast expanse of rolling tundra with lichens abounding on the uplands. Dwarf birch, willows, and grasses grow knee-high in sheltered areas, and along the southern fringes of the area gnarled spruce have a tenuous hold. The landscape is strewn with glacially scarred boulders and pocked with large and small lakes and rivers which flow fast and sinuously to Hudson Bay. Some lakes and rivers contain fish, but seldom during the year are any species abundant. The Caribou Eskimos were able to subsist in the Barrens only because vast herds of caribou came and went twice each year and small herds sometimes lingered there throughout the year. These people are discussed because they lived in the most demanding of all Eskimo-inhabited environments, utilized a single major food resource, and had the simplest material culture found anywhere among Eskimos. Unlike most other Eskimos they lived mainly in an inland setting; they feared the spruce forests to the south and were uneasy along the shores of Hudson Bay.

In all likelihood nearly 600 years ago the ancestors of the Caribou Eskimos lived along the coast where they hunted seals and great whales in addition to ranging inland for caribou. As the earth's crust lifted locally around A.D. 1400, the adjacent arctic seas became so shallow that they were abandoned by great whales and provided a less hospitable environment for seals. Subsequent to this change, persons historically identified as the Caribou Eskimos became committed to inland caribou hunting above any other subsistence activity. Linguistic evidence also suggests that their move from the coast was quite recent since they speak the same Eskimo dialect as the adjacent coastal peoples. Furthermore, the recognized Caribou Eskimo archaeological sites are all of recent origin. Their camp sites yield huge piles of caribou bones but few artifacts, a mute testimony that they had few things to lose or leave behind. They also are fascinating subjects for study because they followed their particular way of life for less than 500 years, during which they had abandoned certain key Eskimo cultural characteristics, such as the toggle-headed harpoon and seal oil lamp.

The Caribou Eskimos were contacted in their homeland in 1878–1880, but because of their extreme physical isolation their way of life had changed comparatively little by the time the Danish ethnographer Kaj Birket-Smith lived among them in 1922–1923. At that time they numbered about 450 persons and were divided into five bands. The largest band included about 110 persons, but rarely did more than 40 persons occupy a single camp site. These people are comparatively short in stature and lean in body build. Eskimos virtually never are fat; they only appear to be so because of their thickly-layered clothing and broad-boned faces. The faces of men were dark from weathering; they wore their hair either long or short, with a tonsured crown quite often. The faces of women were darker than those of the men because women spent many hours in front of smoky cooking fires. Some women had tattoos across their cheeks. The designs were made by pricking the skin and rubbing soot into the openings or by sewing with a needle threaded with a soot-covered hair. Women parted their hair in the middle and braided it. Caribou Eskimos quite naturally smelled of dried caribou skins and rancid caribou fat, the smoke from dwarf-willow fires, and a lifetime of not bathing. These were the honest odors of a hunting people.

The residence unit throughout a year consisted of a nuclear family to which one or two persons related to the adult members might be added.

Table 4.   CULTURE AREAS OF NORTH AMERICA

Eskimo: Eskimo-Aleut (Eskaleutian) languages; sea mammal hunting, caribou hunting and fishing secondary; bilateral descent, largely antonomous families; female infanticide; charismatic leaders; host of good and evil spirits, shaman important, ceremonialism elaborate in west; rectangular driftwood, stone, or sod house in east and west, snowhouse in central area, tailored clothing, elaborate harpoons; dog traction, kayak and umiak, feuds usually caused by disputes over women.

Northern Athapaskan: Na-Dene languages; caribou hunting, fishing for salmon in the west and whitefish elsewhere; bilateral or matrilineal descent; band organization; shamanism, fear of Nakani as a supernatural; double lean-to, or rectangular log frame dwellings covered with earth, spruce root and birch bark baskets, snowshoes, toboggan, bark canoe, semitailored clothing; cannibalism in extreme cases of famine.

Northern Algonkian: Algonkian (Algonkian-Mosan) languages; caribou hunting, fishing; bilateral or patrilineal descent; band organization; shaking-tent for predicting the future, shamanism; conical tent, bark canoe, snowshoes, toboggan, semitailored clothing; mobile small family band organization.

Great Basin-Baja: diverse language families; gathering vegetable foods such as acorns and pine nuts with hunting more secondary; bilateral descent dominant, elaborate female puberty ceremonies; band organization; shaman, ceremonial round poorly developed, diverse supernaturals; temporary dwelling, developed basketry.

Plateau: Salish languages; salmon fishing supplemented by hunting and collecting; bilateral descent; village minimal political unit; diverse spirits, shaman; semisubterranean winter house, summer dwelling of reeds or mats, basketry important, bark fiber clothing.

Northwest Coast: Na-Dene languages in the north, Wakashan languages in the south; salmon fishing, hunting of sea and land mammals; matrilineal descent in the north and patrilineal descent in the south, slaves, commoners, and nobles; rich men as leaders, village maximal political unit; potlatch, secret societies, elaborate winter ceremonial round; large, rectangular, gable-roofed plank houses, totem poles most important in historic times, large dugout canoe, elaborate woodworking technology; stress on the ownership of material goods.

Plains: dominated by Macro-Siouan speakers; bison hunting; descent bilateral but with patrilineal alternative; emphasis on war, alliances of bands, military societies; tipi of bison skin, dog-drawn travois, bison important for skin clothing, bone tools; dung as fuel.

Eastern Woodlands: Macro-Algonkian and Macro-Siouan languages; maize, beans, and squash cultivation supplemented by some hunting and fishing; matrilineal descent groups with outstanding men in these units important; tribal confederations occur; developed ceremonial round often focusing on harvests, secret societies; dome-shaped bark- or mat-covered wigwam dwelling, bark canoe.

Southeast: Macro-Algonkian and Macro-Siouan languages; intensive cultivation of maize, squash, and cane, with hunting and fishing less important; matrilineal descent; confederated groups of ethics, warfare important; elaborate ceremonial life, sun worship important; rectangular dwelling, fortified settlements; domestic turkey.

Southwest: dominated by Hokan and Aztec-Tanoan languages; intensive cultivation of maize, beans, and squash, with hunting less important; matrilineal or bilateral descent; village as basic political unit; complex ceremonial round, kiva-type ceremonial structure, masked dancers; pueblo-type dwelling, elaborate pottery and basketry; cotton raised for garment material, domestic turkey (some peoples in this area, such as the Navajo, had economies based mainly on gathering).

Mexico and Central America: dominated by Aztec-Tanoan, Penutian, and Oto-Manguean speakers; intensive cultivation of maize, beans, and squash; largely bilateral descent; complex governmental organization, powerful confederations of ethnics; extremely elaborate ceremonial life, human sacrifices, complex calendrical systems; rectangular flat or hip-roof house widespread; gold, silver, and copper worked, cotton raised.

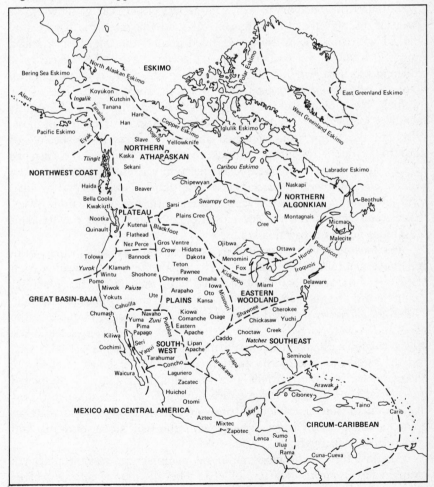

Map 4. CULTURE AREAS AND SELECT ETHNICS OF NORTH AMERICA (CIRCUM-CARIBBEAN DISCUSSED WITH SOUTH AMERICA).

In the summer families lived in conical-shaped tents made of pole frames covered with dehaired caribou skins. In the winter each family lived in the most renowned of all aboriginal dwellings, the dome-shaped snowhouse. In order to construct such a dwelling a field of snow was sought which was firmly but not densely packed or layered. Preferably one man cut the rectangular blocks of snow as another fitted them into place. The first blocks were cut from the area some thirteen feet across which was to be the house floor. After the first circle of blocks was in place, they were trimmed in order to produce an inward slope at the top, and each subsequent row was cut so that it sloped inwardly until the key block was fitted at the top of the structure. The builder, who was encased inside, cut his way out, and this opening, to which an arched passageway of snow blocks was attached, served as the entrance. Any spaces between the blocks were chinked with snow, loose snow was piled around the outer walls, and a snow block above the entrance was replaced with a block of clear ice which served as a window. The major structural feature in the interior was a raised platform of packed snow which occupied the rear half of the dwelling. Here, on top of a twig matting covered with skins, the family members lounged, ate, and slept. The interior was not heated purposefully, but the temperature remained about 25 degrees F. irrespective of how cold it might be outside. Storage rooms were built off the entrance passage, and another room, vented in the roof, was used for cooking. The women cooked foods in rectangular soapstone vessels set on a platform of stones. The vessels were heated with fires built from twigs, mosses, and lichens; oil was never used even though it was the standard fuel among adjacent coastal Eskimos.

Eskimos made the most efficient cold-adapted garments in the world, and those of the Caribou Eskimos were among the best anywhere. Men wore two suits of caribou skin clothing, with the hair of the inner set facing inward and the hair of the outer set facing in the opposite direction. The inner garments included fitted breeches which reached almost to the knees and skin stockings with sewn-in feet which reached above the knees, plus a thigh-length, hooded inner parka. The outer parka fitted loosely, and the same was true of the outer breeches. Winter boots reached the knee, and caribou skin mittens with the hair facing outward completed their dress. The clothing of women was much the same as for men except that a woman wore a very loose-fitting parka in order to accommodate an infant, a single set of baggy trousers with the hair facing outward, and long, very loose-fitting boots.

An inventory of the most important manufactures to be found at a camp included surprisingly few objects. The all-purpose cutting tool of women was the ulu, with a semilunar, ground slate blade and a wooden handle. The man's knife probably consisted of a slate blade set into the end of an antler handle. Meat and fish occasionally were eaten raw, but more often they were cooked in rectangular soapstone vessels suspended over a fire. The meat was retrieved from the pot with an antler fork and served on an oblong wooden tray. The broth from a meal was ladled with a dipper of musk-ox horn and passed from one person to the next to sip. In the winter a snowhouse was lighted with saucer-shaped soapstone lamps which burned caribou fat along a moss wick. Surprisingly enough, even when seal oil was available it was not burned, and the lamp was not used for cooking as among the adjacent coastal Eskimos. Fires were lighted by striking flint against iron pyrites. Water was stored in pails made from skin, and in the spring it was sucked through a birdbone tube in order to prevent one's lips from cracking. The skin-working equipment probably included stone as well as caribou-scapula scrapers, eyed needles made from caribou bone, and caribou sinew as thread.

Winter mobility was facilitated by the use of dog teams. Typically a family owned only three dogs because of the difficulty in obtaining dog food. In the winter dogs slept in the entrance passage of their owner's house and were fed once a day, but in the summer they hunted small animals and ate human feces in order to survive. The attitude of these and many other Eskimos was that dogs could be whipped and beaten, but they were not killed purposefully. Each dog was hitched to a sled with an individual trace, which resulted in a fan-shaped hitching arrangement. The sleds were up to thirty feet in length, with runners made from spliced pieces of wood. Between the runners were lashed wood crosspieces, and the vehicle looked very much like a ladder.

According to these Eskimos, the caribou on which they depended for meat, skins, antler, sinew, and bone at one time did not exist on the earth. Legend records that a man cut a deep hole into the earth to obtain caribou and from this opening so many animals appeared that they nearly covered the earth. It was then that the man covered the hole again. Thus, caribou were literally creatures of the earth; they established their own seasonal movements and were free from direct human or supernatural control. Nonetheless, *Pinga*, "the One up in the Sky," was especially influential concerning the relationships between caribou and men. Pinga was offended when men were careless in handling caribou or wasteful with the meat. The established rules for the treatment of these animals included removing all evidence of a kill, except to leave a piece of meat and fat nearby beneath a stone, and preventing dogs from chewing caribou bones or antler.

The vast herds of caribou wintered to the south of Caribou Eskimo country, and each year in the spring they began to migrate northward. At this time hunters established camps at localities which experience had taught them might be on the migration route. Since food supplies usually were low during their wait, the men hunted ptarmigan, which often were plentiful and were killed easily. These birds were stunned with stones or more often were shot with blunted arrows propelled from bows backed with strengthening cords of sinew. The caribou which arrived first were the cows with yearling calfs, and the last to appear were great bulls. When the first animals approached, the people did not rush to the kill since it made little difference to them whether or not they went hungry for a few more days. Finally the caribou were taken in large numbers, and then the people ate to excess and even more. On their spring movement the animals methodically headed northward, and in the fall they turned to the south in great herds. It was in the fall that their skins were prime, their meat best, and the layer of fat thickest. A great kill in the fall assured a winter of comfort, but if few animals were taken, the possibility of starvation hung veil-like over the people of the Barrens.

In anticipation of intercepting the southbound herds, the Eskimos most often established camps near a narrow spot in a lake or at a river shallow, because these were favored caribou crossing places. Stone cairns, thought by the caribou to be men, often were erected in converging lines to guide the animals into an ambush or into a body of water. In order to take swimming caribou the men deftly maneuvered their kayaks with double-bladed paddles and made their kills with stone-tipped lances. During the October mating season when bulls jealously guarded groups of females, a hunter sometimes disguised himself by holding a set of caribou antlers over his head and grunting like a bull as he approached. With this technique he was more likely to come within effective arrow range, which was about sixty-five feet. If a reasonably heavy snowfall occurred during the time caribou were numerous and relatively unafraid, a pit might be dug in the snow, walled with blocks to a height of ten feet, and covered with slabs of snow. An animal drawn by curiosity to the cairn erected at the spot fell into the pit and was trapped. A pitfall might also be baited with dog or wolf urine, which attracted caribou because of its salt content. By these diverse hunting techniques the people hoped to kill many more animals than they could consume in the immediate future. The surplus meat was placed on the ground over a layer of old bones, which allowed air to circulate beneath; on top of the meat boulders were piled to prevent foxes from pilfering the cache. If a number of large caches were established in one particular sector, a family spent the entire winter camped nearby.

Apart from caribou the only large mammals hunted were muskoxen, but they did not range widely over the Barrens. Because of their

A Caribou Eskimo man in the 1950s. The meat from freshly killed caribou is spread out to dry on rocks in the background (photograph by the author).

poor defensive tactics any herd discovered was annihilated. After a group of musk-oxen had been sighted, dogs were released in order to bait the animals and bring them to bay. The musk-oxen formed a circle with their heads facing outward. In this position the entire herd could be killed with lances and arrows, since a live animal would not abandon those fallen beside him and would charge only if a man approached too closely.

These Eskimos felt that caribou meat was the only decent food; they were not averse to fishing to relieve the monotony of their usual diet or in order to ward off starvation, but fish were not regarded as highly desirable fare. In the winter a hungry man was more likely to continue an unsuccessful search for caribou than to fish through the ice, which was considered an even less profitable activity. To take fish at this time of the year a hole was first chiseled in river or lake ice with a long-handled ice pick tipped with an antler point. Ice constantly reformed at the hole, and to remove it the fisherman used a musk-ox horn or antler scoop. A stone-weighted sinew line was lowered into the hole; to it were attached strips of trout skin or an inflated fish skin. The fisherman stood above the hole jiggling the lure with one hand as his other held a leister poised to strike. When fishing through the ice with a lure and leister combination or with a barbless hook, they hoped to catch trout, tullibee, or whitefish. In the summer when arctic char ascended the rivers to spawn, a weir and an associated dam, both built from stones, were constructed across a shallow stretch of river. When the char were trapped between the two obstructions, they were taken with leisters.

The extreme gregariousness of Eskimos is well documented, and whenever food supplies were abundant or even just adequate, a number of related or friendly families camped together. Within a family and a settlement the division of labor was clear. Men built snowhouses and women pitched tents; both men and women fished and dressed skins; men hunted and drove dog teams, and manufactured everything except skin garments. The other major obligations of women were to prepare the meals and raise the children.

Notable events in an individual's journey from womb to tomb provide insight into the social lives of the group. When a woman realized that she was pregnant, she observed certain rules in an effort to insure a normal delivery. For example, she untied her hair as a symbolic means to promote an unimpeded birth. An offspring was named before birth by the parents, since names were not sex linked. The birth took place in the family dwelling, and the mother observed postnatal restrictions for the next month or more. Infanticide rarely was practiced, probably because the infant mortality rate was high. As an infant grew into childhood, very few restrictions were placed on his behavior. The hare was a "bogey man" with which a child was threatened when he misbehaved, but if an erring child did not respond to the threat, the behavior went unpunished. The toys of children were the implements of adult life in miniature in addition to actual playthings such as bull-roarers and popguns. The latter were made from birdbone tubes; chewed moss was inserted at one end and a rod forced rapidly into the opposite end to propel the moss missile.

The transition from adolescence to adulthood was not formally recognized for males, but at a girl's menarche she was subject to food and behavioral taboos, some of which would apply to all subsequent menstrual periods. When a young man began to hunt and kill caribou efficiently, he was acknowledged to be ready for marriage and the accompanying adult status. Infant betrothals were common, and no formal marriage ceremony existed. The couple was most likely to become attached to the household of the husband (patrilocal residence), but this was not a rigid rule. The Caribou Eskimo attitude toward divorce was casual. If a couple disagreed, they might separate, but if they had children they usually attempted to settle their differences. Men exchanged wives for either short or long periods of time, and these lendings often led to close friendships between the men involved.

Given the physical difficulties of adult life, very few persons reached old age. Old people might be abandoned to die, but senilicide was not practiced, although an old or infirmed person might ask for and be given help in committing suicide by hanging. More taboos surrounded death than any other event in an individual's life. If a person died during the day, the corpse was removed through a special opening made at the rear of the dwelling. If a death occurred during the night, the body was placed at the rear of the dwelling. The corpse of a man was kept in the house for three days and that of a woman for five days. During this time the household members observed innumerable behavioral and food taboos which were designed to prevent the soul of the dead from harming the living. The flexed and shrouded corpse was deposited on the tundra and covered with stones or surrounded by a ring of stones. The person's soul went to Pinga and later returned to earth in human or animal form.

The routine of life had no seasonal highlights in terms of formal social festivities or religious rituals, and cooperative activities which involved more than a few persons were relatively unusual. In a typical camp a man was responsible for his family and was helpful to relatives and friends with whom he had long-term intimacy. Because they lived in small groups each person came to know what to expect of others and accepted idiosyncratic actions so long as they were not bizarre. Clearly conceived behavioral conventions did exist, however; perhaps the most important rule was that when the members of a camp faced starvation, any food obtained was common property and was to be shared equally by all. Furthermore, a man was not to be selfish with food, steal it because he was too lazy to hunt, or abandon his family in a time of food stress. Neither should a person have illicit sexual relations or abuse a wife without due cause. A transgressor first was mildly ridiculed by his friends; this action usually was sufficient to induce him to mend his erring ways. If mild verbal ridicule did not rectify the social imbalance, other means were attempted. One very effective recourse was for someone to compose a derisive song about the offender and to sing it in his presence. The songs, which were pungent and to the point, were listened to with chagrin by an offender and enjoyed by the audience. When confronted with one's failings in this manner, a normal individual began to conform, and the incident soon was forgotten. Since all men are not normal, it sometimes happened that ridicule songs went unheeded, in which case the person was ostracized. If the offensive person were camped in one's midst, the simplest solution was to move camp during the night and leave the transgressor behind. He could not move into any other camp without the permission of those in residence. Occasionally when a ridicule song was sung, the person exposed to derision became so angry that fistfights resulted, but usually a man would literally run away rather than fight a member of his group. In the event of a murder, blood revenge was in theory exacted against the killer or one of his near relatives. Once a second murder had taken place any further retaliation was disallowed.

Among these people few avenues to prestige were open to an individual. If a man were an able hunter who shared his kills freely and willingly, he gained the respect of everyone, but normally he did not attract a following. The most prestigious persons were shamans, who usually were men with charisma. An effective shaman controlled spirits and thereby healed persons who developed natural or supernatural diseases. An apprentice shaman received instructions from an established practitioner, but in order to obtain his own spirit aids he underwent the ordeal of being "killed," "drowned," or exposed to extreme hunger and cold. In his efforts to diagnose a case, a shaman might wander alone for two or three days, during which time he ate little and seldom rested, seeking the aid of Pinga and of Hila, the spirit of the cold, storms, and adversity from the air. Each shaman possessed a wooden shaft which was attached to his belt, and spirits from the ground entered it to be used in divining. Questions were asked of the shaft, and the answers were judged from its seeming change in weight. Shamans at times performed magic; although they knew that they were using tricks to impress their audience, they nonetheless firmly believed in their supernatural powers, and others believed in them as well.

In this sketch I have attempted to illustrate the simplicity of the Caribou Eskimo manufactures in order to counteract the prevailing impression that all Eskimos have a very sophisticated technology. At the same time it has been noted that even a people with an uncomplicated material culture can possess remarkably satisfactory adaptive forms, in this case the snowhouse and caribou skin clothing. It should be noted too that these people had notable blind spots, such as their failure to make effective use of seal oil, even when it was available through trade, and their bias against eating fish except as an emergency food or as a change from the preferred diet of caribou meat. It seems likely that if they had been more willing to fish they might have been able to avoid many of their starvations. Finally, the Caribou Eskimos illustrate the dangers inherent in basing not only an economy but a complete way of life on a single species of migratory big-game animal.

Sources: Birket-Smith 1929; Harp 1961; Hirsch 1954; Rasmussen 1930.

INGALIK VIEWS AND VALUES

An ethnography, as the description of a particular ethnic, presumably should be an account of another people's way of life largely unfettered by our own conventions. Yet we know that this is not the case. Limitations of the field time available or of one's training, interests, and abilities narrow the recordings to an often stock and sometimes stark cluster of findings. We do not often explore or even gain entry to the aesthetic corners (from our perspective) of the minds of ethnics. Occasionally an ethnographer makes us realize what we so often miss or mention only in passing. One such person is Cornelius Osgood, and the people he described so very well were the Ingalik of the lower Yukon River in Alaska.

For the Ingalik the world was created by Denato, whose name is a contraction of their word for "everyone's father." He was largely remote from the course of human affairs, and his distinct characteristics were unelaborated. Yet it is clear that Denato created man, animals, and inanimate objects, which lived together first in another world under the creator's control. The forms in each class shared many of the characteristics of humans and had superhuman qualities as well. In time Denato peopled the earth with all of the forms found later. He first made rock people, tree people, salmon people, and so on, and then finally he made a man and a woman of mud, not clay, and sent them to earth. They were taught by their creator how to survive in the natural world, how to interact with other beings, and which taboos to observe. Another belief, describing the origin of animals, had no association with Denato and is inconsistent with what has preceded. According to this tradition, animals came first from the ground within a mountain, and from here they continue to appear periodically, especially in response to ceremonies performed by men. Thus mountains are pleasant places, and it was among them that people preferred to die.

The universe had four realms which were ordered in relationship to one another. The first was the world of normal life, and the others were spirit worlds. The only spirit that could linger in the natural world was that of a shaman. Usually the spirit of a dead person departed for a realm called "Raven living," which was beneath the surface of the normal world. The journey there took the spirit through a long tunnel; at the end the spirit of a woman was met by Raven, who appeared to be a handsome young man, and the spirit of a man was met by Raven's wife. In each instance the spirit of the dead slept with the supernatural and then was ferried across a river to the land of the dead. Very little was known about "up on top of the sky," the third level, except that it was the spirit home of persons who had frozen to death, been killed in war or murdered, died in childbirth, or committed suicide by any means but drowning. The final realm of existence was the "fish trail"; located beneath "Raven living," the spirits of drowned persons existed there in a village beneath the water of a river.

In life each person was thought to possess three essential qualities: body, spirit, and breath. A person's physical body came from a land of unborn babies and was transferred into its mother's womb. If a neonate died, its body was not buried in the ground but placed in the branches of a young tree in order to facilitate its rebirth. Sooner or later the spirit (yeg) of a person would leave his body, and the individual then died. Death itself resulted from the fact that the supernatural Giyeg had directly or indirectly lured the spirit away, for just as people ate animals in order to survive, Giyeg subsisted on the flesh of humans. The body of a dead person was not feared, but it was a frightening experience to be associated with the dead because of the nearness of Giyeg. The fact that the flesh of a dead person disappeared was taken as evidence that Giyeg had consumed the edible portions. A person, like all other things considered tangible, had a spirit which was invisible except when one stood in the sun, and then it was manifest as one's shadow. This spirit left a person's body to wander during dreams, which made it dangerous to waken a sleeping person. If Giyeg prevailed on the spirit as it wandered, it would depart permanently from the person's body. Each individual's spirit was a unique entity and a force to be protected more than feared. The third life quality was associated with "speech" or breath, and it began to leave the body of a person as the spirit ebbed. The breath of a deceased individual joined others of its kind in a village near the cemetery. Although invisible, the breath people made a sound similar to the tapping of feet. On occasion they attempted to lure the breath of a former friend or relative to join them, which might cause the person's death.

Survival was contingent on dealing successfully with forces intent on human destruction, and the most dangerous of these was Giyeg, who was aided by helpers who were effective in different ways. Although never seen, Giyeg was said to look like a little man in the winter and to assume the appearance of a whirlwind in the summer. As the most important threat to human life, Giyeg was a single force and at the same time had multiple facets. In his efforts to attract a person's spirit he caused dreams or produced illness in a person. He was attracted especially by noise, and it was he who caused a house to creak after the fire had died at night. One means for gaining protection against Giyeg was to burn lamps at night. An alternative name for Giyeg was Eli—a designation used in referring aloud to him, since he was attracted by his real name. At times, however, Eli was considered a distinct being. Giyeg was aided by the spirits of sorcerers; when these forces caused a death, the body was food for Giyeg. Additional helpers were natural forces. For example, the "cold spirit" was not as powerful as Giyeg or the spirit of sorcerers, but it was nonetheless a potent and harmful force. The cold spirit had the ability to heat a winter traveler's blood and deceive him into thinking that he was warm. The man would remove his parka and then his mittens; in time he became tired and slept, only to freeze to death. A "water man" who lived in the water could tip over a man's canoe, and if he chose, this spirit could drown the person.

Some persons referred to Giyeg as Nakani, but the latter appears more often to have been thought of as a helper of Giyeg. A Nakani or "woods man" originated at a time of starvation. During a famine some men and women became insane and were lost, only to develop into Nakani. They were dangerous only in the summer, when their usual practice was to steal children. In order not to attract their attention, people did not talk about them nor did they whistle when they suspected that a Nakani was near because these supernaturals communicated by whistling.

Other forces in the natural world aided man in a positive manner. Animals were made available for hunting through luring them from their home inside a mountain by performing certain ceremonies. Even more important were the "salmon people," for the flesh of this fish was the prime Ingalik staple. Each of the five salmon species lived in a separate village near the "fish trail," the home of the spirits of the drowned. In the late spring the humpback salmon summoned the others to swim up the Yukon River; this was likened to being invited to a potlatch. The number of salmon taken during a summer depended on how many villages the messenger had visited. The humpback salmon arrived first and was followed by other species. The Ingalik believed that the fish swam freely into a man's net; when he lifted it out of the water and struck the fish with a club, its spirit was released to return to its watery home.

As an Ingalik faced the realities of life, he was more concerned with what was "evil" or "bad" than that which was good. Of all evils, perhaps the greatest was to kill someone. It always was evil to kill a woman, but the murder of male enemies was excusable. After any murder the weapons used were burned or otherwise destroyed. For a sorcerer to kill someone was evil, and a revengeful murder of the sorcerer was similarly regarded, if only because it was thought that the killer surely would die as a result of his act. Similarly, to feud or gossip was evil, and aggressive behavior such as biting or kicking was bad. For a person to be economically unproductive was considered bad for several reasons. If a man had broken a taboo which made him unsuccessful in obtaining food, this was bad not only for him but also because the burden of supporting him fell to others. Similarly a lazy person was bad because his energy was wasted. Noise was not just bad but evil, and the important positive value placed on being quiet led to the avoidance on arguments, to walking quietly, and speaking softly.

Goodness was a more passive state of behavior, one that was simply the converse of evil or bad. In addition, it was good to resist change and to be conservative. Life itself was good, and its positive aspects were conveyed in the common expression the "loved fire." The evening fire in the men's house symbolized warmth, security, and togetherness among the members of a village.

Beauty to the Ingalik most often appears to have meant "pretty" and "attractive," but it also referred to an ability to last or endure. Specific characteristics of attractive objects included color contrasts which were in close association, as between red and white skins placed together. Regularity or order was appreciated as was illustrated by the geometric designs formed in the edging on a birch bark basket. Finally smoothness was much valued, as reflected by spruce planks which were regular and even. The most outstanding characteristic of a beautiful woman was her hair, and long hair in particular was especially pretty. Additional physical features which were regarded as desirable in a woman included shortness of stature, stoutness of build, large breasts, and small feet.

With respect to their general behavior patterns, an Ingalik was far more concerned with hearing and seeing the right things than he was with smells. To avoid something because of its smell was unusual. It was felt, however, that people should avoid looking directly into the eyes of another; it was proper to look off to one side or downward. Sounds were kept at a minimum, to the extent that it was improper to yawn loudly or to smack one's lips, and sudden noises were frightening. It was found too that while the emotions of anger, jealousy, fear, and shame were expressed, as we would expect, it was shame that loomed as most important. If a person were noisy or were looked at directly by another, he felt ashamed. This attitude was conveyed in stories too; when something disparaging was said about someone, the accused was ashamed.

Social life was organized around the nuclear family. A man habitually lived in his wife's community after marriage (matrilocal residence), although living in the settlement of the husband was an acceptable alternative. There were no strong feelings about whether one should marry a person from his own or another settlement (agamous communities), and relatives were traced along both the male and female lines (bilateral descent). These people had three distinct social classes, but an individual was capable of shifting from one to another during his lifetime. Persons known as "rich men" along with their families made up about 5 percent of the population. A man achieved this status by being a highly successful provider who accumulated food surpluses and owned material property of value, or by becoming a successful shaman. Rich men led ceremonial activities and were in a position to aid ordinary persons in times of economic or emotional stresses. Common people constituted about 75 percent of the population, and although they were not named as a separate class, yet they clearly stood between rich men and those called "people who do nothing." These were lazy persons who lived off other persons and did not marry. A male numbered among such persons might have been born into a respectable family, but as a child he refused to perform the chores which were expected of him. If he continued to behave in this manner, he was turned out of the house around the age of ten. He might be taken home by a friend who felt sorry for him, but the friend's mother was most likely to turn him away. As the boy became hungrier, he was likely to steal food from his mother's cache. If he returned home, his mother would most likely accuse him of the theft and beat him with a stick, and he would leave again. It was unlikely that such a person would reform; he slept in the men's house, stole food, and was generally despised. Eventually such persons might starve or freeze to death.

The Ingalik spoke a language of the Na-Dene linguistic phylum; speakers of related languages were more widespread than those of any other linguistic phylum in North America. The area of the Na-Dene included the interior of Alaska and much of northwestern Canada, and it extended southward to include small pockets in northern California and a broad area of the southwestern United States. The Ingalik of the Anvik-Shageluk area, who were studied most intensively by Osgood, clearly recognized distinctions in their speech and material culture which set them off from other Ingalik living nearby. Their houses, however, were similar to those built by Ingalik farther down the Yukon River. A winter house was semisubterranean, rectangular in outline, and covered with a nearly flat roof. It was entered through a short tunnel to which an entry-way was attached. These dwellings were framed with spruce posts, and the walls were formed with poles over which dry grass and a layer of dirt were added. Interior benches served for sleeping and lounging, and there was a central fireplace beneath a roof opening which served as a skylight and exit for smoke. A small house was occupied by a single family, whereas larger ones accommodated several families. In the summer people lived in rectangular houses constructed on the ground surface; these dwellings were built near the water's edge at a winter settlement or else at a separate summer village located near good fishing spots. Summer houses had vertical wall planks, and their gabled roofs were built of poles covered with birch bark and topped with a layer of dirt. They were occupied by from one to three families and were entered through a small oval opening in one wall. In the interior were benches as well as a central fireplace.

Life in an Ingalik village focused in the men's house or kashim, as the Russians termed it on the basis of an Eskimo name for a similar structure. A kashim was large, with the main room measuring about twenty-five by thirty-five feet. Framed and walled with logs, the semisub-terranean structure had a cribbed roof and was covered entirely with grass and earth. In the center of the roof was a removable skylight, and through it the smoke from the large central firepit drifted upward. Along one of the longer sides and extending to the firepit was a tunnel beneath the floor; this served as an entrance and exit on occasion. Above it was another exit which led to a porch or entryway connected with steps to the ground surface. Along all four walls were benches some two feet in width. The men's house served as a workshop, and it was here that ceremonies were performed. Men slept in the kashim on the nights when they did not visit their wives, and they also bathed there by building a fire in the fireplace and then removing their clothes to sweat in the dry heat.

These people wore skin clothing all year long. A knee-length musk-rat pelt parka with an attached hood was the standard upper garment for both men and women, and beneath it was an undershirt of squirrel skins. Two pair of caribou skin trousers were worn by men; the inner pair was short and was covered by a belted outer pair which reached from above the waist nearly to the ankles. Women wore undertrousers over which were drawn caribou skin trousers with boots attached. The caribou skin boots of men were knee length, but those which women wore outside the house reached halfway to their hips. Other garments included mittens, hats, and boas, all of skin or fur. The most distinctive items of adornment were the labrets worn by men. Two holes were made in the outer edges of a youth's mouth just beneath his lower lip. Into each of these openings was slipped a labret made of stone or antler. These ornaments were round or oblong and were flanged at both ends to prevent them from slipping out of the openings. Not all males wore labrets, but they were considered attractive and desirable adornments.

Economic welfare was based largely on fishing, and salmon were the most important species harvested. King salmon were taken in gill nets drifted down the river and tended from a canoe, but most others probably were caught in large funnel-shaped fish traps made of wood splints and set in association with weirs. Other fish traps were set for pike, loche, and blackfish; whitefish were taken in gill nets; pike were hooked, and lampreys were dip-netted. Caribou, bears, birds, and small game were snared or else taken in deadfalls. In the winter men hunted on snowshoes, and when traveling with heavy loads they used built-up sleds pulled by people, not by dogs. For summer transportation the birch bark canoe was the most important form of boat. These people are known for the fine quality of their snowshoes as well as for their skill in working wood and birch bark. Indians of the subarctic forests of North America often led very uncertain lives due to the frequent scarcity of food, but because of the diversity and abundance of fish in and near the Yukon River, the Ingalik could live comparatively secure lives in their semipermanent villages.

In spite of the relative abundance of food there were periodic starvations, and the Ingalik were deeply conscious of death. No other single event was of comparable magnitude in terms of personal loss and ceremonial involvements. Signs of approaching death were numerous, and one of the most certain indicators that someone was going to die was the hoot of an owl heard from the forest. To see where a raven had rolled over in the snow beside a trail or to find the frozen body of a particular species of hawk were equally certain signs of death. As the time of an individual's death grew near, he made sounds similar to yawnings. A person who was aware that he was dying might show no outward sign of emotion, or he might weep from fear.

Sources: Osgood 1940, 1958, 1959.

PAIUTE IRRIGATION

One of the most inviting and yet perplexing problems confronting anthropologists is to explain the origins of ideas employed by various peoples. The body of available information about innovations in our society is voluminous, which makes it possible sometimes—but not always—to determine with precision where and when a new form was introduced. The problem of establishing the derivation of a known form among ethnics, whether it is a bow and arrow or the mother-in-law taboo, is fraught with uncertainties. People often borrow ideas from others and forget the donor's identity, or they originate a form but attach no historical importance to the fact. Furthermore, an ethnographer inquires into the origins of a custom often hundreds of years after it was accepted in the cultural matrix of a people, and they cannot be expected to remember the circumstances of the change. Possibly no one would deny that the idea to cultivate plants was of great moment in the economic history of man. Whether the innovation occurred only once or repeatedly is not important in the present context. It is pertinent to ask, "How did it come about?" Archaeologists of course have contributed a great deal to understanding the origins of farming, and yet ethnography too has something to offer, if only because archaeological interpretations must be based on ethnographic analogies. To describe and briefly analyze Paiute irrigation practices provides no absolute answer to the beginnings of farming activities among men, but it does exemplify a possible transition.

On the eastern side of the Sierra Nevada Mountains in central California is a great interior basin, and one of its landlocked watercourses is the Owens River, which flows into Owens Lake. In this region of comparatively little rainfall, hot summers, and relatively cold winters an estimated 1,000 Paiute Indians lived at the onset of historic contact. The population density was about 2.5 persons per square mile, which is low but not out of proportion with densities among other peoples who followed a similar way of life. These Indians depended heavily on pine nuts for food, and during those years of abundant harvests they spent the winter in the mountains near caches of nuts which they had collected. Here they built double lean-tos, one for women and another for men; these structures were framed with posts and poles and covered with pine boughs. When the pine nut yield was small, they wintered in valley bottoms, where more substantial winter houses were constructed. These pole-framed structures were built above a circular pit and were occupied by a number of small families or a single large family. These dwellings looked like broad-based cones in outline and were covered with reed mats or with leaves, boughs, and earth. In the summer they lived in dome-shaped structures built at ground level with bent willow pole frames covered with boughs or sections of woven grass; these valley-bottom dwellings were designed for protection from the sun above all else. Another structure was the sweathouse, which was built on the same general plan as the valley-bottom winter house. Here a bath was made by building a fire in the central firepit, and the male bathers sweated solely from the dry heat. This building also served as a meeting house and as a residence for unmarried or elderly males.

Paiute males wore breechclouts, short-sleeved shirts, and ankle-length pants, all of which were made from dehaired skins. Both sexes wore skin moccasins, and women wore short deerskin skirts, which might be painted with vertical red stripes and have deer hooves included as decorative trim along the lower edges. In the winter woven rabbit skin capes were worn by men and women. These people made a wide variety of coiled and twined baskets which served as carrying and storage containers. Their basketry water containers were coated on the inside with pitch. Given the nature of their seasonal movements, their manufactures tended to be light and portable. They made crude pottery and conical pipes of clay for smoking wild tobacco; their knives had flaked obsidian blades, and they used a hand-rotated drill to kindle a fire.

If people wintered in the mountains, they returned to the valley bottoms in the spring and brought with them any surplus pine nuts they might have. Throughout most of the year they hunted when the opportunity arose, and the bow and arrow was their most important weapon. For small game they used a bow made from a single piece of wood (self bow), but for hunting larger animals the bow was strengthened with sinew (sinew-backed bow). The feathered arrow shafts were tipped with flaked stone or wood points. Deer were hunted by using dogs to bring them to bay or by luring them with disguises or imitations of their calls. At times large numbers of persons participated in cooperative hunts for antelope, deer, mountain sheep, and rabbits. The small game taken by individuals included waterfowl, squirrels, porcupine, and gophers. During the summer fish formed a significant part of their diet, and they were taken by a wide variety of means. A fish poison was made by crushing slim solomon plants and distributing bundles of them in pools; as the fish became stupefied, they were collected in baskets. Fish were shot with featherless arrows and were taken with multipronged spears (leisters) and barbed hooks as well as in gill nets. Furthermore, conical baskets were attached to the openings in the dams built to form pools for poisoning fish, and these served as fish traps.

Piñon grew at elevations ranging from 6,000 to 9,000 feet, and their seeds were the most important staple. Productivity of the trees was unreliable, but in a year of an abundant harvest, enough nuts were collected to last a family through the winter, spring, and early summer. Groves of productive pines were owned by the residents of each locality, and trespassing led to rock-throwing quarrels. In order to harvest the nuts, wooden hooks were tied with thongs to long poles. With these instruments cones were dislodged from trees, and any ripe nuts which fell from the cones were collected on blankets spread beneath the trees. The cones and nuts were carried in baskets and skin bags to the winter settlement, where they were stored in rock-lined pits along hillsides. As seeds were needed, the cones were exposed to the sun so that they would open and the seeds could be dislodged. Cones also were opened by placing them in a bed of coals overnight; with this method the nuts would roast at the same time. Loose nuts were charred in a tray held over a fire. Cooked nuts might be eaten dry, pulverized into a flour, made into a gruel, or added to soups.

During the fall wild seeds from diverse grasses and other plants were collected. The usual pattern was for a group of women to dislodge the seeds from their stalks with seed beaters, which looked rather like tennis rackets, and to catch the seeds in conical carrying baskets. If a variety of seeds were collected at one time, they later were separated by sifting them through a twined basket. The seeds were processed further by grinding them on a flat stone (milling stone, metate) with the aid of a handstone (muller, mano). After being pulverized, they were winnowed if necessary to remove the husks. Probably their most common means of using the resultant flour was to cook it with water in pottery vessels to make a mush or gruel.

In order to increase the number of wild seed plants in certain areas, the Paiute built dams and ditches to divert water into fields, which were up to four miles in length and nearly two miles in width. There were relatively few such irrigated plots due to the nature of the local terrain. In some areas a new irrigator was chosen each year, but in other sectors a local leader held the title permanently. A new dam of boulders, brush, sticks, and mud was built each spring by the irrigator, with the aid of about twenty-five men. A main ditch leading from the dam was cleared and then tended by the irrigator, who also maintained small lateral ditches and lesser dams. In the fall of the year after the seeds had been harvested from a field, the dam was broken. Fish stranded in the irrigation ditch after the water was gone were collected from the dry creek bed, as they had been when the dam was built in the spring. Some plots were flooded on alternate years, probably to allow the seed plants to reestablish themselves. The labor that went into dam construction and harvesting the seeds was communal.

Here is an example of plant irrigation without domestic crops, plantings, or cultivation. The Paiute were not farmers, but seem to have been on the verge of becoming cultivators. Irrigating wild plants might have been an old and widespread practice in the southwestern United States, and might have survived only in eastern California, but there is no evidence to support this logical possibility. It also is possible that the idea of irrigation could have spread to the Paiute from farmers in the Southwest. Yet if this were true, we would expect at least one cultivated species to have been planted, which was not the case.

Possibly the Paiute irrigation system originated among the Indians themselves. Any number of localities flooded naturally, and it would have been rather obvious that these were the sectors in which plants grew best. Given the importance placed on seeds as food, the arid nature of the environment, and the unified sources of water which moistened fields naturally, it seems reasonable that they might perceive how to expand productivity with dams and ditches. Assuming that the Paiute did originate the irrigation system, we need not suggest that it took a genius to conceive of the first network. We know that collectors of wild seeds were careful observers of growing conditions and knew the characteristics of their environmental setting very well. Any number of persons could have formulated the idea to modify the course of a stream purposefully in order to flood an adjacent but comparatively unproductive plot of seed-producing land. Conceivably, if historic contact had not taken place until a few hundred years later, the Paiute might have had a much more elaborate irrigation system, which could have drastically altered their subsistence round. The major point to be considered is that a slight purposeful change in the natural environment had the potential for causing remarkable changes in the field of culture.

Source: Steward 1933.

THE YUROK: SELFISH CAPITALISTS

Along much of the western coast of America, from northern California to the Gulf of Alaska, the coastline is indented with narrow bays, behind which often rise snow-shrouded mountains. An abundance of rainfall and the relatively mild year-round climate have produced huge tracts of great trees and undergrowth so dense that often it is impenetrable. The rivers feeding into the Pacific Ocean usually are short, and they once ran fast and clear from the mountains. Each summer millions of salmon from the Pacific searched for these streams in which to spawn. This environment once was occupied by diverse peoples; although they differed from each other in many ways, most of them shared a dependence on salmon and other products of the sea for their subsistence welfare. It often is written, and probably is true, that among all the ethnics who lived by hunting, fishing, and collecting, those of the Northwest Coast of North America had developed the most complex aboriginal way of life. All the coastal peoples from San Francisco Bay to the Bering Strait depended to a certain extent on their harvest of Pacific salmon, but the species were exploited most intensively from the Klamath River in California and Oregon to the Yukon River in Alaska. Those groups relying heavily on salmon in their economic life included the Tlingit, Haida, Tshimshian, Kwakiutl, Nootka, and Yurok as well as hosts of other Indians of lesser fame. Yurok life exemplifies the typical Northwest Coast Indian concern with wealth and prestige but differs in having no effective political organization and deemphasizing far-flung kinship ties. The Yurok also lacked Northwest Coast Indian totemic associations, a rigidly defined class structure, and involvements with inherited titles validated by great potlatches. Their material culture, by contrast, was most typical of California Indian forms. The Yurok invite consideration because they were an essentially classless people who stressed wealth, personal honor, and individual initiative. Individualism appears to have been a dominant principle which guided their lives. In some notable aspects their life style was similar to that of many contemporary United Statesians.

Most Yurok lived along the banks of the lower Klamath River in northern California; the others occupied a sector of the seacoast adjacent to the river mouth. The aboriginal population numbered about 2,500 persons, and along with their neighbors to the south, the Wiyot, they comprised the only representatives of the Ritwan language family. This linguistic fact is notable because the Yurok and Wiyot were isolated from the speakers of other languages belonging to the same phylum, which in this case was Algonkian-Mosan (Macro-Algonkian), a phylum concentrated in the eastern United States but extending into the center of the continent. If the Ritwan speakers did not exist in fact, it is doubtful that they would be assumed to exist in theory. Here we have an example of a small linguistic enclave which probably became physically detached from the core of the parent phylum thousands of years ago. They shared very few nonlinguistic ties with other Algonkian-Mosan speakers; one similarity of note was the belief that the world was surrounded by a sea partially composed of pitch. Thus, they retained their language but lost the cultural forms and societal norms generally associated with it. An additional point is appropriate with reference to the language and culture of the Yurok and their neighbors. To the east of the Yurok were the Karok, who were Hokan-Siouan (Hokan) speakers; to the north and south of the Yurok were the Tolowa and the Hupa, representing the Na-Dene linguistic phylum. Within a radius of about sixty miles, therefore, were persons who represented three distinct linguistic phyla and yet had very similar material forms. The rather obvious point is that language and culture do not necessarily go hand in hand. Since the Yurok, Hupa, and Karok were socially distinct, it may be seen that in one small sector of the Pacific Northwest the linguistic differences were great, the social divisions clear, but the cultural forms were similar.

The Yurok felt that normal persons stayed near their homes with their friends and relatives; thus they did not freely venture far nor did they welcome strangers who were not introduced by familiar neighbors.

Their provincial perspective was further reflected in their manner of conceiving of the world and their position in it. For them the geographical center of the earth, which was thought to be essentially flat, was near the junction of the Trinity and Klamath rivers; the Klamath was considered the only notable watercourse in the entire world. They believed that from the mouth of this river it was only a twelve-day canoe trip to the other side of the world, a distance of some 150 miles. Their conceptual map depicted an ocean surrounding the country which they occupied with their neighbors; beyond it was a sea of pitch, and at the sky's edge in the northwest was the mystical home of supernaturals, including salmon and a small marine mollusk called dentalium.

Historically a Portuguese expedition probably first visited the Yurok coast in 1595, and the area was revisited by the Spanish in 1775. Effective contact with outsiders was established between 1775 and 1800, and over the next twenty years the local Indians became involved in the sea otter trade. From about 1820 until 1848 very little is recorded about Yurok interactions with foreigners, and contacts probably were infrequent. Gold was discovered along the Trinity River in the 1840s, and this brought the first direct and lasting contact between the Indians and outsiders. When Kroeber began his ethnographic studies of the Yurok in 1900, the oldest Yurok could still recall what was essentially an aboriginal way of life.

Yurok country covered nearly 700 square miles, but the areas fronting the Klamath River and the seacoast were exploited most intensively. A network of trails provided access from these regions to the heavily wooded localities adjacent to them. Settlements, which ranged in size from one to about twenty-five dwellings, were located at the mouths of streams or along coastal lagoons. A typical village consisted of five or six houses, each with about seven residents related through a line of males. Hamlets were abandoned due to flooding, quarrels among the inhabitants, disease, or apparently because residents became bored with living in one place.

The rectangular plank houses had gabled roofs and were built in pits dug in the ground. A roof opening admitted light to the interior and permitted smoke from the fireplace to escape. On one of the shorter sides a round entrance hole was cut near the ground level, and outside the opening paving stones were set. Some four feet behind the entrance and paralleling the front wall was a partition; behind this, driftwood and household goods were stored. Included might be such items as snowshoes, carrying baskets, implements called seed beaters for dislodging seeds from standing plants, and disk-shaped baskets for collecting seeds. In the center of a house, a pit up to five feet in depth was dug, and a notched pole

A group of Yurok houses (Courtesy of Lowie Museum of Anthropology, University of California, Berkeley).

ladder joined the two levels. The center of this sector contained a stone-lined fireplace where meals were prepared; the residents ate in this lower section, and women and children usually slept there. Scattered about were wooden meat-serving trays, twined cooking baskets, spoons of antler, and wooden finger bowls used for washing after meals. The only other furnishings were redwood stools. Often a lean-to of planks, which served as a menstrual hut, was built at one side of a house; at other times a separate structure which served the same purpose was constructed a short distance away. The only other buildings of note were the bath houses, which were associated with from one to three dwellings. It was here that men and boys slept and lounged; although women were not prohibited from entering a bath house, they were not particularly welcome visitors. Bath houses were smaller than dwellings and were set deeper into the ground, but they were of the same general form as the houses. The entrance, however, was in one of the longer sidewalls, and in front of it the ground was paved with stones. Since the floor of a bath house was deep in the ground, a notched pole ladder was placed near the entrance; a separate exit, which was very small, was built into one of the shorter walls. The interior was floored with stones or planks except in the vicinity of the fireplace, and the room was furnished only with redwood pillows. To prepare a bath a fire was built in the fireplace, and the smoke drifted out cracks in the gabled peak of the roof, which was covered with an old canoe turned upside down. Bathers undressed, entered the bath house, and closed the doorways. Each individual lay close to the floor to avoid suffocating from the smoke. After the fire had burned down, they squeezed through the exit, lounged on the stone platform to recover from the effects of the extreme heat, and then swam in a nearby stream.

A clear indication of the importance of salmon as food is the fact that this fish was called "that which is eaten" (Waterman 1920:185). As salmon ascended the Klamath River, they usually were taken in dip nets when they paused to rest at pools near eddies. Gill nets were set in eddies also, and seines were employed. The netting appears consistently to have been fashioned from iris leaf fiber made into cordage. Salmon also were caught in weir and trap combinations as well as with harpoons made by mounting two separate toggling points on a single long wooden shaft. Next to salmon in importance as food was the acorn, which was the prime staple among most Indians in California. As Kroeber (1925:87) noted with brevity and clarity, "Acorns were gathered, dried, stored, cracked, pulverized, sifted, leached, and usually boiled with hot stones in a basket." Meat and other plant products were far less important in the total diet. Large animals such as deer and elk were taken occasionally with arrows shot from sinew-backed bows as well as in snares set along game trails. A single plant, tobacco, was grown on burnt-over hilltops. It apparently was the same species as the wild tobacco which occurred locally, but the leaves from plants growing wild were not smoked for fear that they had grown on graves. Tobacco was smoked in pipes with tubular bowls set at the end of wooden stems; the most avid smokers were likely to be older persons.

In terms of dress and adornments the men wore their hair long and loose, and men as well as women pierced their earlobes and hung a pin of bone or shell in the opening. A man might paint his face with diverse designs; the colors used were indicative of his feelings—white meant mourning, red was for joy, and red and black in combination reflected hostility. Older men wore no clothing, but younger ones wore a skin folded about the hips. The women gathered their hair in two bundles in front of their shoulders and kept it in place with thongs. They wore basketry caps, their chins were tattooed, and around their necks hung necklaces of bones, shells, or small pieces of fruit. From a woman's waist hung a short skin apron fringed with shells, nuts, or pieces of obsidian;

over this garment a somewhat longer skirt habitually was worn. In cold weather persons of either sex wore capes of deerskin; skin moccasins were worn mainly by travelers.

After many years of Yurok studies, Kroeber characterized these Indians as an extraordinarily proud people who were quick to anger and ever reluctant to forgive misdeeds or to make peace with their enemies since they hated with a conviction of their righteousness. They were suspicious, sensitive, greedy, and covetous of material property. While trying always to retain what they possessed, they attempted to gain greater wealth at the expense of others. They plotted constantly to make claims against the wealth of others and to avoid or defer the payment of their own obligations. At the same time they were puritanical in their speech, gestures, and sexual activities.

Since many of their attitudes focused on wealth, the nature of Yurok riches must be described. The most important medium of exchange, which was standardized in value and thus fits an acceptable definition of money, was dentalium shells. These small mollusks produced tusk-shaped shells which might reach three inches in length. They were most abundant in the coastal waters of British Columbia where the Indians used a rake-like device to impale them on the sandy ocean floor. From the western subarctic to southern California these shells were highly prized, and the Yurok graded those that they received into six named types. The longest shells, which were very scarce, were the most valuable, and an eleven-shell string of these was worth about $50.00 during the early period of white contact. A string of similar length but consisting of fifteen smaller shells was worth $2.50 at the same time period. Another monetary unit was the scalp of a redheaded woodpecker; these were small change since they ranged in value from 10 cents to $1.50 each. These birds were taken locally by tying a small funnel-shaped wood trap over the entrance to their nest in a tree. A trap was set in the evening, and the next morning as the birds attempted to fly away, they became wedged in the funnel and could not escape. A finely dressed deerskin was valued at from $50.00 to $100.00, but an albino deerskin was worth as much as $500.00. Finally, large, oblong blades flaked from black obsidian and as much as a yard in length were held in such esteem that their value could not be estimated. Shorter obsidian blades, up to a foot in length, were valued at a dollar an inch. The finest blades, however, rarely passed out of the ownership of a particular family. Money, especially in the form of dentalium shells, was exchanged for artifacts, services, and property. The amount of tobacco that would fill a woman's basketry hat was worth one small shell. A large dugout canoe was worth ten large woodpecker scalps or two twelve-shell strings of dentalium. A house was worth three of the twelve-shell strings, while a shaman's fee for curing was one or two of these strings.

Wealth served three primary functions: Disputes could be settled permanently only if property was exchanged, marriages were validated only when riches passed from the groom to his bride's family, and great prestige was gained only by owning valuable property. Any wrong which served as the basis of a property claim was considered as having been committed by one individual against another person. Physical punishment or violence never was condoned and only led to further claims. In order to settle any wrong, property was awarded to the victim; extenuating circumstances, such as the age, sex, or previous record of an offender, rarely were taken into serious consideration. At the same time, the extent of a property settlement was in part contingent on the wealth of the offender and the social position of the claimant. Once the terms of a settlement had been agreed on and property had changed hands, no further recourse was permitted to the parties involved concerning that particular dispute. The primary grounds for claims were murder, adultery, seduction, trespassing, using the name of a deceased person, or a shaman's refusal to treat someone who was ill. Another grounds for a suit stemmed from every person's right to be ferried across a river if he did not have an available boat; the persons involved might even have been enemies, but the obligation remained.

The Yurok obviously had a well-developed and integrated legal system in spite of the fact that they were nonliterate; the rules and precedents were memorized. Many basic legal concepts which we might expect to find were entirely absent from their code. That there were no offenses against the community as a collectivity suggests weak extrafamilial integration at the settlement or ethnic level. Neither was there any idea of valid physical punishment. While money ideally had a fixed value, more or less might be sought depending on the social position of the person against whom a claim was made and depending on the history of the objects used as the medium of exchange. In other words some money was "clean" and some was "unclean." The conclusion to be drawn from these criteria is that the Yurok had a highly organized and effective legal system, and yet they lacked any formal body politic. Their legal norms were operative in the absence of codification, centralized authority, or a legitimate enforcement body because tradition and public sentiment provided a firm base which no sane Yurok was prepared to defy. It was established by custom that one individual would press a claim against another, who then would resist as vigorously as possible. Sooner or later the aid of intermediaries might be sought and compromises made by both parties until a final settlement could be reached.

As is true of any legal system, the one of the Yurok had many derivative ramifications. For example, a person who was unable to discharge a debt was obligated to become a chattel of his claimant and to labor for this person. Such an owner might give a wife to his debtor, but any children they produced became the property of the owner. Debt slavery, which always involved another Yurok, was rare, however, and slaveholding tended to be unusual. One extraordinarily wealthy man was said to have owned three slaves.

When an individual was ill from a disorder which did not have an obvious physical cause, such as a cut or broken bone, he was treated by a female shaman. The amount of payment was negotiated and was paid in full before the treatment was begun. A cure was expected to follow payment, and if this did not occur, the patient was refunded his property. A shaman could not refuse to treat a patient unless she were demonstrably ill herself. If for some reason a refusal was made and the prospective patient died, the shaman was held responsible for the death.

An individual's existence, even his conception, was conditioned by thoughts about money. Some casual observers of the Yurok assumed that they had a mating season since births generally took place in the spring. The patterning in the time of births resulted from the fact that a man kept his wealth in the house where his wife slept, not in the bath house where he usually slept. Since wealth became tainted by exposure to sexual activities a man tended to copulate with his wife only in the summer when they often slept out-of-doors. A pregnant woman worked diligently and ate very little in the hope that the birth would not be difficult and that her pattern of behavior would be passed on to the offspring. Many child-rearing practices quite clearly promoted adult values. To encourage self-reliance, the legs of an infant were massaged to induce it to crawl at an early age, and it was weaned by the time it was a year old, which is a short nursing period among ethnics. Small children were taught to consume very little food, not to speak at meals, to eat slowly, and to think of money while they ate. A child soon learned not to mention the name of a dead person or to refer to such an individual because litigation against him through his parents would follow. In order to discourage a child's use of words or gestures associated with the dead, nettles might be placed on his lips or hands. Likewise, children were strongly encouraged to acquire adult skills at a youthful age.

Two examples of disputes over property rights illustrate the workings of the system. In one instance a man ferried an acquaintance across a river. It so happened that the carrier's house caught fire when he was so engaged. The man being ferried was held responsible for the loss, less the ferriage, because it was reasoned that the house owner might have prevented the loss if he had not been transporting his acquaintance. The second episode occurred during the early period of United States control and involved a trader. He contracted with five Indians to transport trade goods from the coast to his trading post on the river; all five men were drowned on the trip. During the next few months the relatives debated about the amount of settlement and then presented their claim; their price was equal to about $1,500.00 in gold. The trader refused to pay, maintaining that he only had hired the men to transport the goods and had nothing directly to do with their deaths. The Indians left but returned a few days later prepared to kill the debtor and no doubt loot his store. He had been forewarned, however, and held off their attack. A truce was arranged by a neutral party, and the Indians were deceived into thinking that the trader was sending for money to make the settlement. In actual fact he sent for U.S. Army troops who came to his rescue and stayed for about eight months. During this time the Yurok claimants did nothing, but after the soldiers left, they killed a white even though he had no association with the original confrontation. This case illustrates that an intermediary was used to arrange a settlement, that claimants were patient and calculating, and that any stranger was held accountable for the acts of any other one, suggesting that the Yurok regarded all outsiders as from a single kin group.

The vast importance attached to material property is well reflected in marital negotiations. A man's social standing was determined largely by the amount of property that his father had offered to his wife's relatives at the time of their marriage. Persons at the bottom of the social scale were issue from nonlegitimate matings, and for them no property had been exchanged. The social position of bastards was even beneath that of slaves. Next in rank were individuals whose fathers, because very little had been offered for their daughters, could in turn provide only a small amount of wealth for their sons' marriages. The next level was reached when an honorable and sufficient amount was offered as bridewealth. Finally, the social hierarchy was capped by men whose fathers offered an inordinate amount of wealth for their brides. Each of these arrangements was a "full-marriage," meaning that after the wealth had been exchanged the bride joined the household of her husband (patrilocal residence). Expectably, every potential marital arrangement called for manipulations by the relatives involved to gain the greatest possible personal advantage. A groom could not be expected to possess the necessary wealth without aid from his father and his father's brothers. These men, however, were sometimes so greedy that they would not discharge their obligations to the young man. In this situation, as well as in the case of a poor but honorable male, a "half-marriage" was arranged; this type constituted about 25 percent of all marriages. The groom presented his potential father-in-law with all the property which he was able to assemble even though it was an insufficient amount, and then he moved into the bride's household as a member (matrilocal residence). The children of such a couple were affiliated with the wife's family, not the husband's, and the bridewealth of any daughters born to the couple went to the wife's family. Additionally, the husband was subordinated to his wife to such an extent that she could openly criticize his behavior, supervise his subsistence activities, and control the behavior of their children. Other circumstances which led to half-marriages included a premarital pregnancy which required rapid marital arrangements to avert the birth of a bastard, or marriage into a family which had only daughters. In the latter event an in-marrying man might be declared a legitimate heir by his father-in-law. Furthermore, a selfish man with a daughter who was a successful shaman might force her into a half-marriage in order to have a lasting claim to the earnings from her practice.

Objects of material wealth were not plentiful among the Yurok, and the manner in which they were coveted made it difficult for a poor but ambitious person to improve his social standing. An avenue to riches did exist, but it was a difficult one. The accepted approach was for a young man to think long and hard about money, especially during and after bathing in the intense heat of a bath house. He was to think of money at every possible moment, and to concentrate on dentalium shells alone for ten consecutive days was highly desirable. Such an individual was further obliged to work hard, to fast long and diligently, and to avoid thoughts of sex and women. He said to himself, "I want to be rich," yet he did not invoke the aid of spirits. By following this regimen it was thought that money would come his way, and even if it did not such an individual gained respect among others.

People were litigious where money was involved, but their purpose in seeking increased wealth was the prestige and honor of ownership. Simply to know that one possessed goods of great monetary value and to be able to display them occasionally brought feelings of inordinate pride. The greatest exhibits of riches were made during the climax of dances held following ceremonies designed to assure the continuity of the natural world. The core of these ceremonies was the recitation of an esoteric narrative by a formulist. The dances that followed were held at least once a day for five, ten or more days, and the most dramatic group performances were the Deerskin Dances. The participants were males, and most of them wore knee-length, wrap-around skirts of skin. Around a man's neck were hung masses of dentalium shells, and over his brow was a band of wolf fur. Attached in his hair was a long feather which in fact was a composite of many feathers joined to appear as a single feather of great length. His face was elaborately painted or else his shoulders and arms were adorned with paint. He carried a pole with a stuffed deer's head at the top, and the deer's skin hung down loosely to sway as the pole was moved during a dance. Other more elaborately costumed dancers did not hold deerskins aloft but carried obsidian blades encased in deerskin covers. As the days passed, more and more obsidian blades were held and exposed for all to see. At the last dance of the final day the most priceless treasures finally were exhibited.

Many Yurok gathered together during the ritual involved in the construction of a great fish weir with associated fish traps. The only other occasion when they cooperated intensively with one another was during the annual World Renewal ceremonies held each fall. One was performed at the spot thought to be the geographical center of the world, and others were held at four additional locations scattered about their country. The purpose of these rituals, with their complex components, was to avert natural disasters and disease so that the world might continue to exist in an unchanging fashion. Only in these events was ethnicwide cooperation for the common good reflected.

The individualistic Yurok obviously placed great emphasis on hard work, self-denial, and crass as well as subtle aggression in order to accumulate wealth. As Walter Goldschmidt has observed, the Yurok and other Indians who lived near them had derived a "protestant ethic" with clear capitalistic values even in the absence of a Western cultural background.

Sources: Goldschmidt 1951; Heizer and Mills 1952; Kroeber 1925, 1959; Thompson 1916; Waterman 1920.

TLINGIT TOTEM POLES

Not infrequently we associate a particular trait with a specific area of the world and presume that the form was not only well-established aboriginally but originated during that time period. One reason for these assumptions is that the characteristic often is striking if not dramatic and is "typical" of a particular area. We may fail to consider that some forms presumed to be aboriginal might in fact have been produced as a result of historic contact. Certain forms of totem poles made on the Northwest Coast of North America during historic times illustrate the point.

The northern sector of the Northwest Coast is a land of superlatives. The mountains are towering, the rivers wild, the trees huge, and the natural resources bountiful. It was in this majestic setting that about 10,000 Tlingit Indians lived when they first were contacted by the Russians in the mid-nineteenth century. Even the diversity of available foods was impressive. The richest resource was salmon, and each species came from the north Pacific Ocean by the millions to ascend spawning streams. Each year salmon could be taken from July to December, but the greatest quantities were fished in September. They were harvested by building weirs across streams; at openings in these fences, funnel-shaped fish traps made from splints of wood were placed. Salmon were cleaned and split, after which they were sun dried or smoked for future consumption. At other times of the year the people fished for halibut by setting lines of hooks from their canoes. Women fished for trout by using gill nets in streams, while men chopped holes in winter ice to spear flounder. In addition great quantities of oil-rich candlefish were taken in dip nets as they ascended rivers. Fish were not the only food, for they hunted seals, sea lions, and dolphins with harpoons at sea and took diverse land mammals such as deer, porcupines, and marmots with arrows shot from bows and by setting a wide variety of traps and snares.

The aboriginal Tlingit were tall and lean, and their bodily adornments made them especially striking. A man wore a ring through a hole in his nasal septum, and from his earlobes were suspended pieces of shell, stone, or teeth. Men of renown had small holes along the outer edges of their ears, and in these, pieces of wool or small feathers were placed. Women wore earrings in addition to extremely large medial labrets beneath their lower lip. Facial paintings in red and black were popular, not only because the designs were pleasing but because the paint also served as a protective covering from the heat and cold. Men and women dressed in short-sleeved skin shirts, and in cold weather capes of sea otter skins were added. Women also wore an undergarment of skins which covered their bodies and legs. They went barefooted except when they wore moccasins in cold weather. Their villages, with houses arranged in rows, usually were built along sheltered bays or on the banks of the lower courses of rivers. The square houses built of heavy planks had gabled roofs and lasted for generations. These structures were built around four massive interior corner posts and were entered through an oval doorway which faced the water. In larger houses there was a sunken pit in the center; in the area with a fireplace, a fire was maintained, meals were consumed, and women often worked. On the sides at ground level were compartments enclosed by planks or mats for sleeping. On overhead beams fish might be hung to dry, and here too large artifacts which were not in use were stored. Around a house entrance, or at times surrounding an entire village, were protective palisades. Exploitable areas adjacent to a settlement were owned by the members of particular female lines represented in a village (matrisibs). Closely related persons of a particular matrisib occupied either a single dwelling or ones which were adjacent. The Tlingit area was divided into thirteen or fourteen geographical units called *kons*, each with its recognized boundaries. The matrisibs were divided into two groups (moieties), the Ravens and the Wolves (alternatively Eagles). Thus an individual was identified as a Tlingit, as a member of a particular moiety, as a member of a named matrisib, as belonging to a specific female line within a matrisib (matrilineage), and as a member of a particular household and family.

Economic and individual activities united a household, whose membership centered around a core of brothers and their mother's sisters' sons, who were classed as "brothers." These males as well as other members of their matrilineages and in-marrying spouses cooperated under the direction of the Keeper of the House, an elder among the core of brothers. His superior position within the residence unit was reflected in several important ways. A Keeper of the House supervised the economic activities of members, and he represented the household at ceremonial events. His special privileges included being given the best food to eat and being freed from menial chores. When such a man died, he was replaced by a "brother," either biological or classificatory. Women brought into a household as wives always were from a sib in the opposite moiety (moiety exogamy). An ideal mate was a father's sister, followed in terms of preference by a brother's daughter, or a father's sister's daughter; the latter was the girl that a man was most likely to marry since of the choices, only she was of his own generation.

The elaborations of Northwest Coast Indian ceremonial life are well known, and the potlatch is the most famous of all their festivities. A potlatch was held in order to commemorate some notable event affecting the members of a segment of a sib. The death of an outstanding leader, the completion of a new house, a man's assumption of an honored sib name, or the settlement of a feud all were occasions for holding potlatches. Among the Tlingit these festivities ostensibly were held by local members of one sib to honor those of a competing sib which was of the opposite moiety and was represented in the same or another settlement. In order to hold a memorable potlatch the organizer and his relatives accumulated vast amounts of property and food. Huge feasts were arranged, special songs and ceremonials were held, and valuable gifts were presented to the guests. At a later date they in turn became the hosts and were honor bound to organize an even greater potlatch for their former hosts than the one which they had attended.

In one respect the potlatch and totem poles were always associated: No totem pole could be erected without holding a potlatch to honor the event. All totem poles were made from red cedar, but they assumed many different forms and served distinct functions. The most widespread type on the Northwest Coast was the house pillar; among the Indians of the Queen Charlotte Islands and southward these poles, which were struc-

Mortuary pole and graves in the northern Tlingit area (from Malaspina and De Bustamante y Guerra 1885).

tural supports inside a building, were carved with designs to illustrate mythological events. Among the Tlingit, the house posts themselves usually were plain, but they were faced with carved panels to give the appearance of being carved posts. Some panels were inlaid with pieces of abalone shell, ermine skin, and human hair. The reason the Tlingit house posts themselves were not carved may have been that the large red cedar trees used for posts did not grow in most of the Tlingit area; since the carvings were made by craftsmen at the southern fringe of Tlingit country and had to be imported, it was less expensive to transport them as panels.

Mortuary poles were the second type of totem pole, and they consisted of plain poles, on top of which were placed boxes containing the ashes of the person in whose honor the pole was erected. At a later date the ashes were redeposited in a cavity at the rear, and a totemic figure of the deceased person's sib was carved in wood and placed on top of the pole. This was the most common form of totem pole found among the Tlingit before their intensive exposure to Christian missionaries. Another form, the memorial pole, was erected either in memory of a dead person or to honor someone who was still alive. It usually commemorated the dead, however, and was placed a short distance from a grave. In historic times this form tended to replace the older mortuary poles.

Another type of totem pole was erected at the front center of a house; this was the heraldic pole. The designs carved on such a pole were taken from the mythology of the residents' matrilineage, and a hole in the base served as the doorway. In early historic times heraldic poles were short and broad, but later they became tall and elaborate. The fifth form was the ridicule pole, which was raised by someone who hoped to force an important person to recognize some particular obligation. An example will illustrate the circumstances under which a ridicule pole might be raised. In the household of a ranking member of one particular sib lived three women from another sib whose totemic representation was a frog. These women defied the rules of propriety and slept with slaves belonging to the household head; this man then attempted to make the Frog sib leader, who was responsible for the women, pay for their keep. The head of the Frog sib maintained that the women had so badly disgraced his group that they had been expelled from it, and he refused to recognize the debt. As his only recourse, the reluctant host erected a pole with three frogs sitting side by side on a crosspiece at the top. Whether or not the debt ever was paid is not known.

The sixth and final form was called the potlatch pole, and it was the most elaborate of them all. At the top were from one to three "watchmen," and beneath them was the totemic symbol of the man who had the pole carved and erected. Under this symbol was illustrated a myth important in the traditions of this person. Near the base of the pole was the totemic figure of his wife's sib; this was the only form of pole on which the totems of different sibs were represented.

A totem is any form which is held in special esteem by a particular social group. Although it may be a plant or an object of nature such as the moon, it is most often an animal species. Attitudes toward totemic objects vary widely, from one of great religious respect for the form because of its association with the group's origins to a casual acceptance of it as a symbol of the group without any additional significance. Among the Tlingit the totemic symbols represented on poles were associated with either a moiety or a particular matrisib, and they were derived from the mythology of their users. Thus, persons of the Raven moiety were permitted to symbolize the Raven in their art forms, and had the additional right to use the totems of their sib, such as a frog or sea lion, in their designs.

A weathered and tilted totem pole in an abandoned Tlingit cemetery or village gives the impression of great antiquity. Yet wood exposed to the elements in southeastern Alaska deteriorated rapidly because of heavy rainfall and the fluctuations in temperature. Totem poles are so dramatic in appearance and so overwhelming in size that it is almost inconceivable that they would not have been described if they had been seen by the earliest explorers in the area. Yet none of the early Spanish, Russian, or English explorers mentioned seeing totem poles. Admittedly some of them had only fleeting contacts with the Indians, but others had ample opportunity to explore coastal settlements. However, by the 1790s descriptions of totem poles begin to appear often in accounts. The freestanding form seen most often was the mortuary pole, although other detached forms were mentioned. Carved house posts too are reported, and in all probability they were the earliest form that was made. Around Sitka, in the heart of Tlingit country, no totem poles were seen in 1775, but mortuary poles were abundant by 1805 and remained so almost fifty years later. Apart from these mortuary forms most free-standing poles appear to have been erected from about 1840 to 1880. In the northern Tlingit area, as well as in the extreme south, such as around Vancouver Island, detached totem poles were not carved in any number until about 1880 or even later.

The most elaborate poles are potlatch poles, and observers usually agree that they probably could not have been made prior to the introduction of iron tools. The Tlingit had a sophisticated woodworking technology at the time of historic contact and probably already had salvaged some iron tools from flotsam which drifted ashore. Shortly after the Northwest Coast was discovered, it was visited by many trading vessels from diverse nations. The traders sought one commodity above all others —the pelts of sea otter, which brought high prices in Europe but especially in China. Large numbers of sea otter lived along the Tlingit coastline, and they were killed by the thousands. This new fur trade made it possible for the members of lesser lineages of matrisibs to accumulate great wealth rapidly, and their riches were spent on lavish potlatches climaxed and commemorated by the erection of great potlatch poles. Soon each wealthy man attempted to give a greater potlatch than his rivals and to raise a potlatch pole which dwarfed the one of his competitor both in size and elaborateness. Thus, the florescence of both the potlatch system and the erection of totem poles was a direct response to conditions brought about by early historic contact.

Sources: Keithahn 1963; Krause 1956; Oberg ms.

CROW WARFARE

Hostile activities may occur in nearly any human population. An armed, organized, and murderous conflict between groups of people is war, while purposeful murders on a smaller scale are termed feuds. Probably no people were entirely free from feuding in one way or another, and most societies accommodated both forms of hostility. The reasons offered to account for wars range from economic motivations and religious goals to the offended pride of persons and nations. It also has been reported rather frequently that for some peoples warfare was a game, a deadly one but a game nonetheless. Possibly the most renowned warriors among ethnics were the Plains Indians in the United States. They typify the ideal of proud and determined warriors who fought for personal honor above all else. Contrary to the patterning of conflicts in large-scale societies, Plains Indian wars usually were of brief duration; the soldiers were not drawn from standing armies, and there were no officers with permanent rank.

Among ethnics of the North American Plains information about the Crow is more adequate than for most as a result of the field studies by Robert H. Lowie. As mentioned in the second chapter, the lifeway of the Indians he described was not aboriginal and was similar only in outline to their culture at the early period of historic contact. The introduction of horses, indirectly from Spanish sources in Mexico, made equestrian hunters of these people. The early nineteenth-century Crow were known not only as able horsemen and warriors, but as skilled craftsmen and haughty individuals. In the Upper Missouri River system and in the not-too-distant past, the Crow and Hidatsa were one people, who ranged as far westward as the Rocky Mountains and lived mainly by hunting large game animals. By the early 1800s the Crow numbered about 3,400 persons, of whom some 1,100 were warriors; at that time they owned about 10,000 horses, more than did any other ethnic of the region.

The Crow were Siouan speakers with their closest linguistic ties to the Hidatsa and the Dakota, and they were divided into two groups, the Mountain and River Crow. A position of superior leadership was assumed by a "valiant man," who was wiser and braver than the rest. Such an individual emerged as the head of a camp and appears to have remained in office as long as the band prospered. His primary duties were to decide where and when the camp group should move, and each spring he appointed a particular military society to police the activities of camp members. The most important function of military society members was to supervise cooperative bison hunts. Individuals or small parties who hunted bison alone were likely to scatter the herds and thereby reduce the number of animals available to be taken in a large cooperative hunt. If members of the military society established the fact that a person had hunted illegally, he was whipped, his weapons destroyed, and the game taken from him. The policing force attempted to settle peacefully any disputes between members of the band and to prevent war parties from venturing forth at inauspicious times. They also were in charge of the movement of people from one camp to another.

The Crow lived in tepees, the dwelling form which we associate so intimately with Indian life on the American Plains. These structures were

Mounted Crow scout (Courtesy of the American Museum of Natural History).

framed with four basic poles, to which others were added; over the entire framework was a covering of sewn bison skins, which was pinned together at the front. Two additional outside poles were used to adjust the flaps attached at the smokehole in the top of a tepee. Near the center of a dwelling floor was a fireplace, and at the rear was the seat of honor. The tepee-type dwelling was well suited to a mobile hunting economy. Camp goods were transported on travois pulled by horses and dogs from one camp to the next. The most important animal hunted was bison; other game of significance included antelope, deer, and elk. Crow material culture reflects their dependence on the hunt. The skin garments of men included a shirt, full-length leggings, a G-string, and moccasins; women wore long dresses of skins as well as skin leggings and moccasins. Tools often were made from bone, and containers were fashioned from skins rather than from basketry or pottery. Bows were made from horn or antler, backed with sinew and strung with sinew, while arrows might be tipped with bone points. Shields used in battle were made from bison hide, while spoons and cups were of horn. This list could be expanded, but it is sufficient to emphasize the point that the animals killed by the Crow provided much more than meat.

In their social lives stress was placed on relatives traced through women (matrilineal descent); this is reflected in the fact that children acquired one of thirteen names associated with female lines. Each matrilineal descent group was represented in various sectors of Crow country, and actual blood ties could be traced to some persons in other sectors; to others such bonds were presumed to exist (matrisib). Each sib was responsible for the behavior of its members and in theory was free from internal control by the members of another sib. On occasion disputes arose between the members of different sibs which led to feuds and murders, but when confronted by a common enemy the sibs united. The thirteen named matrisibs were clustered into five groups of two each, plus one group of three. The grouped sibs (phratries) were unnamed, but members of sibs belonging to the same phratry were prohibited from marrying one another. For example, Sore-Lip and Greasy-inside-the-Mouth were the names of paired matrisibs. A man from one could not marry a woman from the other. However, marriage was permitted into the Kicked-in-their-Bellies or Bad-War-Honors sibs, which formed another pair. Sib affiliation not only regulated marriage but also offered physical and moral aid to members. In principle matrilineal descent prevailed, but on occasion sacred objects and ceremonial prerogatives were inherited by an eldest son rather than by a sister's oldest son. Then too an individual felt closely identified with his father and his father's relatives, and when a man married, he and his bride lived near his father's home (patrilocal residence).

War was the dominating and lifelong focal point of activity and interest among the Crow. A male achieved great prestige only in connection with war. Old age was deplored because such men could no longer fight; ideally a warrior died young and in battle. Women shared in the glories of their men, as when a wife danced with the scalps taken by her husband, and mothers prodded the warriors to avenge the battle deaths of their sons. A successful raid yielded not only the material reward of booty and an increased social standing for participants, but it indicated the strong spiritual protection of those involved. Thus, even their religion was intimately linked with conflict. The two reasons most often expressed for going forth to do battle were the desire for revenge and the hope to gain booty, especially in the form of horses. The games of boys stressed weaponry skills, perseverance, and bravery, all of which conditioned them for the conflicts in which they soon would be participants. Given these values, most Crow boys sought to accompany a war party at a youthful age. During their informal initiation they were required to perform menial camp chores and were the butt of practical jokes by experienced warriors.

A typical hostile venture among the Crow is best termed a raid. Each was organized by a "raid-planner" on his own initiative; however, under certain circumstances the military society in charge of a camp could stop the organization of any particular raid. Ideally a raid-planner first had a prophetic dream or vision about the details of the venture, including its successful outcome. If he could convince others that his revelation was a true one, he would be able to enlist a party and make arrangements to set forth. The most important preparation by participants was to have many pairs of moccasins made since the raiders usually set out on foot. The actual departure often was made after the sun had set, and when the territory of an enemy was approached, usually within a matter of days, scouts were dispatched to reconnoiter any camp they found. The warriors then made their final preparations for a raid, attaching sacred objects to their bodies and painting their faces in a manner prescribed in a dream or vision. The planner also offered a prayer to the Sun for the success of the enterprise. Usually the purpose of the raiders was to take as many horses as possible, and the technique was for one or two men to creep into the enemy camp. If many horses were obtained, the raiders were well satisfied and rode away as fast as possible in order to avoid capture. Even the most carefully planned and executed raid was hazardous and exhausting; when all did not go well, the results could be disastrous. If not enough horses were captured to provide each man with a mount, some warriors were obliged to walk back, and this greatly increased the risk of their being killed by pursuers. Warriors traveled so light that they might run out of provisions if something delayed their return; once a sudden snowstorm overtook a Crow raiding party and resulted in the death of most of the men from hunger and exposure.

While a typical raid was organized in order to steal horses, others were fielded for the primary purpose of killing enemies, often as vengeance for the death of a Crow. If the party returned from such a venture "with black face," it meant that at least one enemy had been slain. When the victors returned, dances were held, and each participant invited the people to his tepee to hear his account of the exploit. Additional festivities were held during the following days, and these brought communitywide recognition and attested to the importance of successful martial achievements. The most renowned raid planners were not the men who killed many enemies or captured innumerable horses, but those who did not sustain losses. If one raider was killed, the surviving men did not return into camp until they had at least stolen horses on a second raid. The death of a single Crow warrior plunged the camp into mourning. For the family in which the death had occurred, the mourning rules prevailed until an enemy had been killed.

The social standing of a Crow male was based largely on his achievements against enemies; four different activities were acknowledged to be the most honorable. These were to lead a successful raid, to steal horses picketed in an enemy camp, to "count coup" (meaning to be the first to touch an enemy), and to take a bow or gun from an enemy in hand-to-hand combat. Individual opinions varied on the importance attached to any one of the four brave deeds. Some felt that all were of equal importance, while others judged particular combinations as bravest. Furthermore, each of the four accomplishments was symbolized on the garments of the person involved. A certain degree of variation prevailed, but in general a warrior who counted coup attached wolf tails to the heels of his moccasins. A man who had taken a gun adorned his shirt with ermine skins; the leader of a war party who had returned with booty fringed his leggings with ermine or scalps. An individual who had accomplished each feat at least once was a valiant man and was by definition a leader. Thus social distinctions were based largely on deeds of personal valor, although an individual's position was enhanced further if he had many relatives who would support him.

The best known of Plains Indian war exploits is the concept of "coup." The word was introduced by French-Canadians and means a "blow" or "stroke." In a broad sense "counting coup" meant to kill, scalp, or be the first to strike an enemy. Among the Crow the word would best apply to being the first to touch an enemy. For quite obvious reasons it was a far braver deed to touch an enemy with a special rod, called a

coup stick, than to kill him, and it was far more honorable to have been
the first to touch or strike a particular enemy than to be the second or
third man to do so.

As might be expected, in the confusion of battle two men might feel
that they each had the first claim to a particular coup. In order to settle
such disagreements each disputant might swear by the Sun that his claim
was just. The next time some misfortune befell one of the men he was
judged to be the false claimant. At large gatherings Crow warriors recited
their great accomplishments in battle, and to the four most important
deeds others might be added, such as the number of times a man had
gone into battle, the wounds received, and how many horses had been
captured from an enemy. The Crow took scalps, but such an accomplishment in itself was not considered an event worthy of recitation.

In 1910 when numerous notable chiefs still were alive the first chief
among the Crow was Bell-Rock. His totals in each category were six
unquestioned coups, five captured guns, two tethered horses obtained
without question, and the leadership of at least eleven war parties. Another chief who was respected universally for his bravery was Gray-Bull;
he claimed three feats in each of the categories.

In Crow ideology it was fitting for a warrior to die bravely in battle
at a youthful age, yet when any member of a raiding party was killed, the
venture was considered a failure if not a disaster. The death of a Crow
warrior sometimes led an inconsolable male kinsman to take one of the
greatest of all possible vows—to hold a Sun Dance. Years might pass
between the time of one Sun Dance and another because such an event
involved a great deal of preparation. The Sun was a supreme deity, and
this particular ritual was above all else a prayer for vengeance. Yet if the
bereaved felt strongly enough to make the vow, the positive benefits in
terms of success in battle were considered almost automatic. Instead of
making an outright declaration of intent, the bereaved man's behavior
became a clue to his intent; he ate little and soon acquired a lean and
haggard look. His formal declaration of intent was made just before a
bison hunt when he asked the band chief to save the tongues from all of
the animals slain. Some informants reported that as many as a thousand
tongues were required, and a series of hunts might be undertaken to
provide such a large number. The tongues were necessary in order to feed
people during the ceremony and to pay individuals for special services.
The man who made the vow was called a "Whistler," seemingly because
at certain points during the rituals he blew on an eagle-bone whistle. He
engaged a shaman who supervised the ceremony and provided an extremely sacred and powerful doll for the Whistler to use in visualizing a
dead enemy. The form of such a doll had been given to the shaman in a

vision, or was passed down from one of his ancestors. A sacred doll also was used in one other fashion. Before going off to do battle, a warrior might go to the owner of such a doll and beseech it to bring success to his venture; the owner would make a small replica of the form, which the warrior then wore. This was an important but secondary use of a sacred doll; its greatest importance was that a Sun Dance could not be held without one being present.

The shaman who presided at a Sun Dance was the "father" to his "son," the man who took the vow. The medicine man engaged in preliminary rituals and called on other persons to perform particular tasks, the most important of which were the preparation of garments for the Whistler. He was dressed in a specially made kilt, and his face and body were painted with special designs in white clay. One cross-shaped pattern was painted on his chest and another on his back, each symbolizing the Morning Star, and lightning designs from his eyes represented tears. A necklace of skunk skin and a whistle were hung around his neck, and a plume was attached to the top of his head. He wore a special robe as well as new moccasins blackened with charcoal to represent the slaying of an enemy. Songs were sung after the Whistler was costumed, and later eight warriors recited their war honors.

Following the preliminaries sketched here only in outline, the Whistler passed the night on a special bed of sagebrush and cedar. That evening the shaman selected a site within a few miles of camp where the Sun Dance lodge would be erected. The central post against which the others were leaned was felled by a chaste woman after a great deal of ritual, and it was treated as if it were a slain enemy. Around the center post was built a pole framework which was covered near the top and along the lower section with willows and brush; the broad central band was left open so that the audience could see inside. After the lodge had been completed, the Whistler blew on his whistle and danced slowly toward the lodge from nearby; in one hand he held a hoop made from bent willows, to which were attached eagle feathers painted black. In the center of the hoop the doll, symbolic of the Sun, was fastened. After he entered the lodge, he tied the doll to one of the poles at the level of his face. It was about this time that men who were anxious to receive visions had their bodies daubed with white clay. Lines were attached to the lodge poles, and at the lower ends of these, skewers were attached and passed through slits made in a man's chest or back. A skewered vision-seeker danced and pulled against the skewer until it tore free. The Whistler did not skewer himself, but he did not eat or drink water after he entered the Sun Dance lodge. He gazed at the doll and danced before it as one great warrior after another reenacted his deeds of valor and then described them orally. The

Whistler's necklace, whistle, and head plume were tied to the doll at the end of the day, and he was bedded down in the lodge for the night.

The next day a sham battle was staged as the Whistler began to dance before the doll. He moved slowly and then more rapidly and did not stop as long as women sang; they attempted to drive him to exhaustion. Eventually, but sometimes not for days, the Whistler went into a trance and fell down panting; this was the climax and ended the ceremony. Most Whistlers did not recount the details of their vision until they set off on their quest for an enemy. The Sun Dance was the most important of all Crow ceremonies, and from the description it is quite clear that this most complex religious involvement was associated intimately with war.

The preceding text demonstrates the consuming Crow involvement with warfare and also imparts their ambiguous feelings toward conflicts. Theirs was a curious blend of bravado, bravery, and mournful regret; although death on a battlefield was considered noble, excessive daring more often was admired than imitated. The value which they attached to fighting demonstrates their martial proclivities, and yet it seems possible that all of this emphasis on conflict might be something of a facade, behind which stood a people trying to survive. William W. Newcomb, who studied Plains Indian warfare in detail, suggested that all warfare is economically motivated and is in reality a competitive contest between peoples for survival. Lowie (1920:356), quoted as one of the most respected authorities on the subject, wrote, "The Plains Indian fought not for territorial aggrandizement nor for the victor's spoils, but above all because fighting was a game worth while because of the social recognition it brought when played according to the rules." Most other ethnologists have arrived at similar judgments, although not always in quite so positive a vein. Newcomb derived his contrasting conclusions on the basis of a historical analysis which brought out the following considerations.

In the Plains area before A.D. 1600 lived Indians with two rather different economies. One cluster of peoples was concentrated largely in the arid sectors; these Indians were mobile hunters as well as collectors of plant foods. The other group did some hunting, but they largely were semisedentary horticulturalists who lived along the river valleys that they farmed. Around 1600 Spanish horses were introduced, which made it possible for both groups of peoples to exploit the great bison herds. Effective bison hunting could take place only after a people owned large numbers of horses and could be mobile. Although some of the farmers continued to depend primarily on their crops, even they organized some large-scale bison hunts. The net effect was for the peoples of the Plains to expand the areas over which they hunted. Since hunting effectiveness depended on horses, competition for their ownership became intensive. Somewhat later we also find that the white frontier expanded westward with ever-increasing intensity. This not only forced eastern Indians westward but also opened trade networks through which Indians were supplied with firearms. The peoples with guns and many horses could hunt bison most effectively and at the same time could impinge on their neighbors with the greatest success. It would appear from this resumé that the competition for control of hunting areas was a major cause of Plains Indian warfare, and that it became particularly fierce in the areas where bison were least plentiful. Furthermore, the bison herds shifted their grazing patterns often and were erratic in their year-to-year movements; these factors created an instability in the boundaries of the Indians exploiting the herds. Thus, if virtually all Crow were warriors from the time of their youth, it was to a large degree because the society required as many men as possible to defend their unstable way of life.

Sources: Lowie 1920, 1956; Newcomb 1950.

ZUNI COOPERATION

The word "society," as applied to a human population, means group living with goals and values shared among the participants. The concept also presumes that the persons involved follow common means to achieve their ends and interact with one another for an extended period of time as a collectivity. In these terms all societies are built on principles designed to integrate their members, but a great deal of variability exists in achieving this end. In some societies, as among many Eskimos, an individual functioned within a small family group in his dealings with others, and the activities of one family usually were of little concern to the members of another family. In the Philippines the large Ifugao families were integrated through being starkly competitive with one another. Among other peoples communitywide cooperation was a major social goal. The Zuni of New Mexico illustrate this pattern in which all group members were closely integrated through social, economic, and ceremonial groupings.

Among Indians in the United States those who have followed traditional patterns of behavior most tenaciously and for the longest span of historic time are settled farmers of the Southwest. The Zuni were encountered in 1540 by the Francisco Coronado expedition which was searching for the "Seven Cities of Cibola." One Zuni settlement was taken by force, but even though food was seized, the anticipated gold and other riches were not found. These and the other fabled "cities" were in fact comparatively small villages which the Spanish called pueblos. The Franciscans established a mission among the Zuni in 1629, but within four years some of the missionaries and the soldiers protecting them were killed. Although the Spanish established Santa Fe as an administrative center 200 miles away from the pueblo, they were never able to control the Zuni effectively. These pueblo dwellers, who numbered about 2,500 during the early historic period, actively participated in the Pueblo Revolt of 1680, and before as well as afterwards their acceptance of Spanish mission aims was halfhearted. When their area came under control by the United States, no dramatic changes occurred; in fact, it was not until the 1880s that the first intensive contacts were made. The individuals involved were cattlemen who attempted to encroach on Zuni lands and springs; in time they were prevented from permanent intrusions by the federal government. The long-term and positive association between the Zuni and the ethnographer Frank H. Cushing led to other friendly contacts with sympathetic whites. By the turn of the century diverse Christian missions were established among them, and a federally sponsored school was in operation.

The pueblo of Zuni consisted of a compact community of terraced houses built of adobe. The settlement was near the Zuni River, where little water flowed except after summer storms which made it a rushing torrent. In aboriginal times the people living here subsisted largely on maize, beans, and squash, which they raised by dry farming techniques. These staples were supplemented by meat from the animals they hunted, such as antelope and deer. Additional food resources for which the Spanish were responsible were wheat cultivated in irrigated plots near springs, peach orchards, melon patches, and herds of sheep; each was integrated into the subsistence cycle at a comparatively early date in spite of the general hostility of the Zuni toward the Spanish.

In Zuni society the most important unit by far was the household; its membership core consisted of a group of women related through females (matrilineage). Ideally a household was headed by an old woman, and living with her were her married daughters, their children, and in-marrying males (matrilocal residence). A household might also include divorced or widowed males who were the offspring of a female member. Thus husbands were outsiders in terms of a household core, and they in turn felt close ties with the households of their birth. The women of a household owned land which could not be alienated, and it was tilled mainly by in-marrying husbands. At certain times, such as during a harvest, the men might be unable to perform all the essential tasks. In such cases aid might be offered by their friends, the male relatives of the female household head, or by persons chosen to help by the leaders of

A view of the Zuni pueblo (from Stevenson 1905).

religious organizations. Cooperative work parties of this nature labored hard, but the occasion also was something of an outing, during which stories were recounted, friendly rivalries exhibited, and pranks played. Females of the household took a noon meal to the workers in the fields, and a large meal was served to them when they returned to the village in the evening. The harvested crops were the property of the women after they were brought into the house to be cached in a storeroom. From here they were withdrawn as required for consumption or for trade. Just as men helped one another in farming activities, the women and girls worked together performing domestic tasks. One of their most time-consuming duties was to grind maize into flour. In each household were three sets of grinding stones, manos and metates, of differing coarseness for preparing flour. The women of a house also produced craft items such as pottery, and they raised their children cooperatively.

A household was a small matrilineage, with the members occupying adjacent rooms in the dwelling. Each such unit was a component of a larger social group whose members presumed common ancestry through females (matrisib). In the recent past there were thirteen matrisibs represented at Zuni, and the members of each were obligated to find spouses from a sib other than their own (sib exogamy). Within each sib there was a leading lineage, with an elder female as the guardian of sacred paraphernalia belonging to the sib; a brother or maternal uncle of this woman was the most important sib leader.

With pervasive cooperation as the ideal it is to be expected that wealth differential among families was not great. Although the members of some households were richer than others, conventions prevailed which effectively redistributed much of the wealth. Apart from gifts to needy friends and relatives, a formalized giving occurred during the preparations for the winter solstice ceremonies and events associated with it. In order to serve as host for the impersonators of the gods during winter solstice rituals, the members of a well-to-do family diligently accumulated food and other property during the preceding year. They were aided mainly by persons of their ceremonial society, but all other villagers took part also, in order to receive some of the supernatural benefits and food given to all who participated. During these preparations poor women helped to grind maize and received gifts of food in return. A new house was constructed for the event; after men had hauled the timbers and built the walls, women did the plastering. The house was blessed by ceremonial leaders, and each person involved in the enterprise reaped spiritual as well as material rewards. When gifts were given during these preparations, there was no thought of either short- or long-term reciprocity.

To a large degree communitywide welfare depended on the yield of the cultivated crops. Yet this was a marginal area for most of the dry farming techniques which the people employed. It is little wonder that most Zuni ceremonial activities focused on rain and fertility. A ceremonial society was associated with each of the sibs, and the members held at least one major ceremony during the year. The leader of each society was drawn from the sib represented, but the general membership consisted of persons from diverse sibs. Each of these ceremonies was conducted in a room with an altar, on which sacred objects were arranged; the most important sacred object was an ear of maize, which symbolized the unity of the sib. The associated rituals included chants, prayers, and the smoking of a ceremonial pipe.

Another network of ceremonial involvements focused on the Katcina cult into which each male was initiated before he could be a fully integrated member of the group. Activities of the Katcina cult centered in a ceremonial structure of the type termed a *kiva* among Indians in the Southwest. A kiva served not only as the site of esoteric rituals but also as a workshop and the place where unmarried males lived. Cult activities focused on the impersonation of ancestral spirits, who were powerful supernaturals. These deities brought rain and fertility following the performance of dramatic secret and public rituals, and they were impersonated by men wearing masks and costumes appropriate to each of the many different gods. In addition to the Katcina cult there were other ceremonial associations serving such purposes as curing, conducting warfare, and bringing rain. Control of these groups might be associated with a particular sib, and sometimes the leaders were quite influential. The leadership of a ceremonial group was not actively sought, since this attitude was contrary to Zuni values. Instead individuals usually were groomed for a particular office from the time of their youth.

In a very real sense Zuni life was lived within the framework of a theocracy. The Sun priest, as the head of the priesthood, was acknowledged as the most important voice in civil and religious affairs. He remained subject to the same ideals of behavior which guided the lives of other persons, however, and he might be suspected of practicing witchcraft or causing the failure of crops, in which cases he could be replaced. As the person most responsible for the welfare of the pueblo, he was expected to be the greatest conformist. Thus his role could not be converted into a base for personal power. He was above all else the titular head of a network of religious organizations in which young and old, rich, and poor participated as groups and often *en masse* to harmonize collectively men with the gods.

Political power was in the hands of outstanding officeholders in ceremonial, not secular, organizations. The paramount leader, or "House

Chief," spoke for the religious societies collectively; he was at the same time the Sun priest, the keeper of the Calendar, and the individual most responsible for community welfare. No important ceremony could be held without his participation; he likewise was the person most responsible for appointing other ceremonial leaders. Important decisions were made by a six-man body of ceremonial leaders and were implemented by two Bow priests, men who were outstanding members of the War Society. The council dealt mainly with the appointment of civil officers, the round of ceremonial activities, and the actions necessary in times of calamity or crisis. In their deliberations the council members might seek the advice of any other ceremonial leaders who were influential in the particular area involved. The Bow priests alone dealt with secular disputes, which ranged from conflicts between families to warfare. The civil officeholders were headed by a "governor," an institution formalized through contacts with the Spanish. The civil authorities were appointed by the priests and could be removed from office at any time. They held jurisdiction over complaints such as those involving the boundaries of land, water rights, and inheritances.

The essence of a man was his soul, which was associated with his head, his heart, and his breath. It was in one's head that intelligence and skill were seated, while profound thoughts and emotions were deep in one's heart. Breath symbolized not only life but more, for when one inhaled in the presence of sacred objects, something of their essence entered an individual's body. These were not simply abstract notions of an esoteric nature but were integrated with the concept of self and functioned as a part of daily living. A precise set of behavioral characteristics served as the ideals which each member of the pueblo was expected to follow. An individual was expected to be inconspicuous, unobtrusive, considerate, generous, kind, and forgiving. Deplorable personality traits included personal aggressiveness, driving ambition, the quest for power, outspokenness, and the inability to compromise. Anyone who manifest the latter traits not only was deplored as a person but was quite likely to be accused of the most serious of all crimes, sorcery.

The Zuni felt that most deaths were caused by sorcerers who shot foreign objects into the bodies of victims. Under ordinary circumstances no one ever admitted being a sorcerer, and the practice of witchcraft always was covert. No person was immune to suspicion, however, and anyone suspected of such activity was shunned. If a death was attributed to a witch, the accusation was brought into the open most often by relatives of the person who had died. The Bow priests heard the evidence and interrogated the accused. If he appeared to be guilty, he was tortured into a confession. In itself a confession might be enough to negate his power and lead to his release; an alternative was to execute the sorcerer. In the rare instance when one person killed another and sorcery clearly was not the cause, every effort was made by the families involved to settle the matter quickly and quietly. The same was true of cases involving bodily injury, rape, and theft. Settlements were made promptly in order to avoid a resort to civil authorities, whose judgment might be harsh.

Accusations involving sorcery represented a major social stress, but there were others as well. Marriage, especially during the early years, tended to be quite brittle. A wife might divorce her husband simply by placing his possessions outside the door to indicate that he was no longer welcome as a member of her household. Even when a marriage ended, a man usually was regarded for many years as a suspicious outsider by his wife's relatives. Yet many marriages were lasting, seemingly because open quarrels were distasteful to the husband and wife alike. Stresses sometimes arose between sisters who lived in close association within a single household, especially if one sister disliked the husband of another. If a man was known by his wife to be participating in an adulterous relationship, she might fight with the woman in public as an extreme means for embarrassing her spouse.

The integrated and cooperative nature of Zuni life is apparent in many and highly diverse activities. For example, except when trading with the Navajo, a Zuni did not attempt to take unfair advantage in exchanges. A household's members did not attempt to accumulate and hold more material property than they actually required in ordinary living. No significant amount of property changed hands as a part of marital arrangements. This general deemphasis on economic power as an avenue to personal prestige was accompanied by an emphasis on the heartfelt participation and cooperation of individuals in many ceremonial activities.

The cooperative aspect of a man's social life may be summarized well simply by citing each of the minimal units to which he belonged. He was a lifelong participant in all important events which concerned the matrilineage of his birth; he was an economically important member of his wife's household; he was a member of the Katcina cult and at least one other esoteric religious association. He might also be a member of additional ceremonial associations. Each of these bonds had far-reaching ramifications. For example, as a member by birth of a particular matrilineage within a matrisib, a man was in a large part responsible for the general welfare of his mother and his sister. He brought them food and other gifts, contributed labor in their behalf when necessary, and was very much concerned about the discipline and general welfare of his sister's children. A man also might establish a *kihe* relationship with another person. The individual chosen might be a close childhood friend, someone with a valued skill that the man hoped to acquire, or a person whose closeness was sought for other reasons. In any event the dyad formalized their relationship in a hair-washing ritual and thereby became adopted members in each other's families, with all the accompanying rights and duties. They exchanged gifts but did not trade, and in general extended mutual aid. A kihe relationship was lifelong, and even after the death of one partner, it might be continued by his family.

Sources: Bunzel 1932; Dozier 1970; Goldman 1937; Spicer 1962; Stevenson 1905.

THE NATCHEZ GOD-KING

Complex aboriginal lifeways among ethnics are associated with peoples in central Mexico, Peru, and West Africa, but not in the United States in most people's minds. However, along the lower Mississippi River and in adjacent areas of the Southeast lived Indians with highly developed cultural systems. Comparatively little ethnographic information exists about most of these peoples because they were destroyed in early historic times. A partial exception is the Natchez of Mississippi whose way of life was reported by Antoine S. Le Page du Pratz (1695–1775), a colonist on intimate terms with the Natchez for about eight years after the first intensive contact with the French. The Natchez culture probably was not an indigenous development in the Southeast; it appears that at least some of the core features originated in Mexico. The Natchez possibly numbered about 4,000 persons during the late 1700s, and they appear to have been clustered in nine communities, a few of which were dominated by foreign Indians whom they adopted. The Natchez ethnic was integrated into a powerful political and religious system headed by one man, the Great Sun.

According to their traditions, in the distant past when the core population lived somewhere to the southwest of their historic homeland, two strangers, a man and his wife, arrived among them. These persons were so brilliant in appearance that the people thought they were derived from the sun. The man said that their origins were in the sky and that he would become their leader if the people would accept the rules and dogma to which he subscribed. These were explained to the people, and they agreed to accept them as their own. The man likewise instructed the people to build a temple which would be dedicated to the sun and there they were to maintain a sacred fire which he would bring from the sun. The people again concurred and accepted this man as their ruler; he was the first

Great Sun and the person who led them to their area of historic occupancy.

In Natchez dogma the supreme supernatural was termed the Great Spirit and was personified as a male who was so powerful that all other forces were nothing by comparison. From clay He made a perfect but small image of a man; He blew on the form to give it life and then watched it grow to perfection. A woman also was created as a companion for man. The Great Spirit was the creator of all things seen and unseen which were beneficial, and most lesser spirits were his servants. Some of those of the air, however, were evil. Although their leader was bound by the Great Spirit and therefore could do no evil, his servants remained active in the world. The Great Spirit was intimately associated with a sacred temple fire tended constantly by two of eight male guardians. Through this fire the Great Sun, his direct descendants, and his near-relatives communicated with the Great Spirit.

The Great Sun's dwelling, unlike that of any other person, was built on top of an earthen mound some eight feet in height. The dwelling was twenty-five feet wide and forty feet in length. Apparently when a ruler died, his house was burned, the mound probably was increased in size, and the dwelling of his successor was built on the expanded base. His house, of a style like that of many others, was framed with poles covered with mats and had domed or gabled roofs. In his dwelling the Great Sun sat on a small throne, and at all times he wore special garments. His head was covered with an elaborate headdress consisting of white feathers mounted on a netted base, which was bordered with red and fringed with seeds. When he ventured forth, he was carried on a litter which had a seat mounted on poles and cushioned with deerskins; adorning the litter were leaves and flowers. He was accompanied by sixteen of the greatest and strongest warriors, who carried the litter in relays.

Across a great open plaza from the house mound of the Great Sun was a flat-topped temple mound some eight feet in height. Three sides of it were steep, but the one facing the plaza was gently sloping. On top of the mound was a structure over thirty feet in length; built of heavy logs, it was topped with a gabled roof adorned with three large wooden birds. Inside the rectangular doorway were two rooms; the larger outer room contained a hearth on which the extraordinarily sacred fire burned. Nearby was a coffin made of cane which contained the bones of the most recently deceased Great Sun. The contents of the inner room were not clearly recorded, but it probably contained a stone which reportedly was the remains of the first Great Sun.

In physical appearance the Natchez were distinctive since they had very high foreheads, produced by artificially flattening the heads of infants. A man's hair was tonsured except that a little hair was allowed to grow long at the crown, and to this scalp lock white feathers might be attached. Youths, who often were vain, wore bracelets of deer ribs steamed and bent into circular form and necklaces made from stone beads; they also might carry fans made of turkey feathers. The hair of a woman was cut in bangs in front, and the longer hair at the back was held in a net with tassels at the end. From her pierced ears were hung shell ornaments. Both sexes removed axillary hair, and the hair of a man's beard was plucked. Young males and females alike had lines tattooed over the bridge of the nose, and some females had vertical lines tattooed on their chins. Near relatives of the Great Sun as well as outstanding warriors were elaborately tattooed on their heads, limbs, and bodies with abstract designs as well as figures of suns and serpents. The tattoos were made by pricking the skin and rubbing red or blue pigments or charcoal into the openings. Ordinary women wore knee-length skirts and men wore white breechclouts, both of which were made from deerskin. The breechclouts of chiefs were dyed black, and women of superior standing might wear cloaks made of feathers attached to a netted base. Robes and capes of skin were added in colder weather, and moccasins were worn when traveling.

The Natchez economy was based mainly on the cultivation of two varieties of maize, from which over forty separate dishes were prepared, and on other domestic plants. The cane growing on land to be farmed was cut and burned, after which the ground was prepared for planting with a wooden mattock. Fall hunts were emphasized to obtain deer and bison; the animals were shot with arrows from bows after they had been stalked or hunted cooperatively. The meat was smoked for later consumption. Fishing was even less important than hunting although some species were taken with gill nets, hooks, and arrows.

The social life of these Indians has been an inviting subject for study because of its seemingly anomalous characteristics. Apparently, however, the system was in fact neither unique nor strange; instead, the ethnographic data have been misinterpreted. From a reevaluation of early reports, Carol Mason suggests that at the apex of Natchez social structure were the Great Sun, his siblings, and his mother as well as others closely related in that particular female line (matrilineal descent). These individuals were obligated to marry persons from other lineages (matrilineage exogamy). Since there was matrilineal descent, the children of a Sun man could not belong to the lineage of their father; instead they were members of their mother's lineage. In order to acknowledge the out-of-the-ordinary standing of these children, they were considered as "nobles" or as "honored persons," depending on the nearness of their ties to the central

The burial of Tattooed Serpent, the brother of the Natchez ruler, the Great Sun (from Le Page du Pratz 1947).

figures in the Sun lineage. The title of noble or honored person also could be earned by persons of ordinary birth. For example, through notable success in warfare many men appear to have become honored persons. Likewise at the funeral of a member of the Sun lineage an individual could sacrifice his infant and thereby become an honored person. The keys to the social system were the exogamous nature of the Sun matrilineage and the recognition of no other line as being comparable in rank. Furthermore, a Sun could marry either a common person or a titled individual, provided the latter was not a Sun.

The ceremonies following the death of Tattooed Serpent, the brother of the Great Sun, will serve to illustrate the exalted standing of persons in the Sun lineage. Soon after Tattooed Serpent died, his body was clothed in his finest garments, his face was painted red, and a crown of feathers was placed on his head. Laid out on his bed, his body was surrounded by his weapons and all the peace pipes that he had received. Also standing nearby was a pole from which hung forty-six rings of cane, each of which represented an enemy slain by the deceased. He was surrounded by his primary wife, a secondary wife, his chancellor, chief pipe bearer, physician, some old women who were to be sacrificed as a part of his burial ceremony, and a noblewoman who had volunteered to be killed as a part of the services. The following day the dance of death was held; this appears to have centered around the persons to be killed for the funeral. Comparatively few victims were on hand, apparently because the French discouraged these sacrifices. Each victim was accompanied by eight relatives, and they rehearsed the death ritual twice during the day. The relatives who participated seem to have become honored persons after the sacrifices. At this time too the child of a common couple was killed by its parents, and as a reward for their sacrifice they were elevated to noble standing.

On the day of the burial the ceremonial activities were under the direction of a priest, who had the upper portion of his body painted red, wore a crown of red feathers, and had a knee-length garment decorated at the bottom with red and white feathers. In one hand he carried a cross-shaped staff from which black feathers hung. When he reached the house of the deceased, he saluted the dead man and then began the cry of death which was echoed by the mass of people assembled. The body of the deceased was taken from the house and placed on a litter, which was carried by temple guardians. The priest bearing the staff led the procession and was followed by the oldest warrior, who carried the pole with rings attached in one hand and a pipe of war in the other. The body of Tattooed Serpent came next in the procession, and it was followed by the sacrificial victims. The procession went around the house of the dead man three times and then wound in intersecting circles toward the temple. The body of the sacrificed child repeatedly was thrown on the ground in front of the corpse bearers so that they would walk over it. When the litter reached the temple, the victims, who had been drugged with tobacco, were strangled. The dead man's two wives also were killed and were buried in the grave with him.

Apparently by the time the French arrived, the Natchez had already begun declining in power and in numbers. Even in their eclipsed state, however, the complexity of their culture remained very much in evidence. The existence among them of a god-king who ruled with unlimited power, the occurrence of priests as full-time religious specialists, the permanence of their settlements, and the productivity of their land all are evidence of Natchez sophistication. Although their achievements were hardly equal to those of the Inca in terms of political organization or comparable to the Maya in religious terms, nonetheless Natchez culture was a far more complex way of life than generally is attributed to Indians north of Mexico.

Sources: Le Page du Pratz 1947; Mason 1964; Swanton 1946.

RELIGION OF THE MAYA

The modern Maya population is estimated at two million persons, which makes them one of the most numerous surviving indigenous peoples. They occupy a virtually unbroken expanse from the Yucatan Peninsula of Mexico to Guatemala and adjacent regions; this general area also was their aboriginal homeland. With many other Mesoamerican Indians they shared an economy based on maize, beans, and squash cultivation. They had hieroglyphic writing and a complex permutating calendar, developed markets in which chocolate beans served as money, and made human sacrifices. The Maya area is divided into distinct highland and lowland regions, in which there are well-defined rainy and dry seasons. The highland sector adjacent to the Pacific Ocean is more than 1,000 feet in elevation and is dominated by high volcanic mountains from whose core a thick mantle of ash was deposited over the land, to be overlain by a thin but rich soil cover. At higher elevations pines and grasses grow; farther down the deep ravines are stands of oak. Forests were burned over, and the resulting fields (milpas) were tilled for about ten years, after which they were allowed to lie fallow for as many as fifteen years. In the heart of Maya country, the lowland area extending northward across the Yucatan Peninsula, the setting contrasts greatly with the highlands. The lowlands consist of a great limestone shelf which is occasionally broken by hills. Comparatively few rivers flow through the region, and lakes are uncommon. Swamps and waterholes are sometimes found seasonally, but sinks formed by the collapse of underground caves (cenotes) are the most important source of water for domestic use. The lowlands are hot and dry much of the year; rainfall is not particularly abundant, and years of drought are not uncommon. The landscape is covered with forests comprised of varied species of plants depending on whether the region is generally dry or moist. In some areas deer and peccary are plentiful, spider monkeys common, and jaguars sometimes are found. The lowlanders burned over forests and planted their crops in the blanket of ash, but the yield of any particular field was high for only two plantings. The milpas lay fallow from four to twenty years, and while the areas farmed were productive, a great deal of land was required to sustain the cultivation system.

In Mexico maize was cultivated by about 5000 B.C., and yet reasonably wide-scale farming did not begin in the Mayan area until about 1500 B.C. With the origination of more productive varieties of maize as the possible cause, the amount of farmland increased and grain cultivation was intensified. Maya-speakers appear to have arrived in the area before this time and probably occupied small villages with fields nearby, hunting and collecting in adjacent localities. By about 800 B.C. the farming economy had expanded broadly, and large concentrations of peoples lived in the Maya area. No agreement exists among anthropologists concerning why the Maya had achieved greatness in cultural terms by the end of the first millennium A.D. The fact remains, however, that they had an elaborate calendrical system, esoteric writing, a vast amount of astronomical knowledge, impressive stone buildings, and sophisticated works of art.

At the time of Spanish contact in 1542 the apex of Maya culture had passed, yet their way of life remained one of the most complex reported for the New World. For food they depended most heavily on the crops from their milpas and on garden vegetables as well as fruit trees. Dogs of a number of different varieties were raised. The males of one strain were castrated and fattened for food and sacrifices; another variety was used when hunting. Deer and peccary were taken in drives with the aid of dogs and were killed with bows and arrows. Birds such as wild turkeys, quail, and pigeons were taken with pellets shot from blowguns. Included among their domestic animals in addition to dogs were turkeys and stingless bees. Fish were hooked, netted, and shot with arrows along the sea in Yucatan, while in inland regions dams were constructed to create pools from which fish were taken after first stupefying them with plant poisons.

Among the Maya distinct and separate social classes existed which were ranked internally. Nobles held the highest political offices and owned private lands. They were also the warriors of greatest rank, the richest merchants and farmers, and the holders of the highest religious offices. At the time of historic contact the ranking nobles were descendants of Toltec conquerers of an earlier era. At the head of each major territory was a ruler who inherited his position along the male line. He lived at his capital, and his economic position was assured by tribute received and the products of his land. A regional ruler's male relatives controlled smaller towns through local councils. Commoners were mainly farmers who worked their own lands or the lands of others. Slaves were common persons who had been taken as captives in war. Although they formed a hereditary class, a slave could be ransomed by his relatives.

An individual Maya of Yucatan inherited different rights and duties as well as distinct names from his father's and mother's side of the family (double-descent). There were about 250 names for male lines (patrisibs) at the time of historic contact. An individual was obligated to seek a marriage partner from a male line different from his own (sib exogamy). Property was inherited along the male line, and persons so related formed a mutual aid and protective association. One function of the named female groups (matrisibs) appears to have been the regulation of marriage. A father's sister's daughter or a mother's brother's daughter (cross-cousins) was the favored mate for a young man.

Maya knowledge was most developed in association with religious activities, for among them, as among many peoples, it was the priests who were the society's intellectuals. The extent of Maya achievements makes it apparent that they do not comfortably fit the definition of "ethnic" which has been offered. They wrote many books, which were made by folding pieces of paper bark and dealt with highly varied subjects; only three, which are religious texts, have survived. In addition there are post-conquest descriptions of their way of life, some of which were written in the language of the Maya but using Spanish script.

One of the most remarkable achievements of Mesoamerican Indians was the fact that they devised a numerical system which employed the concept of zero as a place holder; this idea seldom has been conceived in man's intellectual history. The Maya probably borrowed the idea from another people in Mexico, but they elaborated on the system. Our number system is based on counting by tens (decimal), whereas the Maya system was based on twenties (vigesimal). Mathematical calculations were used by merchants, but they were even more important to the priests. The calendar of the Maya was based on two permutating cycles. One of these, comprising 260 days, was derived from a system of thirteen numbers interlocking with twenty days. Each of the days had its own associations for good or evil in what Michael D. Coe (1966:55) has termed "a kind of perpetual fortune-telling machine." This system or Calendar Round meshed with the 365-day count of "Vague Year," so termed since it was not precisely 365 days although the extra quarter of a day was ignored by the Maya. Within the Vague Year were eighteen "months," each with twenty days; the five days added to the end of the series were very unlucky. Any day of the 260-day calendar had a value in the 365-day count. The "Long Count" of the Maya was based on a unit having 360 days; twenty of these units totaled 7,200 days, and twenty of the latter units totaled 144,000 days. The Maya also had a short lunar series which dealt with the phases of the moon and correlated with the Long Count. It is interesting to note that their calculation of a lunar month was 29.53020 days as opposed to a true calculation of 29.53059 days.

Considering the amount of intellectual energy that scholars have put into the study of Maya writing, the rewards have been disappointing. The glyphs with calendrical and astronomical meanings are understood, but the others are not. The difficulty hinges on correlating pictorial signs with the Maya words which they represent. At present it appears that the inscriptions on Maya monuments most likely deal with the rise and fall of ruling lines of nobility.

Considering the intellectual and material elaborations of the Maya it is not surprising that luxury goods and common commodities alike were traded over wide areas. Of all the Maya subgroups none were more renowned as traders than the Putun or Chortal Maya. From their homeland at the western base of the Yucatan Peninsula they emerged as great sea traders shortly after A.D. 1000. From a colony on Cozumel Island near the northeastern sector of the peninsula they proceeded to conquer adjacent mainland areas. In their homeland they had been influenced rather strongly by the Nahautl of central Mexico, some of whom were established as rulers over the Putun before their dispersal. It possibly was a Putun trading vessel that Columbus contacted along the coast of Honduras on his fourth voyage. The canoe had a cabin, and about twenty-five men, as well as a number of women and children, were aboard. The cargo included such diverse items as garments of cotton, copper axes, bells, wooden swords with pieces of flint glued along each side, and a large number of cacao beans. From early historical sources, both archaeological and written, as well as from tracing the origins of particular raw materials used by the Maya, it appears that sea transport was an important part of their trading pattern. Along the eastern coast of the Yucatan Peninsula products arrived from the Nahautl sphere, and from the inland rivers of British Honduras products were carried to the seacoast and then northward along the eastern shore of the peninsula. Among the most important trade items from the highlands were jade, worked lava manos and metates, polished blades of diorite, obsidian blades, and feathers of the quetzal bird. The lowlands produced flint blades, salt, honey, cacao, animal pelts, and a variety of bird feathers. The diversity of products exchanged and the distances over which they were transported indicate the organized and farflung nature of the trading network and the multiplicity of demands that were filled in this manner.

The religious system was headed by priests, who were succeeded in office by their own sons or the second sons of the nobility. The tasks allotted to these men were highly varied and exceedingly important in the organization of Maya life. At the time the Spanish arrived in Yucatan, each of the fifteen politically independent areas was headed by a ruler called a "True Man," who was an ex officio high priest. Immediately beneath him in rank, or perhaps at an equal level, was the highest-ranking priest, called "Rattlesnake-tobacco" or an alternative term. The duties of a Rattlesnake-tobacco included officiating at the most important religious events and teaching novice priests the art of writing, the methods involved in calendrical calculations, and the ways to perform rituals, to divine, and to prophesy. Ordinary priests, perhaps best termed "Diviners," officiated at regular ceremonies at the community level, and in addition some were specialists in prophesying and supervising human sacrifices. Another group of religious functionaries was comprised of old men called "Chacs." There usually were four Chacs, and they cooperated in such activities as holding down a victim for sacrifice. Lesser still were the "Prayermakers," who divined and cured and were in charge of minor rituals. Finally there were the "Vestal Virgins," who lived near the temples and were primarily responsible for tending sacred fires.

Before any major ceremony was performed, it was necessary for the participants to refrain from sexual intercourse, to fast, and often to confess as a form of purification. Certain ceremonies directly or indirectly focused on effigies, and these figures became widely popular in the lowland area during comparatively recent prehistoric times. The effigies, which also were used as incense burners, ranged in size from a few inches to as much as four feet in height. Some were famous and became focal points of shrines, but most were small and probably were kept in homes. They were made of stone or clay, most often the latter. Small effigy incense burners representing different gods were mass-produced in molds. To the basic figures details were added in applique, and after being fired they were painted. Vast quantities of effigy fragments have been recovered from prehistoric sites.

The Maya burned copal, a plant resin, as incense in honor of their gods and recited formal prayers to them as well, but their most dramatic offerings were sacrifices. A very common means of self-sacrifice was to draw one's own blood from the tongue, ears, arms, or penis with the stinger of a ray. The blood was collected on pieces of bark paper and offered to the gods. The sacrifice of persons, especially war captives, to the gods was a long-established custom among the Maya, although it appears to have been more common in recent prehistoric times than during earlier periods. A victim might be placed on an altar with his arms and legs held by Chac priests, or he might be tied to a pole or framework. In these instances an incision usually was made in the chest of the victim and his heart torn out. Other means of sacrificial killing included beating to death with thorns, shooting with arrows, decapitating, or flaying. Some individuals, especially children, were thrown into lakes or cenotes as messengers to the Chac gods who lived at the bottom of bodies of water. Becoming a sacrificial victim assured one of a pleasant afterlife, and when

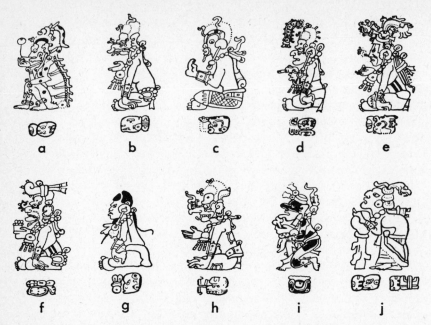

Maya gods and their name glyphs from the Dresden Codex: a. Death God; b. Chac or Rain God; c. North Star God; d. Itzamná; e. Maize God; f. Sun God; g. Young Moon Goddess; h. "Many Lineages" God; i. Merchant God; j. Goddess of Medicine (Courtesy of Thames and Hudson Ltd.; from Coe 1966).

possible fetishes were anointed with the blood of such victims to give the gods strength.

To the Maya the earth was flat, and each of the four cardinal directions was associated with a color, as was the center. The sky was formed of different levels and was held in place by gods or trees associated with a particular quadrant. Thirteen layers, each with its own god, rose above the earth, and beneath it were nine other layers, each associated with a deity. The underworld was a cold and unpleasant land of the dead. Their gods were divine, dignified, and free from virtually all human failings. Their most manlike quality was their desire for human recognition through ritual cleanliness, prayers, rites, and ceremonies. In their physical form most deities were represented by human and animal features in combination. Each deity was assigned to one of the quadrants of the world and was associated with the particular color of that section. In their aspects some were benevolent as well as malevolent, and they might be represented as young or old, male or female, to express their duality.

The deities of creation possibly were the "Begetter of Children" and

"Conceiver of Children"; the "Feathered Serpent" was their son. Alternatively it may have been that Itzamna was the Maya creator, for he certainly was the most important of all the gods. Itzamna lived in the sky, and his tears formed rain. (The Chacs were rain gods as well, but they were important at the village level rather than in the conceptual hierarchy of deities.) He was a single god and many gods, as so often was the case, and he had many alternative names; his prime designation translates "Iguana House." The idea of a house possibly signified that the world, meaning not only the heavens but the earth as well and all of the plants on it, was his dwelling. At the same time he was called "Iguana Earth" or "Iguana House Bountiful Harvest." In different aspects Itzamna was associated with each color quadrant of the earth, and he was the source of everything beneficial, including rain and fertile soil. At the same time he controlled the lesser beings in heaven and on earth.

The sun was the husband of the moon, and both were gods of importance. These were the first individuals to have had sexual intercourse. The Sun (Day) god was an almond-eyed youth and an aged man as well. He was feared because he brought droughts to wither crops, but he also was honored because he originated the system of writing. Furthermore, he was a god of the underworld because of his nightly ventures there. The Moon goddess was associated with weaving, medicine, childbirth, and bodies of water. The Chacs as gods of rain were important only in the lowland area; a lesser function was their association with thunder and lightning. A major Chac was linked with each of the quadrants of the world, and they above all others were most directly responsible for bringing rain to the land.

When death came to a Maya, three destinies were possible. Most persons went to an underworld; some souls went to a heavenly paradise, and those who had been sacrificed in life or died in childbirth or war went to a choice celestial realm. The path to the underworld was long and difficult. At the bottom of the nine layers existence was controlled by the gods of darkness, who were severe. Paradise, perhaps an idea borrowed from the Spanish, was a land of bliss. As there were many gods of life, so it was with gods of death. One of these was symbolized as the planet Venus, who rose from the underworld.

Sources: Coe 1966; Thompson 1970.

SEVEN

SOUTH AMERICA

A wealth of ethnographic data is available for many sectors of South America, although—and as usual—the number of satisfactory aboriginal baseline studies is disappointingly small, especially for areas under early and intensive Spanish influence. Ethnic contrasts are great among these peoples. Nowhere were indigenous elaborations greater than among the Inca. The sophistication of their political organization, the complexities of their religious life, and their metalworking technology are especially worthy of note. In South America too we find simplicity, gatherers who had once been farmers but were forced by other Indians to revert to a simpler way of life; some Kaingang of Brazil serve as an example. The technological simplicity of the Siriono of Bolivia is notable even among incipient farmers. South American peoples were unique among ethnics in comparatively few respects: their developed rubber technology, intensive and complex irrigation networks, manufacture of hammocks, and shrinking of human heads.

Ethnic ways in South America shared one particularly critical complex with North Americans, especially with peoples from central Mexico southward. In both regions complex ways of life were based on maize, beans, and squash cultivation. Furthermore, during early stages in the development of these farming economies it appears that there was considerable contact between peoples in Middle America and those in northwestern South America. Before long, however, each of these major regions began to develop in its own unique direction. The Aztec devoted much of their energy to military conquests and bloody ritualism; the Maya were more aesthetically and theologically oriented, as reflected in their complex religious system, art and architecture; the Inca built a political empire and great public works.

312

The number of distinct ethnics in South America reaches about 3,000, if one is a "splitter," but a more reasonable figure is about 180 distinguishable peoples, with a total population of about 10,000,000. The highest population densities were in the Inca area and elsewhere along the Pacific coasts except at the extreme south and in the very arid sectors of Chile. The most distinctive demographic characteristic of the continent of South America at an aboriginal level is that the population densities were quite low in comparison with the rest of the world. The reason is that in certain localities, such as in the central Andes, large numbers of persons could be supported within small areas but large expanses could not be cultivated. This has remained true to the present time; in Peru only about 2 percent of the land currently is under cultivation. About 750,000 people in aboriginal South America had gathering-based economies; this is a larger number than for any other major geographical area of the world.

The earliest inhabitants of South America entered from North America about 13,000 B.C., if not considerably earlier, and reached southern Chile by about 9000 B.C. Originally the ancestors of these people had entered the New World via the Bering Strait. In a very real sense the land bridge from Siberia to Alaska served as a screen through which peoples with only certain types of lifeways succeeded in passing. They had to have an economy adapted to the subarctic, and in all probability they were big game hunters. They flaked stone in order to fashion spearpoints, knives, and scrapers. They had cold-adapted clothing, and they probably wandered as small family groups in search of game. Even without supporting evidence it seems likely that this way of life spread southward along high mountains in western North America and then on into western South America. To speak of the movement as a "migration" is less fitting than to term it a population spread or drift; it is unlikely that there was ever a mass movement of people or that they had a particular destination in mind when they set out. The major point to be made with regard to the earliest occupants of the Americas is that the cultural ways which they brought with them from the Old World were those of low-level gatherers and that most of the subsequent elaborations, such as learning to farm, were built on this elementary base.

Certain developments in the Old World during prehistoric times quite possibly influenced South American Indians. The information concerning two plants is a case in point. In a Peruvian archaeological site dating about 2000 B.C., remains of a cultivated species of cotton were recovered. This cotton was a cross between an Old World domestic species and a New World wild cotton. It seems unlikely that the Old World domestic cotton seeds could have reached the New World without the aid of man. In Peru, at the same site and at the same time level at which the cotton was recovered, the remains of bottle gourds have been found. Since this species quite clearly is a cultigen from the Old World, it would seem that prior to 2000 B.C. ocean voyages must have been successfully undertaken from Asia to western South America.

The cultural evidence for pre-Columbian human contacts between South America and Asia have tantalized anthropologists, and others, for a long time. For example, blowguns were used in Southeast Asia and in sectors of the Amazon drainage system. The physical form of the blowgun and the accompanying use of poisoned darts is similar in both areas. The possibility, of course, exists that the blowgun originated independently in each area. However, when we note too that in sectors of both Asia and South America are reported the use of panpipes, often in complementary pairs, the chewing of lime or ash with a narcotic, the manufacture of penis covers, and the production of bark cloth, the possibility of trans-Pacific contacts is suggestive. More dramatic still is the striking similarity between the earliest pottery from coastal Ecuador and pottery forms from southern Japan. It has been postulated that about 3000 B.C. fishermen drifted in boats from Japan to coastal Ecuador and subsequently introduced their pottery-making techniques.

When subsistence orientations correspond rather well with environmental potential, we may presume that the people involved had reached a level of technoeconomic stability. In other words, if farmers had expanded to the areal limits possible, given their crops and technology, then a form of equilibrium was attained; such was the case over most of South America. Along the southern coasts of Chile, beyond the range of possible cultivation, the people lived largely by collecting shellfish and by hunting sea mammals and birds. Northward and eastward in arid Patagonia, guanaco and rheas were the most important species hunted. Farther north, in the Gran Chaco, these species gave way in importance to peccaries and tapir, which were hunted. The people here also fished and harvested a wide variety of plant products. Farther north in the Tropical Forest culture area were peoples, such as the Siriono of Bolivia, who subsisted largely by gathering but did some farming; still other Indians, ranging as far northward as the Orinoco River drainage, lived rather like the Siriono or were gatherers exclusively. In general terms these peoples lived in settings where food-getting was comparatively difficult, which meant that the population densities were low, the social units remained small, and the people moved often in search of food. Considering that these Indians were distributed throughout the length of South America but in a broken chain, it is to be expected that their subsistence patterns and other ways would vary by locality. These were small, kin-based societies, with the primary units ranging from nuclear families to descent groups who traced relatives either through males or females.

Most Indians in the tropical and subtropical rain forests cleared lands on which to raise maize, beans, bitter and sweet manioc, squash, and peppers. Furthermore, they cultivated other plants which were culturally important: cotton plants for fiber and others for use in making dyes and fish poisons. The base for their subsistence economy, while adequate, was not sufficient to permit the rise of occupational specialists. As a seemingly essential supplement to the starchy vegetable diet, they took fish in small streams by using arrows, leisters, traps, and poisons; river waters also yielded turtles, dolphins, and caymans. Land mammals, such as agouti, anteaters, capybaras, deer, peccaries, and tapirs, were taken with blowguns, arrows, spears, and traps. Gathering pursuits which required movement over water were facilitated by the use of dugout canoes. A community often consisted of one large thatched dwelling which housed one or more lines of males and in-marrying wives. A man obtained his spouse from a patrilineal unit different from his own. It might be represented in either the same community dwelling or in another with whom his group was on friendly terms. Given the propensity of Tropical Forest peoples for warfare, villagers protected themselves by building palisades around their settlements. Probably their most well-known social norm was the couvade, sometimes termed "male childbirth." This custom required a man to observe food and behavioral taboos, which included resting in his hammock for days on end, after his wife had given birth. The rationale behind the practice was that the welfare of an offspring soon after birth was connected intimately with the father's behavior. Puberty rituals, especially for girls, often were designed to test the fortitude of the initiate and to instruct as well. Other ritual dimensions to life included ceremonies designed to foster village welfare, and shamans functioned as the most important curers.

The characteristics of the Southern Andes culture area will be presented in outline because so little is known about their aboriginal ways that an adequate sketch of a representative ethnic could not be assembled for inclusion in the text. The Atacameno lived in the northern extremity of the Southern Andes culture area in an extremely arid area. Knowledge of their way of life is derived almost exclusively from archaeological recoveries. These people lived in small, isolated groups clustered at defensive settlements around oases. They irrigated plots and raised maize, beans, squash, and peppers. They also collected plant products, but more importantly they raised herds of llamas for their wool, meat, and other products. About their social life very little is known except that the leadership of small settlements passed from father to son; that their religious life was reasonably well developed is indicated by the gravegoods in burials. To the south of these people and largely to the east of the Andes lived the Diaguita. They terraced farmland on a small scale and irrigated the plots. These Indians lived in small, independent villages comprised of stone-walled houses with linked rooms. Each settlement also included a fortified position where people collected in times of attacks. The Diaguita raised llamas and possibly vicunas for their wool, and from it they wove fine garments. They were skilled craftsmen who made excellent pottery and cast knives, clubs, tweezers, and various objects of copper. Leadership appears to have been under the control of the most successful warriors, while religious life focused on thunder and lightning as the greatest supernatural powers. The third group of people in the Southern Andes, the Araucanians, lived in a more fertile area than the peoples just described. They occupied scattered homesteads near their cultivated and sometimes irrigated lands, on which were plots of maize, beans, squash, peanuts, and potatoes; these farmlands were prepared by cooperative groups. Raising llamas possibly was more important than farming. Shamans among them were diviners and curers, but at least some of the groups had the concept of a supreme deity, to whom they prayed and made offerings.

The lifeways of the Indians of the Circum-Caribbean also were destroyed before they were described adequately, but the information is more complete than that for the Southern Andes. The peoples of the Circum-Caribbean and northwestern South America were quite varied in their sociocultural patterns, but an important shared characteristic was that they produced a surplus of food, a factor which led to the emergence of small, class-structured chiefdoms by the time of historic contact. These chiefdoms clustered into two general types. The militaristic ones, found mainly in northwestern South America and Central America, were comprised of groups of relatively autonomous villages whose members united to fight common enemies for glory and for tribute more often than for territory. Captives in war served as sacrificial victims for religious ceremonies and for cannibalistic feasts. The theocratic chiefdoms centered mainly in Venezuela and the Greater Antilles. They placed less stress on warfare, and settlements were integrated largely along religious lines, with leaders considered deities and associated with idols and temples. The economies of both chiefdom types were based on the cultivation of relatively permanent plots, which might be terraced or irrigated. The crops were New World staples, but the particular varieties of plants raised depended on local climatic conditions. Some peoples ate the dogs and Muscovy ducks which they raised, but fish tended to be more important

than meat from either wild game or domestic animals. The technological
achievements of some of these peoples were outstanding and included the
production of fine ceramics, molding and casting metals, and constructing
aqueducts, bridges, and roads.

The Central Andean culture area was the Inca Empire, which represented a major culmination of ethnic life in the New World. Since the
Inca are discussed in a vignette to follow, it is unnecessary to summarize
their characteristics in the present context.

Sources: Honigmann 1959; Steward and Faron 1959.

YAHGAN SUBSISTENCE

The Yahgan, who were the most southerly of all the world's ethnics,
lived along the southern coast of Tierra del Fuego Island at the tip of
South America. The mountains of their homeland rise to about 1,500 feet
and are covered with thick underbrush and beech trees of both evergreen
and deciduous species. The summers are cool, and for snow to fall during
this season is not unusual. The mean winter temperature is close to freezing, and throughout the year the weather often is turbulent. The dense
forests offer few exploitable resources, but sea mammals, birds, fish, and
shellfish usually were plentiful along the coast. The Yahgan were divided
into five dialect groups representing the Tehuelche language family. Although they first were visited in 1624, relatively intensive contacts did not
take place until the nineteenth century; at that time it is estimated that
they numbered about 2,500 persons. By 1913 there were fewer than 100
survivors, and in 1933 the number had dropped to forty.

Members of each of the five mutually intelligible dialect groups
ranged from one camping area to another within their separate territories.
Each small family group occupied a dome-shaped dwelling framed with a
circle of poles bent and tied at the top and covered with grass, bark, skin,
or other available materials. An alternative type of structure was tepee-
shaped and framed with poles or even the trunks of trees. The ground
from a house interior might be removed to a depth of as much as three
feet and the depression floored with a layer of grass or branches. An
entrance faced the sea, and in the center of the floor a fire was built. What
is most notable about the Yahgan dwellings is that in spite of the fact that
the environment was cold, these people built only crude, if not flimsy,
houses. The most important protective garment for either sex was a waist-
length cape of skins. This was worn with the hair or fur facing outward
and was held in place with a tie across the chest. Women also wore a
small pubic apron of skin, but men wore nothing more than a cape, often
omitting even it. These people wore skin moccasins only when traveling

Table 5.   CULTURE AREAS OF SOUTH AMERICA

Southern: Charrua, Guaicuruan, Puelche, and Tehuelche languages; hunters of guanaco or sea mammals, and collectors; social life was organized around small groups in which kinship ties were most important; band organization; life cycle the focus of ritual attention, shamans; housing and technology simple.

Tropical Forest: Arawakan, Cariban, Ge, and Tupian languages; forest root-crop (manioc, sweet potatoes, yams) farming by women, with men as hunters and fishermen; kinship-based social groups; village basic political unit; shamanism, ritual focused on birth, puberty, death, and illness; pole-and-thatch house, loom weaving, blowgun, use of rubber, dugout canoe, hammock (this area includes enclaves of gatherers).

Southern Andes: Araucanian and Atacameno languages; irrigation farmers (maize, beans, squash, potatoes) and pastoralists (llamas); autonomous hamlets or villages, descent possibly traced through males; hereditary hamlet leaders, groups confederated in times of war; shamans very important; rectangular, thatched-roof house of wattle-and-daub; llama as pack animal, skilled weavers and craftsmen in pottery and metalworking.

Circum-Caribbean: Arawakan and Cariban languages dominated; men as farmers of maize, beans, and squash; class organization with military achievements important; small, unstable confederations of chiefdoms; temple-idol cults and ancestor veneration; wattle-and-daub house, hammock, gold and silver work; human sacrifice and cannibalism.

Central Andes: dominated by Quechua speakers; irrigation farming highly developed with some sixty plants cultivated, domestic llama and alpaca; hereditary class system and well-developed craft specializations; complex political hierarchy; ancestor cult, priests, elaborate rituals, and a host of deities; sophisticated metalworking technology, elaborate pottery, rectangular house with thatched roof; monumental public architecture and engineering projects.

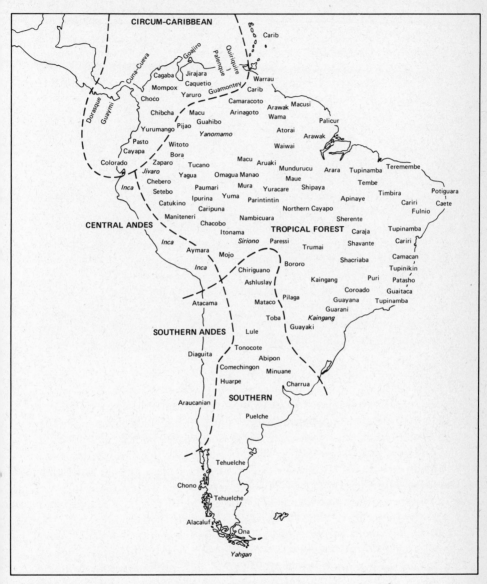

Map 5. CULTURE AREAS AND SELECT ETHNICS OF SOUTH AMERICA.

A Fuegian dwelling (from Hyades and Deniker 1891).

or hunting on land, and they did not wear any covering on their heads. Perhaps better than most ethnics, they illustrate that "essential needs" in terms of housing and clothing may be a cultural concept more than a physiological one. Even though the Yahgan may have developed a cold-adapted physiology, the differences between their ideas of cold protection and those which prevail in most other areas of the world are striking.

These people wore their hair loose in either a tonsured or unaltered style. Hair was cut with the sharp edge of a mussel shell, combed with the toothed jaw of a porpoise or sea otter, and sometimes brushed with bundles of roots. Necklaces were made from sections of bird bones or punctured shells worn on sinew strings, and shell or bone pendants might be added. Bracelets and anklets of sinew or leather also were objects of bodily adornment. The body hair of both sexes was removed by tweezers made from mussel shells. They covered their heads and bodies with oil for protection as well as for beautification and frequently painted their faces and bodies with colors prepared from charcoal, burnt red earth, and white clay. Quite obviously the Yahgan were very much concerned with their

A Fuegian launching
a spear (from Hyades
and Deniker 1891).

grooming, demonstrating that a humble people with few amenities might
have standards of personal appearance as rigorous as our own.

The aboriginal Yahgan probably did not have dogs, and they did not
make pottery, weave, or work metal in any form; they seldom worked
stone except to flake a small number of forms designed to cut. Their
slender inventory of domestic artifacts included coiled baskets of grass,
small containers made of skin or animal bladders, and cylindrical vessels
of bark for carrying and storing water or for bailing canoes. Among the
tools reported were bone awls and chisels, mussel shell scrapers, chipped
stone knives, and bone wedges. The most complex manufacture was a
canoe ribbed with wood and covered with bark from beech trees. These
vessels, which turned up slightly at each end and were propelled with
lanceolate-bladed paddles, averaged fifteen feet in length, were about

three feet across at their widest part, and were as much as two feet in depth. Two to three weeks were required to construct such a vessel. The pieces of bark were sewn with baleen, which they obtained from the mouths of certain species of whales, or with thin strips of wood; the seams were sealed with a mixture of mud and the stems of grass or moss. In the center of each boat a hearth was built. It consisted of a flat stone base on which a piece of turf was turned upside down. The mass of roots and pebbles prevented the fire from burning through, and the fire was kept small so that the sides of the boat would not be burned. Fire was kindled by striking flint against pyrite; the sparks ignited tinder of bird down or dried fungus.

The Yahgan traced their kin along both sides of the family (bilateral descent) and felt quite strongly that a person should not marry a cousin or closer relative. Since they most often camped with relatives, they sought mates from among the members of other camps, but preferred them to be from their own band, i.e., dialect group (band endogamy). Individuals could not marry until they had participated in an initiation ceremony; after being initiated, they were allowed to select their own spouse. A young man gave presents to his potential father-in-law and performed certain services for him, although these obligations were not rigid or formalized as a bride service. Most men had one wife (monogamy), and those with plural wives had most often married sisters (sororal polygyny). Weddings were celebrated by painting the faces of the couple with particular designs and by having dances and feasts. The couple resided briefly with the girl's family (temporary matrilocal residence) and later settled with the husband's family (permanent patrilocal residence). Premarital sexual intercourse and adultery were disapproved, and yet both practices occurred. Divorce was relatively common and was considered justified if a husband were cruel or failed as a provider. Contrary to what might be anticipated, aged persons were treated well and were not abandoned when they became economically unproductive.

Political organization as a patterned area of distinct activities must be considered as nonexistent. Any influence that an individual had over the behavior of others was based on his personality characteristics, network of kinship ties, or these conditions in combination. Each family head was free from the control of any other person, and men were very reluctant to accept the directives of others. Two families were likely to come into conflict only as a result of the murder of a relative. Feuds sometimes led to battles, in which injuries were far more common than deaths; these usually were led by aggressive as well as physically strong individuals. Most often feuds were settled through the auspices of persons friendly to both sides. If a person committed a murder that was regarded as unjustified, he was shunned; a habitual thief was treated in the same manner. Avoidance of a transgressor of conventions was an effective means to bring about conformity in many small-scale societies. The members of one dialect group were hesitant to trespass on the lands of another group except to hunt in times of extreme food stresses, to trade, or to join another people in consuming a whale that had drifted ashore.

When visiting others, even members of the same camp, it was considered proper to paint one's face with particular patterns, and it was incumbent on a host to receive friendly visitors with kindness. It was rude to address anyone by name, and it was ill-mannered to eat a great deal. The most important ceremony was the joint initiation of male and female youths. The component rituals were held annually by local groups and were focused in a special structure built like a house but larger. While under the supervision of adult male and female sponsors, each novice was subjected to a rigorous program which included little food and sleep, daily baths in the sea, and instructions concerning the behavior expected of adults. In the ceremonial structure, which had designs painted on the framework and on special planks, ritual dances were performed by hosts and initiates alike. At the end of the initiation a mock battle took place between men and women. Membership in the *Kina* society was open only to those males who had participated in an initiation. According to a myth, at one time women dominated the men by impersonating spirits and thereby intimidating males, but the men found out the deception and killed all females except one young girl who was unaware of the trickery because she was not yet initiated. The men then took over the Kina rites, which involved the wearing of masks and impersonation of spirits, in order to frighten and control their wives and children.

In the Yahgan diet, mussels were the most important food. Seals were second in value as a food source, and they likewise took diverse species of fish, birds and bird eggs, shellfish apart from mussels, and a few plant products. Even though the diet of these ethnics was varied, in order to obtain enough food they were obliged to move frequently from one coastal camp to another. Surpluses rarely provided more than a few days' reprieve from food-getting activities. The efforts of the women to acquire food appear to have been almost equal in importance to those of men. Whenever weather permitted, the women collected shellfish. Two species of mussels were the primary staple, but the most productive beds, which had the largest mussels, could be harvested only by going out in canoes at low tide when the sea was calm and the water clear. A woman paddled her canoe into position and tied it to kelp, or if her husband accompanied her, he held it in place. The shellfish were removed by using a long pole to which was lashed a short pole with a split distal end. A mussel could be wedged between the prongs of this instrument and lifted into the canoe. Two or three hours were required to obtain a day's supply of mussels in this manner; often, however, weather conditions made this type of collecting impossible. A less desirable technique was to wade into the water and detach the mussels by hand or with the aid of a pointed stick. The mussels were placed in baskets or were piled at the waterline.

Just as the important subsistence activity of women was collecting mussels, men devoted most of their time to hunting sea mammals. Formerly the species taken included the elephant and South American fur seals as well as South American sea lions. Sea lions were the most important species hunted in early historic times since the others were then being depleted by European sealers. One technique for harvesting sea lions was to club them alone or in herds, as they slept along a beach; the latter technique was carried out cooperatively by a group of men. Most often, however, they were hunted in the water from canoes. A frolicking animal might be lured near a canoe by whistling or singing softly and by splashing the water with a paddle. When it was close enough, the hunter launched his harpoon dart. This weapon consisted of a barbed, bone harpoon head fitted into a socket at the end of a wooden shaft; a line was tied between the shaft and the harpoon head. When an animal was struck, the harpoon head cut into its skin, and the barb held it in place. The head detached from the shaft, but the shaft was dragged along by an attachment line. The wounded animal dove and swam for a bed of kelp floating on the surface. The kelp tangled around the shaft, impeding the sea lion's progress, and the hunter paddled near. When the animal finally surfaced, it was killed with a lance or a club. In sectors where there was no floating seaweed a different hunting technique was employed. The hunter attached one end of a long line to the harpoon head but held the opposite end in his hand. Once a sea lion was struck, the line was paid out and the end held fast. The wounded mammal was forced to pull the canoe as it swam, and when it became exhausted, the line was drawn in and the quarry killed. The harpoon with a long line also could be launched from the shore, in which case the hunter tied the free end of the line around his body and gradually pulled the wounded animal ashore.

The meat of whales, both baleen and other forms, was highly desired even though the Yahgan never hunted healthy adult whales. They did make every effort to haul dead whales ashore where they could be butchered, and they hunted sick whales or those which had been injured by killer whales. From their canoes, they launched harpoons and spears into such whales in order to inflict as many large wounds as possible. Some whales withstood these attacks and escaped, at times capsizing canoes in the process. Successful whale hunts appear to have been rather uncommon; they might have been more frequent in aboriginal times before European whalers operating in these waters had depleted the numbers.

Throughout the year, but especially in the summer, women in canoes caught saltwater species of fish with baited lines. These lines were made from kelp stems or were fashioned from sinew. A stone was tied near the bottom of the line as a sinker, and at the end of the line was fastened a bird quill which had a loop at the end to hold a small piece of meat as bait. Tying her canoe to kelp stalks, a woman paid out the line and waited. If a fish swallowed the bait, she gently pulled up on the line until the fish was near the surface of the water, and then with a sharp tug she jerked it into the boat. Sporadically during much of the year herring swam in large schools along the shore of the island, and other fish which preyed on herring then became plentiful, as did birds and sea lions which also fed on the herring. The quantities of herring were so great that they literally were scooped from the water into baskets by hand. On other occasions the herring runs were away from the beaches, and then the fish were scooped into canoes by using special baskets manipulated with detachable pole handles.

Of the many land and sea birds hunted, the most important species in the Yaghan diet were penguins, cormorants, geese, and ducks. Occasionally birds were killed with hand-hurled rocks or with stones propelled from slings, but it was more common to hunt them by other means. Two species of penguins were plentiful on rocks and small islands along the coast. On calm days hunters canoed to these offshore habitats and clubbed the birds to death before they could escape. In order to hunt penguins as they swam in the water, a canoe was maneuvered by a hunter's wife as close to a swimming bird as possible, and the man launched a bird spear at his prey at the most opportune moment. The weapon consisted of a wood shaft to which were bound either one or two points made out of wood or bone and barbed along one side. Four species of cormorants were common. When they were sighted at the water's edge or on the beach, rocks were hurled at them with slings; when they were swimming, these birds were hunted in the same manner as swimming penguins. Some species of cormorants slept uneasily on land during calm nights. At these times a hunter carrying a faintly glowing ember in one hand crept up on the birds and then fanned the ember into a flame. This startled the birds so much that it was possible to club some of them to death before they escaped. On stormy nights cormorants sleeping on the land would tuck their heads beneath one of their wings. A hunter would approach stealthily on his hands and knees, seize a bird, and while holding its head in the sleeping position, he would bite the neck as he simultaneously crushed it with his hands. Many cormorants were killed in this manner, but they were never removed until the following day. The men believed that the birds left alive would return to the spot to roost only if they were not disturbed when sleeping. An additional means for taking cormorants was to capture them with a gorge or toggle. One end of a sinew line was tied to a pole driven into the ground; the opposite end of the line was tied around the center of a piece of bone which had been pointed at each end. The sharpened bone was skewered into the body of a dead fish, and the bait was covered with a thin layer of dried seaweed. When a cormorant swallowed the fish, the gorge toggled in its throat or stomach and cause the bird to either choke or bleed to death.

Geese were a favored food, but the three species represented were difficult to approach in the flat grassy localities which they frequented. In order to take them, a long line was tied between two poles, and along it baleen snares were attached and placed on the ground. As geese walked about, their feet caught in the loops, and the more they pulled the tighter the snare lines were drawn. The hunter lay in wait, and after deciding that he had captured all the geese possible, he went to the snare lines and clubbed or twisted the necks of the trapped birds. Fowl also were taken with the aid of a single baleen snare attached at the end of a long pole. At dusk or at night the hunter looped the snare over the head of a sleeping bird and quickly drew it tight enough to kill the bird; he took one bird after another in this manner until the ones remaining alive became startled and flew off. Alternatively a snare-pole was used by a man concealed in a blind near a spot where birds were known to congregate.

Land animals were not an important source of meat, but the skins of guanaco were utilized for clothing. Guanacos were found in the eastern sector of Yahgan territory, and they were almost always hunted cooperatively by men. Small herds of these cameloids left the high country in the summer and dropped down to lower elevations in order to obtain water. The men stationed themselves at widely separated intervals along a game trail known to have been used recently. When the animals began passing by in single file, a hunter at the upper end of the trail launched his harpoon dart or a spear with an attached, barbed bone point, attempting to strike one of the animals just behind the shoulder blade. The hunters knew that all the guanaco would run down the trail when disturbed, and each man had an opportunity to launch his weapon as the animals passed.

The distinct tendency exists to think of marginal hunting groups as depending almost exclusively on the food-getting efforts of the men to promote survival. Yet this rarely is the case, as the Yahgan example illustrates so well. In order to obtain food in the most efficient manner the efforts of a man complemented those of a woman, and a married couple was not only a conjugal but a subsistence unit. From the ethnographic accounts it would appear that the contribution by women to the daily food supply was quite important if not essential for subsistence welfare. Furthermore, a married couple might form a cooperative unit for getting food, as when a wife paddled the canoe from which her husband hunted. Similarly it is notable that large-scale cooperative hunting was relatively uncommon; this is contrary to the general impression conveyed about the organization of hunting activities among many marginal peoples. One important point to be made concerning the Yahgan food-getting round was the diversity of species on which they depended; if one was in short supply, they had others to which they might turn, which provided a subsistence "cushion." The weapons and devices of these people were simple in form but provided an adequate and reliable harvest. Thus, it is a mistake to presume that technological simplicity correlates with low productivity efficiency. Finally, and perhaps of greatest importance, these Indians had acquired a detailed knowledge of the habits of the species on which they depended. Their artifacts would have been of little value without this sophisticated body of knowledge.

Sources: Cooper 1946; Gusinde 1961.

THE SIRIONO: HUNGRY HUNTERS

Among the Siriono of tropical Bolivia two of the most frequent comments were "my stomach is very empty" and "give me something," meaning food. When a man left camp to hunt, women and children might demand that he bring them back meat. Meals usually were eaten late at night, food was bolted down as quickly as possible, and a person never looked up while eating; these were techniques to avoid sharing one's repast with others. Fights which occurred after drinking honey-based beer often resulted from one person's accusing another of ignoring an obligation to share food. Furthermore, the scope of a man's sexual life was correlated directly with his ability to supply women with food; quarrels were more often over food than over sex. Thus, this was a society in which thoughts about food dominated, yet despite the scarcity of food resources no one ever starved.

These people, who numbered about 2,000 in 1940, occupied a flat area, broken only by scattered hills, in northeastern Bolivia. Fleeting contacts of some bands with Roman Catholic missionaries took place as early as 1693, but intensive interaction with persons of European background was rare prior to the present century. When Allan R. Holmberg (1909–1966) studied the Siriono in the early 1940s, he lived with a small band of persons who were beyond the range of contact with Spanish speakers. At the time Holmberg was among them, growing numbers were being attracted to mission settlements or were working on farms and cattle ranches, often as forced laborers. It is unlikely that any Siriono continue to follow their aboriginal ways at the present time.

In physical appearance the men averaged about five feet four inches in height, and the women were somewhat shorter. Their natural skin color was quite dark, their hair coarse and black, their eyes dark brown, and they had a marked epicanthic fold. One seemingly unique inherited characteristic was that depressions or marks were found on the backs of their ears, and because they habitually picked up objects between the big and second toe, those toes had developed a prehensile quality. It also is notable that about 15 percent of the population was clubfooted. The Siriono wore no clothing, but rarely were they seen without some form of bodily adornment. Red paint, made from the seeds of a particular plant mixed with saliva, was applied most often to the face but was sometimes used over the entire body. The paint was utilized both for supernatural reasons, such as to ward off illness, and for protection from the elements and insects. Colorful feathers decorated their hair on special occasions, necklaces of animal teeth were worn, and cotton strings covered with red paint were wound around sections of their limbs; each of these items served decorative as well as magical purposes.

Given the wandering ways of these people, it is not surprising that their material culture inventory was both highly portable and limited in the number of forms possessed. At their relatively stable, rainy-season camps they built a form of dwelling which consisted of a rectangular framework of poles against which several layers of long palm leaves were arranged in an upright position. The palm leaves, which were about fifteen feet long, leaned inward but did not meet at the top of the structure. Smoke from interior fires drifted skyward through the open top. These dwellings were without either doors or windows; in order to enter, an individual simply separated two palm leaves. One large house was occupied by all the members of a band when they camped at a single location. When family groups traveled alone, they built smaller shelters which were similar in style but were left open on one side. Slung between the upright poles in a large house were hammocks made from bark fibers, and each family had its own fire near its sleeping area. Among the Siriono fire making was a lost art; firebrands were carried when traveling and an ember borrowed from another family if one's own went out.

In and around a household very few manufactures were in evidence. Each family customarily had a single clay pot for boiling food, and gourds served as drinking vessels as well as containers for making mead or storing tobacco, ornaments, and animal teeth. One form of basket was

A Siriono man, his wives, and children (from Holmberg 1950).

woven when needed to carry a particular item, such as meat or fruit, to camp, after which it was discarded. Other baskets were made for storing small objects, and a larger basket was used to transport household goods from one camp to the next. Near a camp mortars were hollowed from fallen logs with the aid of fire, and these served to hold maize or mead for grinding. Among the limited number of tools were digging sticks made for grinding maize in mortars, for planting and cultivating maize, and for removing other food products and clay from the ground. Mussel shells served as planes, while the toothed mandible of one species of fish or a piece of bamboo formed the standard knife. A gouge, made from an incisor tooth hafted to a monkey femur, completes the list of habitually used tools.

The food-getting activities of the Siriono were divided into two dis-

Siriono men returning from a
hunt (from Holmberg 1950).

tinct phases, depending on the time of year they took place. During the
six-month rainy season the people lived in hilly locales which were not
inundated and where wild fruits along with domestic crops provided most
of the food. During the balance of the year they roamed widely, searching
primarily for animals, fish, and honey. It appears that meat and plant
products were of nearly equal importance as year-round food sources.
Unquestionably the most desired food was meat, and men hunted on an
average of every other day throughout the year. During the days when a
man did not hunt, much of his time was occupied in making and repairing
his only manufactured weapon, the bow and arrows. A man constantly
had his bow at his side, even as he slept. The self bows, strung with a
bark fiber cord, were inordinately long, ranging from seven to nine feet.
The reed-shafted and feathered arrows were of two general types. One
form, some eight feet in length, had a barbed wood point and was used
against small game; the second form had a lanceolate head of bamboo on
a nine-foot shaft and was used against large game.

Men tended to venture out alone or in pairs to pursue game, and
each hunter carried about eight arrows. A man ranged silently through the
jungle, luring game as close as possible by seemingly perfect imitations of

their calls. Capuchin monkeys were the animals most likely to be killed since they traveled in large groups and responded well to calling, but they were difficult to hit in the thick forest foliage. When hunting howler monkeys, a man attempted to kill the male first since the females with him, as many as six, would not leave the locality and each could then be taken in turn. Game birds followed monkeys in importance, and then came peccaries. Bands of peccaries were tracked and sometimes encircled by a group of men hunting cooperatively. The largest animal available was the tapir, but because of its nocturnal habits it rarely was taken. Alligators were plentiful, but they were hunted with caution because they tended to die slowly and could be dangerous when wounded.

Wild plant products ranked next to meat in dietary significance, and each person sought these edibles for his family. The most important wild plant was the palm cabbage, which had an edible heart and also produced fruit which could be picked throughout the year. The hearts and fruits of other palms as well as fruits from certain other trees likewise were important. The Siriono prized honey as a food and as the prime ingredient in mead. Honey was sought especially in the dry season, when it was most plentiful. The combs were removed from the hives and the honey squeezed into gourds. Cultivation of plants contributed less to sustenance than did hunting and collecting activities. The reasons cited by Holmberg were that a great deal of effort was required to clear plots for cultivation and that before a planting reached maturity the game in the area often had been so depleted that the planters had abandoned the locality. Crops included maize, sweet manioc, sweet potatoes, papaya, cotton, gourds, and tobacco; the latter two were said to have been recent introductions. In general the edible crops were consumed upon ripening because of the difficulties in storing and transporting the harvest. The only other source of food was fish, but since these were taken only with arrows shot from bows, the harvest tended to be relatively unimportant in terms of the total diet.

From the foregoing description of potential subsistence resources it would seem that the almost constant food stress and the importance of food in the social lives of the Siriono must be exaggerated. Yet this does not appear to be the case due to a number of interlocking factors. One consideration is the technological poverty, particularly with respect to game procurement methods. The fact that the bow and arrow was the exclusive weapon, except for an occasional use of clubs, is quite significant. Bows and arrows, as well as clubs, must necessarily be hand-held and may be employed against a species only when it is close at hand and unguarded. By contrast, snares or traps set for animals work for a hunter in his absence and do not require a direct confrontation. Unlike most gatherers around the world, the Siriono did not employ any such devices. Likewise they could not take advantage of the wide variety of fish present in their setting because they did not know how to make fish traps, hooks, leisters, or nets, or how to prepare fish poisons. Thus, while a great deal of time and energy was devoted to hunting, the rewards were not as great as might be anticipated.

The Siriono knew of virtually no food storage techniques, which is another critical factor contributing to their food stresses. In their setting, if a slain animal was not cooked or treated within half a day, the meat spoiled. The drying and smoking techniques known to them preserved meat for about three days at the most. The only way meat could be kept available was to capture tortoises and then slaughter them as required for food. None of the wild plant foods were preserved; of the domestic crops sweet manioc and sweet potatoes were eaten when they were harvested. Only maize was stored for limited periods.

The social attitude of the people toward food added another dimension to their anxieties over it. Food was cooked by each nuclear family over its own fire and consumed by its members; although members of their extended family might join them, food was not shared widely beyond these units. If a particular food was in temporary abundance, the distinct pattern was to eat and eat until it all was consumed. A man who had collected a number of tortoises might do virtually nothing except eat and sleep for an entire week, and four people might consume a sixty-pound peccary at a single meal. It also is reported that within a span of twenty-four hours a man was able to consume as much as thirty pounds of meat.

A further limitation on food intake stemmed from taboos. The Siriono did not eat snakes because they thought the meat even from nonpoisonous species was poisonous. Neither did they eat bats or insects because of food taboos. Although nearly everyone was allowed to consume edible plant products, numerous prohibitions existed with respect to eating meat. Only the aged were to eat meat from certain animals; however, this restriction often was ignored when people were hungry. In theory, too, a hunter was not permitted to consume any meat from the animals which he had killed because it was felt that to do so would bring bad luck. However, this rule was treated lightly except with respect to the larger species, and these rarely were killed.

Certain food taboos related to the life cycle of an individual. Initially we find that many animals were not to be eaten by a pregnant woman for fear that the offspring would be affected adversely. For example, if a pregnant woman ate toucan meat, the baby might cry a great deal. Some of these taboos applied to the father as well, but the overall intake of food by potential parents apparently was not reduced as a result. The most important function of food taboos in anthropological terms was that they called the attention of the community to the fact that the couple involved was undergoing a change in social status. When a birth was imminent, the father went hunting, and the offspring was named after the first animal that he killed. If the hunt was unsuccessful, the baby was named after some notable physical characteristic that it possessed. No sex distinction existed for names. The first three days after birth were considered especially dangerous for the neonate, and in order to protect its life and to insure its well-being, the parents stayed near their hammocks and observed a number of food taboos. This particular custom falls within the definition of the couvade. Less than half an hour after a baby was born it was given the opportunity to nurse, and for the first year of life it was in almost constant contact with its mother. The offspring could nurse when it chose, and for the first six months it lived on milk alone. After this time the mother offered it prechewed food, which is a common practice among peoples who eat foods which are not easily digested by infants. A woman weaned her child when he was about three years of age by smearing beeswax on her nipples. A good child was rewarded with food delicacies, and misbehavior, such as violating a food taboo, brought a threat that an evil spirit would take the child away or a snake would bite him. As he grew older, a child was told that if he ate prohibited foods he would become diseased or would be abandoned. Children had no toys, but by the time they were three years old boys had miniature bows. Little girls were given small spindles, which were intimately associated with womanhood since adult females spent much of their time spinning cotton thread. Infancy and early childhood were the only times in the lives of these Indians when frustrations and anxieties over food were comparatively few. A boy of eight usually had killed small game, and he began to accompany his father on hunts at about this time. By the age of twelve both boys and girls were ready to assume full adult responsibilities.

Pubescent girls were subject to food taboos with respect to many meat animals. They also could not eat eggs until about a year after they had participated in a puberty ceremony. During this same time they worked hard performing female activities in order to prepare themselves for adult life. Puberty rites with their accompanying taboos and a special period of hard work did not exist for boys. Marriage for a man was ideally with a mother's brother's daughter (asymmetrical or matrilateral cross-cousin marriage), but if such an individual did not exist, some other real or presumed (classificatory) female cross-cousin was married. If a man had more than one wife, the women usually were sisters (sororal polygyny), and a distinct tendency existed for brothers to marry sisters. Mates usually were found within one's own group (band endogamy), and no ceremony was involved in marital arrangements. A couple who were possible spouses had long been aware of their relationship; they had had intercourse; and if they liked one another, they married by announcing their decision to marry. The man then moved his hammock from his parents' area in the house to the section where the wife's parents lived (matrilocal marriage residence). Divorce was uncommon but occurred when a man "cast out" a wife, usually because she had frequent intercourse with a possible spouse or because of her adultery in general. A divorced woman promptly remarried.

When an individual approached thirty years of age, his vigor began to decline, and before he was forty years old he was considered aged. Old people were viewed as a liability since they could not procure food efficiently and slowed a party down on the trail. The food they received was largely leftovers, and when they eventually became ill they often were abandoned to die alone.

Since food was the object of numerous taboos in an individual's life cycle, one might anticipate that it would be a focus of religious activities. If religion is considered to be an integrated system of beliefs and practices centered about the supernatural, then the Siriono had no religion; they had only a series of disarticulated beliefs and practices. The moon was the creator and a culture hero, but it was not worshiped and did not directly affect the lives of the people. They feared monsters and evil spirits which brought harm and hardship, but certain methods of promoting individual or general welfare existed. Men hung bird feathers and the skulls of animals they had killed on house posts or on sticks near the camp in order to supernaturally persuade the species to return. This and a few other magical procedures were carried out by individuals. A single group ceremony of note was held; called *hidai-idákwa*, it was a combined drinking feast and blood-letting ceremony. Only after a person had children could he or she participate in these activities. In theory the ceremony was held each year when there was an abundant supply of honey from which large quantities of beer could be brewed. When the honey-based beer was ready for consumption, men and women drank, sang, and danced in separate groups. After they were drunk, the men pierced each other's arms and the arms of women about six times with an awl. The blood from the punctures was guided into small holes made in the ground. The next morning the men hunted as the women gathered palm cabbages; later in the day the drinking was resumed and continued until the beer supply was exhausted, usually late during the second day. Food taboos were observed at this time, and old clay pots were replaced with new ones as a part of the ceremony. The purposes of the festivities were to rejuvenate the participants and to insure a continuing food supply.

Human minds are capable of focusing on a single aspect of many diverse segments of living, and this orientation becomes a central theme to guide much of what they do. The members of some societies stress prestige and personal honor, while others emphasize the importance of tangible wealth, harmony with the gods, or perhaps even warfare. It is rare that one's daily bread commands such primary attention, but this is what the evidence suggests for the Siriono. They had enough to eat to prevent starvation, but they often endured hunger, rarely had an abundance of food, and had no stored reserve on which they could rely. Hunting, which was stressed, was a precarious and difficult means for obtaining food; consequently it occupied much of their attention. As Holmberg (1950:94) noted of the Siriono,

> The hunter and gatherer must go in search of food at least every other day throughout the year. He must walk long distances, as many as 20 miles a day, in his quest for food. He may be forced to run at top speed through almost impenetrable jungle and swamp to bag a single monkey or coati, and once having bagged his prize he may be forced to climb a tree to retrieve it or the arrow with which he shot it. Game and forest products must always be carried back to camp—sometimes a long distance away. In walking and running through swamp and jungle the naked hunter is exposed to thorns, to spines, and to insect pests; he may fall from a tree (as he frequently does) while harvesting fruits or retrieving game; he is exposed to attacks from jaguars, alligators, and poisonous snakes; he sometimes suffers intensely from heat, cold, and rain. At least 25 percent of the time he returns to camp empty-handed or with insufficient food to completely nourish his family, for which he may be chided by his relatives. In short, while the food quest is differentially rewarding because food for survival is always eventually obtained, it is also always punishing because of the fatigue and pain inevitably associated with hunting, fishing, and collecting food.

A man was anxiety ridden because of the dilemma which he faced almost daily: his and his family's hunger as opposed to the fatigue and frustrations of the hunt. The magic that was practiced usually centered on food, never on sex, and families were bound together for economic reasons above all others. Finally, the most desirable personality traits were to be aggressive, individualistic, and uncooperative, for only with these values could an individual hope to survive at all.

Source: Holmberg 1950.

KAINGANG SEXUAL RELATIONS

Possibly no subject finds a broader and more interested audience among Western readers than that of sex. While descriptions of sexual activities within our own society elicit a large readership, the sexual activities of exotic peoples hold an even greater fascination. However, sex, just as any other form of behavior known to man, must be placed in cultural and social perspective; it is truistic to observe that what is normal among one people may be regarded as strange and even "dirty" among others. Thus it should be informative to sketch sexual relationships and behaviors among a people who were very different from ourselves, and the Kaingang of Brazil have been chosen for this purpose. The group of Kaingang presented depart in significant dimensions from most other peoples described in this volume. Within their traditions, perhaps nearly 400 years ago, they were farmers who lived in settled communities. They were driven from this homeland by powerful enemies and subsequently assumed a wandering way of life in jungle forests as hunters and collectors. With the intrusion of Brazilian colonists these Indians were hunted and killed, but in 1914 the remnants were pacified and settled on reserved lands in the state of Santa Catarina. It was here that Jules Henry (1904–1969) studied them in 1932–1934. At that time the Kaingang once again were becoming farmers, but only 106 persons remained alive in this particular group.

The jungle forest in which the Kaingang had lived was dense and virtually impenetrable except along the banks of some of the innumerable water courses or on temporary trails made by men. During the two-month rainy season it might rain every day for a month, and the streams and rivers would become torrents. The landscape was watery throughout the year, yet these Indians, although they built bridges, did not make boats or rafts. The hazards presented by the environment seem almost overwhelming. Thorns pricked the feet of even those who were wary; the surface of one kind of bamboo cut the skin of anyone who brushed against it; and one species of grass cut so badly that it had to be beaten down before a person could walk through a patch of it. In addition the Kaingang were plagued by dangerous snakes and insects which bit and stung. Thus, it is not surprising that to them the jungle was divided into "dirty places" and those which were "pretty," or largely free from hazards. In the mountainous forests freezing temperatures were common during the winter, yet their clothing was lightweight. The women wore plant fiber skirts, and the men had long shirts of the same material. At night they slept on fern fronds and covered themselves with a net-like robe if they owned one. It is small wonder that people sometimes fell asleep sitting by a fire, complained of sleepless nights, or slept very near each other for warmth.

The most important food was meat from the tapir. Pine nuts were the plant food staple as well as the only type of sustenance which was preserved for future use. In addition to being without boats or seemingly adequate clothing, these Indians did not make traps. They were persistent hunters with bows and arrows in a food quest which was seasonally very unrewarding. They wandered about the jungles in small groups usually consisting of several small families. A man walked ahead with his bow and arrows; in recent times he also carried an ax and a gun. He was followed by his wife who carried most of the family possessions and any extra food in a basket; on top of this load a baby might be perched. Other children walked with their mother, and one of them carried an ember for starting a fire at the next camp. Their houses were lean-tos covered with leaves, and although a couple could build one in half an hour, they were reluctant to do so unless a rainstorm was in the offing. A series of fires were built in front of large lean-tos, one for each family unit. A camp was occupied for a day or for as much as a week, depending on the local availability of food.

Men hunted with the aid of dogs, and their only weapon was a self bow. Some seven feet in length, such a bow could be strung only with great effort. Birds were shot with arrows that were blunted at the point, and arrows which had barbed wooden points were used against monkeys. Iron-pointed arrows with razor-sharp edges were saved for use against tapirs, the species which was sought above all others. A man who returned to camp empty-handed loudly told of his ill luck, but one who had succeeded might say only, "A tapir has been killed." The animal would be carried to the camp that day or the next by the women. The men sought the nests of bees for honey, and they knocked cones from the tall pine trees. The women collected the pine cones from the ground and did most of the other collecting.

Among these people sex was a common topic of conversation and a subject for frequent joking among the young and old alike. Their sexuality was expressed in many ways and often. The genitals of a male were manipulated by his mother before the child could walk, and to the amusement of adults, very small children pretended to copulate. A boy of three might jokingly be asked with whom he had sexual intercourse and he was expected to respond that it was with his grandfather's sister or some such person. An old man might refer to a small boy as a cohusband, or someone might jokingly be accused of wanting to fornicate with a dog. Yet intercourse did not appear to take place between children, and Henry has suggested that it was because children received a great deal of caressing attention from adults. It was common for young men, both married and unmarried, to caress each other during the day for hours on end and to sleep against one another for warmth and body contact at night. This behavior would suggest to us homosexuality, yet no homosexual actions, such as grabbing the genitals of another male, were ever noted or suggested.

Small children of both sexes played roughly together, and in later life males as well as females often were violent in their sexual aggression. As surprising as it may seem to us, if a woman were rejected in her pinching and punching advances, she took no offense. A husband away from camp might suspect that his wife was copulating with another man, and his suspicions probably were well grounded. Gossip about affairs was rampant as long as the offended party was out of hearing range. A woman nursing her nonlegitimate offspring might laugh as another woman related the affairs of her daughter. Parents rarely counseled their children to be faithful to a spouse, and the idea of love for one's marriage partner was a foreign idea. The Kaingang had no form of "love" magic, which is not strange given their aggressive openness about sexual matters. Perhaps it is likewise quite reasonable that when someone awakened in the morning feeling ill, he was prone to think that he had been forced to have sexual intercourse with a supernatural being.

Young couples had numerous sexual affairs, and the only means for distinguishing between a temporary liaison and an arrangement which was relatively permanent (marriage) was an announcement by the couple that they were husband and wife, since no marriage ceremony existed. The boundary between an amourette, an extended liaison, and marriage was at times vague, and a woman sometimes bore an offspring outside of marriage. In this event no stigma whatever was attached to either the mother or the child. Life as a single adult was considered emotionally unrewarding in spite of having repeated affairs, and sooner or later young people married—the man in order to have someone to cook his meals and the girl to have someone's care and affection on a more permanent basis. Youthful philandering led to postmarital adultery, but since adultery was the expectation and the norm, anxieties over it or jealousy were relatively muted or even unimportant. If one of the couple objected strongly to the extramarital activities of the other, a beating of the offending partner might result. If the marriage ruptured, it simply meant leaving one's spouse and living with relatives or friends. No property settlement was involved nor was the decision of any great importance to the community as a whole. Marriages were unstable until a woman had three children; by this time she required the aid of a man in caring for the children and men grew fond of their children. For a couple to separate after they had three children was nearly unheard of.

Food and sex loomed as major and integrated foci in the lives of these people. Not unexpectedly marriage considered in the abstract was thought of in terms of food-providing and food-receiving networks. In other words, how many persons a man would be obligated to feed was weighed against the number of persons from whom one could expect food. Given the small number of persons in the total population the advantageous arrangements varied widely from person to person. In this sense adultery served a positive function. When a single man carried on a protracted affair with the wife of a camp fellow, he was at the same time contributing to the group's food supply. As would be anticipated, the membership of any camp was quite fluid, and each adult was most concerned with his personal welfare and that of his immediate family. Unilineal kinship groups did not exist to bind him to a broader cluster of relatives. Furthermore, small family units were unstable as a result of divorces and deaths. The net result was a form of social integration that was based on the effectiveness with which adults provided one another with sexual satisfaction and food.

In the marital system unions between half-brothers and half-sisters were rare, and marriages between brothers and sisters or parents and children were avoided. In about 60 percent of the marriages the persons involved had a single spouse (monogamy), in 18 percent men had more than one wife (polygyny), in 14 percent women had more than one husband (polyandry), and 8 percent of the couples had reciprocal access to their spouses (joint or group marriage). These statistics are based on records for about 300 marriages which had occurred during the time of the study and nearly 100 years previously. These Indians did not view marital arrangements in terms of choices which formed an integrated system. Instead variations reflected different circumstances and were specific responses to particular situations without consideration of the social form. What would be considered as highly patterned among ourselves was very differently conceived by the Kaingang. For instance, a man might marry a woman and then acquire a second wife because of his abilities as a provider of sex and sustenance. A second man might join the unit as a cohusband, and on the death of the initial husband he might acquire the wives for himself. The women involved might even be a mother and her daughter. The principals would not be concerned about the nature of societal norms but would be doing what was expedient and practical for them at any particular moment.

Another example will further illustrate the practicality of marital arrangements. Small family groups often lived in isolation for years on end. One such camp was composed of a man, his sister, and his friend, each of whom had one spouse. The friend's wife died, and the man accepted him as a cohusband. This was a reasonable move, for it kept the friend in the camp as a companion and as a hunter. Later the friend died, as did the woman that they had shared. The man's sister then suggested that he take her three young daughters as wives, and he did so. The girls had no objections; in fact, they looked forward to participating in sexual activities about which they had heard so much. In time each of the girls bore him a child, and eventually his group joined another which had as a nucleus two men from whom they had departed years before. Two of the man's three wives left him, with one going to each of the newcomers. Thus the principal man, who originally had one wife, again was monogamous. He could have objected to the departure of his wives and children from his household, but the women eventually would have left irrespective of his feelings. He could have become angry with the men who received his wives, but if he had done so, these men and the women would have left, depriving him of their companionship as well as contact with his children by the women involved.

In the context of this discussion it is not difficult to imagine other forms of marital arrangements as having existed. A father and son might share the same wife, one woman might have four husbands at the same time, a youth might marry his stepmother, and so on. In all probability the strongest of Kaingang social ties were between cohusbands in polygynous and group marriages. The men involved were more secure in this marital arrangement than in any other. However, the independent nature of many men led them to avoid this possibility as long as possible, which sometimes was for life. If a man were a part of one such unit as he matured, he was likely to prefer it in later years. The key to the entire system was the fact that wives were formally or informally shared just as food was shared. Jealousy was rare, and when it was expressed, the aggressor was most likely to be left without a spouse as well as deprived of sex and food. Furthermore, his plight became an inviting topic about which others gossiped at great length and with delight.

Another point of considerable importance is that no matter how casual an affair might have been, the persons involved felt long-term responsibilities toward one another. In later years they might provide mutual aid, which was very important given the vicissitudes of their life style. By extension, a person used the term "father" for his biological father and for all of his mother's paramours and other husbands. The term "father" in its broadest sense also was applied to any older male, but the concept of allegiance to the men associated with one's mother was clear.

Given the small size of the Kaingang population, even before their number was so drastically reduced, most persons were related to one another, and therefore marriage between relatives became understandable and not particularly out of the ordinary. Given the insecurity of economic life it is further reasonable that each individual would attempt to maintain a maximum amount of flexibility in residence and marital arrangements. The fortunes of a camp group could change dramatically with the death of one adult, and thus multiple options furthered individual survival. What might not be anticipated was their very lax attitude toward sexual mores and a marital system built more on individual situations than on conventional patterns. When it was a practical necessity to marry near relatives, they did so without being restricted by the boundaries of incest established by most peoples. Kaingang sex life appears to have been a stabilized and continuing pattern. Perhaps above all else their sexual ways illustrate a potential variability which has rarely been explored in cultures around the world. (Surely some readers are quite disappointed in this presentation of data about sex since the discussion does not deal with the exotic and erotic in exciting combination. Yet sexual data in an anthropological context is more often of the type presented than any other.)

Source: Henry 1941.

JIVARO SHRUNKEN HEADS

Anthropologists have the reputation of telling "weird stories about naked savages," but hopefully this view is a distortion of reality. The business of ethnography is to describe the ways of other peoples, and only at times are their norms so far removed from our own that they appear barely comprehensible. Perhaps nothing seems more strange to us than the practice of killing enemies and shrinking their heads, and yet as will be shown, this custom was only one facet of the lives of its Indian practitioners and was quite reasonable in the context of their culture.

When Rafael Karsten (1879–1956) lived among the Jivaro from 1916–1918 and 1928–1929, they dominated the area to the east of the Andes in Ecuador and numbered about 12,000 persons. Knowledge of these people dates from the latter days of aboriginal Inca intrusions into their jungle homeland. The Spanish gained control over portions of the area in 1557, but by the end of the century the Indians had revolted and the Spanish were expelled, although retaliatory expeditions followed for many years. Missionaries, especially Jesuits, attempted to work among the Jivaro in the eighteenth century, but their numbers were few and their efforts were largely unrewarded. They did make some headway but were forced to abandon their efforts in 1768 when an administrative order expelled them. The political turmoil of the Ecuadorian war for independence in 1809 left the Jivaro to themselves, but missionaries returned some sixty years later and were intermittently present from that time forward. By the time of Karsten's work few Jivaro were Christians, although intrusions by whites had become increasingly frequent.

The Jivaro were of medium height, muscular, and arrogant in their manner, as expressed in vehement speech and violent gestures. The long black hair of the men sometimes reached to their waists, and it was formed into three braids, a large one at the back and smaller ones over each temple. They wore a loincloth of locally-made cotton cloth; it reached their knees and was held in place with a belt of hair or snakeskin. In cool weather a man wore a piece of cotton cloth which was slipped over his head and reached down over his back and chest in the manner of a poncho. Women wore their hair shorter than the men, and their primary garment was a long cloth dress, held in place by a piece of material which passed over one shoulder and by a belt at the waist. Not many years before the study was made, clothing reportedly was made from bark cloth. Diverse adornments were favored for their attractiveness and for magical properties. Men usually wore a hair comb as an amulet, and they sometimes wore headdresses made from very colorful feathers. From their pierced earlobes hung bamboo tubes up to ten inches in length, which were decorated with geometric designs. Women wore smaller ear ornaments of the same form and also had cylindrical labrets up to four inches in length hanging from beneath their lower lips. Necklaces and bracelets were worn by both sexes, but those of the women were less elaborate than the ones of men. Necklaces often were made from the teeth of monkeys which the wearer had killed, and old warriors favored necklaces of jaguar teeth. Necklaces beaded from a wide variety of seeds were worn by persons of both sexes.

The settlements were built in the midst of forests where they were less likely to be discovered by enemies, and each dwelling was a defensive structure. The houses were elliptical in outline, up to about sixty-five feet in length and about half as wide. A house was built around a framework of posts and poles and had a low conical roof covered with palm leaf thatching. The outer walls were constructed of stout vertical poles bound in place with vines. Light filtered in through spaces between the poles; there were no windows. The sturdy door at one end of a house was used by men, and one at the opposite end was for women. Each entrance led to the sector of a dwelling occupied by that sex. During periods of intense hostilities they built a second outer wall and constructed small cubicles of poles within a dwelling. A warrior was stationed in each compartment and could extend his weapon through a hole in the wall. The cubicles were the final line of defense in the event that enemies penetrated the outer wall.

Around the interior walls of a house were benches used to sit on during the day and for sleeping at night. The benches in the women's section were separated by partitions, and each compartment was occupied by a woman and her young children. A cooking and heating fire usually was built on the floor adjacent to the sleeping area. When necessary, a fire was kindled by spinning a shaft of wood against a second piece of wood, both of which were from one particular species of tree. It seldom was necessary to use the fire drill, however, because they attempted to keep their fires burning continuously. At each fireplace three or four logs were arranged as the spokes in a wheel, with the fire at the center. As a log burned, it was pushed inward; the arrangement served also as the platform on which cooking pots rested. In the woman's area were gourds which served as water containers as well as unembellished pottery containers for cooking and storing foods and for brewing manioc-based beer. The men's portion of the dwelling contained a distinctive and different cluster of artifacts. Prominent among these was a large signal drum made from a hollowed-out tree trunk; there also were lances, blowguns with quivers containing darts, and shields. Here were kept the low wooden stools used by the men, and here they made baskets, spun cotton thread, and wove cloth on upright looms.

At the time of Karsten's studies the most important cultivated plants were sweet manioc and bananas, but sweet potatoes, maize, and beans also were significant cultigens. Manioc was the staple, and it was most often prepared for consumption by boiling, although it might be roasted in the fire. The most important wild plant food was palm cabbage, which was cut from two different species; the cabbage was either eaten raw or boiled in water in order to prepare a soup. The most important game animals were wild hogs, peccary, monkeys, agouti, and paca, and the wide variety of birds included wild turkeys, toucans, and parrots. Deer and tapir were available but were not eaten. Larger animals were hunted with the aid of dogs and were killed with spears, while small game and birds were shot with darts from blowguns; the bow and arrow were unknown. The Jivaro caught fish, tortoises, lizards, edible frogs, and crabs; they also owned domestic pigs and fowl introduced by the Spanish. Although there were innumerable food taboos, the people had a wide variety of foods from which to choose and never went hungry. The favored beverage was beer made from boiled manioc; the fermentation process was started by chewing some of the cooked manioc enough to combine it thoroughly with saliva and then spitting the mixture into a pot of mashed manioc.

The most important hunting weapon was the blowgun, and from it poisoned darts were propelled. Blowguns were made by the members of only a few Jivaro groups, but they were traded widely. A blowgun was about nine feet in length and was made from a particular species of hardwood. It was fashioned into two separate halves and had a bore which was from eight to ten millimeters in diameter. The end which was blown into was somewhat thicker than the opposite end and was fitted with a mouthpiece made from a jaguar or deer bone. The two halves were bound together, and about nine inches from the mouthpiece a sight made from black wax was attached. The darts were small, round slivers of hard palm wood about ten inches in length. The forward end was smeared with curare poison, and the opposite end was wound with enough wild cotton so that it fitted snugly into the bore. The darts were carried in a bamboo quiver which was suspended around the neck or waist, and attached to the quiver was a small gourd stuffed with cotton. Just before a dart was to be shot a piece of cotton was removed from the container and fitted around the dart. In this manner the base of the blowgun was closed, and it became possible to propel the dart through the tube with a strong breath. On the quiver strap was fastened the claw of a crab, which was used to make a cut near the tip of the poisoned dart. The purpose of the cut was to cause the poisoned tip to break off and remain in an animal struck since some species, especially monkeys, removed the dart from their bodies when hit. The effective range of a blowgun was up to about thirty-five yards, depending on the strength of the poison and the size of the species shot.

The residents of a settlement were related to one another by blood or marriage and lived in a single dwelling. Each household-community was economically and politically self-sufficient. A community was friendly with the members of other settlements to which it was bound by kinship ties; enemies primarily were unrelated Jivaro. The social lives of these people were organized around monogamous or alternatively polygynous families; if a man had two or three secondary wives, they often were sisters (sororal polygyny). Highly successful warriors had four or more wives, some of whom usually were captured as children in raids against enemies. The custom also prevailed whereby a man was obligated to marry the wife of his deceased brother (levirate). However, if the dead man's brother considered this woman an undesirable spouse, he might accuse her of having poisoned her husband. If others tended to concur with this accusation, he was able to avoid taking the woman as a wife. A couple resided with the wife's family (matrilocal residence) immediately following marriage, and if a man received his first wife's sisters as secondary wives, he was likely to continue to live in the house of his father-in-law. However, many men after they began to raise a family of their own tended to establish their residence apart from either of the original families (neolocal residence). An individual was free to select a mate from within his own community or from another settlement (agamous communities), but in either case an ideal marriage partner appears to have been a father's sister's daughter (patrilateral cross-cousins marriage), although seemingly a man might also marry his mother's sister's daughter.

As a rule a young man arranged a betrothal with the parents of a girl who was from about five to ten years of age. Once a potential marriage was negotiated, the youth was obliged to work for the girl's father in order to demonstrate that he was a capable provider and a reliable person. The youth lived with his potential in-laws and helped educate his betrothed in her wifely duties. However, it was not until after a girl's menarche and her participation in the Tobacco Ceremony that she became his wife. Preparations for this ceremony were begun long in advance since two to three years' time was required in order to arrange for the festivities. Larger crops had to be planted and enough chickens and pigs raised to feed the guests. In the interim the girl and her future spouse observed many food taboos; their restraint was designed to promote the growth of the foods for the festivities, all of which were associated with the tobacco spirit. For about eight evenings before the Tobacco Ceremony a dance was performed within the house by boys and young men. During the dance the participants continually mentioned the names of the game hunted and the craft skills of men; the purpose of the dance and these accompanying recitations was to further household welfare. A few days before the ceremony began, manioc was collected in order to brew beer, and the betrothed girl figured prominently in these preparations. The Tobacco Ceremony spanned four days, and during the festivities a great deal of beer and food were consumed. The high point was approached on the second day when the bride, one of her sisters, and another young female relative drank an emetic in order to purge themselves for dreaming. From this time until the end of the festivities these women consumed a minimal amount of food in order to receive the full effects of the *savinya*. It was made from tobacco leaves by an old woman who was a director of the ceremony. She chewed the leaves until they were thoroughly saturated with saliva and then spit the pulp into a small clay pot. The three purged women slept in separate shelters at some distance from the house, and each of them drank some savinya before going to sleep. They were expected to dream about bountiful harvests of crops and fat pigs. The following day these women received the tobacco medicine repeatedly. The old woman and a female assistant then recited the words to songs so that those who did not know them could soon sing with the others. The recitation and singing went on for several hours; the lyrics dealt with crops, especially manioc, from the time a garden was prepared for planting until the plants were harvested. The three drugged females were led to their shelters that night, and after they were wakened in the morning, the pigs were killed ceremonially. The final day included more singing of songs, but on this day the lyrics focused on the Earth-mother Goddess and fertility associated with this supernatural. Finally the fast of the three women was broken, and the hair of the bride was combed first by the old woman and then by her potential husband. The girl's face and body were painted, and she was ceremonially dressed. Later the same day there was a great deal of feasting, and the final farewell to guests was ritually performed the following day.

The Tobacco Ceremony has been presented in outline in order to convey some of the complexities of a key ritual. Tobacco was regarded among the Jivaro as an especially powerful supernatural plant. It was given to the bride in a potent form in order to fill her with its mysterious power and to favorably influence her future life in economic and personal terms. The participation of two close relatives of the girl was designed to further the general welfare of the household group. This ceremony served the further function of emphasizing the pending status change for the young girl and her suitor.

Bravery and skill in warfare were inordinately important values and were impressed on a male child from the time he was very young. A youth was given narcotics to induce dreams in which he would see ancestral spirits; only in this manner could he expect to become a great warrior who would live a long life and kill many enemies. Sons frequently were reminded by their fathers of relatives' deaths and of outrages committed against the family which demanded revenge, even though the episodes might have taken place in the distant past. Tales of this nature were repeated each morning by a father, and youths accompanied raiding parties to gain early exposure to the methods of warfare. In times of peace an elder in each community was the sole authority over household members, but in times of active hostilities an old and respected warrior was granted nearly complete control over the activities of allied community-households. After the immediate danger had passed, his formal control lapsed completely; thus, "war chiefs" existed only during a period of crisis.

The Jivaro sense of individual liberty and freedom knew almost no reasonable bounds. Their independent nature led to frequent quarrels, which could expand abruptly into blood feuds. Concomitantly they considered many if not most deaths to be due to the evil intent of sorcerers, who might be either professional shamans or influential old men. A feud might erupt as the result of a relatively trivial episode. For instance, domestic pigs were permitted to roam about freely during the day, and an animal might find its way into the gardens of a neighboring community and be very destructive. The owner of the ruined crops would demand compensation from the owner of the pig, and a quarrel was likely to erupt between the families involved. If a person in either family then became ill with a disease attributed to sorcery, it was presumed to have been caused by the quarrelsome neighbor. If the person died and it was divined that the neighbor was responsible, it was incumbent on the surviving relatives of the deceased to exact blood revenge. This act was likely to lead to reciprocal murders and result in long-term hostilities between the families involved. A feud might result also if a man killed his wife because she was presumed to have committed adultery. In a case of this nature the relatives of the woman would profess her innocence, and the man might be killed by his father-in-law or brother-in-law.

When a person contracted a disease which was accompanied by violent pains such as headaches and rheumatic afflictions and especially if there was swelling in the painful area, it was thought that sorcery was the cause. If, however, the disease was thought to have been introduced by whites, as smallpox, dysentery, and most fevers, the illness was considered in the contagious category. If a person died from one of the latter diseases, the person identified as the carrier was open to blood revenge in spite of the fact that he might be acknowledged as an innocent host. Compensation often was acceptable in these instances, as it was for accidental deaths caused by someone who was drunk or under the influence of narcotics.

Given the value placed on family solidarity, honor, and vengeance, justice clearly was perceived as an essential social goal. A supernatural dimension also existed, for the soul of a deceased person cried for revenge and was present in the dreams of relatives. Sometimes years passed before an only son was mature enough to avenge the murder of his father, or before an opportune moment to exact revenge occurred. It was not essential to kill the murderer himself; any of his near relatives, either male or female, were potential victims. Immediately after a murder, the possibility of compensation being accepted by the family of the deceased usually was out of the question. But as time passed, the offended family might accept a rifle, an ax, or a good dog as compensation, and the case would be closed. If it happened that a person was killed by another member of his family, the loss was considered as regrettable but not to be avenged. "Trophy" heads never were taken of Jivaro, only of other ethnics, all of whom the Jivaro hoped to exterminate; in victory, however, they did not occupy enemy territories because they feared the supernatural forces which existed there.

In order to protect themselves from enemies they had various means of defense apart from the solid construction of their houses. Around gardens high fences were built so that they could tend their crops in relative security. On the paths which enemies might use, pits were dug, and pointed sticks were placed upright in the bottom in order to impale an enemy who fell through the thin covering. Another method used along a path was to bend a pole back and fit pointed sticks into it. An unwary person tripped the release, and the sticks were driven into his face or body. The people had holes in their house walls to watch for the approach of enemies and were constantly on the lookout for strange footprints which might indicate the nearness of spies. Furthermore, the signal drums served to warn allies of an enemy's approach.

In warfare the spear was the principal offensive weapon and a shield the means of resisting open attack. The shaft and lanceolate head of a fighting spear were fashioned from a single piece of hard palm wood. The circular shield was made from a single piece of light but very strong wood from a particular tree. Large shields were kept in the houses to resist assaults at home, and lighter ones were carried by warriors on raids. Blowguns and poisoned arrows were used exclusively against game; it was felt that if blowguns were employed against men, they would no longer be effective for hunting game. Furthermore, they were not considered effective weapons against men.

When a man decided to undertake a raid of vengeance, he first fasted and took a drug to induce dreams; if these were propitious, he made further plans. A surprise raid might be made on an enemy or he might be warned of the attack. If the potential victim was told of the plans, he might send word that an attack would be welcome; sometimes this was enough to make the planners end their preparations. If the plans went forward, war dances were held, beer was drunk, and tobacco was smoked in order to strengthen the raiders both naturally and supernaturally. The day before the attack, they painted their bodies black. The actual attack might take place at the house of the victim just before dawn; they waited until the accused came out to relieve himself and then rushed forth to make the kill. As a more frequent alternative, they attempted to ambush him away from his house. After a successful raid the killers observed food and other taboos for two to three months.

The preparations for fights with non-Jivaro were much more elaborate and first involved the selection of a war leader, a man who was an elderly and successful warrior. The secret preparations included taking narcotics in order to induce favorable dreams, and lengthy discussions were held to interpret these dreams. Spies were dispatched to determine the strengths and weaknesses of the intended victims. As the time for an attack approached, detailed plans were formulated by the war leader, and war dances were held. These were accompanied by a shouted dialogue between warriors, which served to encourage the participants and was a magical means to assure success. A war song likewise was designed to bring victory. One of these is as follows (Karsten 1935:285–286).

> My brother, my brother,
> Let us make war together!
> To my son also I have said:
> My son, my son,
> Make you strong, make you brave!
> Me they won't kill!
> I will not die!
> Myself I will kill my enemy!
> I have dreamed and my dreams have been good.
> I have seen the Old Ones [ancestral spirits]!
> I will capture my enemy!
> I have him already!
> Presently I will be engaged in fighting!
> All right, may my enemy come, may he come!
> And may he take my life if he can!
> If he kills me,
> My sons will certainly see (that it will be avenged).
> May he kill some one else!

As with the war dance a war song was sung just before setting forth, and it was intended to serve as a magical means for gaining victory. The ritual preparations further included drinking beer and smoking tobacco.

The warriors set off in a single line, and as long as they were on the march, whether for a few days or weeks, they spoke in a whisper and only when necessary. The war leader was privileged to speak loudly in order to give instructions, and at the camping sites he reviewed the plan of attack and offered words of encouragement, especially to inspire novice warriors. In making preparations for an attack, each man carefully arranged his clothing and braided his hair in three long pigtails which were adorned with toucan feathers, human hair, and a brightly colored plant bast. The latter was added because of its magical properties as well as to distinguish friends from enemies. Each warrior put on a monkey skin cap, very long ear ornaments, and a necklace of jaguar teeth. Finally he coated his face, chest, arms, and legs with black paint. The goal of these preparations was threefold: to gain magical aid, to be able to identify friends in the confusion of battle, and to terrify foes.

Although enemies were taken unaware outdoors if possible, it was more often necessary to launch a surprise attack against a house. The raiders stationed themselves around a house at night or early in the morning in the hope that someone would come outside. If this happened, they killed the individual immediately and rushed in the open door to massacre the residents. Otherwise they set fire to the roof thatching and then killed the residents as they fled.

Not infrequently the enemy was warned that potential attackers were in the vicinity. The barking of dogs or the cackling of chickens might give them away. The householders would immediately beat their signal drums to bring friends to their aid. The attackers then were forced to choose between retreating rapidly or launching their attack and hoping that relief would not arrive in time to aid the beleaguered villagers. The people in a house might attempt to flee to another house in the vicinity, for they could not depend on the arrival of friends in time to give them aid. In the confusion some or all of the people in a house might succeed in escaping. The persons most often killed were old, and an attack might be given up at this point. It might happen, however, that the warriors within a house being threatened would sally forth prepared for fierce hand-to-hand fighting. In general an attack was completely successful if all the people in a house were murdered; the victors also might kill some of their domestic animals. The victims were not tortured, but every effort was made to take their heads and to mutilate their bodies. If any persons were spared, they were most likely to be young girls. Women were spared less often, for they might never forgive the murder of their families.

The major goal of an attack on other ethnics was to obtain one or more heads. The usual pattern was for a warrior to return home with the head of a victim and begin the long and involved preparations necessary for a victory feast. If an individual was poor, he might forgo the celebration, and the same was true of a great warrior who had taken many heads. Such a man had so many enemies that most of his time was spent defending himself against their attacks. In general, however, a man who had taken a head, or *tsantsa*, would hold the desired celebration because only in this manner could he be assured of fame, additional victories, and a long life. The celebration also was an avenue to material wealth and had deep religious significance.

The head of a victim was detached from as near the body as possible, and preparation of the tsantsa was begun within a short time. Ritual practices were followed before the initial step in preparing the head was undertaken; then a vertical line was cut down the back of the head, after which the scalp and facial skin were peeled from the skull. The skull and adhering flesh was discarded without ceremony. The head skin was immersed in a pot of boiling water briefly; this served to contract it somewhat and to sterilize it. The skin was then cooled on top of an upright stick, after which a ring of vine was attached temporarily at the base of the neck. The circumference of the vine ring was the same as that of the reduced form; the incision at the back of the head was then sewn together with a needle and fiber thread. Three stones then were heated in a fire, and one at a time they were placed in the tsantsa and rolled around in order to burn off any blood or other matter adhering to the inner surface. After the last stone was removed, the cavity was filled about halfway with hot, fine sand which was shaken around. After the sand cooled, it was taken out and reheated; the process was repeated many times. In between the applications of sand, a knife was used to carefully scrape away the burned inner surface. Repeated heatings shrank the head skin, and as it was shrinking, the operator molded the skin with his fingers in order to preserve the victim's original features in diminished perspective. The tsantsa required days or even weeks to process into final form, which was about one-fourth its original size. When the head was shrunk fully, the lips were closed with wooden pins which had strings attached to them, and the face was covered with charcoal. Particular attention was paid to the hair on the head since it was the locus of the victim's soul.

The supernatural potency of a tsantsa depended on the victim's qualities when he was alive. If he was old, had fought with honor, and held tenaciously to life while being killed, the head was of great esteem. Some heads of women were processed, and of more significance, the heads of sloths were prepared in the same manner. The feasts held to celebrate taking a sloth head were as numerous and as important as those for human heads. The significance of a sloth's head is explained by the belief that in primeval times sloths, along with all other animals, were Jivaro. The sloth was singled out for particular attention because it was thought to have been a lineal survivor from this ancient era. His ancestor was a Jivaro but from a foreign group and thus an enemy. The great antiquity of sloths was demonstrated by the fact that they moved slowly, their hair was partially gray, and when wounded they were difficult to kill. A sloth head was reduced only slightly in size since it was small in its natural form, but after it was processed it looked quite human.

Soon after he had killed an enemy, a warrior was obligated to fast and eat only mashed manioc. He cooked for himself and ate with a small wooden utensil in order to prevent his fingers from coming in contact with the food. Since he had the blood of an enemy on his hands, he might die if

A Jivaro warrior prepares to enter his house for the first time wearing the head that he took (Courtesy of Societas Scientiarum Fennica; from Karston 1935).

his fingers touched the food he ate. Neither was he permitted to wash himself or his garments or clean his spear until he passed through a purification ceremony at his home village. Furthermore, it was not until after another ceremony was held, months later, that he was permitted to sleep with a woman or even in the same room with one.

The ceremonies to which a successful warrior was subjected were drawn out and complex. The knowledge that he had taken a head preceded his arrival at his home community, and he could return only after the tsantsa had been prepared. He entered the community dwelling with his hair taken down and without adornments or body paint. An old warrior, as ceremonial host, hung the shrunken head suspended from a cord around the killer's neck. The host and then the other men present stroked the hair of the head as the killer was greeted by the women, who joined him in a victory dance. He was the center of attention, but he shared the role with his wife and one of his daughters. After the dance the head was hung from a spear placed just inside the door; at this point the initial dangers associated with its arrival had been dispelled. During the Washing of the Blood Ceremony the slayer's legs were decorated with the blood of a chicken in order to ritually purify him; he then bathed and washed his clothing and weapon for the first time since he had taken the head. The man's wife and daughter went through the bathing ritual with him because they had had contact with the head when it was still dangerous. The feast that followed was not elaborate, since only a short period of time was available to make the necessary preparations. Between this feast and a much more elaborate one some months later, the warrior dressed plainly and was subject to many food and behavioral taboos. He was permitted to consume only certain foods; he did not hunt or venture far from the settlement. This was an especially dangerous period because the soul of the tsantsa was not yet under his control, and it could cause his death, kill members of his family, or cause his crops to fail and his pigs to die. Three or four months later a separate ceremony, Painting with Blackening, accompanied by a more elaborate feast, was performed. This ceremony was highlighted by washing the shrunken head in a magical solution which made the soul of the deceased the servant of the murderer. The three to four days of feasting were concluded by painting the slayer's body with a vegetable blackening.

The final ceremony was sometimes called the Eating of the Tsantsa, to imply that the soul of the shrunken head passed under the complete control of the slayer. Preparations for the event required two to three years, and a few months before the celebration the warrior again began to wear simple clothing without adornments and observe the food and behavioral taboos mentioned earlier. The slayer alone was responsible for the pending celebration, and it was he and his housemates who made all the necessary preparations. Many clay pots were made to hold the beer which was to be brewed, a special tobacco-based liquid was made, special benches were constructed to accommodate household guests, and enough food and firewood were collected to last for fifteen days. Guests were ceremonially invited to attend, and the honored ritual specialists began to arrive. The festivities began with a dance held by the householders to dispel and further negate the potential danger of the head and at the same time to increase its powers for the possessor. When the guests were assembled in all their finery, introductory speeches were made about the event, and beer was distributed. The tsantsa was the focal point of the celebrations, and all of the activities were designed to give the slayer even greater control over the head for his general prosperity. The tobacco juice preparation was taken in order to help protect the warrior and his relatives. The balance of the opening activities revolved around drinking bouts, feasting, and dancing all night; during this stage the events surrounding the head-taking were recounted at length. Early the following day a narcotic-based liquid was drunk and vomited on three occasions by all adults who chose to partake of it with the warrior, his wife, and daughter. The persons who drank the infusion slept after losing the third dosage and were expected to have dreams which were favorable portents for the future. After waking they recounted their dreams and ate as other persons drank beer and danced until nearly dawn. The following day a tobacco juice preparation was taken by the slayer and the other principals after they had been seated ceremonially. The old warrior who led the ceremony cut the strings and removed the pins which closed the mouth of the tsantsa and hung it around the slayer's neck, an action accompanied by songs and dances performed by the women. The shrunken head then was taken outside the house and washed in a special solution, after which its hair was dressed with combs which had extraordinary power. After this event the soul of the tsantsa was considered under the almost complete control of the killer. Further fasting, beer drinking, and dancing concluded the several years of preparations necessary to make the soul of an enemy amenable to the power of the slayer.

Jivaro ceremonials surrounding shrunken heads appear to have been quite uniform among all the local groups. The ceremonies were predicated on the assumption that the soul of the dead person was represented in the trophy, especially in its hair, and yearned to revenge its death by harming the killer or anyone associated with him. Through the series of rituals the soul first was neutralized and then brought under the control of the murderer. Furthermore, those persons who aided in the ceremonies gained supernatural aid, and this was especially important for the wife and daughter of the successful warrior in their efforts to raise good crops. Thus, the general economic welfare of the entire household was advanced when a man took a tsantsa and performed the rituals necessary to gain control over it.

This comparatively long discussion of Jivaro head-shrinking ceremonies has been included in order to demonstrate that the custom was more than a bizarre set of rituals among a particular people. Despite the apparent strangeness of the practice, it clearly was intended as a means to further the general welfare of the household involved. The tsantsa itself simply fulfilled a role in reaching these goals more effectively than any other means known to the Indian participants.

Source: Karsten 1935.

DRUGS AMONG THE YANOMAMO

A question asked with increasing frequency and concern is whether we are able to satisfactorily accommodate the unrestricted use of psycho-active drugs in our culture. Opinions tend to be age-specific and vary from vehemently positive to singularly negative. The widespread use of such drugs is a new cultural experience to us, and we are finding it difficult to grapple with the situation objectively, partially because we have no context in which to place the pattern. One reasonable means by which to broaden our understanding of the subject is to consider drug usage in the context of another culture, one in which the use of hallucinogens is well established and normal, even in quite ordinary situations.

The Yanomamo (Yạnomamö), with whom effective contact was not established until the mid-1950s, are one of the largest groups of aboriginal South American peoples to remain unaffected by outsiders until recent times. Their population is estimated at 10,000, and their homeland is in the jungles of southern Venezuela and adjacent sectors of Brazil. George J. Seitz studied a segment of the Yanomamo which he identified as the Waika during repeated visits from 1956 to 1965, and Napoleon A. Chagnon spent nineteen months among various groups in the mid-1960s. In the very recent past the Yanomamo occupied more than 125 scattered villages, with an average of about eighty persons each. Most villages were at relatively low elevations, and no matter whether there were adjacent hills, ridges, or plains, jungle vegetation was everywhere except along the water courses and at their farming plots. Their permanent dwellings were built at well-drained sites, such as on a slight rise, and the members of an entire village occupied one large house. A village dwelling was built in segments, with each man constructing the particular portion his family was to occupy. These houses were circular, framed with posts and poles, and covered with thatch in the shape of a cone. The smaller ones had comparatively steep sides and a small opening at the top, but the sides of the larger structures gently sloped to a large central opening at the top. A house was inhabited for about two years at the most, for by this time the roof was so badly infested with insects that they dropped down whenever the thatch was jarred. A house then was abandoned and a new one constructed, again in a piecemeal manner.

Within a house hammocks were suspended from the structural posts, and clay cooking pots were scattered about. Food was cooked in these vessels by the men, since women were considered so clumsy that they were not even permitted to touch the pots. Fires were built by twirling a wooden shaft against a flat piece of wood on which cotton tinder was placed. A knife for light work was bladed with an agouti tooth attached to a wooden handle with resin and fiber. Another knife form consisted of the lower jaw of a wild pig, with the canine teeth functioning as the blade. The self bow, which was the primary weapon, was made from hard palm wood and strung with a twisted fiber cord. One form of arrow, which was made from cane and feathered, was pointed with a sliver of palm wood some fifteen inches in length. The point was covered with curare poison, and lateral grooves were cut into the point so that it would break off in a wounded animal or man. Extra arrowpoints were carried in a short bamboo quiver which was hung from a string around a hunter's neck.

A large amount of their food, about 85 percent, was produced in garden plots. These were cleared by cutting down the brush and small trees and ringing larger trees, which also were burned at the base. Later the man who was preparing the plot burned the dead vegetation and began his planting. The most important crops were four varieties of plantains and bananas, both started by taking cuttings from established gardens. They also raised maize, sweet manioc, taro, sweet potatoes, a fruit-producing palm, and a few other food crops of minor importance. A host of other plants were cultivated for their magical qualities. For example, the dried leaves of one plant and a fragrant wood were powdered and blended to produce a "female charm" which most men carried with them. If the opportunity presented itself, the powder was held against the nostril of a female and she was forced to breathe it, after which she was expected to be very susceptible to seduction. The people also raised tobacco, which was chewed, and a cotton was produced from which hammocks were fashioned. Once a garden had been established for a few years, it produced crops yearlong, but before it reached this peak, there might be periods of hunger. This danger could be offset in part by planting crops which matured rapidly, such as maize. Except when warfare forced the residents of a village to flee a locality, gardens were sustained in the same area for many years by clearing adjacent plots as needed to replace those which declined in productivity and had to be abandoned.

Nearly as much time was spent in hunting and collecting foods as in gardening, but the rewards were much smaller. The animals most often killed were monkeys, wild turkeys, wild pigs, tapir, deer, and small rodents. All game was taken with bows and arrows, and men usually hunted alone. The curare-tipped arrows usually were used against monkeys. Lanceolate bamboo points were fixed to arrows to kill large animals, which might be taken with the aid of dogs, and a barbed arrowpoint was employed against birds. The people also collected fruit from wild palms, honey, grubs, caterpillars, and ants. Obtaining food posed no great problem given the productivity of the environment and the exploitative technology of these Indians. The animals of the jungle normally were not dangerous; the greatest uncertainties in life were posed by other Yanomamo.

Since a tremendous amount of effort was required in order to clear and establish new gardens, members of any particular community would remain in one area, farming nearby plots indefinitely, if not threatened seriously by raids from enemies. In order for a village to remain cohesive, the population had to be about 150 persons. The members of smaller settlements were obligated to group themselves into uncertain alliances with their neighbors. A village with fewer than about 50 persons could not field enough warriors to defend it in a raid; on the other hand a community could become too large to function. If the population grew to about 250 persons, the village soon would fragment because of internal conflicts. These developed from accusations of adultery, which resulted in bitter fights and violent feuds. The villagers attempted to maintain their autonomy by limiting all marriages to members of the community (village endogamy). One descent line of males (patrilineage) offered its women to the members of another patrilineage in the settlement (patrilineage exogamy), and the second lineage reciprocated in kind. Thus a man who received a wife from a particular patrilineage was obligated to offer a woman to that lineage. The ideal marriage partner was the daughter of one's mother's brother or father's sister (cross-cousin marriage).

In this male-dominated society a strong positive value was placed on physical violence. A wife was expected to anticipate the demands of her husband, and when she did not, he might routinely vent his displeasure by hitting her with his hand or with a piece of firewood. A truly irate husband might shoot his wife in the buttocks with a barbed arrow or burn her with an ember. When a woman was suspected of marital infidelity, her ears might be cut off or her ear ornaments grasped in order to rip the lobes. One important factor which tempered a husband's treatment of his wife was the presence of her brothers, for they were likely to come to her defense. Hostile feelings toward neighboring Yanomamo sometimes erupted, but in general networks of trade relations were maintained with nearby villages. Local craft items were exchanged for others which were made elsewhere, and in this manner weak and strong alliances were developed and maintained between settlements in the area. When animosities developed, they were kept secret as much as possible until they could be acted on. Persons from a community might be invited to a feast held in their honor, only to have the men murdered and the women seized by their hosts. Furthermore, a time when most of the men from a village were off on a raid of vengeance was an ideal moment for "allies" to raid the settlement, kill the men who were left to defend it, and escape with as many women as possible. Even when a feast held for visitors from another village actually was a friendly gesture, the visitors often made gluttons of themselves and then attempted to intimidate their hosts. Such behavior might lead to chest-pounding duels, to fights with clubs, or even to murders with bows and arrows.

The most important inhabitants of the spirit world of these people were tiny, humanlike demonic beings who lived on rocks and mountains. Fundamentally they were hostile to humans, but if they could be controlled and induced to live in a man's chest, he then could cause as well as cure illness. Many men aspired to be shamans, and about half of them succeeded, some much more effectively than others. An aspirant to shamanistic powers abstained from sexual relations, fasted, took drugs, and after days of contemplation established rapport with spirits. Later, when called on, these demonic creatures could remove a hostile spirit in the body of a friend or be sent to eat the souls of the children in hostile villages.

The most important hallucinogenic drug used by the Yanomamo was processed from the resin in the bark of a tree belonging to the genus *Virola*; from this resin a powdered snuff termed *ebene* was derived. After the outer bark of a tree had been removed, the inner bark containing the resin was scraped free and then kneaded between the palms along with wood ashes and saliva. After the mass had been worked into a pliable wad, the moisture was removed by heating it on a piece of broken clay pot. The residue was ground into powder, which was brushed onto a leaf with a feather. This was the most common form of ebene, although on occasion it was made from the bark, leaves or seeds of other plants; thus ebene was a generic term.

In order to take ebene a small quantity was placed inside a hollow cane tube; one end of the tube was held in a nostril of the man taking the drug, and another man blew on the opposite end. The process usually was repeated for the other nostril. The immediate response to the drug-laden blast of air was pain, choking, and coughing. As this subsided, the man's nose ran with mucus, his eyes watered, he perspired profusely, and he might vomit. Usually within a few minutes the recipient had difficulty focusing his eyes, and he gave the impression of being intoxicated. The drug produced color visions and enabled the taker to contact spirit aids, which he invited into his chest. This invitation was expressed through a stamping dance step, singing, and sporadic shouts which lasted nearly an hour. During this time he was not in a complete stupor, as indicated by his dancing and singing. Descriptions indicate that the taker of ebene felt like a giant and saw everything surrounding him as magnified greatly in size. This gave him the feeling of being superhuman, and the spirits which he contacted gave him a sense of power.

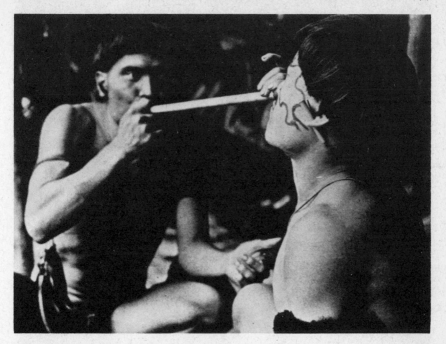

A Yanomamo man blowing ebene into the nostril of another man (Courtesy Holt, Rinehart and Winston, Inc.; from Chagnon 1968).

Hallucinogenic drugs were taken only by men, and the time chosen most often was in the late afternoon. The effects lasted for an hour or more, and afterwards the man bathed to wash away the mucus and vomit. An overdose made a man violent, and he might carry his weapons about the village threateningly as people fled. Someone, however, usually managed to disarm him before harm could be done to others. In spite of the pain involved, most men took drugs. Some did not do so, however, because they disliked the unpleasant effects. None of the drugs taken by the Yanomamo were habit-forming; persons who were accustomed to taking them could and did abstain for weeks at a time. On the other hand the reaction to being without tobacco was one of great stress. The first activity of the day for men, women, and children was to chew tobacco; to it they clearly were addicted.

Superficially it might appear that Yanomamo drug-taking practices produced the excessive violence which dominated their lives, but more careful study makes this conclusion seem ill-grounded and inappropriate. Many other diverse factors led to the emergence of their extremely aggressive behavior patterns. The use of drugs did on occasion lead to

A Yanomamo in a hallucinogenic stupor (Courtesy Holt, Rinehart and Winston, Inc.; from Chagnon 1968).

violent acts against one's own people and against enemies, but such examples seem to have been rare. The hallucinogenics no doubt offered a welcome escape from reality to some men, but they served a far more important function than that in terms of the culture as a whole. It was through the use of drugs that a man was able to invoke supernatural powers to act in his behalf. Thus the use of ebene gave the men extra power and confidence to deal with the enemies surrounding them.

Sources: Chagnon 1968; Chagnon *et al.* 1971; Seitz 1967.

THE INCA EMPIRE

The empire of the Inca has been described by some commentators as the most enlightened and successful socialistic government ever implemented by man. Others have interpreted Inca life as a rigidly confined social order which if it was not oppressive, was at least very restrictive and extremely authoritarian. Irrespective of the striking differences between these interpretations, this empire was one of the most remarkable political achievements of man. A rather unusual aspect of their history is that we have records of the Inca verbal traditions, which span hundreds of years, about the rise of their empire. Although the tales of their genesis and early existence are quite fanciful, accounts of the hundred years just prior to historic contact appear to be factual; between the two periods fact and fancy often are combined. Information about the past was preserved in genealogical accounts and narrative poems which were memorized and verbally passed from father to son by specially trained oral historians. In spite of the difficulty in distinguishing between myths and oral history, it seems highly fitting to describe the Inca largely in terms of their own views about their past.

Manco Capac, the first Inca or ruler, presumably lived around A.D. 1200, and by the time of the Spanish conquest in 1532 he was thought of as a founder who was more godlike than human. One version of Inca origins reports that a short distance from the future capital of Cuzco was a hill with three openings, which perhaps were caves. Manco Capac, his three brothers, and his four sisters emerged from the central cavity, and they assumed the role of leaders for those persons who came from the lateral openings. The people were organized into ten *ayllus* or patrilineal descent groups, each of which would in time occupy a distinct area (patrilineal clans); furthermore, each ayllu was an endogamous unit (clan endogamy). After their emergence on earth the clans wandered about under the leadership of Manco Capac; during this time the second Inca, Sinchi Roca, was born to the original Inca and his eldest sister. The group journeyed about seeking an area with fertile land where they might become established. As they moved from place to place, they tested the quality of the soil with a golden staff. When they neared the site of the future city of Cuzco, they found that the soil was fertile, and the locality was considered desirable for settlement. Other peoples already lived there, however, and they prepared to battle the Inca. Before this time Manco Capac had disposed of two of his brothers; one became trapped in the emergency opening when he was sent back for a sacred llama, and the second brother was turned into stone. The third brother, who was extraordinarily powerful, helped rid the Cuzco locality of its settlers by an unusual display of strength. He killed one of the local inhabitants, cut out the man's lungs, and inflated them; after seeing this the other people fled. The Inca and his four sisters built their first permanent houses on the spot where the Temple of the Sun would in time be erected. Other origin myths offer contrasting views about the founding of the Inca line, and it is possible that this one may have been fabricated by later rulers to give both mystery and substance to their Inca heritage.

The first eight Incas, who reigned from about 1200 to 1438, apparently controlled only the area around Cuzco. There were conflicts and wars with the other local Indians, but no one people dominated the land beyond Cuzco. This situation is described in accounts of the reign of the fourth Inca, Mayta Capac. When he was one year old, Mayta Capac reportedly was as large as an eight-year-old, and within a few years he successfully warred against adjoining peoples. Despite the fact that he had defeated neighboring groups, he does not appear to have expanded Inca control beyond the immediate Cuzco region. When the eighth ruler, Viracocha Inca, assumed power, local peoples who had been conquered had not yet been controlled. This led to their return to power and further wars of conquest. In his prime, Viracocha was able to extend control over an area about twenty-five miles from Cuzco by placing Inca officials in control of defeated peoples and stationing soldiers in their midst. During this era there were a number of local chiefdoms of almost equal power. Two groups among them often allied against a third power and crushed it, but they soon fell in turn to a similar alliance. However, near the end of the reign of Viracocha only the chiefdom of Chanca continued to rival that of the Inca. When the Chanca attacked, Viracocha and Urcon, the son he had chosen as his successor, believed that their defeat in open battle was almost inevitable, and they prepared to defend one particular fortress. However, two other royal sons, one being Yupanqui, with the aid of two old generals chose to meet the invaders in an open battle. Against great odds the Chanca were defeated, and their power soon faded. When the eighth Inca died, Inca Urcon succeeded him, but his reign was cut short when Yupanqui, the leader of the successful war against the Chanca, had himself enthroned and ordered that Urcon's name be striken from the list of rulers. Yupanqui assumed the new name of Pachacuti, which literally meant "cataclysm." He lived up to his name and became one of the most remarkable leaders of all times.

With the reign of Pachacuti between 1438 and 1471 the oral traditions become much more historical than legendary, and one account tends to be similar to the next. This man was above all else a great conqueror, organizer, and planner. Early during his rule Pachacuti sought to gain complete control of those non-Inca in the local area. Peoples who refused to acknowledge Inca power were attacked, and all but old women and children were killed in a display of vengeance. Pachacuti carried his next campaign to the north, then another to the west, and one to the south; after this he ventured even farther north as a conquerer. After fifty years of expansion under Pachacuti and his son Topa Inca (the tenth Inca

Topa Inca and his queen riding in a litter (from Rowe 1946).

ruler), the empire extended from northern Ecuador to central Chile, a distance of nearly 3,000 miles, and it embraced about 380,000 square miles of territory. By the time of historic contact the empire of the Inca included about four million persons.

The pattern of Inca expansion under Pachacuti was to draw a foreign people into his sphere by political manipulations. If these efforts failed, an army was sent forth to conquer refractory peoples. Troops were drawn from among the Inca followers, but they consisted largely of warriors from subject peoples and were controlled by their own leaders, with overall command in the hands of an Inca trusted by the ruler. Early in the reign of Pachacuti the conquered Chanca supplied warriors who fought extremely well and wondered aloud whether they were not in fact more capable in battle than the Inca. When Pachacuti heard of their arrogance, he ordered the Chanca leaders killed, but they learned of the plot and fled. An army under Pachacuti's brother Capa Yupanqui was sent in pursuit with orders not to advance beyond a particular boundary. The brother disobeyed the order and conquered a more distant people, returning with a great deal of booty. Pachacuti had him executed, ostensibly for allowing the Chanca to escape and for disobeying his orders but in fact because he had come to rival Pachacuti's power. In later years the ruler was successful in conquering old enemies who lived along the shores of Lake Titicaca. As he aged, Pachacuti came to depend increasingly on his favored son Topa Inca to lead military ventures among autonomous peoples as well as to quell rebellions, which he did with striking success.

Although the conquests of Pachacuti were grandiose in scale, another dimension to his reign was also of great importance for the future of the empire. During the first years of his rule, Pachacuti's attention was devoted to local problems, and he remained at Cuzco. Later, as was the custom for new rulers, he made an extended tour of the empire to familiarize himself with local conditions, to check on administrators, and to serve as a final court of appeal in the administration of justice. It was after this tour that he ordered the villages around Cuzco leveled for a distance of some six miles and the construction of a planned city. Because of the mountainous conditions around Cuzco the amount of arable land was comparatively limited, and he directed the construction of a great series of terraces to provide additional farmland. He is credited with enlarging the Temple of the Sun and building roads, fortresses, palaces, and a series of great public works. It is quite possible that at least some of these projects were begun by earlier rulers, but Pachacuti clearly was instrumental in initiating architectural planning on a grand scale.

The tenth Inca succeeded his father Pachacuti in 1471 and married his sister. Brother and sister marriages were arranged in order to assure the greatest possible purity of the royal blood line, and while it has been assumed that earlier rulers married their sisters, it is almost an incontestable fact that Topa Inca actually did so. The new Inca soon embarked on conquests which took his armies into the tropical forests to the east of the Andes. While he was thus engaged, the people in the Lake Titicaca region, reasoning that this was an opportune moment to break away from Inca control, revolted. Topa Inca, because of his well-established communications network, was able to shift his soldiers from the jungles to the high Andes rapidly enough to quell the insurrection, a good indication of the administrative efficiency and mobility of the armies. He was not satisfied with consolidating his territorial gains but sought to expand them further. Additional military ventures took him and his armies into Bolivia and down into Chile until they were stopped by the fierce Araucanians at the Maule River in central Chile. After these major campaigns, he turned to the construction of a great fortress at Cuzco. He is credited with introducing the practice of dividing all lands into three parts: one for the government, another for the state religion, and a third for the local people. Topa Inca is also reported to have conducted the first empire-wide census, which was kept up-to-date through a new administrative hierarchy which he introduced, and he replaced the traditional and hereditary chiefs by appointed administrators called *curacas*. The achievements of Pachacuti and Topa Inca climaxed the greatest days of the Inca empire.

The eleventh Inca, Huayna Capac, reigned from 1493 until 1525, but by this time the empire had become so large that it was difficult to administer effectively from Cuzco, especially since all important decisions had to be made by the Inca himself. The new ruler was very young when he assumed power, and dissidents plotted to displace him but failed in their effort. As he matured, he suppressed the usual revolts at distant corners of his realm and added even more territory; yet his conquests were meager compared with those of his father and grandfather. Just before he died a dispute erupted concerning his successor; this was the first and last such challenge of consequence. The rightful heir was Huascar, the son of Huayna Capac's younger sister; his older sister-wife had produced no children. The old ruler's favorite son, however, was Atahuallpa, who possibly was the son of the ruler and the daughter of a defeated chief. Atahuallpa lived with his father at Quito in Ecuador, which the old ruler found to be a more pleasant setting than Cuzco. It appears that Huayna Capac planned to divide the empire into two portions, with Atahuallpa controlling the northern area and Huascar reigning in the south, but he made no clear final judgment before his death. Huascar was installed as the leader in Cuzco, but Atahuallpa had the support of the north. Soon the animosity between the half-brothers grew to such proportions that a clash between them was inevitable, and in anticipation of the conflict each began to assemble his followers. When the armies from the north and south clashed, Atahuallpa was victorious in a terrible battle in which thousands were killed. He now was no longer content to hold half an empire but was determined to have it all. In the final decisive contest Huascar was seized and his soldiers fled from the battlefield. Atahuallpa ordered that all of his half-brother's wives and offspring be killed and attached to poles lining the road from Cuzco, and Huascar was forced to witness the murders. Soon thereafter Atahuallpa prepared to travel to Cuzco and formally become the thirteenth ruler. However, this was the year 1532, and Pizarro landed in Peru with his 180 followers. He soon seized Atahuallpa and held him for ransom. Although the Inca was released for a roomful of gold, which possibly was worth about eight million dollars, on August 29, 1533, he was subsequently tried and killed by the Spanish, bringing an end to the days of the Inca empire.

At the time of historic contact Inca subsistence was based on farming in a mountainous region were arable land was limited. The Inca had expanded the area for cultivation by constructing extensive terraces, and water was at times channeled through elaborate networks of irrigation ditches for many miles. Soil to be planted was loosened first with a long-handled digging stick which had a footrest near the point (foot plow) and was further broken up with an adz-like hoe which with its short handle and chisel-shaped bronze blade served as a general-purpose farming instrument. When it was time to prepare the fields for a new crop, the lands belonging to the government and the religious organization were tilled first. Each male taxpayer was assigned a section which he broke up with his digging stick; his wife followed him with her hoe in order to prepare the soil further. The men formed long lines and worked in groups with their wives, chanting as they labored. Later the lands of the community were cooperatively tilled in the same fashion. Potatoes and the grain quinoa were important crops at relatively high altitudes, while at lower elevations maize, squash, and chili peppers were added. The fields were fertilized with animal or bird dung in some areas and with human feces or small fish in other localities. The most critical time in the horticultural year was the dry season after crops had been planted. When anticipated rains failed to fall, people appealed to the Thunder God for moisture by parading in mourning garb and wailing; black llamas and dogs were tied in public places and not fed, their cries of hunger being designed to gain the compassion of the rain deity. As the plants grew, the fields were weeded and watched in order to protect the crops from destruction by animals.

From low, hot valleys the Inca imported cotton, gourds, and coca along with a host of other cultivated plant products. In terms of local foods wild plant products were comparatively unimportant, and hunting was rigidly regulated. Deer and guanaco, which were killed for their meat, usually were taken by using slings or with bolas. Vicuna were captured alive, shorn or their fleece, and released since their wool was more important than their meat. The Inca or his representative controlled group hunting, which was largely a sport. One particular hunt which has been described involved 10,000 persons who formed a huge circle and drove all the game toward the center. As the circle grew smaller, concentric rings

Planting activities among the Inca (from Rowe 1946).

of beaters formed. Certain hunters killed a given number of the animals caught in the inner circle—in this instance 11,000 animals—and the others were released. Among the domestic animals llamas were of greatest importance; they were raised for their wool, as meat sources, and for carrying burdens. As pack animals they could carry only light loads, and they traveled slowly. Alpacas were raised only for their wool, which was of superior quality to that of the llama. The only domestic meat animal of any consequence was the guinea pig; kept as household scavengers, these little animals were eaten after they had been fattened.

The people in and around Cuzco lived in rectangular houses with thatched and gabled roofs. The windowless walls were constructed either of stones set in mud or of adobe. An extended family usually lived in a small cluster of houses surrounded by a stone or adobe wall through which there was a single opening. The houses were furnished sparsely, with a chimneyless clay stove as the most notable item. Some people might have slept on beds, but the more common practice seems to have been to sleep

An Inca girl carrying a load of wood (from Rowe 1946).

on the floor, clothed and covered with a blanket. Their garments were woven from wool, and the standard clothing items for a man were a breech-clout and a sleeveless, knee-length tunic. Over these a cloak was worn on special occasions and in cold weather. Men and women alike wore leather-soled sandals held in place with wool cords. A woman wore a wraparound, ankle-length dress made from a rectangular piece of cloth that fitted beneath the arms, was attached with pins along one side, and was belted at the waist. Women's cloaks were held in place with pins at the chest, while those of men were tied at the chest or over one arm.

In the recent past the term ayllu or community was applied to a cluster of unrelated, extended Inca families who lived in a restricted area, were bound together by rather informal patterns of leadership, and followed certain rules in common. It appears that in early historical times the term ayllu meant "kin group" above all else. More specifically it ideally was a kin group tracing descent to a presumed common ancestor and was endogamous in terms of marriage. When the matter of descent was important, as in the inheritance of political office, it was traced along the male line. An ayllu usually was named after a place or person, but there was no system of family names or precise rules for naming children. An ayllu was identified with a specific area, and each couple cultivated ayllu lands. These lands were redistributed yearly according to need and in order to rotate crops. Ideally the ayllus within each province were divided into two sections (moieties). For census and taxation purposes individuals were grouped according to twelve age-grades; the important grade was that of able-bodied adult.

In planning large-scale construction projects such as great buildings, terraces, or roads, small clay or stone models were made. Builders used measuring rods to determine distances and the plumb bob as a leveling device, but little is known about their actual construction methods. Common tools included diverse forms of bronze chisels, crowbars of bronze or wood, and hard hammerstones for working stone. The massive stone architecture for which the Inca are famous often entailed transporting huge precut stones over considerable distances to construction sites. The stones were moved on rollers and wooden pry bars by large numbers of men pulling on ropes attached to the stones. In order to fit stones in place when constructing high walls, ramps were built to an appropriate height. Large structures usually were a single story in height and were covered with thatched roofs, but sometimes two- or even three-story buildings were erected. Many Cuzco buildings were constructed of adobe, and in these instances adjoining walls were bonded by fitting pieces of wood between the adobe bricks in interior corners. Lintels were made of poles and were plastered over, and the interior walls were covered with plaster.

The network of Inca roads is in many ways more impressive than their public buildings. One main road ran the length of the empire along the coast, and another was located in the highlands. These were connected to each other by crossroads and were linked to major towns as well. The highland road was the more outstanding engineering feat since it required the construction of stone causeways in localities which flooded or were marshy, switch-backs on steep slopes, and stone pavements or steps when appropriate. Narrow rivers were bridged with beams to which crosspieces were attached, and wide rivers were spanned with suspension bridges hung from towers on opposite banks. The roads were used by men alone or with llamas serving as pack animals, and therefore they tended to be narrow. It was possible to travel great distances at a rapid rate, and with runners stationed at frequent intervals along a road a message could be conveyed over a distance of 150 miles in a single day.

The Inca are renowned for the diversity of their loom-woven cloth as well as for their extraordinary pottery. An even more important gauge to their technological skills is the complexity of the metalworking techniques which were known to them. The Inca mined copper, gold, silver, and tin, and each source of metal became a shrine to which the people prayed for a continuing supply and in whose honor religious festivals were held. The most commonly worked metals were copper and bronze, the latter being made by adding a small percentage of tin to copper. Among the metallurgical processes known were annealing, casting, smelting, soldering, and riveting. Luxury objects made from gold or silver included hammered sheets with raised designs, decorative pins, and cast figures of peoples and llamas. Utilitarian products were made from copper or bronze and included axes, chisels, knives, and bolas.

The Inca developed a mnemonic device termed a "knot" or quipu. It consisted of a main cord to which strings were attached, and these strings were knotted at intervals. Often the strings were of different colors or of a different manufacturing style. Some quipus were used to record numbers in a decimal system not unlike our own. On any string the knot most distant from the main cord represented units; then came knots representing tens, hundreds, and so on. In this manner it appears that sums up to tens of thousands were recorded. The sets of objects counted and the meaning of the color or manufacturing style of the string were memorized by specialists, and their knowledge was passed from one generation to the next. Quipus also were employed as memory aids for recording genealogies, narrative verse, and other texts.

The Inca ruler was a god and a king; he was worshiped as a divine being during his life and had absolute control over his subjects. Although his clothing was of much the same style as that of an ordinary man, it was of much finer material. His braided headdress was elaborately ornamented with tassels and small tubes of gold as an important symbol of his authority. He wore very large earplugs, carried a gold-headed staff, and sat on a small stool which was his throne. Before he received any person, irrespective of his rank, the individual was obligated to remove his sandals and wear a small burden on his back. Usually the visitor did not see the ruler, who sat behind a screen; it was a special honor to meet him face to face. Each new ruler was isolated and fasted for three days before he was crowned in a public ceremony at which each noble swore him allegiance. When a ruler died members of the entire empire mourned his death. His entrails were removed, and his body was wrapped and placed in his palace, where it was preserved with great care. He was waited on in death as he had been in life, even to the point of having women attendants keep flies off his bundled body.

A new royal ayllu originated with each ruler; the membership core was composed of his primary wife, secondary wives, and their descendants along the male line. Each ruler built a new palace, and after his death the members of his ayllu were charged with keeping the palace in repair and maintaining a religious cult in his memory. Persons who were closely related to a ruler were members of the nobility and were privileged to wear particular forms of headdress as well as large earplugs as symbols of their position. They held the highest administrative posts in the empire. The curacas were a hereditary class of secondary nobles who held less important administrative posts. Their number included the rulers of assimilated peoples as well as persons who presumably were distant relatives in the royal line or whose ancestors had originally been made curacas because of their administrative abilities. The nobles and curacas were supported by the harvests from government fields and were exempt from taxation. Outstanding service of a noble or curaca was rewarded by such gifts from the ruler as luxury goods and secondary wives.

Under such a powerful ruler, ordinary persons had little opportunity to make meaningful decisions concerning the course of their lives, and yet each ruler was obligated by custom to keep the welfare of his subjects in the foreground of his decision making. One institution of extreme importance in the development and administration of the empire was the taxation system, which was in terms of service due to the state. Each taxpayer was obligated to help till the fields belonging to the government and state religious organization as well as to labor on public works, serve in the army, and render personal service to the nobility and the ruler. The work performed annually for the ruler was termed *mita*, and the amount of labor was fixed by the ruler. The labor levies were drawn according to the population within each administrative unit. The Inca were able to draw on their labor force in an orderly and equitable manner because they were able to keep accurate population records.

Among the distinctive Inca means for controlling subject peoples was their practice of taking the sons of the ruler of any recently conquered people to Cuzco. Their presence in the capital insured the support of the newly assimilated population, and after the sons were taught Inca ways, they were sent back to rule their homeland. It also was a general practice not to disrupt the religious system of a defeated people so long as it was not in gross conflict with Inca standards. They likewise instituted the practice of moving persons from newly acquired regions to other areas within the empire. The depopulated regions in turn were resettled with peoples whom the Inca felt that they could trust. In this manner the likelihood of rebellions at their borders was decreased.

The control and assimilation of conquered peoples was achieved by an orderly process through an established institutional network. After a people had been defeated, their territory was surveyed, and relief maps were prepared in clay to show the major geographical features. A population census by age-grade was recorded on quipus, and this information along with a report by the conquering general were studied by the ruler and his advisers. Occupied fortresses in the conquered territory were abandoned, and people were settled near their fields. The small, scattered communities in existence were consolidated, and a provincial capital was selected. Here administrative buildings were constructed, and the existing leaders, who were integrated into the curacas class, continued as administrators, although an Inca governor was appointed in overall control. The sacred objects of a conquered people were held by the Inca and could be worshiped only when any of them traveled to Cuzco. A further means for integrating a newly acquired group was to force all of their governmental officials to learn the language of the Inca and to dress as did their conquerers. Each assimilated ethnic, however, retained its local headdress as an identifying badge. By methods such as these, as well as through a rigorous administrative system, the expanding empire was kept united. The despotic power of the ruler was absolute, justice was harsh by our terms, and yet a pervasive paternalism guided the governmental decisions. While there was no privation among the people, at the same time there were few opportunities open to an individual to make meaningful decisions concerning his life.

Sources: Mason 1957; Rowe 1946.

EIGHT

LEARNING
FROM ETHNOGRAPHY

When Western man first ventured
from Europe, he felt secure in the belief that his were the most proper
customs. As the Crusades brought exposure to infidels, the experience
reinforced his conviction that Christian ways were truly good and right.
Then maritime explorers discovered ethnics at nearly every landfall, and
these people were observed as living under sets of rules which were different for each group and contrasted especially with European ways. Initially the ethnics were associated with little more than placenames on
maps. The information about them was superficial, which in itself made
them intriguing but also categorized them as barely known savages in
distant lands. As a growing number of books appeared, the adventures of
travelers were disseminated broadly, and aborigines were captured and
exhibited for all to see. Europeans might still consider their homeland as
the intellectual hub of the world, but because of advances in cartography
and printing, they now realized that peoples with radically different life
styles were far more numerous than themselves. In time the humanness of
such peoples was established, thanks largely to a group of persons whose
chosen task was to observe and describe plants, animals, and other peoples.

The opening chapters of this book, in which the history of ethnography is sketched, were considered as an essential prelude to the discussion
of particular ethnics. It was reasoned that only after understanding the
emergence of ethnography, by placing it in its chronological and topical
framework, could our current awareness of and attitudes toward ethnics
truly be appreciated. An implicit thesis is that we rarely have understood
them very well and only recently have begun to realize the magnitude of

their accomplishments. There is clear irony in the fact that we are beginning to comprehend the ways of ethnics at a time when we nearly have
destroyed them. Another compelling reason for the inclusion of ethnographic history is more strictly anthropological. Other books which describe the emergence of anthropology devote comparatively little attention to developments in the approaches to data collection. I am not
referring to the recent rash of "how-to-do-it" manuals, but to an overview
of the rise of ethnography as a discipline. The opening chapters represent
a preliminary effort to place into focus this largely ignored aspect of
anthropological history. A third purpose of the historical information is to
associate ethnographers and other recorders with particular ethnics, some
of whom are described in the core of the text. Given the varying attitudes
and diverse training of observers which affected their reports, this history
is vital if only to prevent ethnographic reports from being considered as
timeless abstract descriptions.

Euro-Americans unquestionably are the most successful cultural
imperialists known in the history of mankind. We long have been accustomed to exporting a veritable cornucopia of manufactured goods to
ethnics and others who are different from ourselves, and they usually
accepted our offerings, if not with gratitude, at least with comparatively
little reluctance. Over most of the earth, too, we have marketed our own
brands of religion and political organization, but these efforts have met
with considerably less lasting success. As attuned as we are to disseminat-
ing our ideas and products, we have been only reluctant recipients of
ideas derived from beyond our cultural tradition. Although we have borrowed many if not most dimensions of our culture and society from others,
we have been hesitant to admit this fact. In spite of our initial successes
as cultural imperialists, we are criticized by others and by ourselves with
increasing frequency. Our goals, standards, ideals, or ethos if you will,
have become fragmented and confused. We ask with ever-increasing
concern—what are we, where are we going, and do we honestly have the
right to direct the lives of other peoples? We seek a reformulation of our
identity, and this gives every indication of resulting in a major break with
those values which we have cherished so dearly in the recent past. Our era
gives promise of becoming a time when individual differences in behavior
and values will be more acceptable than ever before in the existence of
man. If this be so, we may profit greatly by comprehending the ways of
other peoples, if only to maximize our own potential opportunities and
find greater quality satisfactions in our individual life styles. It is con-
tended that many of the customs and values expressed in the ethnographic
sketches which have been presented, may serve as useful points to consider when thinking about the future of various individual life styles in

our society. Might it not be our turn to pick and choose from the customs of others to enrich or redirect our lives in other ways?

Is it not possible to learn something about material "needs" by thinking of what the Tasmanians did without? Could the automobile ever serve to enrich our lives as did outrigger canoes among the Puluwatans? Cannot the Toda teach us something about the peaceful quality of living? Might we not consider sexual life in a different light by knowing Chukchi and Kaingang customs? Does not the Yanomamo use of drugs carry a message for us? Might we not despair less about the manners of our teenagers if we relate them to those of the Gusii? Could it be that we find more identity with the Yurok than with the Zuni, and what does this tell us about ourselves? Would we profit by comparing the political order of the Inca with our own? Hopefully it is questions such as these which will help us rethink our own ways, and possibly we can profit significantly from an awareness of the realities of living in the lives of peoples called ethnics.

For contemporary and past cultural anthropologists, ethnographic findings served other purposes. These data made it possible to appreciate the breadth of cultural learnings among ethnics. Once the general range had been perceived, field investigators continued to fill in ethnographic gaps as well as to obtain new data bearing on particular problems. Others attempted to organize the diverse findings, and several systematic frameworks were devised in order to clarify the ways of ethnics in comparative terms for a fuller understanding of observed differences and similarities.

EARLY CLASSIFICATIONS

Ethnographers have been and continue to be a group of diligent data collectors. From the days of Morgan to the present time a staggering amount of information has been published about ethnics. For example, as of 1958 the number of worthwhile published sources dealing with the Navajo Indians totalled about 640, and for the Iroquois Indians about 600 sources existed (Murdock 1960:234–246, 329–342, 390). Some of these publications predate the work of Morgan, and many were written by nonanthropologists, but each contains significant ethnographic information. The number of published accounts about ethnics does not appear to be diminishing; in fact, the volume of writings remains impressively great. However, anthropologists have not simply assembled descriptive information about diverse peoples at various points in time. In addition they have compared and classified their findings in order to better comprehend and interpret the vast range of recorded diversity.

The immediate goal of any classification is the systematic arrangement of ideas on the basis of one or more shared characteristics in order to determine similarities and to establish subgroups on the basis of differences. An overall goal of any classification is to group phenomena which are judged as more similar to each other than to other phenomena of the same level. The ultimate goal of scientific classification is to facilitate generalizations about structure, function, and process. Classifications are a means to ends, not ends in themselves, and one must ask not only what is the basis of the classification, but also what purpose a particular classification is designed to fulfill in the broad and narrow contexts of understanding.

Each ethnic as well as every nation represents a unique sociocultural system. When Europeans became reasonably familiar with persons from other societies, comparisons were made and judgments rendered about the particular niche in which these foreigners belonged. During the Middle Ages most European writers classified themselves and their near neighbors as civilized but considered persons with distinctly different cultures as savages, pagans, natives, barbarians, inhabitants, and the like. Comparisons made at this time among ethnics simply pointed out their gross similarities, and rankings of a more discriminating nature would not be made for many years to come. The early comparative statements about peoples were based on their conditions at a particular moment in history; they addressed themselves to matters of gross structure and function as they existed in a static combination. Once the time element was added and comparisons were made at different periods of time within one group, we move from static categories to a concern with social and cultural change. It was not historians or natural scientists who originally conceived of grand designs in an effort to explain human diversity; this was a task achieved first by philosophers and theologians. Philosophical speculations and theological pronouncements about why men were different required no body of substantive information for their support.

Early in European history the Roman poet Lucretius (98–55 B.C.), an Epicurean, had composed a work titled *On the Nature of Things*; in part, it was an inferential explanation for the cosmological system in terms of successive stages in which life forms arose spontaneously from the earth:

> First of all the earth gave birth to the tribes of herbage and bright verdure all around the hills and over all the plains, the flowering fields gleamed in their green hue, and thereafter the diverse trees were started with loose rein on their great race of growing through the air. Even as down and hair and bristles are first formed on the limbs of four-footed beasts and the body of fowls strong of wing, so then the newborn earth

raised up herbage and shrubs first, and thereafter produced the races of mortal things, many races born in many ways by diverse means. For neither can living animals have fallen from the sky nor the beasts of earth have issued forth from the salt pools. It remains that rightly has the earth won the name of mother, since out of earth all things are produced. And even now many animals spring forth from the earth, formed by the rains and the warm heat of the sun; wherefore we may wonder the less, if then more animals and greater were born, reaching their full growth when earth and air were fresh. First of all the tribe of winged fowls and the diverse birds left their eggs, hatched out in the spring season, as now in the summer the grasshoppers of their own will leave their smooth shells, seeking life and livelihood. Then it was that the earth first gave birth to the race of mortal things. For much heat and moisture abounded then in the fields; thereby, wherever a suitable spot or place was afforded, there grew up wombs, clinging to the earth by their roots; and when in the fullness of time the age of the little ones, fleeing moisture and eager for air, had opened them, nature would turn to that place the pores in the earth and constrain them to give forth from their opened veins a sap, most like to milk; even as now every woman, when she has brought forth, is filled with sweet milk, because all the current of her nourishment is turned towards her paps. The earth furnished food for the young, the warmth raiment, the grass a couch rich in much soft down. But the youth of the world called not into being hard frosts nor exceeding heat nor winds of mighty violence: for all things grow and come to their strength in like degrees (Bailey 1921:212–213).

Much later, in the Middle Ages of Europe, one popular explanation for the differences among peoples was that ethnics once had been civilized but had fallen from the grace of God. Other commentators attributed cultural differences to distinctions of race. One of the first persons who attempted to explain man's diverse ways in a reasonably systematic manner by employing empirical data was Giambattista Vico (1668–1744), an Italian professor of rhetoric. In a book which appeared in 1725 titled *New Science* (1948), he attempted to formulate "natural laws of the peoples," which he contrasted with the "natural law of the philosophers." He sought to establish the universal basis of history. Vico began with the "age of the gods" when family life began, and from this stage he postulated an "age of heroes" which led eventually to the rise of a feudal aristocracy. In the ensuing conflict the patricians had the power, but the plebeians finally succeeded in pressing for equal rights and establishing the "age of men." As the stage progressed, however, equality among men led to their softness and decline so that men reverted to a barbarous state and the cycle began anew (Fisch and Bergin 1944:46–53). Although Philip Bagby (1963:12) labeled Vico "a half-educated Neapolitan literary hack," Stephen Toulmin and June Goodfield (1966:125–129) likened the advances Vico made in the study of society to those of Gregor J. Mendel in the field of biology; Toulmin and Goodfield appear somewhat closer to a just evaluation of Vico and his contribution.

The year before *New Science* appeared, Father Joseph-Francois Lafitau published *Customs of American Savages Compared with Those of Earliest Times*. In this two-volume work Lafitau not only described Indian life in unprecedented detail and with unparalleled sophistication, but as the title suggests, he compared Indian customs with those prevalent in the early stages of Western society. He considered differences in cultures to be caused by degeneration. In his view as a Jesuit, God had created men with a single religion, but as they wandered over the earth, in time peoples lost touch with the true religion and proper way of life. If diverse peoples demonstrated certain similarities, Lafitau reasoned that these were remnants of the original universal unity. He employed ethnographic information about Indians as a means to interpret the past. He wrote,

> I was not content with knowing the nature of the Indians, and with informing myself about their customs and practices. I sought in these practices and customs vestiges of the most remote antiquity. I read carefully the works of the earliest authors who dealt with the customs, laws, and usages of the peoples with whom they had some acquaintance. I compared these customs, one with the other, and I confess that whereas the ancient authors have given me some light to support several happy conjectures concerning the Indians, the customs of the Indians have provided me with light for understanding more clearly and for explaining several things which appear in the ancient writers (Fenton 1969:179).

Lafitau was an early cultural relativist; one of the first thorough ethnographers, in a sense he was the originator of the comparative method in the interpretation of ethnographic information (Fenton 1969:173–187). Thus, a French Jesuit priest had been a leader in crossing three major thresholds in the history of anthropological thought. Admittedly he did not make a significant impact on the thinking of his time, but Lafitau was a harbinger of the future.

Lucretius reconstructed the past of man in reasoned terms and offered a framework which was developmental. Vico drew on historical sources in a rather disorderly, subjective manner to derive his grand design. Lafitau compared former European customs with those of Indians, focusing mainly on empirical comparisons and remaining within the general Christian, theological explanation of how and why man had changed. The next step would be to bring field accounts about ethnics into a systematic, comparative framework based more on reason than on traditional Christian theology. From the common-sense Scottish school of history and social progress arose a keystone leading to a broad-scale comparative study of ethnics. The eighteenth-century Scottish historians conceived a model which was designed to explain social growth and stability. In this grand plan, which arose from Protestant theology but combined it with current knowledge, "progress" toward civilization had left the ethnics of the world behind. The original unity of mankind was accepted, and from this common base it was felt that some men had progressed by growing intellectually as others remained unenlightened. Some of the information used to exemplify the nature of man's changing ways was taken from descriptions of primitive peoples. The result of this approach was a unilineal evolutionary system to accommodate differential sociocultural development (Pearce 1965:82–86).

Prominent in the development of this Scottish model was William Robertson (1721–1793), the son of a Presbyterian minister and himself trained in the ministry at the University of Edinburgh. The younger Robertson became the principal of this institution in 1762, partially on the basis of a book he published in 1759 titled *History of Scotland*. In 1777 he published a two-volume work, *History of America*, which subsequently appeared in innumerable editions published in England and in the United States. E. Adamson Hoebel (1966:509–510) states without hesitation that "cultural anthropology was finally born" with the apearance of this book on American history. Unquestionably Robertson achieved a major synthesis of information about American Indians, especially those of Mexico and Peru. In his typology three progressive stages were postulated—savagery, barbarism, and civilization, a trichotomy borrowed from Montesquieu (1949:276). According to his classification, savages lacked writing, metalworking, and domestic animals; thus most Indians in the Americas were savages. In Mexico and Peru, however, were people who had developed cities and intensive farming, and he considered them to be at an advanced stage of barbarism. He argued that since most American Indians did not have knowledge of such forms as the plow and forge, they must have been derived from peoples who were equally rude in their achievements and suggested that New World Indians had arrived from Asia in the vicinity of Bering Strait. As a further indication of this route, he noted that many of the same species of animals were distributed widely in northern Eurasia and northern North America, suggesting a land passage between the Old World and the New World. Robertson was not interested in ethnographic details about aboriginal Americans, and in his broad sweep he considered that all those who lived north of Mexico were much the same in their lifeways. In discussng ethnics he stated, "In every inquiry concerning the operations of men when united together in society, the first object of attention should be their mode of subsistence. Accordingly as that varies, the laws and policy must be different" (Robertson 1777:vol. 1, 324). He then set out to offer a composite sketch of Indians in terms of their physical appearance, "qualities of their minds," domestic state, political life, warfare, arts, and religion. He concluded that Indians had attained a low level of accomplishment because of the hardships which they faced in their environment and because of their physical isolation. This is one of the early integrated and documented studies attempting to explain why savages and civilized men were similar physical beings and yet stood poles apart in the cultural history of mankind (Hoebel 1960:648–655; Pearce 1965:76–91).

As a pertinent aside, Erwin H. Ackerknecht (1954:117–125) offers the intriguing idea that the comparison of one people with another arose in part from the popularity of comparative anatomy. His reasoning is that when anthropology was in its undifferentiated stage many of the leaders in the field were trained as medical doctors, and they applied the comparative techniques they had learned for their own field to their new subject for study. By the middle of the nineteenth century, physical and cultural anthropology had become distinct, with specialists in each field. At this time physical anthropologists began taking an evolutionary approach to their data, and comparative anatomy provided the evidence to support their theories. When cultural anthropologists subsequently turned to biological evolution as a model for cultural developments, their efforts met with initial success but soon were disdained and even ridiculed.

Laugh, smile, sigh, or cry, as you will, but the concept of evolution is one of the most important abstract ideas recently conceived by Western man. The proposition that everything is subject to orderly change is comparable in impact to the origination of the alphabet or of Hebrew-Christian-Mohammedan monotheism. Evolution is descent and irreversible transformations through time; it is a continuum of changes and modifications leading to increasingly divergent forms. In modern biological concepts evolution is thought to depend on changes in gene frequencies between ancestral and descendant populations. At present it is exceedingly difficult to measure changes in gene frequencies directly, and therefore morphological differences which reflect different gene frequencies are studied in order to plot the course of organic evolution. A critical problem confronting persons interested in sociocultural evolution is to determine whether the theories and units for analysis in organic evolution are in fact applicable to superorganic evolution, and if so, whether they may be used to plot its course reliably.

R. W. Gerard and others (1956:10) prepared a useful summary of the parallels between biological and cultural evolution; this is reproduced in Table 6. The biological units are well established, and for each is listed a cultural analogue. Analogies of this nature are helpful guides to thoughts about cultural evolution.

FROM SAVAGERY TO CIVILIZATION: MORGAN

The natural history of man moved toward becoming a science of man when its proponents made concerted efforts to generalize broadly about sociocultural differences without considering divine force as the primary cause of change. Hoebel (1960) singles out Robertson as the first essentially modern sociocultural anthropologist, and his choice seems quite justified.

Table 6. CORRESPONDENCES BETWEEN BIOLOGICAL AND CULTURAL EVOLUTION (after Gerard *et al.* 1956:10).

Biological Evolution	Cultural Evolution
Distinct species and varieties	Distinct cultures and subcultures
Morphology, structural organization	Directly observable artifacts and customs distinctive of cultures
Physiology, functional attributes	Functional properties attributable to directly observable cultural characteristics
Genetic complex determining structures and functions	"Implicit culture" (i.e., the inferred cultural structure or "cultural genotype")
Preservation of species but replacement of individuals	Preservation of cultures but replacement of individuals and artifacts
Hereditary transmission of genetic complex, generating particular species	"Hereditary" transmission of idea-custom-artifact complexes, generating particular cultures
Modification of genetic complex by mutations, selection, migration, and "genetic drift"	Culture change through invention and discovery; adaptation; diffusion and other forms of culture contact; "cultural drift"
Natural selection of genetic complexes generally leading to adaptation to environment	Adaptive and "accidental" (i.e., historically determined) selection of ideas, customs, and artifacts
Extinction of the maladapted and maladjusted species	Extinction of maladapted and maladjusted cultures

However, it was not until one hundred years after *History of America* first appeared that a detailed evolutionary framework was offered in order to explain man's social and cultural development. This monumental contribution was *Ancient Society*, which appeared first in 1877 and was written by Lewis H. Morgan. Robertson had anticipated Morgan, but the knowledge which had been accumulated during the intervening century made Morgan's synthesis possible. This increased ethnographic information and the principles of evolution were combined by Morgan in a perceptive analysis. He first made a synthesis based on a wealth of original field data; this was his comparative study of kinship systems. While revising his manuscript about kinship, *Systems of Consanguinity and Affinity of the Human Family*, Morgan formulated his evolutionary approach. It is worthwhile to examine the background to this critical event.

Morgan collected Ojibwa kin terms at Marquette, Michigan, in 1858, as noted previously, and he realized the similarity between these terms and those of the Iroquois. He soon began to collect similar schedules from other Indian tribes, and he distributed questionnaires about kinship terms to persons around the world in order to assemble parallel information about diverse peoples. In 1865 Morgan completed a draft of *Systems* and submitted it to the Smithsonian Institution for publication. Joseph Henry, the head of the Smithsonian, sent the manuscript to Joshua McIlvaine for review. At the time McIlvaine taught ethnology and philology at Princeton. Although he was one of Morgan's oldest and best friends, he was nonetheless an ideal reader for the manuscript because not only was he acquainted with Morgan's research but as a philologist he was familiar with the nature of the problems Morgan faced. One major difficulty with the original manuscript was Morgan's inability to explain why the two major groupings of kinship terms which he identified, classificatory and descriptive, had come into being. In his classificatory systems close relatives were lumped into a small number of categories. For example, an individual might refer to his father, his father's brother, and his mother's brother by the same term, and the word for mother was extended to mother's sister as well as to father's sister. Furthermore, brother and sister terms might be extended to include persons we would identify as first cousins. The systems called descriptive have fewer such lumpings; the terminology which prevails in the United States today serves as an example. In 1864 McIlvaine had suggested to Morgan that classificatory systems developed because in primeval human times people were promiscuous and thus all men were potential fathers, which in logical turn made all children brothers and sisters. Morgan spent most of 1866 revising his manuscript but did not accept McIlvaine's suggestion until 1867. In May of that year he formulated a sequence of changes in his classification of family life, which led from the primitive horde, characterized by complete sexual promiscuity through fifteen developmental stages to the monogamous family; this work was included in *Systems* when it appeared in 1870 (Morgan 1870; Resek 1960:73, 90–99).

Given Morgan's evolutionary explanation for the changes in kinship terminologies, his increasing involvement with anthropological studies after *Systems* was published, and the success of evolutionary explanations in biology, it is not surprising that he again utilized an evolutionary framework to articulate diverse ethnographic facts when he wrote *Ancient Society*. In this volume we have the first detailed framework in which the evolution of cultural systems is based on changes in modes of subsistence. The work also includes lengthy discussions about the development of political and social life, family forms, and kinship systems. Today it is not difficult to find fault with Morgan's use of ethnographic data, the integrity of the levels in his system, and many of the conclusions which he drew. His explanations for the changing of people from one stage to another usually are inadequate; his findings often are poorly integrated and incorrectly interpreted; he failed to understand the relationship between social life and modes of subsistence, and his reconstructions of technological developments often are incorrect. In spite of these most serious failings, Morgan's evolutionary classification is the brightest star in the search for a grand design to encompass the rise and development of culture and society.

Morgan summarized his sequence for the development of culture and society at the beginning of *Ancient Society*, which is reproduced as Table 7. At the hypothetical beginning level, the Lower Status of Savagery, men possessed speech; the period ended with the use of fire and with subsistence based on fishing. No extant people were in this level at the time of historic contact. Morgan conjectured that language set men apart as distinct from all other species and that it was an implicit groundwork on which culture was built, but he did not elaborate on this thesis in *Ancient Society* (1877:5). Was he correct? No one really knows. Some investigators have suggested that language is a comparatively recent development among men (Livingstone 1969), whereas others have argued that the beginnings of culture and language took place at essentially the same point in time. Is the use of fire a significant divider? It would seem to be. When men first controlled fire, nearly a million years ago, the introduction must have been a major step forward. Fire possibly was employed as a weapon against game; to cook food, making it more easily digested and likely to preserve longer; to provide warmth, and to extend man's day, thereby permitting him to break the physiological cycle of bedding down at sunset. One of the more important uses of time made possible by fire would be the leisure to think and to plan. The acquisition of fire surely must be heralded as a significant contribution toward the development of human culture.

Morgan suggested that men first subsisted on fruits and nuts and lived in a tropical or subtropical setting. Most anthropologists today would deny that cultural man originated in the tropics and would consider meat more important than plant food in the diet of early man. Morgan (1877:19–21) thought that animal foods "entered from a very early period into human consumption," but he did not know whether animals were sought during his fruits and nuts stage. From either point of view it is most unlikely that fish were a dominant food at an early stage in human times. Man appears to have lived by collecting and hunting long before he turned to fish as a primary source of food. It is possible to hunt animals and to collect plants over most of the earth, but only in comparatively few areas might fish have served as the food staple. Thus, Morgan offered reasoned speculations about the origins of culture, and even today when considering the same problem, we must deal more often in conjecture than with fact.

The Middle Status of Savagery, which began with fish and fire, ended with the invention of the bow and arrow. By this time men had spread over the earth, and the people represented at this level included Australians and most Polynesians at the time of their historic contact. Morgan

Table 7. MORGAN'S SUMMARY OF THE EVOLUTIONARY STAGES IN THE DEVELOPMENT OF SOCIOCULTURAL BEHAVIOR (Morgan 1877:10–12).

I. *Lower Status of Savagery*
This period commenced with the infancy of the human race and may be said to have ended with the acquisition of a fish subsistence and of a knowledge of the use of fire. Mankind were then living in their original restricted habitat, and subsisting upon fruits and nuts. The commencement of articulate speech belongs to this period. No exemplification of tribes of mankind in this condition remained to the historical period.

II. *Middle Status of Savagery*
It commenced with the acquisition of a fish subsistence and a knowledge of the use of fire, and ended with the invention of the bow and arrow. Mankind, while in this condition, spread from their original habitat over the greater portion of the earth's surface. Among tribes still existing it will leave in the Middle Status of savagery, for example, the Australians and the greater part of the Polynesians when discovered. It will be sufficient to give one or more exemplifications of each status.

III. *Upper Status of Savagery*
It commenced with the invention of the bow and arrow, and ended with the invention of the art of pottery. It leaves in the Upper Status of Savagery

the Athapascan tribes of the Hudson's Bay Territory, the tribes of the valley of the Columbia, and certain coast tribes of North and South America; but with relation to the time of their discovery. This closes the period of Savagery.

IV. *Lower Status of Barbarism*

The invention or practice of the art of pottery, all things considered, is probably the most effective and conclusive test that can be selected to fix a boundary line, necessarily arbitrary, between savagery and barbarism. The distinctness of the two conditions has long been recognized, but no criterion of progress out of the former into the latter has hitherto been brought forward. All such tribes, then, as never attained to the art of pottery will be classed as savages, and those possessing this art but who never attained a phonetic alphabet and the use of writing will be classed as barbarians.

The first subperiod of barbarism commenced with the manufacture of pottery, whether by original invention or adoption. In finding its termination, and the commencement of the Middle Status, a difficulty is encountered in the unequal endowments of the two hemispheres, which began to be influential upon human affairs after the period of savagery had passed. It may be met, however, by the adoption of equivalents. In the Eastern hemisphere, the domestication of animals, and the Western, the cultivation of maize and plants by irrigation, together with the use of adobe-brick and stone in house building, have been selected as sufficient evidence of progress to work a transition out of the Lower and into the Middle Status of barbarism. It leaves, for example, in the Lower Status the Indian tribes of the United States east of the Missouri River and such tribes of Europe and Asia as practiced the art of pottery but were without domestic animals.

V. *Middle Status of Barbarism*

It commenced with the domestication of animals in the Eastern hemisphere, and in the Western with cultivation by irrigation and with the use of adobe-brick and stone in architecture, as shown. Its termination may be fixed with the invention of the process of smelting iron ore. This places in the Middle Status, for example, the Village Indians of New Mexico, Mexico, Central America, and Peru, and such tribes in the Eastern hemisphere as possessed domestic animals but were without a knowledge of iron. The ancient Britons, although familiar with the use of iron, fairly belong in this connection. The vicinity of more advanced continental tribes had advanced the arts of life among them far beyond the state of development of their domestic institutions.

VI. *Upper Status of Barbarism*

It commenced with the manufacture of iron, and ended with the invention of a phonetic alphabet, and the use of writing in literary composition. Here civilization begins. This leaves in the Upper Status, for example, the Grecian tribes of the Homeric age, the Italian tribes shortly before the founding of Rome, and the Germanic tribes of the time of Caesar.

VIII. *Status of Civilization*

It commenced, as stated, with the use of a phonetic alphabet and the production of literary records, and divides into *Ancient* and *Modern*. As an equivalent, hieroglyphical writing upon stone may be admitted.

(1877:8–9, 21) reasoned that man originated in one area of the world and that as he acquired increasingly human ways his successes made farflung dispersal possible. He theorized that as men wandered about the world, different populations experienced similar conditions and responded to them in a nearly uniform manner. All of this seems reasonable, especially if the words "nearly uniform" are stressed. Note, however, that Morgan considered the presence of the bow and arrow as a critical technological marker to usher in the Upper Status of Savagery. His choice of this single form, as important as it might have been in many areas of the world, was unfortunate. The reason is that any people who lack this weapon must be classed as middle level savages no matter what other characteristics they manifest. Only a few people of Australia possessed the bow and arrow, and they all retained a very simple way of life compared to that of most other peoples. The Bushmen in South Africa depended heavily on the bow and arrow, but in subsistence activities their way of life was similar to that found among the aboriginal Australians. In fact, Bushman religion was even simpler than that reported for the Australians. In most of Polynesia the bow and arrow was not used, but the sociocultural complexity of the Polynesians was far greater than that reported for either the Australians or the Bushmen.

Many more problems, similar to those cited, are evident in any contemporary interpretation of Morgan's evolutionary system. Nonetheless, the framework which he developed is a clear historical first, and even more important it was a coalescence of ideas which served as a base to be destroyed or built upon as other researchers considered the same general problem. His general stages from savagery to barbarism and civilization have endured, while the specific details have been largely rejected. His broad insights into the relationships between technical accomplishments and changes in other aspects of living remain; his discussions of the rise of different kinship terminologies, family forms, and political systems have provided a fertile base on which other investigators have expanded.

ETHNIC ANALOGUES

Lafitau compared the Iroquois with early historic Europeans in order to better understand European customs. Robertson compared aboriginal Americans with each other in order to establish a sequence of human development. Morgan followed the lead of Robertson but added many refinements. Any discussions of two or more peoples at one point in time or temporally, involve comparisons and judgments about these differences and similarities. The most important supposition among evolutionists is that ethnics at the time of historic contact pursued lifeways which were in varying degrees reflections of the earlier stages of more complex societies. The label given to the use of ethnographic data in this manner, "conjectural or theoretical history," appears to have been coined in 1815 by Dugald Stewart (1854:vol. 1, 4). Conjectural history is based on a "comparative method" of analysis. It implies that in the past human nature has been much the same everywhere and that all peoples have followed the same general line of development. Thus, by recording the ways of ethnics who developed at a slower rate than civilized peoples, we should be able to unveil the earlier stages leading to civilization. As pointed out by Lewis (1955:259–292), the disadvantage of the term "comparative method" is that it applies not only to the use of comparisons in our daily lives, but to other diverse comparisons within and beyond the scope of anthropology. For a general label he therefore prefers "comparisons in anthropology." Although to Boas and his students the comparative method referred to the works of cultural evolutionists, Lewis stresses that the term has come to refer to highly diverse forms of sociocultural comparisons. I prefer to use the words *ethnic analogues* to refer to the comparative dimensions that Morgan had in mind. The assumption is that the customs of modern ethnics are analogous to the ways of other peoples at other points in time. In this sense the Bushmen of South Africa and the indigenous peoples of Australia represent a general stage or level through which the members of more complex societies passed long ago. In other words the simpler sociocultural forms preceded and are older than those which are complex and recent. Marvin Harris (1968:152) traces this line of reasoning to the Enlightenment idea of "progress" with reference to the differing ways of men and to the Great Chain of Being in biology.

What is wrong with the idea of ethnic analogues? Boas and his students felt that they had discovered a basic flaw in comparisons of this nature. They reasoned that the lifeways of even the most primitive of modern ethnics had great antiquity and must have changed in remarkable ways from the original conditions which they were considered to represent. In other words it would not be possible for "peoples whom time had forgotten," or truly primitive contemporaries, to exist among modern ethnics. Therefore, such peoples could not represent the sociocultural systems of primeval man in an evolutionary or any other broad-scale framework.

If we were to take the Australians at the time of historic contact as representative of the stage of middle-range savagery, how might we demonstrate that their ways of life might be broadly similar to those of primordial man? To begin with, their relatively simple Upper Paleolithic technology is broadly representative of developments which have been found much earlier in the archaeological record in many other areas of the world. In any archaeological sequence most of the forms that the Australians made are found preceding the manufactures of farmers and city dwellers. The economy of the Australians was based on collecting and hunting, and this is the underlying stage for those economies based on pastoralism or farming in the overall archaeological record. Thus, these simple designs for living found among historic Australian aborigines are paralleled in the earlier time periods unearthed for more complex societies. Furthermore, aboriginal Australians had no developed economic specializations of the degree or complexity reported among farmers and industrialists.

Have the aboriginal Australians changed at all during the last 20,000 years? Most certainly, but because of their geographical isolation they received few new ideas from beyond the subcontinent which might stimulate change, and their environment limited the local development of complex patterns for living. For example, no animals indigenous to Australia had any potential as domestics, and the same is true of plants; no wild grasses could be developed into cereal crops comparable to wheat, maize, or similar grains, either by aboriginal Australians or by modern farmers in the area. Are there any aspects of aboriginal Australian life which are more complex than those found among hunters and collectors elsewhere in the world at the time of historic contact? The answer is yes. The spear-thrower or throwing-board used by some Australians is more complex in its configuration than similar forms reported anywhere else, and among hunters the diversity of spear forms is unusually great. Certain aspects of the Australians' religious life seem quite elaborate too in comparison to their economic level. These complexities are best understood in terms of the physical isolation of Australia. The people brought few forms with them to the subcontinent, and although they elaborated on these, they were not prepared for a quantum leap in their technology or economy because of their isolation and the virtual absence of external stimuli.

One important reason for the Boasian rejection of evolutionary classifications and the ethnic analogues on which they were based, was that the frameworks, such as the one proposed by Morgan, soon were exposed as having gross and obvious shortcomings. One major failing was that Morgan and others underestimated the degree of cultural diversity among modern ethnics. Furthermore, not only were the available ethnographic reports often inadequate, but the degree to which contact with complex societies had changed the ways of life of many ethnics before their adequate description was not realized.

In this discussion of ethnic analogues it is not implied that the course of change always is toward more complex forms. In fact we know that entire populations or segments of established populations may revert to simpler, less elaborate forms. For example, in colonial America when families from along the eastern seaboard crossed the Appalachian Mountains into the Ohio country they left behind most of the frills and many of the cultural forms which they previously had considered as necessities. The frontier settler was forced to fend for himself and also to defend himself because he was beyond the effective political control of the colonial administration. Frontier life was organizationally simpler than the life that the pioneer had left behind. The end product was a simpler culture, a compromise one, which was accepted temporarily in the hope that the necessities and amenities which were left behind could in time be regained. Similarly the Maya Indians of Yucatan had developed an elaborate cultural system in prehistoric times, but by the time the Spanish arrived among them, their manner of living had retrogressed to a simpler form. The same was true of the Kaingang of Brazil, the Caribou Eskimos of central Canada, and many other peoples at the time of historic contact.

LEVELS OF SOCIAL COMPLEXITY: COON

The reader might feel that to leap from a discussion of *Ancient Society* published in 1877 to the appendix of a work which appeared in 1948 is not just a cavalier treatment of ethnic classifications but borders on irresponsibility, but I would argue that this is not so. The pervasive influence of Boas, the rapid proliferation of little Boasians, and the positions of academic power that they achieved long delayed any further broad-scale temporal classifications of peoples around the world. In 1948 Carleton S. Coon published *A Reader in General Anthropology*, which is primarily a series of ethnographic sketches drawn from diverse original sources. Through his method of organizing the text and in an appendix Coon sets forth a general framework for the analysis of human behavior and presents a formula designed to measure the complexity of contemporary and historically documented societies which existed without the use of coal, gunpowder, and steam engines. The criteria for placing a people in this classification were: the specialization of individuals, the number of institutions to which an individual may belong, the complexity of the institutions, and the amount of trade. The purpose of Coon's system was to make quantitative comparisons of peoples' ways, assuming only that the long-range trend in culture has been from simple to complex and that societies may be most fruitfully studied as integrated wholes. He did not attempt to classify peoples on the basis of their technology because he felt that this was Morgan's mistake. Coon cites the Lapps of Scandinavia and the Pygmies of Africa as examples of peoples who used iron tools which they obtained by trade. Because they did not make some of the sophisticated tools which they possessed, a classification which included these tools would lead to a distorted interpretation of the peoples' cultural level. He also calls attention to the environment, which is regarded as a critical variable in the development of cultural systems; this factor is not explicitly accounted for, however, in the classification. Coon (1948:vi–vii, 563, 611–614) was cautious and did not stress that peoples at the lower levels of his classification represented earlier stages of social development. The evolutionary nature of his system is clear, however, because he selected peoples who were from historically unrelated areas of the world and then ranked one against another. He does not attempt to explain why peoples were at different levels except to suggest that differential settings held unequal potentialities for man's exploitation and that environmental limitations could be offset in part by trade relations.

COMMUNITY PATTERNING: BEARDSLEY AND OTHERS

In 1955 Richard K. Beardsley, Preston Holder, Alex D. Krieger, Betty J. Meggers, and John Rinaldo (1956:129–157) cooperatively set out to formulate a broad-scale classification of cultures. Their aim was to derive a system which would accommodate archaeological and ethnographic data and have functional integrity as well as evolutionary significance. The primary unit in their classification is the community, defined "as the largest grouping of persons in any particular culture whose normal activities bind them together into a self-conscious, corporate unit, which is economically self-sufficient and politically independent" (Beardsley et al. 1956:133). They derived a mobility scale for communities, with categories ranging from those groups whose members wandered freely and almost continually to permanently sedentary aggregates. At particular points along the continuum "community patterns" or networks of sociocultural behaviors were isolated and identified. In order to explain the differences in patterned mobility it was reasoned that peoples became increasingly sedentary when the opportunity presented itself and that persons in the more stable physical settlements were likely to live longer than persons in wandering communities; thus there was adaptive advantage in residential stability. The major variable leading to increased stability was improvement in the means of subsistence.

Seven levels or types of community patterns were identified, and the conditions giving rise to each were detailed. The first type, designated *Free*

Wandering, is largely conjectured and might be expected to occur most often when a people expanded into an unoccupied area or when a population declined rapidly in numbers—for instance, as a result of European contact. Suggestively territoriality did not exist at this level, but since nonhuman primates usually have defined territories, it was recognized that this level possibly was more hypothetical than real. The stage is characterized by few food resources and low population densities. The Alacaluf Indians of Tierra del Fuego are the only people identified at this level, and their patterning resulted from depopulation following European contact.

In the next stage, *Restricted Wandering*, a specific territory was occupied and defended against trespassers or was claimed exclusively by a people for certain food resources. The community population was fewer than 100 persons, and they traveled in monogamous nuclear or extended family groups for all or part of each year. The economic base was hunting, fishing, and collecting, but since food storage methods were negligible, the people were on the move in search of local harvests most of the time. If the status of chief existed, it was as an adviser above all else, and in general, status differentiations were few. The group frequently had a shaman, but any supernatural belief system was ill-defined. Hunting and curing magic were important, and puberty ceremonies ranged from being absent to being well developed.

If a people established themselves at a particular location for weeks or months during the year, they became *Central-Based Wanderers*. This pattern developed when a storable food product such as acorns was available, when a people became farmers but reaped only small harvests, or when there was a locally abundant food such as shellfish. The gatherers of shellfish were decidedly more settled than any other peoples at this level because of the year-round dependability of their major food resource. The others became stable because they cultivated plants or had derived methods to prepare foods for storage. The population density was much the same as at the previous level, and the people were still organized as nuclear or extended families. They formed more cohesive units at their central base, however, reverting to self-sufficient smaller groups only when they were dispersed. A chief symbolized group unity but had no coercive power, and status distinctions were minor. In the realm of supernatural matters shamans attempted to cure with the aid of magic; group ceremonies varied from being important to absent, and the dead were remembered in a ceremonial manner.

An even more complex pattern arose when the members of a community remained in a single location from one year to the next and moved from one dwelling site to another only infrequently. Such relative permanence was achieved by salmon fishermen on the Northwest Coast of North America, but elsewhere in the world these partially sedentary peoples were farmers who lived in areas where the soil was moderately productive. In this, the *Semi-Permanent Sedentary* stage, population density was relatively low because it was necessary to cultivate large areas in order to support the community, and yet villages numbering from 500 to 1000 persons were known. As at simpler levels each village was independent and self-sufficient, but a temporary confederation was formed in times of crises. A division of labor was well established; men hunted and cleared plots for cultivation while women harvested the crops and prepared foods for consumption. Surplus food products were redistributed at ceremonies and feasts but were not accumulated by individuals. Here for the first time we see the emergence of village or tribal craft specializations and the importance of local trade. At the same time unilineal descent groups such as clans and moieties began to emerge as important, and a chief was influential or ineffective depending on his personal qualifications. Individuals acquired prestige as superior craftsmen, warriors, and shamans. In the realm of supernatural matters forest spirits and ghosts of the dead existed; the dead frequently were buried under house floors. Ceremonies included masked dances and folk drama as a means for promoting success in farming. Although shamans were at times powerful because of their rapport with spirits, they remained primarily curers.

Simple Nuclear Centers were permanent groupings of relatively isolated self-sufficient towns (undifferentiated) or were clusters of villages and hamlets which supported a market or ceremonial nucleus (differentiated) which was not self-sufficient. These centers arose when efficient cultivation of plants and the employment of soil conservation techniques increased harvests so that dependable food surpluses were produced. As many persons became freed from farming activities, the rise of full-time specialization occurred along technological, administrative, and ceremonial lines; membership in any such unit typically was hereditary. While kinship ties were important between families, social stratification led to great differences among segments of the population. The chief, as the epitome of his class, possessed coercive power; he and other persons of high status occupied dwellings which were superior to those of lesser persons. Religion emerged as an organized system, with temples, a calendar of events, public ceremonies, elaborate paraphernalia, and sacrifices to the gods.

In the *Advanced Nuclear Centered* community pattern, greater agricultural surpluses were reaped, and the power of the ruling elite was stabilized through an increased ability to coerce the populace. Craft specialization intensified, the chief often became a king, and great planned cities came into being. In general this level represented an elaboration of features which were clearly present in the previous level.

In the final stage, the *Supra-Nuclear Integrated*, the centers and other lesser units were joined by conquest. As nuclear centers vied with one another for food, commodities, raw materials, prestige, and the like, one fell to another, and the conquered people were joined into the political and economic network of the victors, thereby integrating different cultural traditions. Taxes, tribute, standardized mediums of exchange, an effective military organization, a state religion, and a king who also was a god emerged to guide the destinies of these empires.

Beardsley and others identify the nature of archaeological remains to be expected at each level and offer archaeological as well as ethnographic examples for each of the different stages. Furthermore, they have added a classification for pastoral nomads, which parallels that of farmers, to the Simple Nuclear Centered level. However, since most if not all pastoralists are part-societies, attached by trading or raiding to sedentary farmers, the pastoralists might be viewed as complementary to and dependent on some form of center. Each community pattern is considered a result of the peoples' subsistence efforts, which in turn depend on the food resources, the environmental potential, and the techniques of exploitation available. In evolutionary terms, one stage usually is viewed as having developed from the previous level, with the changes achieved through the realization of new subsistence goals.

BANDS TO CHIEFDOMS: SERVICE

Elman R. Service (1962) has formulated a classification in which he draws on baseline and reconstructed ethnographic data in order to present stages of cultural evolution. In the development of his system Service utilizes the evolutionary perspective of Leslie White and Steward's specific distinctions made about the organization of small-scale ethnics. Service's earliest and most basic level is the *patrilocal band*. Members select brides from other bands, but the newly married couple joins the male's residence group. Within a band the basic unit is the nuclear family—a man, his wife, and their children; this group may be expanded to include an aged person. Small families of this nature may live dispersed from one another or join in a relatively permanent manner. As many as 30 to 100 persons may remain together in times of plenty and during cooperative hunts or group ceremonies. If the band's memberhip becomes dispersed widely, then ties most likely are maintained through common myths, ceremonies, and acknowledged kinship bonds.

From the patrilocal band arose the *tribe*; the transition to this level most likely occurred after man had domesticated plants and animals and thereby gained dependable food sources. The change to the tribal level may have taken place in response to competition for space since, if nothing else, a more concentrated population could defend itself better than a dispersed people. Unity of an unprecedented nature was achieved through tribal sodalities, which were represented in each band. A sodality, as defined by Service (1962:21), is "a nonresidential association that has some corporate functions or purposes"; kindred, clans, segmentary lineages, or associations based on age-grade, secret, or curing interests serve as examples. At the tribal level sodalities are nonlocal; that is, they do not comprise residential units. They are named, however, and by their use of insignia, the assumption of common descent, and participation in ceremonies, tribal unity is achieved and maintained. For this reason distinctions between tribes were rather clear and precise. The egalitarian nature of band society is characteristic also of tribal societies; leadership is charismatic and is for special purposes, such as providing guidance in times of hostilities and direction when conducting ceremonies. Tradition provides the key guide to behavioral norms. Feuds among groups are the prime source of internal disruptions, and hostilities against other tribes, which are ever-present, are the greatest source of external conflict. With the population of a tribe more concentrated than that of a band, in-marrying groups are not scattered widely, and thus intermittent cooperation is possible among males even when they live in different residential units.

The third and highest level of the classification, the *chiefdom*, is distinguished from the tribe by having far greater economic productivity and consequently unprecedented population concentrations. Furthermore, a chiefdom was highly organized along economic, social, and religious lines, although it did not have a government backed by legal force. The rise of chiefdoms is not directly attributable to technological changes, although these did occur and at times were important. Instead it was the total environmental situation which led to specialized production and the redistribution of goods from a center. Specialization probably arose most commonly in regions with diverse ecological zones in which the localized resources were exploited by particular residence groups. At the band and tribal levels a people might move from one zone to another in order to exploit localized products, but farming peoples tended to settle permanently, thus necessitating a reciprocal exchange among peoples occupying different zones. As the quantity of production increased, the distributional networks became more elaborate and better organized. This in turn led to more intensive ecological specialization and fostered individual specialization of labor, with an accompanying loss of the self-sufficiency known at the tribal level and the production of superior craft products. In time outstanding craftsmen were subsidized, sometimes at a redistributional center. A chief could support craftsmen, multiple wives, and retainers from the stores of food he obtained as a result of his role in the redistributional network. The next step was for the position of chief to become a permanent office, and it was then that social differences arose to distinguish the chief and his relatives from the balance of the population. Once the office of chief had become hereditary and a precise means for establishing succession had developed, a social hierarchy was created. As the authority of a chief increased, he was able to organize public labor, and this was extremely important in expanding agricultural productivity, especially through the construction of irrigation networks. Equally as important was the chief's ability to wage war successfully; this warfare was an intensification of the antagonisms found among tribal societies. A chief and his followers might exterminate or displace a conquered population, or they might integrate a defeated people into the chiefdom. When confronted by civilized peoples, the members of a chiefdom often were reduced to conditions not dissimilar to those which prevailed in tribes or even in bands. In some areas, such as along the Northwest Coast of North America, where the impact of civilization was largely commercial and involved relatively few individuals, the social organization of old tended to remain intact, but rivalry for status intensified greatly.

A true *state* is distinguished from a chiefdom by the presence of leaders who maintain a monopoly on the legal use of legitimate force. Any personal or individual recourse to force is nongovernmental and thereby illegal. In states we also find that political classes are crystallized and formalized to a degree unknown in chiefdoms. Service does not elaborate his discussion of the state but feels that much confusion has resulted from the fact that the state is ordinarily not distinguished from the chiefdom.

The span of time between the appearance of *Ancient Society* in 1877 and the publication of Coon's evolutionary classification in 1948 is striking but understandable. The Boasians who prevailed in the United States during the interim felt that it was most important to collect detailed information about particular peoples and that if comparisons were offered, they must be limited in scope. The functionalists in England also preferred to consider particular societies in detail and to avoid all-encompassing comparisons. They were in part reacting against the imaginative but now discredited diffusionist schemes of William H. Rivers in his later years, of Grafton Elliot Smith, and of Wilhelm Schmidt. It was almost inevitable that evolution would again become an ethnological focus. Ronald Cohen (1962:321–348) suggests that evolutionary thinking is now a focal point because of our search for an all-encompassing framework which will unite the diverse dimensions of anthropology. The successes of biologists impress us greatly, and some aspects of anthropology have long been linked with the studies of biologists. Likewise, given the rapidly changing nature of the modern world, it is natural and fitting that we should seek an explanatory design to accommodate the changes; evolutionary thoughts are inviting in this regard.

Why is it that peoples change from one level to another? Lucretius felt that a spontaneous force was behind the emergence of successive stages in life forms. In later times other persons have credited a divine engineer with the underlying patterning. Some have sought to explain cultural differences on the basis of the potentialities inherent in racial groups. Clear or vague recourse has been made to conditions of the atmosphere, climate, or geography as well as to nonracial differences in mental or physical qualities. The tendency has been to seek one general explanation applicable to all cultural change. In a discussion of "prime-movers" in cultural evolution Service (1968:396–409) labels Morgan's system as a technologically deterministic view: With the mounting production of goods the resulting trade and accumulation of property led to accompanying changes in the nature of family life and the state. Morgan's introductory thesis to explain change, however, was one of "mentalistic-idealistic determinants"; the change arose from mental qualities and free will, or as stated by Service (1968:398), "Civilized man literally thought himself out of savagery." The latter approach leads nowhere, or at least not very far, in understanding cultural evolution, but a technological basis for change has had considerable appeal.

Karl Marx and Friedrich Engels seized on the technological determinism in *Ancient Society* and carried Morgan's thesis much further: With the development of economic productivity and private property, the state arose to protect capitalism, the workers became exploited, and religion served as a means to justify the social order. This was the first theory in which technology, social structure, and function were integrated to explain processual change in culture. However, the mentalistic ideal was retained in this view, for once workers developed an awareness of the system in which they found themselves, they then could free themselves from the pattern and consciously guide their own futures.

Leslie White has linked technology and energy utilization in his efforts to explain evolutionary developments. *"Culture advances as the amount of energy harnessed per capita per year increases, or as the efficiency or economy of the means of controlling energy is increased, or both"* (White 1959:56). Through technology energy was harnessed with ever-increasing effectiveness, which led to expanding cultural development on a worldwide basis. Service (1968:406–407) interprets the techno-economic deterministic views as failing to predict evolution in all societies and therefore feels that they cannot be viewed as prime-movers:

> To be sure, some kind of technological production of necessities, especially of food, is required for any society. In the context of evolution, such production is an *enabler*, so to speak, without which an increase in size and density could not take place. But a necessity or enabler is not necessarily a mover. Many stabilized societies could produce much more than they do, but it does not follow that they necessarily will, nor that if they did that they would necessarily "evolve" in some sense.

To quote Harris (1969:202), "One of the main tasks of modern anthropology is to give quantitative expression to the tendency for demo-techno-econo-environmental parameters to constrain and shape social organization and ideology."

CULTURE AREA CLASSIFICATION: MASON

The broad interpretation of ethnographic data initially was oriented toward developing an evolutionary framework, partially in an attempt to emulate the successes of biologists in advancing the concepts of evolution. Boas and his students challenged this position and emphasized a more extensive collection of data, with interpretations being of secondary significance and limited to restricted frameworks. Only after a great deal of information had been assembled and the evolutionary approach had been discredited temporarily did the culture area classification emerge.

In anthropological writings Boas usually is credited with having originated the culture area approach to the organization of ethnographic data when in 1893 he arranged the exhibits at the World's Columbian Exposition, held in Chicago, on a geographical basis (e.g., Spier 1959:151). In the interest of historiography a quotation from an article by William H. Holmes (1893:432) about the exhibit is as follows:

> Prof. O. T. Mason, representing the National Museum, explained the plan on which the ethnologic exhibit was made. The well-known map of linguistic families north of Mexico, prepared by Major J. W. Powell, was taken as a basis on which to assemble the materials. The aim was to have each leading linguistic stock of peoples represented by collections of art products and industries arranged serially in the alcoves.

On this basis it is reasonable to credit Otis T. Mason (1838–1908) with formulating the culture area concept, especially since he authored the earliest definitive statement on the subject.

In 1896 Mason published a classification of American Indians which, based on a combination of environmental and cultural factors, resulted in the delineation of eighteen environments or "culture areas" in the Americas. The criteria considered in distinguishing the areas are as follow: 1. climate and physiography; 2. predominant minerals, vegetables, animals; 3. foods, drinks, narcotics, stimulants, medicines; 4. clothing and adornment of the body; 5. house, fire, furniture, utensils; 6. arts in stone, clay, plants, animal tissues; 7. implements and utensils of fishing, hunting, and war; 8. locomotion (Mason 1896:647). Note that Mason defined his areas largely on the basis of cultural factors and with an almost complete reliance on manufactures. This emphasis on artifacts is understandable in part because of his lifelong interest in material culture. Furthermore, when little is known about an area, it is more likely that representative artifacts exist than that a broad range of sociocultural information is available. If Mason had attempted to consider the diversity in dance, mythology, religion, political or social life, his task would have been almost insurmountable. The problem of distinguishing culture areas on the basis of diverse aspects of culture has never been resolved satisfactorily; thus Mason does not stand alone in his failings. It is further worthy of note that he did not employ linguistic data as a means for defining the areas, probably because the geographical basis of the classification could not be realized by using linguistic stocks, since some are represented in noncontiguous areas. In 1907 Mason returned to the culture area concept with special reference to North America north of Mexico and revised his original presentation slightly. The geographical areas he presented were much the same as those advanced in 1896, and again he defined the areal characteristics largely on the basis of material culture. He mentioned the correspondence between climatic zones and "ethnic environments" but did not dwell on the parallels (Mason 1907:427).

The name of Clark Wissler (1870–1947), a student of Boas, most often is associated with the subsequent development of the culture area classification. Wissler set forth his approach in an article which appeared in 1914, and he developed it further in a book, *The American Indian*, which appeared in 1917 and was revised for two subsequent editions (1922, 1938). In the original article Wissler pointed out that studies of material culture were not then very fashionable. Nonetheless, this was his focus, and he noted that dealing with a great number of tribes on a comparative basis was more feasible with reference to their manufactures than on the basis of social or religious activities. Wissler listed diverse categories of material objects which were necessary for comparison and then defined culture areas largely on the basis of regional similarities in manufactures. In certain respects it is not difficult to defend the emphasis on material culture over all other aspects when classifying peoples. The reason is that all societies must possess manufactures which enable them to obtain food from their environment. Thus, material goods, especially those items concerned with subsistence activities, are everywhere important in furthering survival directly.

The most notable continentwide culture area classifications are by Clark Wissler (1917), Harold E. Driver and William C. Massey (1957) for North America; Wissler (1938), Julian H. Steward and Louis C. Faron (1959) for South America; Melville J. Herskovits (1924) for Africa; Elizabeth Bacon (1946), Alfred L. Kroeber (1947), and Raoul S. Naroll (1950) for Asia; and Douglas L. Oliver (1952) for Oceania.

A detailed discussion of culture area studies, with special emphasis on North America, has been presented by Driver (1962). He defined a culture area as "a geographical area occupied by a number of peoples whose cultures show a significant degree of similarity with each other and at the same time a significant degree of dissimilarity with the cultures of the peoples of other such areas" (Driver 1961:12). Implicit in this and other similar definitions is the fact that one particular time period is involved. Most often, for the New World at least, the classifiers have attempted to establish culture areas as they existed in the aboriginal period, before any disruptions by the arrival of Europeans or Americans. Thus they have sought aboriginal baseline ethnographic information as the basis for their classifications. In this effort one problem has been paramount; the peoples of different areas did not experience their first contacts at the same time. Direct historic contact for Indians of the Caribbean area began in 1492, for the Valley of Mexico in 1521, for Eskimos of the Coronation Gulf area of Canada in 1913, and for some Yanamamo of Brazil in 1958. The problem has been resolved with the concept of a *sliding historical time scale*. Because the peoples within any particular region had their first contacts at about the same time, they will fit into one period on the scale, and the temporal baseline can be changed from area to area.

The concept has proved to be of comparatively limited value. The reasons are as follow: Even when primary stress is on material culture, it is difficult to weigh the significance of the presence or absence of traits; qualitative judgments rather than quantitative measures have been the basis for establishing boundaries; a single culture area may include peoples with many seemingly important differences; one area often tends to blend into another; and classifiers rarely agree on all boundaries. The most valuable service rendered by the culture area classification is that it provided a base from which other concepts for ethnographic data interpretation were derived.

Culture centers Wissler (1923:61–63) identified these as contiguous or at least localized tribal groups whose traits typify a culture area and are unlike those of other areas. Tribes located beyond a culture center may blend the characteristics of two different areas. The tribes representing a culture center are much more distinct from those of another center than are the peripheral tribes distinct from similarly located tribes in other areas. It further appears that tribes moving outward from centers develop intermediate material inventories, whereas those joining a center emerge as typical of the culture center, suggesting the vitality of the centrally developed forms.

Culture climax If a culture center is viewed in terms of development through time, it becomes a climax. Thus a culture climax or culmination is a center considered in terms of a temporal dimension. This concept was presented and elaborated by Kroeber (1939:5, 222–225) and was integrated with the idea of cultural intensity. Intensity refers to the elaboration of forms to a greater degree among one or more tribes in an area than among the other peoples of the same area. Among the people of a climax tribe, we expect to find the general characteristics known among adjacent peoples but richer in content, more elaborate in form, and more fully integrated into the overall sociocultural system. Furthermore, a climax locality is a center out of which ideas spread. The members of a climax tribe also have a greater capacity to assimilate foreign ideas than do adjacent peoples of the same culture area.

Cotradition Wendell C. Bennett (1948:1–7), an archaeologist, defined cotradition as a culture area with time depth. This is a very useful idea if only because it encourages consideration of archaeological assemblages as units with temporal continuity rather than as isolates at particular times and places. The major concern is not how long a culture existed in the area but whether or not continuity is evidenced through time.

Crosscultural type Steward (1955:88–92) originated this concept in order to distinguish patternings in particular cultures which are reported from historically unrelated areas of the world. If two peoples with distinct traditions nontheless share certain key characteristics, regularities are said to be exhibited. These regularities, or convergences, are not exhibited in the total range of the sociocultural forms involved, but are restricted to major units such as social structure, religion, or political government, and even then not in terms of every detail. It is the "cultural core" which is similar. Note that with this concept we move away from the analysis, in theory, of cultural totalities. This is a major step because of the explicit assumption that some dimensions of culture are more important than others for comparative understanding.

Culture clusters In an effort to compare systematically select characteristics of different peoples around the world, Murdock (1967:3-6) was confronted with the difficulty of choosing peoples for inclusion. If his sample included two or more peoples with very close cultural ties, then the comparative conclusions drawn would be weighted because the related peoples represented variations on a single type. Therefore, he grouped people who were closely related into clusters; each cluster was then considered as a single unit in a worldwide sample. Murdock reasoned that two people with a common background would become distinct enough to be considered as independent if they had been separated a thousand years. In order to establish the separation, historical records and linguistic data were of prime importance. Furthermore, proximal but linguistically distinct peoples might be included in a single cluster because of mutual borrowings. To determine which peoples should be grouped, he derived the "three degree rule," which refers to three degrees of latitude anywhere in the world and three degrees of longitude in the tropics, a measure of distance which approaches being 200 miles. As Murdock (1967:4) notes, the rule "assumes that a distance of 200 miles between the geographical centers of two societies belonging to different clusters will ordinarily be sufficient to assure a degree of independence comparable to that achievable by genetically related societies over a span of 1,000 years."

Before and after the culture area concept came into being, some ethnologists compared and ranked ethnics in terms of their relative cultural and social complexity at the time they first were contacted by literate foreigners. The resultant classifications from Morgan to Service presume that some clusters of peoples have developed at a more rapid rate than others. The simplicity of particular cultures usually has been explained in terms of their geographical isolation (Australians and Bushmen), the limitations of environmental exploitations (Eskimos and Amazonian farmers), or cultural blindness (the failure of early historic Tasmanians to utilize fish as food even though many species were readily available). Contemporary anthropologists would reject any suggestion that the differences in achievements among peoples are based on racial or "innate" personality characteristics.

Why have so many attempts been made to formulate sociocultural classifications, evolutionary or otherwise, if we cannot prove that any of the reconstructions did exist in fact? One reason is simply intellectual curiosity about our past. It is engaging to seek to illuminate the development of cultural behavior, not only because it is unique to men but because of our lasting curiosity about ourselves and how we came to be what we are. Another consideration is that by better understanding the past in reasoned but not absolute terms, we may come to have a fuller appreciation of the directions in which we may be moving. In this sense the future must be derived from the past, and the past becomes at least partially a precedent for the future.

Much has been written about classifications, yet there is no reason to believe that any existing taxonomy adequately comes to grips with *why* there have been major advances in culture. By contrast the answers to *where* and *when* increasingly complex designs for living emerge are reasonably clear, and the *range* of cultural achievements by ethnics has been rather well established. In order to probe the question of why man changed, we must seek new approaches to old ideas. One inviting possibility is to return to a materialistic framework for cultural evolution, as proposed by Lewis Henry Morgan. We tend to lose sight of one fact that he stressed so well: Man is a cultural being because he is a technological animal. The key to changes in humanness clearly is enmeshed in tchnological accomplishments; all else is secondary. Somewhere within the essence of their technology rests the answer to why all men are what they are.

BIBLIOGRAPHY*

Aberle, David F., *et al.*, 1950, "The functional prerequisites of a society," *Ethics*, 60:100–111.

Ackerknecht, Erwin H., 1954, "On the comparative method in anthropology," in Robert F. Spencer, ed., *Method and Perspective in Anthropology*. Minneapolis, Minn.: University of Minnesota Press, pp. 117–125.

———, 1955, "George Forster, Alexander von Humboldt, and ethnology," *Isis*, 46:83–95.

Alsop, Richard, 1967, *Narrative of the Adventures and Sufferings of John R. Jewitt*. Fairfield, Wash.: Ye Galleon Press. (original edition, 1815)

American Ethnological Society, 1845, *Transactions of the American Ethnological Society*, vol. 1. New York: Bartlett & Welford.

Anderson, Charles R., 1939, *Melville in the South Seas*. New York: Columbia University Press.

Ashley Montagu, M. F., 1942, "Bronislaw Malinowski (1884–1942), *Isis*, 34: 146–150.

Bacon, Elizabeth, 1946, "A preliminary attempt to determine the culture areas of Asia," *SJA*, 2:117–132.

Bagby, Philip, 1963, *Culture and History*. Berkeley: University of California Press. (original edition, 1958)

Bailey, Cyril, trans., 1921, *Lucretius on the Nature of Things*. Oxford: Clarendon Press.

Barton, Roy F., 1919, "Ifugao law," *UCPAAE*, 15:no. 1.

———, 1922, "Ifugao economics," *UCPAAE*, 15:no. 5.

———, 1938, *Philippine Pagans*. London: Routledge & Kegan Paul Ltd.

---

*Abbreviations:

AA	American Anthropologist
SJA	Southwestern Journal of Anthropology
UCPAAE	University of California Publications in American Archaeology and Ethnology

Batchelor, John, 1927, *Ainu Life and Lore*. Tokyo: Kyobunkwan.

Beaglehole, John C., ed., 1955, *Journals of Captain James Cook on His Voyages of Discovery*, vol. 1. Cambridge: Hakluyt Society.

Beardsley, Richard K., *et al.*, 1956, "Functional and evolutionary implications of community patterning," in Robert Wauchope, ed., *Seminars in Archaeology: 1955*. Society for American Archaeology Memoir No. 11, pp. 129–157.

Bennett, Wendell C., 1948, "The Peruvian co-tradition," in Wendell C. Bennett, ed., *A Reappraisal of Peruvian Archaeology*. Society for American Archaeology Memoir No. 4, pp. 1–7.

Berndt, Ronald M., 1963, "Groups with minimal European associations," in Helen Sheils, ed., *Australian Aboriginal Studies*. Melbourne: Oxford University Press, pp. 385–408.

Berreman, Gerald D., 1966, "Anemic and emetic analyses in social anthropology," AA, n.s., 68:346–354.

Birket-Smith, Kaj, 1929, "The Caribou Eskimos," *Report of the Fifth Thule Expedition*, 5:part 1.

Bleek, Dorothea F., 1929, "Bushman folklore," *Africa*, 2:302–312.

Blow Snake, Sam, 1926, *Crashing Thunder: the Autobiography of an American Indian*, Paul Radin, ed. New York: Appleton-Century-Crofts. (issued first as UCPAAE, 16:no. 7, 1920)

Boas, Franz, 1905, "The Jesup North Pacific Expedition," *International Congress of Americanists*. Easton, Pa. Eschenbach Printing Co., pp. 91–100.

——— 1937, "Waldemar Bogoras," AA, n.s., 39:314–315.

———, 1943, "The American Ethnological Society," *Science*, 97:7–8.

———, 1966, *Kwakiutl Ethnography*, Helen Codere, ed. Chicago: University of Chicago Press.

Bodine, John J., 1969, "A field experience: Taos and Taos Pueblo," *Abstracts of the 1969 Joint Meeting of the Southern Anthropological Society and the American Ethnological Society*, vol. 2. New Orleans, La.: Tulane University and Baton Rouge: Louisiana State University. (mimeographed)

Bogoras, Waldemar, 1904–9, "The Chukchee," *Jesup North Pacific Expedition*, vol. 7, American Museum of Natural History Memoir, vol. 11.

Bonner, T. D., 1965, *Life and Adventures of James P. Beckwourth*. Minneapolis, Minn.: Ross & Haines, Inc. (original edition, 1856)

Bonwick, James, 1870, *Daily Life and Origin of the Tasmanians*. London: F. Low, Son, and Marston.

Bourne, Edward G., 1907, "Columbus, Ramon Pane and the beginnings of American anthropology," *Proceedings of the American Antiquarian Society*, n.s., 17:310–348.

Bruwer, J. P. van S., 1958, "Matrilineal kinship among the Kunda," *Africa*, 28:207–224.

Bunzel, Ruth L., 1932, "Introduction to Zuni Ceremonialism," *Forty-seventh Annual Report of the Bureau of American Ethnology*, 467–1086.

Burrow, J. W., 1963, "Evolution and anthropology in the 1860's," *Victorian Studies*, 7:137–154.

Casson, Stanley, 1939, *Discovery of Man*. New York: Harper & Row, Publishers.

Chagnon, Napoleon A., 1968, Ya̧nomamö, the Fierce People. New York: Holt, Rinehart and Winston, Inc.

———, et al., 1971, "Ya̧nomamö hallucinogens: anthropological, botanical, and chemical findings," Current Anthropology, 12:72–74.

Chamberlain, Alexander F., 1892, Language of the Mississaga Indians of Skugog. Philadelphia: Press of MacCalla & Co.

Cheyne, Andrew, 1852, A Description of Islands in the Western Pacific Ocean. London: J. D. Potter.

Codere, Helen, 1959, "The understanding of the Kwakiutl," in Walter Gold-schmidt, ed., Anthropology of Franz Boas. American Anthropological Association Memoir No. 89, pp. 61–75.

Coe, Michael D., 1966, Maya. New York: Frederick A. Praeger, Inc.

Cohen, Felix S., 1960, Legal Conscience. Lucy K. Cohen, ed. New Haven: Yale University Press.

Cohen, Ronald, 1962, "The strategy of social evolution," Anthropologica, n.s., 4:321–348.

Conklin, Edwin G., 1948, "A brief history of the American Philosophical Society," American Philosophical Society Year Book 1947. Philadelphia: George H. Buchanan Co., pp. 7–26.

Conklin, Harold C., 1955, "Hanunoo color categories," SJA, 11:339–344.

Coon, Carleton S., 1948, A Reader in General Anthropology. New York: Holt, Rinehart and Winston, Inc.

Cooper, John M., 1946, "The Yahgan," Handbook of South American Indians, vol. 1, Bureau of American Ethnology Bulletin 143:81–106.

Covey, Cyclone, 1961, Cabeza de Vaca's Adventures in the Unknown Interior of America. New York: P. F. Collier, Inc. (original edition, 1542)

Crone, Gerald R., 1937, Voyages of Cadamosto. London: Hakluyt Society.

Cushing, Frank H., 1875, "Antiquities of Orleans County, New York," Annual Report of the Smithsonian Institution for 1874, pp. 375–377.

———, 1884–5, "Zuni Breadstuffs," Millstone, Indianapolis, Ind. (reprinted, Heye Foundation, 1920)

———, 1901, Zuni Folk Tales. New York: G. P. Putnam's Sons. (reprinted 1931)

Dapper, Olfert, 1933, "Kaffraria or land of the Kafirs," in I. Schapera and B. Farrington, ed. and trans., Early Cape Hottentots. Cape Town: Van Riebeeck Society, 1–77. (original edition, 1668)

Degerando, Joseph-Marie, 1969, Observations of Savage Peoples. F. C. T. Moore, trans. Berkeley: University of California Press.

Dercum, Francis X., 1927, "The origin and activities of the American Philosophical Society and an address on the dynamic factor in evolution," Proceedings of the American Philosophical Society, 66:19–45.

Dozier, Edward P., 1954, "The Hopi-Tewa of Arizona," UCPAAE, 44:no. 3.

———, 1966, Hano: A Tewa Indian Community in Arizona. New York: Holt, Rinehart and Winston, Inc.

———, 1970, Pueblo Indians of North America. New York: Holt, Rinehart and Winston, Inc.

Driver, Harold E., 1961, *Indians of North America*. Chicago: University of Chicago Press.

———, 1962, "The contribution of A. L. Kroeber to culture area theory and practice," *Indiana University Publications in Anthropology and Linguistics Memoir 18*.

———, and William C. Massey, 1957, "Comparative studies of North American Indians," *Transactions of the American Philosophical Society*, n.s., vol. 47, part 2.

Dupree, Anderson H., 1957, *Science in the Federal Government*. Cambridge: Harvard University Press.

Eggan, Fred R., and W. Lloyd Warner, 1956, "Alfred Reginald Radcliffe-Brown, 1881–1945," AA, n.s., 58:544–547.

Elkin, Adolphus P., 1964, *Australian Aborigines*. New York: Doubleday & Company, Inc. (original edition, 1938)

Emory, Kenneth P., 1959, "Origin of the Hawaiians," *Journal of the Polynesian Society*, 68:29–35.

Evans-Pritchard, Edward E., 1962, *Social Anthropology and other Essays*. New York: The Free Press.

Fenton, William N., 1951, "Iroquois studies at mid-century," *Proceedings of the American Philosophical Society*, 95:296–310.

———, 1969, "J-F. Lafitau (1681–1746), precursor of scientific anthropology," SJA, 25:173–187.

Firth, Raymond, 1936, *We, The Tikopia*. London: George Allen & Unwin Ltd.

———, 1959, *Social Change in Tikopia*. London: George Allen & Unwin Ltd.

———, 1960, "Introduction: Malinowski as scientist and as man," in Raymond Firth, ed., *Man and Culture*. London: Routledge & Kegan Paul Ltd., pp. 1–14.

Fisch, Max H., and Thomas G. Bergin, 1944, *Autobiography of Giambattista Vico*. Ithaca: Cornell University Press.

Fison, Lorimer, and Alfred W. Howitt, 1880, *Kamilaroi and Kurnai*. Melbourne: G. Robertson.

Fletcher, Alice C., and Francis La Flesche, 1911, "The Omaha tribe," *Twenty-seventh Annual Report of the Bureau of American Ethnology*.

Fortes, Meyer, 1969, *Kinship and the Social Order*. Chicago: Aldine Publishing Co.

Frake, Charles O., 1961, "The diagnosis of disease among the Subanun of Mindanao," AA, n.s., 63:113–132.

———, 1962, "The ethnographic study of cognitive systems," in Thomas Gladwin and William C. Sturtevant, eds., *Anthropology and Human Behavior*. Anthropological Society of Washington, pp. 72–85.

Frazer, James G., 1920, "Fison and Howitt," *Sir Rodger de Coverley and other Literary Pieces*. London: Macmillan & Co., Ltd., pp. 210–259.

Freilich, Morris, ed., 1970, *Marginal Natives*. New York: Harper & Row, Publishers.

Fürer-Haimendorf, Christopher von, 1943, "The Chenchus," *Aboriginal Tribes of Hyderabad*, vol. 1. London: Macmillan & Co., Ltd.

Gerard, R. W., *et al.*, 1956, "Biological and cultural evolution," *Behavioral Science,* 1:6–34.

Gilbertson, Albert N., 1914, "In memoriam: Alexander Francis Chamberlain," *AA,* n.s., 16:337–348.

Gladwin, Thomas, 1970, *East Is a Big Bird.* Cambridge: Harvard University Press.

Godley, Alfred D., 1920, *Herodotus,* 4 vols. New York: G. P. Putnam's Sons.

Golde, Peggy, ed., 1970, *Women in the Field.* Chicago: Aldine Publishing Co.

Goldman, Irving, 1937, "The Zuni Indians of New Mexico," in Margaret Mead, ed., *Cooperation and Competition among Primitive Peoples.* New York: McGraw-Hill, Inc., pp. 313–353.

Goldschmidt, Walter, 1951, "Ethics and the structure of society," *AA,* n.s., 53:506–524.

Grevenbroek, Johannes G., 1933, "An elegant and accurate account of the African race," in I. Schapera and B. Farrington, ed. and trans., *Early Cape Hottentots.* Cape Town: Van Riebeeck Society, 161–299. (written, 1695)

Gruber, Jacob W., 1967, "Horatio Hale and the development of American anthropology," *Proceedings of the American Philosophical Society,* 111:5–37.

Gusinde, Martin, 1961, *Yamana,* Frieda Schutze, trans. New Haven: Human Relations Area Files. (original edition, 1937, as *Die Yamana*)

Haddon, Alfred C., ed., 1901–35, *Reports of the Cambridge Anthropological Expedition to Torres Straits,* 6 vols. Cambridge: Cambridge University Press.

Harp, Elmer, 1961, "The archaeology of the lower and middle Thelon, Northwest Territories," *Arctic Institute of North America, Technical Papers,* no. 8.

Harris, Marvin, 1967, Review of Bronislaw K. Malinowski's *A Diary in the Strict Sense of the Term. Natural History,* 76(7):71,74.

——, 1968, *Rise of Anthropological Theory.* New York: Thomas Y. Crowell.

Hart, Charles W. M., 1954, "The sons of Turimpi," *AA,* n.s., 56:242–261.

——, and Arnold R. Pilling, 1960, *Tiwi of North Australia.* New York: Holt, Rinehart and Winston, Inc.

Hart, Henry H., 1950, *Sea Road to the Indies.* New York: The Macmillan Company.

Hearne, Samuel, 1958, *A Journey from Prince of Wales's Fort in Hudson's Bay to the Northern Ocean.* Richard Glover, ed. Toronto: The Macmillan Co. of Canada, Ltd. (original edition, 1795)

Heizer, Robert F., and John E. Mills, 1952, *Four Ages of Tsurai.* Berkeley: University of California Press.

Henderson, George C., 1931*a, Fiji and the Fijians, 1835–1856.* Sydney: Angus & Robertson, Ltd.

——, 1931*b, Journal of Thomas Williams,* A Missionary in Fiji, 1840–1853, 2 vols. Sydney: Angus & Robertson, Ltd.

Henry, Frances, and Satish Saberwal, eds., 1969, *Stress and Response in Fieldwork.* New York: Holt, Rinehart and Winston, Inc.

Henry, Jules, 1941, *Jungle People.* Locust Valley, N.Y.: J. J. Augustin, Inc.

Herskovits, Melville J., 1924, "A preliminary consideration of the culture areas of Africa," AA, n.s., 26:50–63.
———, 1930, "The culture areas of Africa," *Africa*, 3:59–76.
———, 1945, *Backgrounds of African Art*. Denver: Denver Art Museum.
Himmelfarb, Gertrude, 1962, *Darwin and the Darwinian Revolution*. New York: Doubleday & Company, Inc.
Hirsch, David I., 1954, "Glottochronology and Eskimo and Eskimo-Aleut prehistory," AA, n.s., 56:825–838.
Hodge, Frederick W., 1916, *McGee Memorial Meeting of the Washington Academy of Sciences*, Baltimore: The Williams & Wilkins Company, 63–68.
Hodgen, Margaret T., 1964, *Early Anthropology in the Sixteenth and Seventeenth Centuries*. Philadelphia: University of Pennsylvania Press.
Hoebel, E. Adamson, 1960, "William Robertson: An 18th century anthropologist-historian," AA, n.s., 62:648–655.
———, 1966, *Anthropology*. New York: McGraw-Hill, Inc.
Holm, Gustav, 1914, "Ethnological sketch of the Angmagsalik Eskimo," in William Thalbitzer, ed., The Ammassalik Eskimo. *Meddelelser om Gronland*, 39:1–147.
Holmberg, Allan R., 1950, "Nomads of the long bow," *Smithsonian Institution, Institute of Social Anthropology Publication*, no. 10.
Holmes, William H., 1893, "The World's Fair Congress of Anthropology," AA, 6:423–434.
———, 1900, "In memoriam, Frank Hamilton Cushing," AA, n.s., 2:356–360.
Honigmann, John J., 1959, *World of Man*. New York: Harper & Row, Publishers.
Howitt, Alfred W., 1904, *Native Tribes of South-East Australia*. London: Macmillan & Co., Ltd.
Huddleston, Lee E., 1967, *Origins of the American Indians*. Austin: University of Texas Press.
Hyades, P., and J. Deniker, 1891, *Mission Scientific du Cap Horn*. Paris: Gauthier-Villars et Fils.
Jacobs, Melville, 1964, *Pattern in Cultural Anthropology*. Homewood, Ill.: Dorsey Press.
Jane, Cecil, 1930, *Select Documents Illustrating the Four Voyages of Columbus*, vol. 1. London: Hakluyt Society.
Jenkins, Claude, 1926, "Christian pilgrimages, A.D. 500–800," in Arthur P. Newton, ed., *Travel and Travelers of the Middle Ages*. New York: Alfred A. Knopf, pp. 36–69.
Jochelson, Waldemar, 1933, "The Yakut," *Anthropological Papers of the American Museum of Natural History*, 33:part 2.
Jones, Howard M., 1964, *O Strange New World*. New York: The Viking Press, Inc. (original edition, 1952)
Jongmans, Douwe, and Peter C. Gutkind, eds., 1967, *Anthropologists in the Field*. Assen, Holland: Van Gorcum & Co.
Judd, Neil M., 1967, *Bureau of American Ethnology*. Norman, Okla.: University of Oklahoma Press.

Junod, Henri A., 1966, *Life of a South African Tribe*, 2 vols. New York: University Books, Inc. (original edition, 1926)

Kaberry, Phyllis, 1960, "Malinowski's contribution to fieldwork methods and the writing of ethnography," Raymond Firth, ed., *Man and Culture*. London: Routledge & Kegan Paul Ltd., 71–91.

Kardiner, Abram, and Edward Preble, 1963, *They Studied Man*. New York: New American Library of World Literature, Inc.

Karsten, Rafael, 1935, "The Head-hunters of Western Amazonas," *Commentationes Humanarum Litterarum*, vol. 7.

Keesing, Felix M., 1939, "The Menomini Indians of Wisconsin," *Memoirs of the American Philosophical Society*, vol. 10.

Keith, Arthur, 1917, "How can the institute best serve the needs of anthropology?," *Journal of the Royal Anthropological Institute of Great Britain and Ireland*, 47:12–30.

Keithahn, Edward L., 1963, *Monuments in Cedar*. Seattle, Wash.: Superior Publishing Co.

Kenton, Edna, ed., 1927, *Indians of North America*, 2 vols. New York: Harcourt Brace Jovanovich, Inc.

Kiger, Joseph C., 1963, *American Learned Societies*. Washington, D. C.: Public Affairs Press.

Kluckhohn, Clyde, 1953, "Universal categories of culture," in Alfred L. Kroeber, ed., *Anthropology Today*. Chicago: University of Chicago Press, pp. 507–523.

Kolben, Peter, 1731, *Present State of Cape of Good-Hope*, 2 vols. London: W. Innys.

Krause, Aurel, 1956, *Tlingit Indians*, Erna Gunther, trans. Seattle: University of Washington Press.

Kroeber, Alfred L., 1908, "Ethnology of the Gros Ventre," *Anthropological Papers of the American Museum of Natural History*, 1:part 4.

———, 1925, "Handbook of the Indians of California," *Bureau of American Ethnology Bulletin* 78.

———, 1939, "Cultural and natural areas of native North America," *UCPAAE*, vol. 38.

———, 1947, "Culture groupings in Asia," *SJA*, 3:322–330.

———, 1948, *Anthropology*. New York: Harcourt Brace Jovanovich, Inc.

———, 1949, "The concept of culture in science," *Journal of General Education*, 3:182–196.

———, 1957, "What ethnography is," *UCPAAE*, 47(2):191–204.

———, 1959, "Yurok national character," *UCPAAE*, 47(3):236–240.

Kroeber, Theodora, 1961, *Ishi in Two Worlds*. Berkeley: University of California Press.

Kuykendall, Ralph S., 1947, *Hawaiian Kingdom, 1778–1854*. Honolulu: University of Hawaii Press.

Lamb, Daniel S., 1906, "The story of the Anthropological Society of Washington," *AA*, n.s., 8:564–579.

Langness, Lewis L., 1965, *Life History in Anthropological Science*. New York: Holt, Rinehart and Winston, Inc.

La Vega, Garcilaso de, 1966, *Royal Commentaries of the Incas*, 2 vols., Harold V. Livermore, trans. Austin: University of Texas Press. (original edition, 1616–1617)

Lee, Richard B., 1965, "Subsistence Ecology of the Kung Bushmen." Ph.D. dissertation, University of California, Berkeley.

Lee, Sidney, 1929, "The American Indian in Elizabethan England," in Frederick S. Boas, ed., *Elizabethan and other Essays*. Oxford: Clarendon Press, pp. 263–301.

Leeds, Anthony, 1965, "Reindeer herding and Chukchi social institutions," in Anthony Leeds and Andrew P. Vayda, eds., *Man, Culture, and Animals*. Washington, D. C.: American Association for the Advancement of Science, pp. 87–128.

——, and Andrew P. Vayda, eds., 1965, *Man, Culture, and Animals*. Washington, D. C.: American Association for the Advancement of Science.

Le Page du Pratz, Antoine S., 1947, *History of Louisiana*. New Orleans: Pelican Press. (original edition, 1774)

Le Vine, Robert A., and Barbara B. Le Vine, 1963, "Nyansongo: A Gusii community in Kenya," in Beatrice B. Whiting, ed., *Six Cultures, Studies of Child Rearing*. New York: John Wiley & Sons, Inc., pp. 15–202.

Lewis, Oscar, 1942, *Effects of White Contact upon Blackfoot Culture*. Locust Valley, N. Y.: J. J. Augustin, Inc.

——, 1951, *Life in a Mexican Village: Tepoztlan Restudied*. Urbana, Ill.: University of Illinois Press.

——, 1955, "Comparisons in cultural anthropology," in William L. Thomas, ed., *Yearbook of Anthropology—1955*. New York: Wenner-Gren Foundation, pp. 259–292.

——, 1960, *Tepoztlán: Village in Mexico*. New York: Holt, Rinehart and Winston, Inc.

Livingstone, Frank B., 1969, "Genetics, ecology and the origins of incest and exogamy," *Current Anthropology*, 10:45–49.

Lorant, Stefan, 1965, *New World, the First Pictures of America*. New York: Duell, Sloan & Pearce-Meredith Press. (original edition, 1946)

Lowie, Robert H., 1920, *Primitive Society*. New York: Liveright Publishing Corporation.

——, 1936, "Alfred L. Kroeber: II. Professional appreciation," in Robert Lowie, ed., *Essays in Anthropology Presented to A. L. Kroeber*. Berkeley: University of California Press, pp. xix–xxiii.

——, 1937, *History of Ethnological Theory*. New York: Holt, Rinehart and Winston, Inc.

——, 1956, *Crow Indians*. New York: Holt, Rinehart and Winston, Inc. (original edition, 1935)

——, 1959, *Ethnologist*. Berkeley: University of California Press.

Lurie, Nancy O., 1966, "Women in early American anthropology," in June

Helm, ed., *Pioneers of American Anthropology*. Seattle: University of Washington Press, pp. 29–81.

Malaspina, D. Alejandro, and Don Jose, De Bustamante y Guerra, 1885, *Potical-Scientific Trip around the World* (translated title). Madrid: Press of the Widow and Children of Abienzo.

Malinowski, Bronislaw K.,

——, 1926, *Crime and Custom in Savage Society*. London: Routledge & Kegan Paul Ltd.

——, 1932, "Social anthropology," *Encyclopaedia Britannica*, 14th ed., 20: 862–870.

——, 1935, *Coral Gardens and Their Magic*, 2 vols. London: George Allen & Unwin Ltd.

——, 1961, *Argonauts of the Western Pacific*. New York: E. P. Dutton & Co., Inc. (original edition, 1922)

——, 1963, *Family among the Australian Aborigines*. New York: Schocken Books. (original edition, 1913)

——, 1967, *A Diary in the Strict Sense of the Term*. New York: Harcourt Brace Jovanovich, Inc.

Mallery, Garrick, 1886, "Pictographs of the North American Indians; a preliminary paper," *Fourth Annual Report of the Bureau of Ethnology*, 3–256.

——, 1893, "Picture-writing of the American Indians," *Tenth Annual Report of the Bureau of Ethnology*, pp. 3–807.

Malo, David, 1951, *Hawaiian Antiquities*, Nathaniel B. Emerson, trans. Honolulu: Bishop Museum. (original edition, 1903)

Man, Edward H., 1883, "On the aboriginal inhabitants of the Andaman Islands," *Journal of the Anthropological Institute of Great Britain and Ireland*, 12:69–116, 117–175, 327–434.

Marett, Robert R., 1931, "Memoir," in Robert R. Marett and Thomas K. Penniman, eds., *Spencer's Last Journey*. New York: Oxford University Press, pp. 14–46.

Marquis, Thomas B., 1928, *Memoirs of a White Crow Indian*. New York: Appleton-Century-Crofts.

Mason, Carol, 1964, "Natchez class structure," *Ethnohistory*, 11:120–133.

Mason, J. Alden, 1957, *Ancient Civilizations of Peru*. Baltimore: Penguin Books, Inc.

Mason, Otis T., 1896, "Influence of environment upon human industries or arts," *Annual Report of the Smithsonian Institution for 1895*, pp. 639–665.

——, 1907, "Environment," Handbook of American Indians north of Mexico, part 1, Frederick W. Hodge, ed. *Bureau of American Ethnology Bulletin* 30:427–430.

Mason, Philip P., ed., 1958, *Schoolcraft's Expedition to Lake Itasca*. East Lansing, Mich.: Michigan State University Press.

Mathur, Mary E. F., 1969, "The Iroquois in ethnography," *Indian Historian*, 2(3):12–18.

Mead, Margaret, 1930, *Growing Up in New Guinea*. New York: William Morrow & Company, Inc.

————, 1932, *Changing Culture of an Indian Tribe*. New York: Columbia University Press.

————, 1956, *New Lives for Old*. New York: William Morrow & Company, Inc.

Mealing, S. R., ed., 1967, *Jesuit Relations and Allied Documents*. Toronto: McClelland and Stewart, Ltd.

Montesquieu, Charles L., 1949, *Spirit of the Laws*, Thomas Nugent, trans. New York: Hafner Publishing Company.

Morgan, John, 1967, *Life and Adventures of William Buckley*. Melbourne: William Heinemann, Ltd. (original edition, 1852)

Morgan, Lewis H., 1851, *League of the Ho-de-no-sau-nee, or Iroquois*. Rochester, N.Y.: Sage & Bros.

————, 1870, "Systems of Consanguinity and Affinity of the Human Family," *Smithsonian Contributions to Knowledge*, vol. 17.

————, 1877, *Ancient Society*. New York: Henry Holt and Company.

Munro, Neil G., 1962, *Ainu Creed and Cult*, B. Z. Seligman, ed. London: Routledge & Kegan Paul Ltd.

Murdock, George P., 1945, "The common denominator of cultures," in Ralph Linton, ed., *Science of Man in the World Crisis*. New York: Columbia University Press, pp. 123–142.

————, 1959, *Africa, Its People and Their Culture History*. New York: McGraw-Hill, Inc.

————, 1960, *Ethnographic Bibliography of North America*, 3d ed. New Haven, Conn.: Human Relations Area Files.

————, 1967, *Ethnographic Atlas*. Pittsburgh, Pa.: University of Pittsburgh Press.

Murray, Alexander H., 1910, "Journal of the Yukon, 1847–48," *Publications of the Canadian Archives*, no. 4.

Naroll, Raoul S., 1950, "A draft map of the culture areas of Asia," *SJA* 6:183–187.

————, and Ronald Cohen, 1970, *A Handbook of Method in Cultural Anthropology*. Garden City, N. Y.: Natural History Press.

Newcomb, William W., 1950, "A re-examination of the causes of Plains warfare," *AA*, n.s., 52:317–330.

————, 1961, *Indians of Texas*. Austin: University of Texas Press.

Newman, Philip L., 1965, *Knowing the Gururumba*. New York: Holt, Rinehart and Winston, Inc.

Notes and Queries on Anthropology, 1951, London: Routledge and Kegan Paul, Ltd.

Nowell, Charles E., 1962, *Magellan's Voyage Around the World*. Evanston, Ill.: Northwestern University Press.

Oberg, Kalervo, 1937, "The Social Economy of the Tlingit Indians," MS., Ph.D. dissertation, University of Chicago.

Okladnikov, A. P., 1970, *Yakutia*, Henry N. Michael, ed. Montreal: McGill-Queen's University Press.

Oliver, Douglas L., 1952, *Pacific Islands*. Cambridge: Harvard University Press.

d'Olwer, Luis N., n.d., "Fray Bernardino de Sahagun," Handbook of Middle American Indians, Working Papers, Library of Congress.

Ortiz, Alfonso, 1969, Tewa World. Chicago: University of Chicago Press.

Osborn, Chase S., and Stellanova Osborn, 1942, Schoolcraft—Longfellow—Hiawatha. Tempe, Ariz.: Jaques Cattell Press.

————, 1943, "Schoolcraft and the American Ethnological Society," Science, n.s., 97:161–162.

Osgood, Cornelius, 1936a, "The distribution of the Northern Athapaskan Indians," Yale University Publications in Anthropology, no. 7.

————, 1936b, "Contributions to the ethnography of the Kutchin," Yale University Publications in Anthropology, no. 14.

————, 1937, "The ethnography of the Tanaina," Yale University Publications in Anthropology, no. 16.

————, 1940, "Ingalik material culture," Yale University Publications in Anthropology, no. 22.

————, 1953, Winter. New York: W. W. Norton & Company, Inc.

————, 1958, "Ingalik social culture," Yale University Publications in Anthropology, no. 53.

————, 1959, "Ingalik mental culture," Yale University Publications in Anthropology, no. 56.

Ottenberg, Simon, and Phoebe Ottenberg, eds., 1960, Cultures and Societies of Africa. New York: Random House, Inc.

Paley, William, 1802, Natural Theology; or, Evidence of the Existence and Attributes of The Deity. London: R. Faulder.

Pearce, Roy H., 1965, Savages of America. Baltimore: The Johns Hopkins Press. (original edition, 1953)

Pehrson, Robert N., 1951, "Reindeer herding among the Karesuando Lapps," American-Scandinavian Review, 39:271–279.

————, 1954a, "Bilateral kin groupings as a structural type: a preliminary statement," Journal of East Asiatic Studies, 3:199–202.

————, 1954b, "The Lappish herding leader: a structural analysis," AA, n.s., 56:1076–1080.

————, 1956, "North Lappish kinship terminology in relation to working organization," Congres International des Sciences Anthropologiques et Ethnologiques, 3:81–86.

Pennimann, Thomas K., 1965, A Hundred Years of Anthropology. London: Gerald Duckworth & Co., Ltd. (first edition, 1935)

Polack, Joel S., 1840, Manners and Customs of the New Zealanders, 2 vols. London: Ames Madden & Co.

Poole, E. H. Lane, 1949, Native Tribes of the Eastern Province of Northern Rhodesia. Lusaka: Government Printer.

Porter, Charles T., 1954, "Personal Reminiscences," in League of the Ho-de-no-sau-nee or Iroquois, 2:153–161. New Haven: Human Relations Area Files. (original edition, 1901, Herbert M. Lloyd, ed. New York: Dodd, Mead & Company, Inc.)

Powell, John W., 1900, "In memoriam, Frank Hamilton Cushing," AA, n.s., 2:360–367.

Putnam, Patrick, 1948, "The Pygmies of the Ituri Forest," in Carleton S. Coon, ed., A Reader in General Anthropology. New York: Holt, Rinehart and Winston, Inc., pp. 322–342.

Pyke, William T., 1916, Thirty Years among the Blacks of Australia. Melbourne: E. W. Cole.

Quiggin, A. H., and E. S. Fegan, 1940, "Alfred Court Haddon, 1855–1940," Man, 40:97–100.

Radcliffe-Brown, Alfred R., 1948, Andaman Islanders. New York: The Free Press. (original edition, 1922)

———, 1952, Structure and Function in Primitive Society. New York: The Free Press.

Rasmussen, Knud, 1930, "Intellectual culture of the Caribou Eskimos," Report of the Fifth Thule Expedition, vol. 7, no. 2.

Rattray, Robert S., 1923, Ashanti. New York: Oxford University Press.

Ray, Verne F., and Nancy O. Lurie, 1954, "The contributions of Lewis and Clark to ethnography," Journal of the Washington Academy of Sciences, 44:358–370.

Redfield, Robert, 1930, Tepoztlan, A Mexican Village. Chicago: University of Chicago Press.

———, 1941, Folk Culture of Yucatan. Chicago: University of Chicago Press.

———, 1950, A Village that Chose Progress. Chicago: University of Chicago Press.

Resek, Carl, 1960, Lewis Henry Morgan, American Scholar. Chicago: University of Chicago Press.

Richards, Audrey I., 1960, "The concept of culture in Malinowski's work," in Raymond Firth, ed., Man and Culture. London: Routledge & Kegan Paul, Ltd., 15–31.

Richards, Cara B., 1957, "Matriarchy or mistake: the role of Iroquois women through time," Cultural Stability and Cultural Change, 36–45. Proceedings of the American Ethnological Society.

———, 1967, "Huron and Iroquois residence patterns 1600–1650," in Elizabeth Tooker, ed., Iroquois Culture, History, and Prehistory. New York State Museum and Science Service, pp. 51–56.

Rivers, William H. R., 1900, "A genealogical method of collecting social and vital statistics," Journal of the Anthropological Institute of Great Britain and Ireland, 30:74–82.

———, 1906, Todas. London: Macmillan & Co., Ltd. (reprinted in 1967)

Robertson, William, 1759, History of Scotland. London: Roxburghe.

———, 1777, History of America, 2 vols. Dublin: Whitstone et al.

Robinson, George A., 1966, Friendly Mission, N. J. B. Plomley, ed. Tasmanian Historical Research Association. Kingsgrove, New South Wales: Halstead Press, Ltd.

Rockhill, William W., 1900, Journey of William of Rubruck. London: Hakluyt Society.

Rohner, Ronald P., 1966, "Franz Boas," in June Helm, ed., *Pioneers of American Anthropology.* Seattle: University of Washington Press, pp. 149–222.

Roscoe, John, 1966, *Baganda.* New York: Barnes & Noble, Inc. (original edition, 1911)

Ross, John, 1819, *A Voyage of Discovery.* London: John Murray.

Roth, Walter E., 1897, *Ethnological Studies among the North-West-Central Queensland Aborigines.* Brisbane: Edmund Gregory, Government Printer.

Rowe, John R., 1946, "Inca culture at the time of the Spanish conquest," *Handbook of South American Indians,* vol. 2. *Bureau of American Ethnology Bulletin* 143:183–330.

Schapera, Isaac, 1930, *Khoisan Peoples of South Africa.* London: Routledge & Kegan Paul, Ltd. (reprinted in 1951)

———, and B. Farrington, eds. and trans., 1933, *Early Cape Hottentots.* Cape Town: Van Riebeeck Society.

Scheffer, Johannes, 1673, *Lapponia.* Frankfurt. (trans. and published as *History of Lapland* in 1704)

Schoen, Ivan, 1969, "Contact with the stone age," *Natural History,* 73(1): 11–18, 66–67.

Schoolcraft, Henry R.,

———, 1819, *A View of the Lead Mines of Missouri.* New York: John Wiley & Sons, Inc.

———, 1821, *Narrative Journal of Travels.* Albany: E. & E. Hosford.

———, 1839, *Algic Researches,* 2 vols. New York: Harper & Row, Publishers.

———, 1848, *Indian and His Wigwam.* New York: Dewitt & Davenport.

Seitz, George J., 1967, "Epena, the intoxicating snuff powder of the Waika Indians with the Tucano medicine man, Agostino," in Daniel H. Efron, *et al.,* eds., *Ethnopharmacologic Search for Psychoactive Drugs.* Public Health Service Publication No. 1645, pp. 315–338.

Service, Elman R., 1962, *Primitive Social Organization.* New York: Random House, Inc.

———, 1968, "The prime-mover of cultural evolution," *SJA,* 24:396–409.

Shimony, Annemarie A., 1961, "Conservatism among the Iroquois at the Six Nations Reserve," *Yale University Publications in Anthropology,* no. 65.

Shinichiro, Takakura, 1960, "The Ainu of northern Japan," John A. Harrison, ed. and trans., *Transactions of the American Philosophical Society,* n.s., 50, part 4.

Sibiya, Christina, 1948, *Zulu Woman,* related by Rebecca H. Reyher. New York: Columbia University Press.

Simmons, Leo W., 1942, *Sun Chief, the Autobiography of a Hopi Indian.* New Haven, Conn.: Yale University Press.

Slotkin, J. S., 1965, "Readings in early anthropology," *Viking Fund Publications in Anthropology,* no. 40.

Smith, Marian W., 1943, "Centenary of the American Ethnological Society," *AA,* n.s., 45:181–184.

———, 1959, "Boas' 'natural history' approach to field method," in Walter

Goldschmidt, ed., *Anthropology of Franz Boas*. American Anthropological Association Memoir No. 89, pp. 46–60.

Smith, Michael G., 1962, "History and social anthropology," *Journal of the Royal Anthropological Institute of Great Britain and Ireland*, 92:73–85.

Souter, Gavin, 1963, *New Guinea, The Last Unknown*. Sydney: Angus and Robertson.

Spencer, Robert F., and Elden Johnson, 1968, *Atlas for Anthropology*. Dubuque, Iowa: William C. Brown Company, Publishers.

Spencer, Walter B., 1914, *Native Tribes of the Northern Territory of Australia*. London: Macmillan and Co., Ltd.

———, and Frank J. Gillen, 1899, *Native Tribes of Central Australia*. London: Macmillan and Co., Ltd.

———, and ——— ,1904, *Northern Tribes of Central Australia*. London: Macmillan and Co., Ltd.

———, and ———, 1927, *Arunta: A Study of a Stone Age People*. 2 vols. London: Macmillan and Co., Ltd.

Spicer, Edward H., 1962, *Cycles of Conquest*. Tucson: University of Arizona Press.

Spier, Leslie, 1959, "Some central elements in the legacy," in Walter Goldschmidt, ed., *Anthropology of Franz Boas*. American Anthropological Association Memoir No. 89, pp. 146–155.

Spindler, George D., ed., 1970, *Being an Anthropologist*. New York: Holt, Rinehart and Winston, Inc.

Squier, Ephraim G., and Edwin H. Davis, 1848, "Ancient monuments of the Mississippi Valley," *Smithsonian Contributions to Knowledge*, vol. 1.

Stern, Bernhard J., 1931, *Lewis Henry Morgan*. Chicago: University of Chicago Press.

Stevenson, Matilda C., 1905, "The Zuni Indians," *Twenty-Third Annual Report of the Bureau of American Ethnology*, pp. 1–608.

Steward, Julian H., 1933, "Ethnography of the Owens Valley Paiute," *UCPAAE*, 33:part 3.

——— 1938, "Basin-plateau aboriginal sociopolitical groups," *Bureau of American Ethnology Bulletin* 120.

———, 1955, *Theory of Culture Change*. Urbana: University of Illinois Press.

———, 1961, "Alfred Louis Kroeber," *AA*, n.s., 63:1038–1061.

———, and Louis C. Faron, 1959, *Native Peoples of South America*. New York: McGraw-Hill, Inc.

Stewart, Dugald, 1854, *Dissertation Exhibiting the Progress of Metaphysical, Ethical, and Political Philosophy*, vol. 1, William Hamilton, ed. Edinburgh: Thomas Constable and Co.

Stocking, George W., 1960, "Franz Boas and the founding of the American Anthropological Association," *AA*, n.s., 62:1–17.

———, 1964, "French anthropology in 1800," *Isis*, 55:134–150.

———, 1965, "From physics to ethnology," *Journal of the History of the Behavioral Sciences*, 1:53–66.

Sturtevant, William C., 1966, "Anthropology, history, and ethnohistory," *Ethnohistory*, 13:1–51.

Swanton, John R., 1946, "The Indians of the Southeastern United States," *Bureau of American Ethnology Bulletin* 137.

Sweet, Louise E., 1965, "Camel pastoralism in north Arabia and the minimal camping unit," in Anthony Leeds and Andrew P. Vayda, eds., *Man, Culture, and Animals*. Washington, D.C.: American Association for the Advancement of Science, pp. 129–152.

Tanner, J. M., 1959, "Boas' contributions to knowledge of human growth and form," in Walter Goldschmidt, ed., *Anthropology of Franz Boas*. American Anthropological Association Memoir No. 89, pp. 76–111.

Tax, Sol, 1965, "From Lafitau to Radcliffe-Brown," in Fred Eggan, ed., *Social Anthropology of North American Indian Tribes*. Chicago: University of Chicago Press, pp. 443–481.

Ten Rhyne, William, 1933, "A short account of the Cape of Good Hope," in Isaac Schapera and B. Farrington, eds. and trans., *Early Cape Hottentots*. Cape Town: Van Riebeeck Society, pp. 81–157. (original edition, 1686)

Tetens, Alfred, 1958, *Among the Savages of the South Seas*, Florence M. Spoehr, trans. Stanford, Calif: Stanford University Press. (adapted from a volume published by Tetens in 1888)

Thalbitzer, William, ed., 1914, "The Ammassalik Eskimo," *Meddelelser om Gronland*, vol. 39.

Thompson, J. Eric, 1970, *Maya History and Religion*. Norman, Okla.: University of Oklahoma Press.

Thompson, Lucy, 1916, *To The American Indian*. Eureka, Calif.: Cummins Print Shop.

Thwaites, Reuben G., 1896–1901, *Jesuit Relations and Allied Documents*, 73 vols. Cleveland: Burrows Bros.

Tokarev, S. A., and I. S. Gurvich, 1964, "The Yakuts," in M. G. Levin and L. P. Potapov, eds., *Peoples of Siberia*. Chicago: University of Chicago Press, pp. 243–304.

Toulmin, Stephen, and June Goodfield, 1965, *Discovery of Time*. New York: Harper & Row, Publishers.

Turi, Johan, 1931, *Turi's Book of Lappland*, Emilie D. Hatt, ed., E. Gee Nash, trans. New York: Harper & Row, Publishers.

Turnbull, Colin M., 1965, "The Mbuti Pygmies: an ethnographic survey," *Anthropological Papers of the American Museum of Natural History*, 50: part 3.

Vico, Giambattista, 1948, *New Science of Giambattista Vico*. Thomas G. Bergin and Max H. Fisch, eds. and trans. Ithaca, N.Y.: Cornell University Press.

Watanabe, Hitoshi, 1968, "Subsistence and ecology of northern food gatherers with special reference to the Ainu," in Richard B. Lee and Irven DeVore, eds., *Man the Hunter*. Chicago: Aldine Publishing Co., pp. 69–77.

Waterman, T. T., 1920, "Yurok Geography," *UCPAAE*, 16:no. 5.

Webb, Malcolm C., 1965, "The abolition of the taboo system in Hawaii," *Journal of the Polynesian Society*, 74:21–39.

White, Leslie A., 1959, *Evolution of Culture*. New York: McGraw-Hill, Inc.

Williams, Thomas, 1858, *Fiji and the Fijians*, 2 vols. London: Alexander Heylin.

Winsor, Justin, 1889, *Narrative and Critical History of America*, vol. 2. Boston: Houghton Mifflin Company.

Wissler, Clark, 1917, *American Indian*. New York: Douglas C. McMurtrie. (1922 and 1938 editions)

———, 1923, *Man and Culture*. New York: Thomas Y. Crowell Company.

———, 1942, "The American Indian and the American Philosophical Society," *Proceedings of the American Philosophical Society*, 86:189–204.

Wright, John K., 1925, "The geographical lore of the time of the crusades," *American Geographical Society Research Studies*, no. 15.

NAME INDEX

Smith, Michael G., 69–70
Smithson, James, 85–87
Solomon (Zulu king), 32
Speck, Frank G., 56, 76
Spencer, Walter B., 57–58
Spicer, Edward H., 77
Spier, Leslie, 56
Squier, Ephraim G., 86
Steward, Julian H., 71–72, 393, 399, 400
Stewart, Dugald, 387
Stocking, George W., 83
Sturtevant, William C., 73
Sweet, Louise E., 73
Swinburne, Algernon C., 88

Talayesva, Don C., 32
Tattooed Serpent (Natchez leader), 304–305
Tax, Sol, 52
Ten Rhyne, William, 28, 114
Te Rangihiroa (See Buck, Peter H.)
Tetens, Alfred, 28
Thompson, John, 29–30
Thompson, Lucy, 33
Thwaites, Reuben G., 38
Tipperary (a Tiwi), 211, 214
Topa Inca (Inca ruler), 363–365
Toulmin, Stephen, 378
Turi, Johan O., 33

Turimpi (a Tiwi), 211 ff.
Tylor, Edward B., 58

Urcon (Inca noble), 362

Vaca, Cabeza de, 21–22, 25
Vayda, Andrew P., 72
Vega, Garcilaso de la, 33
Vespucci, Amerigo, 40
Vico, Giambattista, 377–378
Viracocha Inca (Inca ruler), 362
Vittoria, Francis of, 40

Webb, Malcolm C., 242
Westermark, Edward, 66
White, John, 34
White, Leslie, 393, 396–397
White, Martin, 66
Wilkes, Charles, 85
Wilkin, Anthony, 51, 52
Williams, Billy, 71
Williams, Thomas, 39
Wilson, Henry, 28
Wissler, Clark, 3–4, 27, 38, 39, 398–399, 400
Wreede, George F., 113–114

Yupanqui (See Pachacuti)

Zeisberger, David, 39

*Definitions indicated by italicized numbers.